C++: The Complete Reference

C++: The Complete Reference

Herbert Schildt

Osborne **McGraw-Hill**

Berkeley   New York   St. Louis   San Francisco
Auckland   Bogotá   Hamburg   London   Madrid
Mexico City   Milan   Montreal   New Delhi   Panama City
Paris   São Paulo   Singapore   Sydney
Tokyo   Toronto

Osborne **McGraw-Hill**
2600 Tenth Street
Berkeley, California 94710
U.S.A.

For information on translations or book distributors outside of the U.S.A., please write to Osborne **McGraw-Hill** at the above address.

C++ The Complete Reference

890 DOC 9987654

ISBN 0-07-881654-8

CONTENTS AT A GLANCE

TABLE OF CONTENTS

I have been programming in C for many years and writing about C for the past 7 years. I have seen many fads come and go. When it comes to programming, it takes a lot to get me excited, so I do not make the next statement lightly. I believe that C++ is the most important advance in the art and science of programming since the invention of C itself! I can write with confidence that it will change the way you approach the task of programming.

C++ represents a major step forward in programming. Based upon the C language, C++ adds extensions that support object-oriented programming. These extensions also dramatically increase the power of the language. Programming languages and methodologies have constantly evolved since they first were invented in the 1950s. C++ represents the next step in the evolution of C. While a description of object-oriented programming is found later in this book, the point of it is to let you, the programmer, manage increasingly larger and more complex programs. Towards this end, C++ succeeds very well.

It is important to understand, however, that C++ is not only useful for object-oriented programming. Because of its advanced features, it makes the writing of non-object-oriented programs easier, too.

At the time of this writing, C is the language of choice of professional programmers. Because C++ is an enhanced version of C, the popularity of C++ is expected to increase sharply in the next few years. In fact, many industry analysts predict that the 1990s will be the decade of C++. Frankly, the power and versatility of C++, combined with the fact that it is based on the already popular C language, virtually assures its success.

This book covers both the C-like aspects of C++ and the C++-specific features. However, the greatest emphasis is on those features specific to C++. Since many readers are already familar with and proficient in C, the C-like features are discussed separately from the

C++-specific features. This approach prevents the knowledgable C programmer from having to "wade through" reams of information he or she already knows. Instead, the experienced C programmer can simply turn to the sections of this book that cover the C++-specific features.

Part One of this book covers the features of C++ that it has in common with C. Part Two discusses in detail the extensions and enhancements to C added by C++. Part Three shows practical examples of applying C++ and object-oriented programming.

Diskette Offer

There are many useful and interesting functions, classes, and programs contained in this book. If you're like me, you probably would like to use them, but hate typing them into the computer. When I key in routines from a book, it always seems that I type something wrong and spend hours trying to get the program to work. For this reason, I am offering the source code for all the functions and programs contained in this book on diskette for $24.95. Just fill in the order blank on the next page and mail it, along with your payment, to the address shown. Or, if you're in a hurry, just call (217) 586-4021 (the number of my consulting office) and place your order by telephone or fax (217) 586-4779 (Visa and Mastercard accepted).

Please send me _____ copies, at $24.95 each, of the programs in "C++: The Complete Reference" on an IBM-compatible diskette.

Foreign orders only: Checks must be drawn on a U. S. bank, and please add $5 for shipping and handling.

_____

name

_____

address

_____   _____   _____

city   state   zip

_____

telephone

Diskette size (check one): 5 1/4″ _____ 3 1/2″ _____

Method of payment: check _____ Visa _____ MC _____

Credit card number: _____

Expiration date: _____

Signature: _____

Send to:
      Herbert Schildt
      RR 1, Box 130
      Mahomet, IL 61853

      or phone: (217) 586-4021
      fax: (217) 586-4997

This offer subject to change or cancellation at any time.

C++ Basics: The C-Like Features

**P
A
R
T

O
N
E**

Part One of this book discusses the C-like features of C++. As you probably know, C++ is an enhanced version of ANSI standard C. For this reason, any C++ compiler is by definition a C compiler. Because C++ is built upon C, you cannot program in C++ unless you know how to program in C. Further, many of the fundamental concepts that form the basis for C also form the foundation for C++ and these are covered in this part of the book. Since C++ is a superset of C, everything described in this part of the book is applicable to C++. The C++-specific features of C++ are detailed in Part Two of this book. The reason that the C-like features of C++ are covered in their own section is to make it easier for the experienced C programmer to quickly and easily find information about C++ without having to "wade through" reams of information that he or she already knows.

Note: Part One of this book is excerpted from my book *C: The Complete Reference*, 2nd Edition, (Osborne/McGraw-Hill, 1990). If you are particularly interested in C, you will find this book helpful. It covers the complete ANSI C standard as well as all of the standard C library functions. It also contains several example applications of C.

1

An Overview of C

The Origins of C
C Is a Middle-Level Language
C Is a Structured Language
C Is a Programmer's Language
The Form of a C Program
The Library and Linking
Separate Compilation

The purpose of this chapter is to present an overview of the C programming language, its origins, its uses, and its underlying philosophy. Since C++ is built upon C, this chapter also provides an important historical perspective on the roots of C++.

The Origins of C

C was invented and first implemented by Dennis Ritchie on a DEC PDP-11 that used the UNIX operating system. C is the result of a development process that started with an older language called BCPL. BCPL was developed by Martin Richards, and it influenced a language called B, which was invented by Ken Thompson. B led to the development of C in the 1970s.

For many years the de facto standard for C was the version supplied with the UNIX operating system. It is described in *The C Programming Language* by Brian Kernighan and Dennis Ritchie (Englewood Cliffs, N.J.: Prentice-Hall, 1978). With the popularity of microcomputers, a large number of C implementations were created. Because no standards existed at that time, there were discrepancies and incompatibilities between implementations. To alter this situation, ANSI established a committee in the beginning of the summer of 1983 to create an ANSI standard that would define once and for all the C language. The ANSI C standard has now been adopted and all major C and C++ compilers have already implemented this standard.

C Is a Middle-Level Language

C is often called a middle-level computer language. This does not mean that C is less powerful, harder to use, or less developed than a high-level language such as BASIC or Pascal, nor does it imply that C is similar to assembly language and that it presents the user with the associated troubles. C is thought of as a middle-level language because it combines elements of high-level languages with the functionalism of assembly language. The following shows how C fits into the spectrum of languages:

Highest level	Ada
	Modula-2
	Pascal
	COBOL
	FORTRAN
	BASIC
Middle level	C
	FORTH
	Macro-assembler
Lowest level	Assembler

As a middle-level language, C allows the manipulation of bits, bytes, and addresses—the basic elements with which the computer functions. C code is very portable. Portability means that it is possible to adapt software written for one type of computer to another. For example, if a program written for an Apple Macintosh can be moved easily to an IBM PC, then that program is portable.

All high-level programming languages support the concept of data types. A data type defines a set of values that a variable can store along with a set of operations that can be performed on that variable. Common data types are integer, character, and real. Although C has five basic built-in data types, it is not a strongly typed language in the sense of Pascal or Ada. C will allow almost all type conversions. For example, character and integer types may be intermixed freely in most expressions. C performs no run-time error checking such as array-boundary checking. These types of checks are the responsibility of the programmmer.

C is special in that it allows the direct manipulation of bits, bytes, words, and pointers. This makes it well suited for system-level programming, where these operations are common. Another important aspect of C is that it has only 32 keywords (27 from the Kernighan and Ritchie de facto standard, and 5 added by the ANSI standardization committee), which are the commands that make up the C language. As a comparison, consider that BASIC for the IBM PC contains about 159 keywords!

C Is a Structured Language

Although the term "block-structured language" does not strictly apply to C, C is commonly referred to simply as a structured language. It has many similarities to other structured languages, such as ALGOL, Pascal, and Modula-2. (Technically, a block-structured language permits procedures or functions to be declared inside other procedures or functions. In this way the concepts of global and local are expanded through the use of scope rules, which govern the "visibility" of a variable or procedure. However, since C does not allow the creation of functions within functions, it cannot formally be called block structured.)

The distinguishing feature of a structured language is compartmentalization of code and data. This is the ability of a language to section off and hide from the rest of the program all information and instructions necessary to perform a specific task. One way that you achieve compartmentalization is by using subroutines that employ local (temporary) variables. By using local variables, you can write subroutines in such a way that the events that occur within them cause no side effects in other parts of the program. This capability makes it very easy for your C programs to share sections of code. If you develop compartmentalized functions, you need to know only what a function does, not how it does it. Remember, excessive use of global variables (variables known throughout the entire program) may allow bugs to creep into a program by allowing unwanted side effects. (Anyone who has programmed in BASIC is well aware of this problem.)

A structured language allows you a variety of programming possibilities. It directly supports several loop constructs, such as WHILE, DO-WHILE, and FOR. In a structured language, the use of GOTO is either prohibited or discouraged and is not the common form of program control that it is in traditional BASIC. A structured language allows you to indent statements and does not require a strict field concept (as early versions of FORTRAN did).

Here are some examples of structured and nonstructured languages.

Nonstructured	Structured
FORTRAN	Pascal
BASIC	Ada
COBOL	C
	Modula-2

Structured languages tend to be modern. In fact, a mark of an old computer language is that it is nonstructured. Today, most programmers consider structured languages easier to program in.

C's main structural component is the function: C's stand-alone subroutine. In C, functions are the building blocks in which all program activity occurs. They allow the separate tasks in a program to be defined and coded separately, thus allowing your programs to be modular. After you have created a function, you can rely on it to work properly in various situations without creating side effects in other parts of the program. Being able to create stand-alone functions is extremely critical in larger projects where it is important that one programmer's code not accidentally affect another's.

Another way to structure and compartmentalize code in C is through the use of code blocks. A code block is a logically connected group of program statements that is treated as a unit. In C, you create a code block by placing a sequence of statements between opening and closing curly braces. In this example

```
if(x < 10) {
  printf("too low, try again\n");
  scanf("%d", &x);
}
```

the two statements after the **if** and between the curly braces are both executed if **x** is less than 10. These two statements together with the braces represent a code block. They are a logical unit: one of the statements cannot execute without the other also executing. Note that every statement can be either a single statement or a block of statements. Not only do code blocks allow many algorithms to be implemented with clarity, elegance, and efficiency, but they also help the programmer conceptualize the true nature of the routine.

C Is a Programmer's Language

Surprisingly, not all computer programming languages are for programmers. Consider the classic examples of "nonprogrammer's" languages, COBOL and BASIC. COBOL was not designed to make the programmer's lot better, to improve the reliability of the code produced, or even to improve the speed with which code can be written. Rather, COBOL was designed in part to enable nonprogrammers to read and presumably (however unlikely) understand the program. BASIC was created essentially to allow nonprogrammers to program a computer to solve relatively simple problems.

In contrast, C, as well as C++, were created, influenced, and field-tested by real, working programmers. The end result is that C gives the programmer what the programmer wants: few restrictions, few complaints, stand-alone functions, and a compact set of keywords. By using C, you can nearly achieve the efficiency of assembly code combined with the structure of ALGOL or Modula-2. It is no wonder that C is easily the most popular language among top-flight professional programmers.

The fact that C can often be used in place of assembly language is a major factor in its popularity among programmers. Assembly language uses a symbolic representation of the actual binary code that the computer executes directly. Each assembly language operation maps into a single task for the computer to perform. Although assembly language gives you the potential for accomplishing tasks with maximum flexibility and efficiency, it is notoriously difficult to work with when developing and debugging a program. Furthermore, since assembly language is unstructured, the final program tends to be spaghetti code—a tangled mess of jumps, calls, and indexes. This lack of structure makes assembly language programs difficult to read, enhance, and maintain. Perhaps more important, assembly language routines are not portable between machines with different central processing units (CPUs).

Initially, C was used for systems programming. A systems program is part of a large class of programs that forms a portion of the operating system of the computer or its support utilities. For example, the following are usually called systems programs:

Operating systems
Interpreters
Editors
Assembly programs
Compilers
Database managers

As C grew in popularity, many programmers began to use it to program all tasks because of its portability and efficiency. Because there are C compilers for almost all computers, you can take code written for one machine and compile and run it with few or no changes on another. This portability saves both time and money. C compilers also tend to produce very tight, fast object code—object code that is tighter and faster than that of most BASIC compilers, for example.

Perhaps the most significant reason that programmers use C in all types of programming tasks is because they like it! C offers the speed of assembly language and the extensibility of FORTH, with few of the restrictions of Pascal or Modula-2. Each C programmer can create and maintain a unique library of functions that have been tailored to his or her own personality and that can be used in many different programs. Because it allows—indeed, encourages—separate compilation, C enables programmers to manage large projects easily, with little duplication of effort.

The Form of a C Program

Table 1-1 lists the 32 keywords that, combined with the formal C syntax, form the C programming language. Of these, 27 were defined by the original version of C. These five were added by the ANSI committee: **enum, const, signed, void,** and **volatile.**

In addition, many C and C++ compilers have added several keywords that are used to take better advantage of the memory organization of the 8088/8086 family of processors, and that support inter-language programming and interrupts. The most commonly used extended keywords are shown in Table 1-2. Your compiler may also support other extensions that help it take better advantage of its specific environment.

All C keywords are lowercase. In C uppercase and lowercase are different: **else** is a keyword; ELSE is not. A keyword may not be used for any other purpose in a C program—that is, it may not serve as a variable or function name.

All C programs consist of one or more functions. The only function that absolutely must be present is called **main( )**, and it is the first function called when program execution begins. In well-written C code, **main( )** contains what is, in essence, an outline of what the program does. The outline is composed of function calls. Although **main** is technically not part of the C language (that is, it is not a reserved word), treat it as if it were. If you use **main** as the name of a variable, you are likely to confuse the compiler.

auto	double	int	struct
break	else	long	switch
case	enum	register	typedef
char	extern	return	union
const	float	short	unsigned
continue	for	signed	void
default	goto	sizeof	volatile
do	if	static	while

Table 1-1.   The 32 Keywords Defined by the ANSI C Standard

asm	_ cs	_ ds	_ es
_ ss	cdecl	far	huge
interrupt	near	pascal	

Table 1-2. Some Common C/C++ Extended Keywords

The general form of a C program is illustrated in Figure 1-1, where **f1( )** through **fN( )** represent user-defined functions. The rest of this book examines details of the general form of a program.

global declarations

return-type main(*parameter list*)
{
   statement sequence
}

return-type f1(*parameter list*)
{
   statement sequence
}

return-type f2(*parameter list*)
{
   statement sequence
}

   .
   .
   .

return-type fN(*parameter list*)
{
   statement sequence
}

Figure 1-1. The general form of a C program

The Library and Linking

Technically speaking, you can create a useful, functional C program that consists solely of the statements that you actually created. However, this is quite rare because C does not, within the actual definition of the language, provide any method of performing input/output (I/O) operations. As a result, most programs include calls to various functions contained in C's standard library. All C compilers come with a standard C library that provides functions to perform most commonly needed tasks. The ANSI C standard specifies a minimal set of functions that will be contained in the library; however, your compiler will probably contain many other functions. For example, because computing environments vary widely, the ANSI C standard does not define any graphics functions, but your compiler will probably include some.

The implementors of your compiler have already written most of the general-purpose functions that you will use. When you call a function that is not part of the program you wrote, the compiler "remembers" its name. Later, the linker combines the code you wrote with the object code already found in the standard library. This process is called linking. Some compilers have their own linker, and others use the standard linker supplied by their operating system.

The functions in the library are in relocatable format. This means that the memory addresses for the various machine-code instructions have not been absolutely defined—only offset information has been kept. When your program links with the functions in the standard library, these memory offsets are used to create the actual addresses used. There are several technical manuals and books that explain this process in more detail. However, you do not need any further explanation of the actual relocation process to program in C.

In the standard library you will find many of the functions that you will need as you write programs. These functions act as building blocks that you simply combine. If you write a function that you will use repeatedly, you can place it into a library, too. Some compilers allow you to place your function in the standard library; others require you to create an additional library. Either way, the code will be there for you to use over and over.

Remember that the ANSI standard specifies only a *minimum* standard library. Most compilers supply libraries that contain far more functions than those defined by ANSI. Also, some functions found in the original UNIX version of C are not defined by ANSI because they are redundant, but these functions may also be present in your compiler's library.

Separate Compilation

Most short C and C++ programs are completely contained within one source file. However, as a program's length grows, so does its compile time (and long compile times make for short tempers). Hence, C allows you to break a program into pieces contained in many files and to compile each file separately. Once you have compiled all files, they are linked, along with any library routines, to form the complete executable code. The advantage of separate compilation is that if you change the code of one file, you do not need to recompile the entire program. On all but the simplest projects, this saves a substantial amount of time. The user manual to your C++ compiler will contain instructions on compiling multifile programs.

Expressions

The Five Basic Data Types
Modifying the Basic Types
Identifier Names
Variables
Access Type Modifiers
Storage Class Type Modifiers
Variable Initializations
Constants
Operators
Expressions

This chapter examines the most fundamental element of the C language: the expression. As you will see, in C, the expression is substantially more general and more powerful than it is in most other languages. Expressions are formed from the atomic elements of C: data and operators. Data may be represented either by variables or by constants. C, like most other computer languages, supports a number of different types of data. Since data is at the core of all expressions, this discussion begins with an examination of C's basic data types.

The Five Basic Data Types

There are five atomic data types in C: character, integer, floating point, double floating point, and valueless (**char**, **int**, **float**, **double**, and **void**, respectively). As you will see, all other data types in C are based upon one of these base types. The size and range of these data types vary with each processor type and with the implementation of the C compiler. Although a character is generally 1 byte long and an integer is often 2 bytes long, you cannot assume this if you want your programs to be portable to the widest range of computers. The ANSI C standard stipulates only the minimal *range* of each data type, not its size in bytes. (The minimal range of each data type is found in Table 2-1.)

The exact format of the floating-point values will depend upon how they are implemented. Integers will generally correspond to the natural size of a word on the host computer. Values of type **char** are, in theory, restricted to the defined ASCII characters. Values outside that range may be handled differently between C and C++ implementations.

The ranges of **float** and **double** types are given in digits of precision. The **float** and **double** magnitudes will depend upon the method used to represent the floating-point numbers. Whatever the method, the number will be quite large. The ANSI C standard specifies that the minimum range for a floating-point value is 1e−37 to 1e+37.

The type **void** has two uses. It either explicitly declares a function as returning no value or creates generic pointers. Both of these uses are discussed in subsequent chapters.

Type	Approximate Size in Bits	Minimal Range
char	8	−127 to 127
unsigned char	8	0 to 255
signed char	8	−127 to 127
int	16	−32,767 to 32,767
unsigned int	16	0 to 65,535
signed int	16	Same as **int**
short int	16	Same as **int**
unsigned short int	16	0 to 65,535
signed short int	16	Same as **short int**
long int	32	−2,147,483,647 to 2,147,483,647
signed long int	32	Same as **long int**
unsigned long int	32	0 to 4,294,967,295
float	32	6 digits of precision
double	64	10 digits of precision
long double	128	10 digits of precision

Table 2-1. Data Types Defined by the C ANSI Standard

Modifying the Basic Types

With the exception of type **void**, the basic data types may have various modifiers preceding them. You use a *modifier* to alter the meaning of the base type to more precisely fit the needs of various situations. The list of modifiers is shown here.

signed
unsigned
long
short

These modifiers may all be applied to character and integer base types. However, **long** may also be applied to **double**.

Table 2-1 shows all allowed combinations of data types and modifiers along with their minimal ranges and approximate bit-widths.

The use of **signed** on integers is redundant, but allowed, because the default integer declaration assumes a signed number. The most important use of **signed** is to modify **char**.

The difference between signed and unsigned integers is in the way the high-order bit of the integer is interpreted. If you specify a signed integer, the C compiler generates code that assumes that the high-order bit of an integer is to be used as a *sign flag*. If the sign flag is zero, the number is positive; if it is one, the number is negative.

In general, negative numbers are represented by using the *two's complement* approach, which reverses all bits in the number (except the sign flag), adds 1 to this number, and sets the sign flag to 1.

Signed integers are important for a great many algorithms, but they have only half the absolute magnitude of their unsigned brothers. For example, here is 32,767:

0 1 1 1 1 1 1 1   1 1 1 1 1 1 1 1

If the high order bit were set to 1, the number would then be interpreted as −1. However, if you had declared this an **unsigned int**, the number becomes 65,535 when the high order bit is set to 1.

Identifier Names

In C/C++ the names of variables, functions, labels, and various other user-defined objects are called *identifiers*. An identifier can vary from one to several characters. The first character must be a letter or an underscore; subsequent characters must be letters, numbers, or an underscore. Here are some examples of correct and incorrect identifier names:

Correct	*Incorrect*
count	1count
test23	hi!there
high _ balance	high .. balance

The ANSI C standard states that an identifier may be of any length but that at least the first six characters in the name must be significant if the identifier will be involved in an external link process. The standard refers to these as *external names*, and they include function names and global variables that are shared between files. If the identifier is not used in an external link process, the ANSI C standard requires that the first 31 characters be significant. This type of identifier is called an *internal name*. However, in C++, there is no limit to the length of an identifier and all characters are significant. This difference may be important if you are converting a program from C into C++.

In C, upper- and lowercase are treated as distinct. Hence, **count**, **Count**, and **COUNT** are separate identifiers. In some environments, the case of function names and global variables may be ignored if the linker is not case sensitive. However, most contemporary environments support case-sensitive linking.

An identifier may not be the same as a C or C++ keyword, and it should not have the same name as a function that you wrote or that is in the C or C++ library.

Variables

As you probably know, a *variable* is a named location in memory that is used to hold a value which may be modified by the program. All C variables must be declared before they are used. The general form of a declaration is

   type variable _ list;

Here, *type* must be a valid C data type plus any modifiers, and *variable _ list* may consist of one or more identifier names with comma separators. Some examples of declarations are

```
int i,j,l;

short int si;

unsigned int ui;

double balance, profit, loss;
```

Remember, in C, the name of a variable has nothing to do with its type.

Where Variables Are Declared

There are three basic places where variables will be declared: inside functions, in the definition of function parameters, and outside all functions. These variables are called local variables, formal parameters, and global variables.

Local Variables

Variables that are declared inside a function are called *local variables*. In some C literature, these variables may be referred to as *automatic* variables, in keeping with C's use of the (optional) keyword **auto** that you can use to declare them. This book uses the term "local variable" because it is more common. Local variables may be referenced only by statements that are inside the block in which the variables are declared. Stated another way, local variables are not known outside their own code block. Remember that a block of code begins with an opening curly brace and ends with a closing curly brace.

It is important to understand that local variables exist only while the block of code in which they are declared is executing. That is, a local variable is created upon entry into its block and destroyed upon exit.

The most common code block in which local variables are declared is the function. For example, consider the following two functions:

```
void func1(void)
{
  int x;

  x = 10;
}
void func2(void)
{
  int x;

  x = -199;
}
```

The integer variable **x** was declared twice, once in **func1( )** and once in **func2( )**. The **x** in **func1( )** has no bearing on or relationship to the **x** in **func2( )**. Each **x** is known only to the code that is within the same block as the variable's declaration.

The C language contains the keyword **auto**, which you can use to declare local variables. However, since all nonglobal variables are, by default, assumed to be **auto**, it is virtually never used and is not used in this book. (It has been said that **auto** was included in C to provide for source-level compatibility with its predecessor, B. Further, **auto** is supported in C++ to provide compatibility with C.)

For reasons of convenience and tradition, most programmers declare all the variables used by a function immediately after the function's opening curly brace and before any other statements. However, local variables may be declared within any code block. The block defined by a function is simply a special case.

For example, examine this function carefully:

```
void f(void)
{
  int t;

  scanf("%d",&t);

  if(t==1) {
    char s[80];   /* this is created only upon
                     entry into this block */
    printf("enter name:");
    gets(s);
    /* do something ... */
  }
}
```

Here, the local variable **s** will be created upon entry into the **if** code block and destroyed upon exit. Furthermore, **s** is known only within the **if** block and may not be referenced elsewhere—even in other parts of the function that contains it.

One advantage of declaring variables within the block of code that uses them is that it helps prevent unwanted side effects. Since the variable does not exist outside the block in which it is declared, it cannot be altered accidentally.

There is an important difference between C and C++ as to where you can declare local variables. In C, you must declare all local variables at the start of the block in which they are defined, prior to any program statements. For example, the following function is in error if compiled by using a C compiler:

```
/* This function is in error if compiled using
   a C compiler, but perfectly acceptable to a
   C++ compiler.
*/
void f(void)
{
  int i;

  i = 10;

  int j;   /* this is an error in C, but not C++ */

  j = 20;
}
```

However, in C++, this function is perfectly valid because you can define local variables at any point in your program. (The topic of C++ variable declaration is discussed in depth in Part Two of this book.)

Because local variables are created and destroyed with each entry and exit from the block in which they are declared, their content is lost once the block is left. This is especially important to remember in terms of a function call. When a function is called, its local variables are created, and upon its return they are destroyed. This means that local variables cannot retain their values between calls. (However, you can direct the compiler to retain their values through the use of the **static** modifier.)

Unless otherwise specified, storage for local variables is on the stack. The fact that the stack is a dynamic and changing region of memory explains why local variables cannot, in general, hold their values between function calls.

You can initialize a local variable to some known value. This value will be assigned to the variable each time the block of code in which it is declared is entered. For example, the following program prints the number 10 ten times:

```
#include "stdio.h"

void f(void);

main()
{
  int i;

  for(i=0; i<10; i++)  f();

  return 0;
}

void f(void)
{
  int j = 10;

  printf("%d ", j);

  j++;  /* this line has no lasting effect */
}
```

Formal Parameters

If a function is to use arguments, it must declare variables that will accept the values of the arguments. These variables are called the *formal parameters* of the function. They behave like any other local variables inside the function. As shown in the following program fragment, their declaration occurs after the function name, inside parentheses:

```
/* Return 1 if c is part of string s; 0 otherwise */
is_in(char *s, char c)
{
  while(*s)
    if(*s==c) return 1;
    else s++;

  return 0;
}
```

The function **is_in( )** has two parameters: **s** and **c**. This function returns 1 if the character specified in **c** is contained within the string **s**,
zero if it is not.

You must tell C what type of variables these are by declaring them
as just shown. Once you have done this, you may use them inside the
function as normal local variables. Keep in mind that as local variables,
they are also dynamic and are destroyed upon exit from the function.

As with local variables, you may make assignments to a function's
formal parameters or use them in any allowable C expression. Even
though these variables perform the special task of receiving the value of
the arguments passed to the function, you can use them like any other
local variable.

Global Variables

Unlike local variables, *global variables* are known throughout the entire
program and may be used by any piece of code. Also, they will hold their
value during the entire execution of the program. You create global
variables by declaring them outside of any function. Any expression may
access them, regardless of what block of code that expression is in.

In the following program fragment, you can see that the variable
count has been declared outside all functions. Although its declaration
was before the **main( )** function, you could have placed it anywhere
before its first use, as long as it was not in a function. However, it is
most common to declare global variables at the top of the program.

```
#include "stdio.h"

int count;  /* count is global  */

void func1(void);
void func2(void);

main()
```

```
{
  count = 100;
  func1();

  return 0;
}

void func1(void)
{
  int temp;

  temp = count;
  func2();
  printf("count is %d", count); /* will print 100 */
}

void func2(void)
{
  int count;

  for(count=1; count<10; count++)
    putchar('.');
}
```

Look closely at this program fragment. Notice that although neither
main( ) nor **func1( )** has declared the variable **count**, both may use it.
func2( ) has, however, declared a local variable called **count**. When
func2( ) references **count**, it will be referencing only its local variable,
not the global one. Remember that if a global variable and a local
variable have the same name, all references to that variable name inside
the code block where the local variable is declared will refer to that local
variable and will have no effect on the global variable. This is convenient, but forgetting it can cause your program to act very strangely,
even though it looks correct.

Storage for global variables is in a fixed region of memory set aside
for this purpose by the C compiler. Global variables are very helpful
when you use the same data in many functions in your program. Avoid
using unnecessary global variables, however, for three reasons: they
take up memory the entire time your program is executing, not just
when they are needed; using a global where a local variable will do
makes a function less general because it relies on something that must
be defined outside itself; and using a large number of global variables
can lead to program errors because of unknown and unwanted side
effects. A major problem in developing large programs is the accidental

changing of a variable's value because it was used elsewhere in the program. This can happen in C if you use too many global variables in your programs.

Access Type Modifiers

There are two type modifiers that may be used to control the ways in which variables may be accessed or modified: These modifiers are **const** and **volatile**. If present, they must precede the type modifiers and the type names they modify.

const

Variables of type **const** may not be changed by your program. (A **const** variable can be given an initial value, however.) The compiler is free to place variables of this type into read-only memory (ROM). For example,

```
const int a=10;
```

will create an integer variable called **a** with an initial value of 10 that may not be modified by your program. However you can use the variable in other types of expressions. A **const** variable receives its value either from an explicit initialization or by some hardware-dependent means.

Variables of type **const** have one very important use—they can protect the arguments to a function from being modified by that function. That is, when a pointer is passed to a function, it is possible for that function to modify the actual variable pointed to by the pointer. However, if the pointer is specified as **const** in the paramenter declaration, the function code will not be able to modify what it points to. For example, the **sp_to_dash( )** function in this short program prints a dash for each space found in its string argument. That is, the string "this is a test" will be printed as "this—is—a—test". Using **const** in the parameter declaration ensures that the code inside the function cannot modify the object pointed to by the parameter.

```
#include "stdio.h"

void sp_to_dash(const char *str);

main()
{
  sp_to_dash("this is a test");

  return 0;
}

void sp_to_dash(const char *str)
{
  while(*str) {
    if(*str==' ') printf("%c", '-');
    else printf("%c", *str);
    str++;
  }
}
```

If you had written **sp_to_dash( )** in such a way that the string would be modified, it would not compile. For example, if you had coded **sp_to_dash( )** as follows, an error will be reported and the program will not compile.

```
/* this is wrong */
void sp_to_dash(const char *str)
{
  while(*str) {
    if(*str==' ') *str = '-'; /* can't do this */
    printf("%c", *str);
    str++;
  }
}
```

Many functions in the C standard library use **const** in their parameter declarations. For example, the **strlen( )** function has this prototype:

    int strlen(const char *str);

Specifying **str** as **const** ensures that **strlen( )** cannot modify the string pointed to by **str**. In general, when a standard library function has no need to modify an object pointed to by a calling argument, it is declared as **const**.

You can also use **const** to provide verification that your program does not, in fact, modify a variable. Remember, a variable of type **const** can be modified by something outside your program; for example, a hardware device may set its value. However, by declaring a variable as **const**, you can prove that any changes to that variable occur because of external events.

volatile

The modifier **volatile** tells the compiler that a variable's value may be changed in ways not explicitly specified by the program. For example, a global variable's address may be passed to the clock routine of the operating system and used to hold the real time of the system. In this situation, the contents of the variable are altered without any explicit assignment statements in the program. This is important because most C compilers will automatically optimize certain expressions by assuming that the content of a variable is unchanging if it does not occur on the left side of an assignment statement. Also, some compilers will change the order of evaluation of an expression during the compilation process. The **volatile** modifier will prevent these changes.

You can use **const** and **volatile** together. For example, if 0x30 is assumed to be the value of a port that is changed only by external conditions, the following declaration would prevent any possibility of accidental assignments to **port** by your program.

```
const volatile unsigned char *port=0x30;
```

Storage Class Type Modifiers

The four storage class modifiers supported by C are

```
extern
static
register
auto
```

You use them to tell the compiler how to store the subsequent variable. The storage specifier precedes the rest of the variable declaration. Its general form is

storage _ specifier type var _ name;

extern

Because C allows separately compiled modules of a large program to be linked in order to speed up compilation and aid in the management of large projects, there must be some way of telling all the files about the global variables required by the program. Although C allows you to declare a global variable more than once, it is not good practice; and in C++, you may only declare a global variable once. How, then, do you inform all the files in your program about the global variables used by the program? The solution is to declare all of your globals in one file and use **extern** declarations in the other, as shown in Figure 2-1.

File 1	File 2
```int x, y;```	```extern int x, y;```
```char ch;```	```extern char ch;```
```main()```	```void func22(void)```
```{```	```{```
` .`	`   x = y/10;`
` .`	`}`
` .`	
```}```	```void func23(void)```
	```{```
```void func1(void)```	`   y = 10;`
```{```	```}```
`  x = 123;`	
```}```	

Figure 2-1.   Using global variables in separately compiled modules

In file 2, the global variable list was copied from file 1 and the **extern** specifier was added to the declarations. The **extern** specifier tells the compiler that the following variable types and names have already been declared elsewhere. In other words, **extern** lets the compiler know what the types and names are for these global variables without actually creating storage for (that is, declaring) them again. When the linker links the two modules, all references to the external variables are resolved.

The **extern** keyword has this general form:

extern *var-list*;

Here, *var-list* is a comma-separated list of variables declared elsewhere in your program.

When you use a global variable inside a function that is in the same file as the declaration for the global variable you can use **extern**, although it is rarely done. Here is an example:

```
int first, last;  /* global definition of first
                     and last */

main()
{
  extern int first;  /* optional use of the
                        extern declaration */
  .
  .
  .
}
```

Although **extern** variable declarations can occur inside the same file as the global declaration, they are not necessary. When the compiler finds a local variable that has not been declared inside the current block, the compiler checks if it matches any of the variables declared in any enclosing blocks. If it does not, the compiler checks the global variables. If a match is found, the compiler assumes that the global variable is being referenced.

static Variables

static variables are permanent variables within their own function or file. They differ from global variables because they are not known outside their function or file but they maintain their values between calls. This makes them useful when you write generalized functions and function libraries that other programmers may use; **static** has different effects upon local variables than upon global ones.

static Local Variables

When you apply the **static** modifier to a local variable, the compiler creates permanent storage much the same as it does for a global variable. The key difference between a **static** local variable and a global variable is that the **static** local variable remains known only to the block in which it is declared. In simple terms, a **static** local variable is a local variable that retains its value between function calls.

static local variables are very important to the creation of stand-alone functions because several types of routines must preserve a value between calls. If **static** variables were not allowed, you would have to use globals, opening the door to possible side effects. For example, a function requiring such a variable would be a number-series generator that produces a new number based on the last one. You could declare a global variable for this value. However, each time the function is used in a program, you would have to remember to declare that global variable and make sure that it did not conflict with any other global variables already declared. Using a global variable would also make this function difficult to place in a function library. The better solution is to declare the variable that holds the generated number to be **static,** as in the following program fragment:

```
series(void)
{
  static int series_num;

  series_num = series_num+23;
  return(series_num);
}
```

In this example, the variable **series_num** stays in existence between function calls, instead of coming and going the way a normal local variable would. This means that each call to **series( )** can produce a new member of the series based on the last number without declaring that variable globally.

You can give a **static** local variable an initialization value. This value is assigned only once—not each time the block of code is entered, as with normal local variables. For example, this version of **series( )** initializes **series_num** to 100:

```
series(void)
{
  static int series_num = 100;

  series_num = series_num+23;
  return(series_num);
}
```

As the function now stands, the series will always begin with the value 123. While this is acceptable for some applications, most series generators will need to let the user specify the starting point. To give **series_num** a user-specified value, you can make **series_num** a global variable and then set its value as specified. However, not defining **series_num** as global was the point of making it **static**. This leads to the second use of **static**.

static Global Variables

Applying the specifier **static** to a global variable instructs the compiler to create a global variable that is known only to the *file* in which you declared the **static** global variable. This means that even though the variable is global, routines in other files will have no knowledge of it and may not alter its contents directly, keeping it free from side effects. Therefore, for the few situations where a local **static** cannot do the job, you can create a small file that contains only the functions that need the global **static** variable, compile that file separately, and use it without fear of side effects.

To illustrate a global **static**, the series generator example from the previous section is recoded so that a starting seed value initializes the series through a call to a second function called **series_start( )**. The entire file containing **series( )**, **series_start( )** and **series_num** is shown here:

```
/* this must all be in one file - preferably by itself */

static int series_num;
```

```
void series_start(int seed);
int series(void);

series(void)
{
  series_num = series_num+23;
  return(series_num);
}

/* initialize series_num */
void series_start(int seed)
{
  series_num = seed;
}
```

Calling **series_start( )** with a known integer value initializes the series generator. After that, calls to **series( )** will generate the next element in the series.

To review: the names of local **static** variables are known only to the function or block of code in which they are declared, and the names of global **static** variables are known only to the file in which they reside. For the preceding example, this means that if you place the **series( )** and **series_start( )** functions in a library, you can use the functions, but you cannot reference the variable **series_num**; it is hidden from the rest of the code in your program. In fact, you may even declare and use another variable called **series_num** in your program (in another file, of course) and not confuse anything. In essence, the **static** modifier allows variables to exist that are known to the functions that need them, without confusing other functions.

static variables enable you to hide portions of your program from other portions. This is a tremendous advantage when you are trying to manage a very large and complex program. The **static** storage specifier lets you create very general functions that can go into libraries for later use.

register Variables

C has one last storage specifier that has traditionally applied only to variables of types **int** and **char**. This is the **register** storage modifier. However, the ANSI C standard has broadened the definition of **register** so that you can apply it to any type of variable. Originally, the **register** specifier requested the C compiler to keep the values of variables declared with this modifier in the register of the CPU rather than in memory, where normal variables are stored. This meant that operations on **register** variables can occur much faster than on variables stored in memory because the value of these variables are actually held in the CPU and do not require a memory access to determine or modify their values. However, since the ANSI C standard allows any type of variable to be modified by **register**, it has changed the definition of **register**. The standard simply states "that access to the object be as fast as possible." In practice, characters and integers are still stored in registers in the CPU. Larger objects like arrays obviously cannot be stored in a register, but they may still receive preferential treatment by the compiler. Depending upon the implementation of the C compiler and its operating environment, **register** variables may be handled in any way deemed fit by the compiler's implementor (for example, storage in cached memory). The ANSI C standard also allows a compiler to, in essence, ignore the **register** modifier and treat variables modified by it as if they weren't, but this is seldom done in practice.

You can apply the **register** specifier only to local variables and to the formal parameters in a function. These are, by default, **auto** variables. Hence, global **register** variables are disallowed. The next example shows how to declare a **register** variable of type **int** and use it to control a loop. This function computes the result of M^e for integers:

```
int_pwr(int m,  register int e)
{
  register int temp;

  temp = 1;

  for(; e; e--) temp = temp * m;
  return temp;
}
```

In this example, both **e** and **temp** are declared as **register** variables because both are used within the loop. Because **register** variables are optimized for speed, they are ideal for loop control. In general practice, you use **register** variables where they will do the most good—in places where many references will be made to the same variable. This is important because while you can declare any number of variables as being of type **register**, not all will receive the same access speed optimization.

The exact number of register variables actually optimized for speed allowed within any one code block is determined by both the environment and the specific implementation of C that you are using. Don't worry about declaring too many **register** variables, though, because the C compiler will automatically make **register** variables into nonregister variables when the limit is reached. (This ensures portability of C code across a broad line of processors.)

Throughout this book, most loop control variables will be of type **register**. Usually at least two **register** variables of type **char** or **int** can actually be held in the registers of the CPU. Because environments vary widely, consult your compiler's user manual to determine if you can apply any other types of optimization options.

Because a **register** variable may be stored in a register of the CPU, **register** variables do not have addresses. That is, you may not find the address of a **register** variable by using the **&** operator (discussed later in this chapter).

Note: Although the ANSI standard has broadened the description of **register**, in practice it is still generally implemented along the lines of its original definition and achieves meaningful decreases in access time only for integer and character types. Thus, you should probably not count on much substantial speed improvement for other types of variables. (As hardware improves, this situation is expected to change.)

Variable Initializations

You can give variables in C a value at the same time that they are declared by placing an equal sign and a constant after the variable name. The general form of initialization is

type variable_name = constant;

Here are some examples:

```
char ch = 'a';
int first = 0;
float balance = 123.23
```

Global and **static** global variables are initialized only at the start of the program. Non-**static** local variables are initialized each time the block in which they are declared is entered. However, **static** local variables are initialized only once. Local and **register** variables that are not initialized may have unknown values before the first assignment is made to them.

Constants

In C, constants refer to fixed values that may not be altered by the program. Constants are so intuitive that they have been used in one form or another by all the preceding sample programs. However, the time has come to cover them formally.

C constants can be of any of the basic data types. The way each constant is represented depends upon its type. Character constants are enclosed between single quotes. For example, 'a' and '%' are both character constants.

Integer constants are specified as numbers without fractional components. For example, 10 and −100 are integer constants. Floating-point constants require the use of the decimal point followed by the number's fractional component. For example, 11.123 is a floating-point constant. C also allows you to use scientific notation for floating-point numbers.

There are two floating-point types: **float** and **double**. There are also several variations of the basic types that you can generate by using the type modifiers. By default, the compiler fits a numeric constant into the smallest compatible data type that will hold it. Therefore, **10** is an **int** by default, but **60000** is **unsigned** and **100000** is a **long**. Even though the value 10 could be fit into a character, the compiler will not do this because it means crossing type boundaries. The only exception to the smallest-type rule is floating-point constants, which are assumed to be **doubles**.

For most of the programs that you will write, the compiler defaults are adequate. However, you can specify precisely the type of constant you want by using a suffix. For floating-point types, if you follow the number with an F, the number is treated as a **float**. If you follow it with an L, the number becomes a **long double**. For integer types, the U suffix stands for **unsigned** and the L for **long**. Here are some examples:

Data Type	Constant Examples
int	1 123 21000 −234
long int	35000L −34L
short int	10 −12 90
unsigned int	10000U 987U 40000
float	123.23F 4.34e−3F
double	123.23 12312333 −0.9876324
long double	1001.2L

Hexadecimal and Octal Constants

It is sometimes easier to use a number system based on 8 or 16 instead of 10. The number system based on 8 is called *octal*; it uses the digits 0 through 7. In octal, the number 10 is the same as 8 in decimal. The base 16 number system is called *hexadecimal* and uses the digits 0 through 9 plus the letters A through F, which stand for 10, 11, 12, 13, 14, and 15. For example, the hexadecimal number 10 is 16 in decimal. Because these two number systems are used frequently, C allows you to specify integer constants in hexadecimal or octal instead of decimal if you prefer. A hexadecimal constant must begin with 0x (a zero followed by an *x*) followed by the constant in hexadecimal form. An octal constant begins with a zero. Here are some examples:

```
int hex = 0x80;   /* 128 in decimal */

int oct = 012;    /* 10 in decimal */
```

String Constants

C supports one other type of constant: the string. A *string* is a set of characters enclosed by double quotes. For example, "this is a test" is a string. You have seen examples of strings in some of the **printf( )** statements in the sample programs. Keep in mind that, although C allows you to define string constants, it does not formally have a string data type in the way a language like BASIC does.

You must not confuse strings with characters. A single character constant is enclosed by single quotes, as 'a'. However, "a" is a string containing only one letter.

Backslash Character Constants

Enclosing character constants in single quotes works for most printing characters, but a few, such as the carriage return, are impossible to enter from the keyboard. For this reason, C contains the backslash character constants.

C supports several special backslash codes (listed in Table 2-2) so that you can enter these special characters easily as constants. Use the backslash codes instead of their ASCII equivalents to help ensure portability.

For example, the following program outputs a newline and a tab and then prints the string "this is a test":

```
#include "stdio.h"

main()
{
  printf("\n\tThis is a test");

  return 0;
}
```

Code	Meaning
\ b	Backspace
\ f	Form feed
\ n	Newline
\ r	Carriage return
\ t	Horizontal tab
\ "	Double quote
\ '	Single quote character
\ 0	Null
\ \	Backslash
\ v	Vertical tab
\ a	Alert (rings the computer's bell)
\ N	Octal constant (where N is an octal constant)
\ xN	Hexadecimal constant (where N is a hexadecimal constant)

Table 2-2.   The C Backslash Codes

Operators

C is rich in built-in operators. It places significantly more importance on operators than do most other computer languages. C defines several broad classes of operators: arithmetic, relational, logical, and bitwise. In addition, C has some special operators for particular tasks. Let's begin with one of C's most important operators: the assignment.

The Assignment Operator

In C, you can use the assignment operator within any valid C expression. This is not the case with most computer languages (including Pascal, BASIC, and FORTRAN) which treat the assignment as a special case statement. The general form of the assignment is

variable _ name = expression;

where an expression may be as simple as a single constant or as complex as you require. Like BASIC and FORTRAN, C uses a single equal sign to indicate assignment. (This is in contrast to Pascal or Modula-2, which use the := construct.) The *target*, or left part, of the assignment must be a variable or a pointer, not a function or a constant.

Frequently in literature on C and in compiler error messages you will see these two terms: *lvalue* and *rvalue*. Simply put, an *lvalue* is any object that can occur on the left side of an assignment statement. For all practical purposes, *lvalue* means "variable." The term *rvalue* refers to expressions that can occur on the right side of an assignment and simply means the value of an expression.

Type Conversion in Assignments

Type conversion refers to the situation in which variables of one type are mixed with variables of another type. When this occurs in an assignment statement, the type conversion rule is very easy. The value of the right side (expression side) of the assignment is converted to the type of the left side (target variable), as in this example:

```
int x;
char ch;
float  f;

void func(void)
{
   ch = x;     /* line 1 */
   x = f;      /* line 2 */
   f = ch;     /* line 3 */
   f = x;      /* line 4 */
}
```

In line 1, the left high-order bits of the integer variable **x** are lopped off, leaving **ch** with the lower 8 bits. If **x** were between 256 and 0 to begin with, then **ch** and **x** would have identical values. Otherwise, the value of **ch** would reflect only the lower order bits of **x**. In line 2, **x** will receive the nonfractional part of **f**. In line 3, **f** will convert the 8-bit integer value stored in **ch** to the same value, but in the floating-point format. This also happens in line 4, except that **f** will convert an integer value into floating-point format.

When converting from integers to characters and long integers to integers, the basic rule is that the appropriate number of high-order bits will be removed. In many environments, this means 8 bits will be lost when going from an integer to a character and 16 bits will be lost when going from a long integer to an integer.

Table 2-3 summarizes these assignment type conversions. Remember that the conversion of an **int** to a **float**, or a **float** to a **double**, and

Target Type	Expression Type	Possible Info Loss
signed char	char	If value > 127 then target will be negative
char	short int	High-order 8 bits
char	int	High-order 8 bits
char	long int	High-order 24 bits
int	long int	High-order 16 bits
int	float	Fractional part and possibly more
float	double	Precision, result rounded
double	long double	Precision, result rounded

Table 2-3.   Common Type Conversions (assuming a 16-bit word)

so on, will not add any precision or accuracy. These kinds of conversions will only change the form in which the value is represented. Remember also that some C compilers (and processors) will always treat a **char** variable as positive, no matter what value it has, when converting it to an **int** or **float**. Other compilers will treat **char** variable values greater than 127 as negative numbers when converting. Generally speaking, use **char** variables for characters, and use **ints**, **short ints**, or **signed chars** when needed to avoid a possible portability problem in this area.

To use Table 2-3 to make a conversion not directly shown, simply convert one type at a time until you finish. For example, to convert from a **double** to an **int**, first convert from a **double** to a **float** and then from a **float** to an **int**.

Multiple Assignments

C allows you to assign many variables the same value by using multiple assignments in a single statement. For example, the following fragment assigns **x**, **y**, and **z** the value 0:

```
x = y = z = 0;
```

Professionally written programs often use this format to assign variables common values.

Arithmetic Operators

Table 2-4 lists C's arithmetic operators. In C, the operators **+**, **−**, *****, and **/** all work the same as in most other computer languages. You can apply these operators to almost any built-in data type allowed by C. When you apply **/** to an integer or character, any remainder will be truncated; for example, 5/2 will equal 2 in integer division.

The modulus operator **%** also works in C as it does in other languages, yielding the remainder of an integer division. You cannot use it on floating-point types. The following code fragment illustrates **%**:

```
int x, y;

x = 5;
y = 2;

printf("%d", x/y);    /* will display 2 */
printf("%d", x%y);    /* will display 1, the remainder of
                          the integer division */

x = 1;
y = 2;

printf("%d %d", x/y, x%y); /*  will display 0 1 */
```

The last line prints a 0 and 1 because 1/2 in integer division is 0 with a remainder of 1.

The unary minus multiplies its single operand by −1. That is, any number preceded by a minus sign switches its sign.

Increment and Decrement Operators

C allows two operators not generally found in other computer languages, the increment and decrement operators + + and − −. The operation + + adds 1 to its operand, and − − subtracts 1. Therefore,

```
x = x+1;
```

is the same as

```
++x;
```

Operator	Action
−	Subtraction; also unary minus
+	Addition
*	Multiplication
/	Division
%	Modulus division
− −	Decrement
+ +	Increment

Table 2-4.   Arithmetic Operators

and

```
x = x-1;
```

is the same as

```
x--;
```

Increment and decrement operators may either precede or follow the operand. For example,

```
x = x+1;
```

can be written

```
++x;
```

or

```
x++;
```

There is, however, a difference when you use these operators in an expression. When an increment or decrement operator precedes its operand, C performs the increment or decrement operation before obtaining the operand's value. If the operator follows its operand, C obtains the operand's value before incrementing or decrementing it. Consider the following:

```
x = 10;
y = ++x;
```

In this case, **y** will be set to 11. However, if the code had been written as

```
x = 10;
y = x++;
```

y would have been set to 10. Either way, **x** is still set to 11; the difference is when it happens. There can be significant advantages in being able to control when the increment or decrement operation takes place.

Most C compilers produce very fast, efficient object code for increment and decrement operations—code that is better than the code
generated by using the equivalent assignment statement. For this reason, it is a good idea to use increment and decrement operators when
you can.

Here is the precedence of the arithmetic operators:

highest	++ −−
	− (unary minus)
	* / %
lowest	+ −

Operators on the same precedence level are evaluated by the compiler
from left to right. Of course, you may use parentheses to alter the order
of evaluation. Parentheses are treated by C as they are by virtually all
other computer languages: They force an operation, or set of operations,
to have a higher precedence level.

Relational and Logical Operators

In the terms *relational operator* and *logical operator, relational* refers
to the relationships that values can have with one another and *logical*
refers to the ways that these relationships can be connected. Because
the relational and logical operators often work together, they will be
discussed together here.

The key to relational and logical operators is the concept of true
and false. In C, true is any value other than zero. False is zero.
Expressions that use relational or logical operators will evaluate to zero
for false and 1 for true.

Table 2-5 shows the relational and logical operators. The truth table
for the logical operators is shown here, using 1's and 0's:

p	q	p && q	p ‖ q	!p
0	0	0	0	1
0	1	0	1	1
1	1	1	1	0
1	0	0	1	0

Relational Operators	
Operator	**Action**
>	Greater than
> =	Greater than or equal
<	Less than
< =	Less than or equal
= =	Equal
! =	Not equal
Logical Operators	
Operator	**Action**
&&	AND
‖	OR
!	NOT

Table 2-5.   Relational and Logical Operators

Both the relational and logical operators are lower in precedence than the arithmetic operators. This means that an expression like 10 > 1+12 is evaluated as if it were written 10 > (1+12). The result is, of course, false.

You may combine several operations into one expression, as shown here:

10>5 && !(10<9) ¦¦ 3< =4

This expression will evaluate true. For a more practical example, although C does not contain an exclusive-OR (XOR) logical operator, you can easily create a function that performs this task by using the other logical operators. The outcome of an XOR operation is true if and only if one (but not both) operand is true. The following program contains the function **xor( )**, which returns the outcome of an exclusive-OR operation performed on the two arguments.

```
#include "stdio.h"

int xor(int a, int b);

main()
{
  printf("%d", xor(1, 0));
```

```
   printf("%d", xor(1, 1));
   printf("%d", xor(0, 1));
   printf("%d", xor(0, 0));

   return 0;
}

/* Perform a logical XOR operation using the
   two arguments. */
xor(int a, int b)
{
   return (a || b) && !(a && b);
}
```

The following table shows the relative precedence of the relational and logical operators.

```
Highest    !
           > >= < <=
           ==    !=
           &&
Lowest     ||
```

As with arithmetic expressions, you can use parentheses to alter the natural order of evaluation in a relational and/or logical expression. For example,

!0 && 0 || 0

is false. However, when the same expression is parenthesised as shown next, the result is true.

!(0 && 0) || 0

Remember that all relational and logical expressions produce a result of either zero or 1. Therefore, the following program fragment is not only correct, but it will also print the number 1 on the display.

```
int x;

x = 100;
printf("%d", x>10);
```

Bitwise Operators

Unlike many other languages, C supports a complete complement of bitwise operators. Since C was designed to take the place of assembly language for most programming tasks, it needed the ablility to support all (or at least many) operations that can be done in assembler. *Bitwise operations* refer to the testing, setting, or shifting of the actual bits within a character or integer type. Bitwise operations may not be used on type **float, double, long double, void,** or other more complex types. Table 2-6 lists these operators.

The bitwise AND, OR, and NOT (one's complement) are governed by the same truth table as were their logical equivalents, except that they work on a bit-by-bit level. The exclusive OR ^ has the truth table shown here:

p	q	p ^ q
0	0	0
1	0	1
1	1	0
0	1	1

As the table indicates, the outcome of an XOR is true only if exactly one of the operands is true; otherwise, it is false.

Bitwise operations are often applied in device drivers, such as modem programs, disk file routines, and printer routines, because you can use the bitwise operations to mask off certain bits, such as parity. (The parity bit confirms that the rest of the bits in the byte are unchanged. It is usually the high-order bit in each byte.)

Operator	Action
&	AND
¦	OR
^	Exclusive OR (XOR)
~	One's complement
>>	Shift right
<<	Shift left

Table 2-6. The Bitwise Operators

Think of the bitwise AND as a way to clear a bit. That is, any bit that is zero in either operand will cause the corresponding bit in the outcome to be set to zero. For example, the following function reads a character from the modem port by using the function **read_modem( )** and will reset the parity bit to zero.

```
char get_char_from_modem(void)
{
  char ch;

  ch = read_modem(); /* get a character from the
                        modem port */
  return(ch & 127);
}
```

Parity is often indicated by the eighth bit, which is set to zero by ANDing it with a byte that has bits 1 through 7 set to 1 and bit 8 set to zero. (This bit pattern is 127 in decimal.) The expression **ch & 127** means to AND the bits in **ch** with the bits that make up the number 127. The net result is that the eighth bit of **ch** will be set to zero. In the following example, assume that **ch** had received the character 'A' and had the parity bit set.

```
  Parity bit
  ↓
    1 1 0 0 0 0 0 1   ch containing an 'A' with parity set
    0 1 1 1 1 1 1 1   127 in binary
&   _____  do bitwise AND
    0 1 0 0 0 0 0 1   'A' without parity
```

The bitwise OR, as the reverse of AND, can be used to set a bit. Any bit that is set to 1 in either operand will cause the corresponding bit in the outcome to be set to 1. For example, the following is 128 | 3:

```
    1 0 0 0 0 0 0 0   128 in binary
    0 0 0 0 0 0 1 1   3 in binary
|   _____  bitwise OR
    1 0 0 0 0 0 1 1   result
```

An exclusive OR, usually abbreviated XOR, will set a bit on if and only if the bits being compared are different. For example, 127 ^ 120 is

```
    0 1 1 1 1 1 1 1   127 in binary
    0 1 1 1 1 0 0 0   120 in binary
^   _____  bitwise XOR
    0 0 0 0 0 1 1 1   result
```

char x;	x as each statement executes	value of x
x = 7;	0 0 0 0 0 1 1 1	7
x = x << 1;	0 0 0 0 1 1 1 0	14
x = x << 3;	0 1 1 1 0 0 0 0	112
x = x << 2;	1 1 0 0 0 0 0 0	192
x = x >> 1;	0 1 1 0 0 0 0 0	96
x = x >> 2;	0 0 0 1 1 0 0 0	24

Each left shift multiplies by 2. Notice that information has been lost after x << 2 because a bit was shifted off the end.

Each right shift divides by 2. Notice that subsequent divisions do not bring back any lost bits.

Table 2-7.   Multiplication and Division with Shift Operators

Remember, relational and logical operators always produce a result that is either zero or 1, whereas the similar bitwise operations may produce any arbitrary value in accordance with the specific operation. In other words, bitwise operations may have values other than zero or 1, while logical operators will always evaluate to zero or 1.

The shift operators >> and << move all bits in a variable to the right or left as specified. The general form of the shift right statement is

variable >> *number of bit positions*

The general form of the shift left statement is

variable << *number of bit positions*

For unsigned values, as bits are shifted off one end, zeroes are brought in the other end. Remember, a shift is *not* a rotate. That is, the bits shifted off one end do not come back around to the other. The bits shifted off are lost, and zeroes are brought in. However, a right shift of a negative value causes 1's to be shifted in.

Bit-shift operations can be very useful when you are decoding external device input, like D/A convertors, and reading status information. The bitwise shift operators can also multiply and divide integers quickly. A shift left effectively multiplies a number by 2, and a shift right divides it by 2, as shown in Table 2-7. The program shown here illustrates the use of the shift operators:

```
/* A bit shift example. */

#include "stdio.h"

main()
{
  unsigned int i;
  int j;

  i = 1;

  /* left shifts */
  for(j=0; j<4; j++) {
    i = i << 1;  /* left shift i by 1,
                which is same as a multiply by 2 */
    printf("left shift %d: %d\n", j, i);
  }

  /* right shifts */
  for(j=0; j<4; j++) {
    i = i >> 1;  /* right shift i by 1,
                which is same as a division by 2 */
    printf("right shift %d: %d\n", j, i);
  }
  return 0;
}
```

The one's complement operator ~ reverses the state of each bit in the specified variable. That is, all 1's are set to zero, and all zeroes are set to 1.

The bitwise operators are often used in cipher routines. If you wished to make a disk file appear unreadable, you could perform some bitwise manipulations on it. One of the simplest methods would be to complement each byte thus reversing each bit in the byte, as shown:

Original byte	0	0	1	0	1	1	0	0	
After 1st complement	1	1	0	1	0	0	1	1	Same
After 2nd complement	0	0	1	0	1	1	0	0	

Notice that a sequence of two complements in a row always produces the original number. The first complement represents the coded version of that byte. The second decodes it to its original value.

You could use the **encode( )** function shown here to encode a character:

```
/* A simple cipher function. */
char encode(char ch)
{
  return(~ch); /* complement it */
}
```

The ? Operator

C allows a very powerful and convenient operator that replaces certain statements of the if-then-else form: the **?**. The ternary operator **?** takes the general form

Exp1 **?** *Exp2* : *Exp3*;

where *Exp1*, *Exp2*, and *Exp3* are expressions. Notice the use and placement of the colon.

The **?** operator works like this: *Exp1* is evaluated. If it is true, *Exp2* is evaluated and becomes the value of the expression. If *Exp1* is false, *Exp3* is evaluated and its value becomes the value of the expression. For example, in

```
x = 10;

y = x>9 ? 100 : 200;
```

y will be assigned the value 100. If **x** had been less than or equal to 9, **y** would have received the value 200. The same code written by using the if-else statement would be

```
x = 10;

if(x>9) y = 100;
else y = 200;
```

See Chapter 3, "C Statements," for a further discussion of the **?** operator in relation to C's other conditional statements.

The & and * Pointer Operators

A *pointer* is the memory address of a variable. A *pointer variable* is a variable that is specifically declared to hold a pointer to its specified type. Knowing a variable's address can be of great help in certain types of routines. However, pointers have three main functions in C. First, they provide a very fast means of referencing array elements. Second, they allow C functions to modify their calling parameters. Third, they support linked lists and other dynamic data structures. Chapter 5 is devoted exclusively to pointers, but this chapter discusses the two operators that are used to manipulate pointers in order to complete the discussion of C operators.

The first operator is &, a unary operator that returns the memory address of its operand. (Remember that a unary operator requires only one operand.) For example,

```
m = &count;
```

places into **m** the address of the variable **count**. This address is the computer's internal location of the variable. It has nothing to do with the *value* of **count**. The operation of the & can be remembered as returning the "the address of." Therefore, the preceding assignment statement could be verbalized as "m receives the address of count."

To better understand this assignment, assume that the variable **count** uses memory location 2000 to store its value. Also assume that **count** has a value of 100. Then, after the assignment, **m** will have the value 2000.

The second operator is *, the complement of &. It is a unary operator that returns the value of the variable located at the address that follows. For example, if **m** contains the memory address of the variable **count**,

```
q = *m;
```

places the value of **count** into **q**. Further, **q** now has the value 100 because 100 is stored at location 2000, the memory address that was stored in **m**. The operation of the * can be remembered as "at address." In this case, you could read the statement as "q receives the value at address m."

Unfortunately, the multiplication sign and the "at address" sign are the same, and the bitwise AND and the "address of" sign are the same.

These operators have no relationship to each other. Both **&** and ***** have a higher precedence than all other arithmetic operators except the unary minus, with which they are equal.

Variables that will hold pointers must be declared as such. Variables that will hold memory addresses—or pointers, as they are called in C—must be declared by preceding the variable name with ***** to indicate to the compiler that it will hold a pointer to that type of variable. For example, to declare a pointer type variable for a **char ch**, write

```
char *ch;
```

Here, **ch** is not a character but rather a pointer to a character— there is a big difference. The type of data that a pointer will be pointing to, in this case **char**, is called the *base type* of the pointer. However, the pointer variable itself is a variable that will be used to hold the address to an object of the base type. Hence, a character pointer (or any pointer, for that matter) will be of sufficient size to hold an address as defined by the architecture of the computer that it is running on. Remember, however, that a pointer should only point to data that is of that pointer's base type.

You can mix pointer and nonpointer directives in the same declaration statement. For example,

```
int x, *y, count;
```

declares **x** and **count** to be integer types and **y** to be a pointer to an integer type.

In the next example, the ***** and **&** operators are used to put the value 10 into a variable called **target**. As expected, this program displays the value 10 on the screen.

```
#include "stdio.h"

main()
{
  int target, source;
  int *m;

  source = 10;
  m = &source;
  target = *m;

  printf("%d", target);
  return 0;
}
```

The sizeof Compile-Time Operator

sizeof is a unary compile-time operator that returns the length, in bytes, of the variable or parenthesized type specifier it precedes. For example, assuming that integers are 2 bytes and **floats** are 4 bytes,

```
float f;

printf("%d ", sizeof f);
printf("%d", sizeof(int));
```

displays **4 2.**

To compute the size of a type, you must enclose the type name in parentheses (like a cast). This is not necessary for variable names, although there is no harm done if you do so.

The ANSI standard defines a special type called **size_t**, which corresponds loosely to an **unsigned** integer. Technically, the value returned by **sizeof** is of type **size_t**, but you can use it as if it were an **unsigned** value.

Primarily, **sizeof** helps to generate portable code when that code depends upon the size of the C built-in data types. For example, imagine a database program that needs to store six integer values per record. If you want to port the database program to the widest variety of computers, you must not assume the size of an integer. Instead, you should determine its actual length by using **sizeof**. In this case, the following routine could write a record to a disk file:

```
/* write 6 integers to a disk file */
void put_rec(int rec[6], FILE *fp)
{
  int len;

  len = fwrite(rec, sizeof rec, 1, fp);
  if(len<>1) printf("write error");
}
```

The key point of this example is that, coded as shown, **put_rec( )** compiles and runs correctly on any computer, no matter how many bytes are in an integer.

One final point: **sizeof** is evaluated at compile time, and the value it produces is treated as a constant within your program.

The Comma Operator

The comma operator strings together several expressions. The left side of the comma operator is always evaluated as **void**. This means that the expression on the right side becomes the value of the total comma-separated expression. For example,

```
x = (y=3, y+1);
```

first assigns **y** the value 3 and then assigns **x** the value 4. You need the parentheses because the comma operator has a lower precedence than the assignment operator.

Essentially, the comma causes a sequence of operations. When you use it on the right side of an assignment statement, the value assigned is the value of the last expression of the comma-separated list.

The comma operator has somewhat the same meaning as the word "and" in normal English in the phrase "do this and this and this."

The . and −> Operators

The . (dot) operator and the −> (arrow) operator are used to reference individual elements of structures and unions. *Structures* and *unions* are compound data types that may be referenced under a single name (see Chapter 7, "Structures, Unions, Enumerations, and User-Defined Types").

The dot operator is used when working with the actual structure or union. The arrow operator is used when a pointer to a structure or union is used. For example, given this global structure:

```
struct employee {
  char name[80];
  int age;
  float wage;
} emp;

struct employee *p = &emp; /* address of emp into p */
```

to assign the value **123.23** to element **wage** of structure **emp**, you would write

```
emp.wage = 123.23;
```

However, the same assignment using a pointer to structure **emp** would be

```
p->wage = 123.23;
```

The [] and ( ) Operators

In C, parentheses are operators that increase the precedence of the operations inside them.

Square brackets perform array indexing (see Chapter 6, "Functions"). Simply, given an array, the expression within the square brackets provides an index into that array. For example,

```
#include "stdio.h"

char s[80];

main()
{
  s[3] = 'X';
  printf("%c", s[3]);
  return 0;
}
```

first assigns the character **X** to the fourth element (remember that all arrays in C begin at zero) of array **s** and then prints that element.

Precedence Summary

Table 2-8 lists the precedence of all C operators. Please note that all operators except the unary operators and **?** associate from left to right. The unary operators **∗**, **&**, and **−**, and the **?** operator associate from right to left.

Note: C++ defines a few additional operators, which are discussed at length later in this book.

Highest	() [] – >.
	! ~ ++ – – – (type) * & sizeof
	* / %
	+ –
	<< >>
	<<= >> =
	== !=
	&
	^
	¦
	&&
	¦¦
	?
	= += –= *= /= %= <<= >>=
Lowest	,

Table 2-8.   The Precedence of C Operators

Expressions

Operators, constants, and variables are the constituents of expressions. An *expression* in C is any valid combination of those pieces. Because most expressions tend to follow the general rules of algebra, they are often taken for granted. However, a few aspects of expressions relate specifically to C.

Order of Evaluation

The ANSI C standard stipulates that the order in which the subexpressions of an expression are evaluated is unspecified. This means that a C or C++ compiler is free to rearrange an expression to produce the most optimal code. It also means that your code should never rely upon the order in which subexpressions are evaluated. For example, the expression

```
x = f1() + f2();
```

does not ensure that **f1( )** will be called before **f2( )**.

Type Conversion in Expressions

When constants and variables of different types are mixed in an expression, they are converted to the same type. The compiler converts all operands "up" to the type of the largest operand. This is called *type promotion*. This is done on an operation-by-operation basis, as described in the following type conversion algorithm:

IF an operand is a **long double**
THEN the second is converted to **long double**
ELSE IF an operand is a **double**
THEN the second is converted to **double**
ELSE IF an operand is a **float**
THEN the second is converted to **float**
ELSE IF an operand is an **unsigned long**
THEN the second is converted to **unsigned long**
ELSE IF an operand is **long**
THEN the second is converted to **long**
ELSE IF an operand is **unsigned**
THEN the second is converted to **unsigned**

There is one additional special case: if one operand is **long** and the other is **unsigned**, and if the value of the **unsigned** cannot be represented by a **long**, then both operands are converted to **unsigned long**.

Once these conversion rules have been applied, each pair of operands will be of the same type, and the result of each operation will be the same as the type of both operands.

For example, let's consider the type conversions that occur in Figure 2-2.

First, the character **ch** is converted to an integer and **float f** is converted to **double**. Then the outcome of **ch/i** is converted to a **double** because **f*d** is **double**. The final result is **double** because, by this time, both operands are **double**.

Casts

You can force an expression to be of a specific type by using a construct called a *cast*. The general form of a cast is

(type) expression

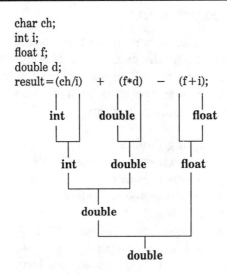

Figure 2-2.   A type conversion example

where *type* is a valid C data type. For example, if you wished to make sure the expression **x/2** would be evaluated to type **float,** you could write

```
(float) x/2
```

Casts are often considered operators. As an operator, a cast is unary and has the same precedence as any other unary operator.

Although casts are not usually used a great deal in programming, they can be very useful at times. For example, suppose you wish to use an integer for loop control but to perform computation on it requires a fractional part, as in the following program:

```
#include "stdio.h"

main() /* print i and i/2 with fractions */
{
  int i;

  for(i=1; i<=100; ++i)
```

```
    printf("%d / 2 is: %f\n", i, (float) i /2);

  return 0;
}
```

Without the cast (**float**), only an integer division would have been performed; the cast ensures that the fractional part of the answer is displayed.

Spacing and Parentheses

You can add tabs and spaces to a C expression to make it easier to read. For example, the following two expressions are the same:

```
x=10/y~(127/x);

x = 10 / y ~(127/x);
```

Redundant or additional parentheses will not cause errors or slow down the execution of the expression. You should use parentheses to make clear the exact order of evaluation, both for yourself and for others. For example, which of the following two expressions is easier to read?

```
x=y/2-34*temp&127;

x = (y/3) - ((34*temp) & 127);
```


C Shorthand

C has a special shorthand that simplifies the coding of a certain type of assignment statement. For example,

```
x = x+10;
```

can be written, in C shorthand, as

```
x += 10;
```

The operator pair **+ =** tells the compiler to assign to **x** the value of **x** plus 10.

This shorthand works for all the binary operators in C (that is, those that require two operands). The general form of this expression,

var = var operator expression

is the same as this shorthand

var operator = expression

For another example,

```
x = x-100;
```

is the same as

```
x -= 100;
```

Shorthand notation is used widely in professionally written C programs; you should become familiar with it.

C Statements

True and False in C
Selection Statements
Iteration Statements
Jump Statements
Expression Statements
Block Statements

This chapter discusses C's rich and varied program statements. The ANSI C standard categorizes C statements into these groups.

selection
iteration
jump
label
expression
block

Included in the selection statements are **if** and **switch**. (The term "conditional statement" is often used in place of "selection statement." However, this book follows the ANSI standard's use of "selection.") The iteration statements are **while, for,** and **do-while**. These are also commonly called loop statements. The jump statements are **break, continue, goto,** and **return**. The label statements include **case** and **default** (discussed along with the **switch** statement) and the label statement (discussed with **goto**). Expression statements are simply statements made up of a valid C expression. Block statements are simply blocks of code. (Remember, a block begins with { and ends with }.)

True and False in C

Many C statements rely upon a conditional expression that determines what course of action is to be taken. A conditional expression evaluates to either a true or a false value. Unlike many other computer languages that specify special values for true and false, a true value in C is any nonzero value, including negative numbers. A false value is zero. This approach to true and false allows a wide range of routines to be coded extremely efficiently.

Selection Statements

C supports two types of selection statements: **if** and **switch**. In addition, the ? operator is an alternative to **if** in certain circumstances.

if

The general form of the **if** statement is

if(*expression*) *statement*;
else *statement*;

According to C syntax, a statement may consist of one of the following: a single statement, a block of statements, or nothing (in the case of empty statements). The **else** clause is optional.

If the **if** expression evaluates to true (anything other than zero), the statement or block that forms the target of the **if** is executed; otherwise, if it exists, the statement or block that is the target of the **else** is executed. Remember, only the code associated with the **if** or the code associated with the **else** will execute—never both.

According to the ANSI standard, the conditional expression controlling the **if** must produce a scalar result. A *scalar* is an integer, a character, a floating-point, or a pointer type. However, it is rare to use a floating-point value to control a conditional statement because execution time is slowed considerably. It takes the CPU several instructions to perform a floating-point operation. Relatively few are needed to perform an integer or character operation.

Consider the following program, which plays a very simple version of the "guess the magic number" game. It prints the message ** **Right** ** when the player guesses the magic number. It generates the magic number using C's random number generator **rand( )**, which returns an arbitrary number between zero and 32,767.

```
/* Magic number program #1. */

#include "stdio.h"
#include "stdlib.h"

main()
{
  int magic; /* magic number */
  int guess; /* user's guess */

  magic = rand();   /* generate the magic number */

  printf("guess the magic number: ");
  scanf("%d", &guess);

  if(guess == magic) printf("** Right **");
  return 0;
}
```

Taking the magic number program further, the next version illustrates the use of the **else** statement to print a message when the wrong number is tried.

```
/* Magic number program #2. */

#include "stdio.h"
#include "stdlib.h"

main()
{
  int magic; /* magic number */
  int guess; /* user's guess */

  magic = rand();   /* generate the magic number */

  printf("guess the magic number: ");
  scanf("%d", &guess);

  if(guess == magic) printf("** Right **");
  else printf("Wrong");

  return 0;
}
```

Nested ifs

A *nested* **if** is the target of another **if** or **else**. Nested **ifs** are very common in programming. Remember that in C, an **else** statement always refers to the nearest **if** statement that is within the same block as the **else** and that is not already associated with an **else**. For example,

```
if(i) {
  if(j) statement 1;
  if(k) statement 2; /* this if */
  else  statement 3; /* is associated with this else */
}
else statement 4; /* associated with if(i) */
```

As the comments describe, the final **else** is not associated with **if(j)** because it is not in the same block. Rather, the final **else** is associated with **if(i)**. Also, the inner **else** is associated with **if(k)** because it is the nearest **if**.

The ANSI standard specifies that at least 15 levels of nesting must be supported. In practice, most compilers allow substantially more.

You can use a nested **if** to add a further improvement to the magic-number program. This addition provides the player with feedback about a wrong guess.

```
/* Magic number program #3. */

#include "stdio.h"
#include "stdlib.h"

main()
{
  int magic;  /* magic number */
  int guess;  /* user's guess */

  magic = rand(); /* get a random number */

  printf("guess the magic number: ");
  scanf("%d", &guess);

  if (guess == magic) {
    printf("** Right **");
    printf(" %d is the magic number\n", magic);
  }
  else {
    printf("Wrong, ");
    if(guess > magic) printf("too high\n");
    else printf("too low\n");
```

```
    }

    return 0;
}
```

Multiple Nested Ifs: The if-else-if Ladder

A common programming construct is the *if-else-if ladder,* sometimes called the *if-else-if staircase* because of its visual appearance. Its general form is

```
if (expression) statement;
else
    if (expression) statement;
    else
        if (expression) statement;
    .
    .
    .
            else statement;
```

The conditions are evaluated from the top down. As soon as a true condition is found, the statement associated with it is executed, and the rest of the ladder is bypassed. If none of the conditions are true, the final **else** will be executed. That is, if all other conditional tests fail, the last **else** statement is performed. If the final **else** is not present, no action will take place if all other conditions are false.

Although the indentation of the general form of the if-else-if ladder is technically correct, it can lead to excessive indentation. Therefore, the if-else-if ladder is generally indented like this:

```
if (expression)
    statement;
else if (expression)
    statement;
else if (expression)
    statement;
    .
    .
    .
else
    statement;
```

With an if-else-if ladder, the magic number program becomes

```
/* Magic number program #4. */

#include "stdio.h"
#include "stdlib.h"

main()
{
  int magic; /* magic number */
  int guess; /* user's guess */

  magic = rand(); /* generate the magic number */

  printf("guess the magic number: ");
  scanf("%d", &guess);

  if(guess == magic) {
    printf("** Right ** ");
    printf("%d is the magic number", magic);
  }
  else if(guess > magic)
    printf("Wrong, too high");
  else printf("Wrong, too low");

  return 0;
}
```

The ? Alternative

You can use the ? operator to replace **if-else** statements of the general form

> if (*condition*)
>   *expression*
> else
>   *expression*

The key restriction is that the target of both the **if** and the **else** must be a single expression, not another C statement.

? is called a *ternary operator* because it requires three operands and takes the general form

> *Exp1* ? *Exp2* : *Exp3*

where *Exp1, Exp2,* and *Exp3* are expressions. Notice the use and placement of the colon.

The value of a ? expression is determined as follows: *Exp1* is evaluated. If it is true, *Exp2* is evaluated and becomes the value of the entire ? expression. If *Exp1* is false, *Exp3* is evaluated and its value becomes the value of the expression. For example, consider

```
x = 10;

y = x>9 ? 100 : 200;
```

In this example, **y** is assigned the value **100**. If **x** had been less than **9, y** would have received the value **200**. The same code written using the **if-else** statement would be

```
x = 10;

if(x>9) y = 100;
else y = 200;
```

The following program uses the ? operator to square an integer value entered by the user. However, this program preserves the sign. That is, **10** squared is **100** and **−10** squared is **−100**.

```
#include "stdio.h"

main()
{
  int isqrd, i;

  printf("enter a number: ");
  scanf("%d", &i);

  isqrd = i>0 ? i*i : -(i*i);

  printf("%d squared is %d", i, isqrd);

  return 0;
}
```

The use of the ? operator to replace **if-else** statements is not restricted to assignments only. Remember, all functions (except those declared as **void**) may return a value. Hence, it is permissible to use one or more function calls in a C expression. When the function's name is encountered, the function is, of course, executed so that its return value may be determined. Therefore, you can execute one or more function calls using the ? operator by placing them in the expressions that form the operands, as in

```
#include "stdio.h"

int f1(int n);
int f2(void);

main()
{
  int t;

  printf("enter a number: ");
  scanf("%d", &t);

  /* print proper message */
  t ? f1(t) + f2() : printf("zero entered");

  return 0;
}

f1(int n)
{
  printf("%d ",n);
  return 0;
}

f2(void)
{
  printf("entered");
  return 0;
}
```

In this simple example, if you enter a zero, the **printf( )** function is called and the **zero entered** message appears. If you enter any other number, then both **f1( )** and **f2( )** are executed. Note that the value of the ? expression is discarded in this example. It is not necessary to assign it to anything.

A word of warning: Some C compilers rearrange the order of evaluation of an expression in an attempt to optimize the object code. This could cause functions that form the operands of the ? operator to execute in an unintended sequence.

With the ? operator, it is possible to rewrite yet again the magic number program:

```
/* Magic number program #5. */

#include "stdio.h"
```

```
#include "stdlib.h"

main()
{
  int magic;
  int guess;

  magic = rand(); /* generate the magic number */

  printf("guess the magic number: ");
  scanf("%d", &guess);

  if(guess == magic) {
    printf("** Right ** ");
    printf("%d is the magic number", magic);
  }
  else
    guess > magic ? printf("High") : printf("Low");

  return 0;
}
```

Here, the ? operator causes the proper message to be displayed based on the outcome of the test **guess > magic.**

The Conditional Expression

Sometimes newcomers to C are confused by the fact that you can use any valid C expression to control the **if** or the **?** operator. That is, the type of expression need not be restricted to only those involving the relational and logical operators (as is the case in languages like BASIC and Pascal). The only requirement is that the expression evaluate to either a zero or nonzero value. The next program reads two integers from the keyboard and displays the quotient. To avoid a divide-by-zero error, an **if** statement, controlled by the second number, is used.

```
/* Divide the first number by the second. */

#include "stdio.h"

main()
{
  int a, b;

  printf("enter two numbers: ");
  scanf("%d%d", &a, &b);
```

```
if(b) printf("%d\n", a/b);
else printf("cannot divide by zero\n");

return 0;
}
```

This approach works because if **b** is zero, the condition controlling the **if** is false and the **else** executes. Otherwise, the condition is true (nonzero) and the division takes place. It is both unnecessary and considered extremely bad style to write this **if** as follows:

```
if(b != 0) printf("%d\n", a/b);
```

It is redundant and potentially inefficient.

switch

C has a built-in multiple-branch selection statement called **switch**. The **switch** successively tests the value of an expression against a list of integer or character constants. When a match is found, the statement or statements associated with that constant are executed. The general form of the **switch** statement is

```
switch(expression) {
  case constant1:
    statement sequence
    break;
  case constant2:
    statement sequence
    break;
  case constant3:
    statement sequence
    break;
    .
    .
    .
  default:
    statement sequence
}
```

The value of *expression* is tested, in order, against the values of the constants specified in the **case** statements. When a match is found, the statement sequence associated with that **case** is executed until the **break** statement is reached or the end of the **switch** statement is reached. The **default** statement is executed if no matches are found. The **default** is optional, and if it is not present, no action takes place if all matches fail.

The ANSI standard specifies that a **switch** can have at least 257 **case** statements. In practice you should limit the number of **case** statements to a smaller amount for efficiency. Although the ANSI standard categorizes the **case** as a label statement, it cannot exist by itself, outside of a **switch**.

The **break** statement is one of C's jump statements. You can use it in loops as well as in **switch** statements. (See the section "Iteration Statements.") When **break** is encountered in a **switch**, the program execution jumps to the line of code following the **switch** statement.

It is important to remember three things about the **switch** statement:

- The **switch** statement differs from the **if** statement in that **switch** can test only for equality, but the **if** can evaluate a relational or logical expression.

- No two **case** constants in the same **switch** can have identical values. Of course, an enclosed **switch** statement and its outer switch may have **case** constants that are the same.

- If character constants are used in the **switch** statement, they are automatically converted to their integer values.

The **switch** statement is often used to process keyboard commands, such as menu selection. As shown here, the function **menu( )** displays a menu for a spelling checker and calls the proper procedures:

```
void menu()
{
  char ch;

  printf("1. Check Spelling\n");
  printf("2. Correct Spelling errors\n");
  printf("3. Display Spelling Errors\n");
  printf("Strike Any Other Key to Skip\n");
```

```
printf("      Enter your choice: ");

ch=getchar();  /* read the selection from
                  the keyboard */

switch(ch) {
  case '1':
    check_spelling();
    break;
  case '2':
    correct_errors();
    break;
  case '3':
    display_errors();
    break;
  default :
    printf("No option selected");
  }
}
```

Technically, the **break** statements inside the **switch** statement are optional. They terminate the statement sequence associated with each constant. If the **break** statement is omitted, execution continues on into the next **case**'s statements until either a **break** or the end of the **switch** is reached. The function shown here makes use of the "drop through" nature of the **cases** to simplify the code for a device-driver input handler:

```
/* Process a value */
void inp_handler(int i)
{
  int flag;

  flag = -1;

  switch(i) {
    case 1:  /* these cases have common statement */
    case 2:  /* sequences */
    case 3:
      flag = 0;
      break;
    case 4:
      flag = 1;
    case 5:
      error(flag);
      break;
    default:
      process(ch);
  }
}
```

This routine illustrates two aspects of the **switch**. First, you can have empty conditions. In this case, the first three **case**s will all execute the same statements:

```
flag = 0;
break;
```

Second, execution continues into the next **case** if no **break** statement is present. If **i** matches 4, **flag** is set to 1, and because there is no **break** statement at the end of that **case**, execution continues and the statement **error(flag)** is executed. If **i** had matched 5, **error(flag)** would have been called with a **flag** value of −1.

The fact that **case**s can be run together when no **break** is present prevents the unwarranted duplication of code, resulting in very efficient code.

Nested switch Statements

You can have a **switch** as part of the statement sequence of an outer **switch**. Even if the **case** constants of the inner and outer **switch** contain common values, no conflicts will arise. For example, the following code fragment is perfectly acceptable:

```
switch(x) {
  case 1:
    switch(y) {
      case 0: printf("divide by zero error");
              break;
      case 1: process(x,y);
    }
    break;
  case 2:
    .
    .
    .
```

Iteration Statements

In C, as in all other modern programming languages, interation statements (commonly called *loops*) allow a set of instructions to be repeatedly performed until a certain condition is reached. This condition may be predefined, as in the **for** loop, or open ended, as in the **while** and **do** loops.

The for Loop

The general format of C's **for** loop is found in all procedural programming languages. In C, however, it has unexpected flexibility and power.

The general form of the **for** statement is

for(*initialization*; *condition*; *increment*) *statement*;

Most commonly, the *initialization* is an assignment statement used to set the loop control variable. The *condition* is a relational expression that determines when the loop will exit. The *increment* defines how the loop control variable will change each time the loop is repeated. These three major sections must be separated by semicolons. The **for** loop continues to execute as long as the condition is true. Once the condition becomes false, program execution resumes on the statement following the **for**.

For example, the following program prints the numbers 1 through 100 on the console:

```
#include "stdio.h"

main()
{
  int x;

  for(x=1; x<=100; x++) printf("%d ", x);

  return 0;
}
```

In the program, **x** is initially set to **1**. Since **x** is less than 100, **printf( )** is called, and **x** is increased by 1 and tested to see if it is still less than or equal to 100. This process repeats until **x** is greater than 100, at which point the loop terminates. In this example, **x** is the *loop control variable,* which is changed and checked each time the loop repeats.

The following example of a **for** loop contains multiple statements:

```
for(x=100; x!=65; x-=5) {
  z = x*x;
  printf("The square of %d, %f",x,z);
}
```

Both the squaring of **x** and the call to **printf( )** are executed until **x** equals **65**. Note that the loop is *negative running:* **x** is initialized to 100 and 5 is subtracted from it each time the loop repeats.

In **for** loops, the conditional test is always performed at the top of the loop. This means that the code inside the loop may not execute at all if the condition is false to begin with. For example,

```
x = 10;

for(y=10; y!=x; ++y) printf("%d", y);

printf("%d", y);
```

This loop will never execute because **x** and **y** are in fact equal when the loop is entered. Since this causes the conditional expression to evaluate to false, neither the body of the loop nor the increment portion of the loop executes. Hence, **y** will still have the value **10** assigned to it, and the output will be only the number 10 printed once on the screen.

for Loop Variations

The previous discussion described the most common form of the **for** loop. However, several variations in the form of the **for** loop are allowed that increase its power, flexibility, and applicability to certain programming situations.

One of the most common variations uses the comma operator to allow two or more variables to control the loop. (Recall that the comma operator strings together a number of expressions in a "do this and this" fashion. See Chapter 2, "Expressions.") For example, this loop uses the variables **x** and **y** to control the loop, with both being initialized inside the **for** statement:

```
for(x=0, y=0; x+y<10; ++x) {
  y = getchar();
  y = y-'0';        /* subtract the ASCII code for 0
                       from y */
  .
  .
  .
}
```

Here, commas separate the two initialization statements. Each time **x** is incremented, the loop repeats, and **y**'s value is set by keyboard input. Both **x** and **y** must be at the correct value for the loop to terminate. **y** must be initialized to zero so that its value is defined prior to the first evaluation of the conditional expression. If **y** is not defined, **y** could (by chance or earlier program usage) contain a 10, thereby making the conditional test false and preventing the loop from executing.

An interesting use of multiple loop control variables is found in the **converge( )** function shown next. The purpose of **converge( )** is to display a string by printing characters from both ends at the same time, converging in the middle at the specified line. This requires positioning the cursor at various disconnected points on the screen. Because of the wide variety of environments that C runs under, neither the ANSI C standard nor the AT&T C++ specification defines such a function. However, virtually all C compilers supply one, although the name of the function may vary. This program uses Turbo C++'s **gotoxy( )** function to position the cursor. (It requires the header CONIO.H.)

```
#include "stdio.h"
#include "conio.h" /* non-standard header file */
#include "string.h"

void converge(int line, char *message);

main()
{
  converge(10, "This is a test of converge().");

  return 0;
}

/* This function displays a string starting at the left
   side of the specified line.  It writes characters
   from both the ends converging at the middle.  It
   uses Turbo C++'s gotoxy() function to position the
   cursor.
*/
void converge(int line, char *message)
{
  int i, j;
```

```
  for(i=1, j=strlen(message); i<j; i++, j--) {
    gotoxy(i, line); printf("%c", message[i-1]);
    gotoxy(j, line); printf("%c", message[j-1]);
  }
}
```

If you use a different C++ compiler, check your user manuals to see what the cursor-positioning function is called.

In **converge( )**, the **for** loop uses two loop control variables, **i** and **j**, to index the string from opposite ends. As the loop iterates, **i** is increased and **j** is decreased. The loop stops when **i** is equal to **j**, thus ensuring that all characters have been written.

The conditional expression does not necessarily have to involve testing the loop control variable against some target value. In fact, the condition may be any relational or logical statement. This means that you can test for several possible terminating conditions. For example, you could use the following function to log a user onto a remote system. The user has three tries to enter the password. The loop terminates when either the three tries are used up or the correct password is entered.

```
void sign_on(void)
{
  char str[20];
  int x;

  for(x=0; x<3 && strcmp(str, "password"); ++x) {
    printf("enter password please:");
    gets(str);
  }
  if(x==3) return;
  /* else log user in ... */
}
```

This function uses **strcmp( )**, which is the standard library function that compares two strings and returns zero if they match.

Remember, each of the three sections of the **for** loop may consist of any valid C expression. They need not actually have anything to do with what the sections are usually used for. With this in mind, consider the following example:

```
#include "stdio.h"

int sqrnum(int num);
int readnum(void);
int prompt(void);
```

```
main()
{
  int t;

  for(prompt(); t=readnum(); prompt())
    sqrnum(t);

  return 0;
}

prompt(void)
{
  printf("enter a number: ");
  return 0;
}

readnum(void)
{
  int t;

  scanf("%d", &t);
  return t;
}

sqrnum(int num)
{
  printf("%d\n", num*num);
  return num*num;
}
```

If you look closely at the **for** loop in **main( )**, you will see that each part of the **for** is made up of function calls that prompt the user and read a number entered from the keyboard. If the number entered is zero, the loop terminates because the conditional expression will be false; otherwise, the number is squared. Thus, in this **for** loop, the initialization and increment portions are used in a nontraditional but completely valid sense.

Another interesting trait of the **for** loop is that pieces of the loop definition need not be there. In fact, there need not be an expression present for any of the sections—the expressions are optional. For example, this loop will run until a 123 is entered:

```
for(x=0; x!=123; ) scanf("%d", &x);
```

Notice that the increment portion of the **for** definition is blank. This means that each time the loop repeats, **x** is tested to see if it equals 123, but no further action takes place. If, however, you type **123** at the keyboard, the loop condition becomes false and the loop terminates.

It is not uncommon to see the initialization occur outside the **for** statement. This happens most frequently when the initial condition of the loop control variable must be computed by some complex means, as in this example:

```
gets(s);  /* read a string into s */
if(*s) x = strlen(s); /* get the string's length */

for( ;x<10; ) {
  printf("%d",x);
  ++x;
}
```

Here, the initialization section has been left blank and x is initialized before the loop is entered.

The Infinite Loop

Although you can use any loop statement to create an infinite loop, the **for** is traditionally used for this purpose. Since none of the three expressions that form the **for** loop are required, you can make an endless loop by leaving the conditional expression empty, as shown here:

```
for(;;) printf(" this loop will run forever.\n");
```

When absent, the condition is assumed to be a true value in C. Although you may have an initialization and increment expression, C programmers usually use the **for(;;)** construct to signify an infinite loop.

Actually, the **for(;;)** construct does not necessarily create an infinite loop because C's **break** statement, when encountered anywhere inside the body of a loop, causes immediate termination (**break** is discussed in detail later in this chapter). Program control then resumes at the code following the loop, as shown here:

```
ch='\0';

for(;;) {
  ch = getchar();  /* get a character */
  if(ch=='A') break;  /* exit the loop */
}

printf("you typed an A");
```

This loop will run until you type an **A** at the keyboard.

for Loops with No Bodies

A statement, as defined by the C syntax, may be empty. This means that the body of the **for** loop (or any other loop) may also be empty. This fact can be used to improve the efficiency of certain algorithms, as well as to create time-delay loops.

One of the most common tasks in programming is the removal of spaces from an input stream. For example, a database may allow a query such as "show all balances less than 400." The database needs to have each word fed to it separately, without spaces. That is, the data-base input processor recognizes "show" but not " show" as a command. The following loop removes leading spaces from the stream pointed to by **str**.

```
for( ; *str==' '; str++) ;
```

As you can see, there is no body to this loop—and no need for one, either.

Programs often use *time-delay loops*. The following shows how to create one by using **for**:

```
for(t=0; t<SOME_VALUE; t++) ;
```

The while Loop

The second loop available in C is the **while**. The general form is

> while (*condition*) *statement*;

where *statement*, as stated earlier, is either an empty statement, a single statement, or a block of statements that is to be repeated. The *condition* may be any expression, with true being any nonzero value. The loop iterates while the condition is true. When the condition becomes false, program control passes to the line after the loop code.

The following example shows a keyboard input routine that simply loops until the character **A** is typed.

```
wait_for_char(void)
{
  char ch;

  ch = '\0';  /* initialize ch */
  while(ch != 'A')  ch = getchar();
  return ch;
}
```

First, **ch** is initialized to null. As a local variable, its value is not known when **wait_for_char( )** is executed. The **while** loop then begins by checking to see if **ch** is not equal to **A**. Because **ch** was initialized to null beforehand, the test is true and the loop begins. Each time a key is pressed on the keyboard, the test is tried again. Once an **A** is typed, the condition becomes false because **ch** equals **A**, and the loop terminates.

As with the **for** loop, **while** loops check the test condition at the top of the loop, which means that the loop code may not execute at all. This eliminates having to perform a separate conditional test before the loop. This is illustrated by the function **pad( )**, which adds spaces to the end of a string up to a predefined length. If the string is already at the desired length, no spaces are added.

```
#include "stdio.h"
#include "string.h"

void pad(char *s, int length);

main()
{
  char str[80];

  strcpy(str, "this is a test");
  pad(str, 40);
  printf("%d", strlen(str));

  return 0;
}

/* add spaces to the end of a string */
void pad(char *s, int length)
{
  int l;

  l = strlen(s);  /* find out how long it is */
```

```
while(l<length) {
  s[l] = ' ';    /* insert a space */
  l++;
}
s[l]='\0';  /* strings need to be
                terminated in a null */
}
```

The two arguments to **pad( )** are **s**, a pointer to the string to lengthen, and **length**, the number of characters that **s** will be lengthened to. If the string **s** is already equal to or greater than **length**, the code inside the **while** loop will never execute. If **s** is less than **length**, **pad( )** adds the required number of spaces onto the string. The **strlen( )** function, which is part of the standard library, returns the length of the string.

If several separate conditions need to terminate a **while** loop, a single variable commonly forms the conditional expression. The value of this variable is set at various points throughout the loop. In this example,

```
void func1(void)
{
  int working;

  working = 1;   /* i.e., true */

  while(working) {
    working = process1();
    if(working)
      working = process2();
    if(working)
      working = process3();
  }
}
```

any of the three routines may return false and cause the loop to exit.

There need not be any statements at all in the body of the **while** loop. For example,

```
while((ch=getchar()) != 'A') ;
```

simply loops until the character **A** is typed at the keyboard. If you feel uncomfortable putting the assignment inside the **while** conditional expression, remember that the equal sign is really just an operator that evaluates to the value of the right-hand operand.

The do-while Loop

Unlike the **for** and **while** loops, which test the loop condition at the top of the loop, the **do-while** loop checks the condition at the bottom of the loop. This means that a **do-while** loop always executes at least once. The general form of the **do-while** loop is

```
do {
    statement;
} while (condition);
```

Although the braces are not necessary when only one statement is present, they improve readability and avoid confusion (to the reader, not the compiler) with the **while**. The **do-while** iterates until *condition* becomes false.

This **do-while** reads numbers from the keyboard until one is less than or equal to 100:

```
do {
  scanf("%d", &num);
} while(num > 100);
```

Perhaps the most common use of the **do-while** is in a menu-selection routine. When a valid response is typed, it is returned as the value of the function. Invalid responses cause a reprompt. The following code shows an improved version of the spelling-checker menu developed earlier in this chapter:

```
void menu(void)
{
  char ch;

  printf("1. Check Spelling\n");
  printf("2. Correct Spelling Errors\n");
  printf("3. Display Spelling Errors\n");
  printf("    Enter your choice: ");

  do {
    ch = getchar();  /* read the selection from
                        the keyboard */
    switch(ch) {
      case '1':
        check_spelling();
        break;
```

```
      case '2':
        correct_errors();
        break;
      case '3':
        display_errors();
        break;
    }
  } while(ch!='1' && ch!='2' && ch!='3');
}
```

In the case of a menu function, you will always want it to execute at least once, making it perfect for the **do-while** loop. After the options have been displayed, the program loops until a valid option is selected.

Jump Statements

C has four statements that perform an unconditional branch: **return, goto, break,** and **continue.** Of these, you may use the **return** and **goto** statements anywhere in your program. You may use the **break** and **continue** statements in conjuction with any of the loop statements. (You may also use the **break** with the **switch,** as discussed earlier in this chapter.)

The return Statement

The **return** statement is used to return from a function. It is categorized by the ANSI C standard as a jump statement because it causes execution to return (that is, jump back) to the point at which the call to the function was made. If the **return** has a value associated with it, that value is the return value of the function. In C, a function that is not declared as returning **void** does not technically have to return a value. If no return value is specified, a garbage value is returned. (Some C compilers automatically return zero if no value is specified, but you should not count on this.) In C++, however, a function not declared as returning **void** *must* return a value. Even in C, if a function is declared as returning a value, it is good programming practice that a value be returned.

The general form of **return** is

return *expression*;

The *expression* is only present if a function is declared as returning a value. If the function is declared as returning **void** no value may be returned.

You can have as many **return** statements as you like within a function. However, the function stops executing as soon as the first **return** is encountered. The } that ends a function also causes the function to return. It is the same as a **return** without any specified value.

A function declared as **void** may not contain a **return** statement that specifies a value. (See Chapter 6, "Functions," for more information on **return**.)

The goto Statement

There are no programming situations that require the use of the **goto** statement. C has a rich set of control structures and allows additional control by using **break** and **continue**, so there is little need for the **goto**. It has a tendency to confuse a program and render it nearly unreadable. However, since C was designed to be a replacement for assembly code, its inclusion is justified. If used wisely, it can benefit certain programming situations.

The **goto** statement requires a label for operation. A *label* is a valid C identifier followed by a colon. (The ANSI standard refers to this type of construct as a *label statement*.) Furthermore, the label must be in the same function as the **goto** that uses it—you cannot jump between functions. The general form of the **goto** is

goto *label*;
  .
  .
  .
label:

where *label* is any valid label, which may be either before or after the *goto*. For example, a loop from 1 to 100 could be written by using a *goto* and a label as shown here:

```
x = 1;

loop1:
  x++;
  if(x<100) goto loop1;
```

The break Statement

The **break** statement has two uses. The first is to terminate a **case** in the **switch** statement, as explained earlier in this chapter. The second is to force immediate termination of a loop, bypassing the normal loop conditional test.

When the **break** statement is encountered inside a loop, the loop is immediately terminated and program control resumes at the next statement following the loop, as in this example:

```
#include "stdio.h"

main()
{
  int t;

  for(t=0; t<100; t++) {
    printf("%d ", t);
    if(t==10) break;
  }

  return 0;
}
```

This code prints the numbers 0 through 10 on the screen and then terminates because the **break** causes immediate exit from the loop, overriding $t < 100$, the conditional test built into the loop.

Programmers often use the **break** statement in loops in which a special condition can cause immediate termination. For example, here a keypress can stop the execution of the **look＿up( )** routine:

```
look_up(char *name)
{
  do {
    /* look up names ... */
    if(kbhit()) break;
  } while(!found);
  /* process match */
}
```

If the file is very long, you can press a key and return from the function early. The **kbhit( )** function returns zero if no key has been pressed, nonzero otherwise. Because of the wide differences between computing environments, the ANSI standard does not define **kbhit( )**, but you will almost certainly have it (or one with a slightly different name) supplied with your compiler.

A **break** will cause an exit from only the innermost loop. For example,

```
for(t=0; t<100; ++t) {
  count = 1;
  for(;;) {
    printf("%d ", count);
    count++;
    if(count==10) break;
  }
}
```

prints the numbers 1 through 10 on the screen 100 times. Each time the **break** is encountered, control passes back to the outer **for** loop.

A **break** used in a **switch** statement affects only that **switch** and not any loop that the **switch** happens to be in.

The exit Function

Just as you can break out of a loop, you can break out of a program by using the standard library function **exit( )**. This function causes immediate termination of the entire program. In effect, **exit( )** acts as if it were breaking out of the entire program. Functionally, **exit( )** is the equivalent to a **return** from **main( )**.

The general form of the **exit( )** function is

void exit(int *return_code*);

The value of *return_code* is returned to the calling process, which is usually the operating system. By convention, returning 0 indicates normal termination. Other arguments are used to indicate some sort of error.

Programmers frequently use **exit( )** when a mandatory condition for the program's execution is not satisfied. For example, imagine a computer game that requries a color graphics card in the system. The **main( )** function of this game might look like this,

```
main()
{
  if(!color_card()) exit(1);
  play();

  return 0;
}
```

where **color_card( )** is a user-defined function that returns true if the color card is present. If the card is not in the system, **color_card( )** returns false, and the program terminates.

This version of **menu( )** uses **exit( )** to quit the program and return to the operating system:

```
menu(void)
{

  char ch;

  printf("1. Check Spelling\n");
  printf("2. Correct Spelling Errors\n");
  printf("3. Display Spelling Errors\n");
  printf("4. Quit\n");
  printf("     Enter your choice: ");

  do {
    ch=getchar();  /* read the selection from
                       the keyboard */
      switch(ch) {
        case '1':
          check_spelling();
          break;
        case '2':
          correct_errors();
          break;
        case '3':
          display_errors();
          break;
        case '4':
          exit(0);  /* return to OS */
      }
  } while(ch!='1' && ch!='2' && ch!='3');
}
```

The continue Statement

In many ways, the **continue** statement is the complement to the **break** statement. But instead of forcing termination, **continue** forces the next iteration of the loop to take place, skipping any code in between. For the **for** loops, **continue** causes the conditional test and then the increment portions of the loop to execute. For the **while** and **do-while**, program control passes to the conditional tests. For example, this program counts the number of spaces contained in the string entered by the user:

```
/* Count spaces */

#include "stdio.h"

main()
{
  char s[80], *str;
  int space;

  printf("enter a string: ");
  gets(s);
  str = s;

  for(space=0; *str; str++) {
    if(*str!=' ') continue;
    space++;
  }
  printf("%d spaces\n", space);

  return 0;
}
```

Each character is tested to see if it is a space. If it is not, the **continue** statement forces the **for** to iterate again. If the character is a space, **space** is incremented.

As you can see in the following example, you can use **continue** to expedite the exit for a loop by forcing the conditional test to be performed sooner:

```
void code(void)
{
  char done, ch;

  done = 0;
  while(!done) {
    ch = getchar();
    if(ch=='$') {
      done = 1;
      continue;
    }
    putchar(ch+1);  /* shift the alphabet one
                       position */

  }
}
```

You could use this function to code a message by shifting all characters one letter higher; for example, an "a" would become a "b." The function terminates when a $ is read. No further output will occur because the conditional test, brought into effect by **continue**, will find **done** to be true and will cause the loop to exit.

Expression Statements

Chapter 2 covers C expressions thoroughly. However, a few special points are mentioned here. An expression statement is simply a valid C expression followed by a semicolon, as in these examples:

```
func();  /* a function call */

a = b+c; /* an assignment statement */

b+f();   /* a valid, but do-nothing statement */

;        /* an empty statement */
```

The first expression statement executes a function call. The second is an assignment. The third expression, although strange, is evaluated by the compiler because the function **f( )** may need to perform some necessary task. The final example shows that C allows a statement to be empty (sometimes called a *null statement*).

Block Statements

Block statements are simply groups of related statements that are treated as a unit. The statements that make up a block are logically bound together. A block is begun with { and terminated with }. Programmers commonly use a block statement to create a multistatement target for some other statement, like the **if**. However, you may place a block statement anywhere you would put any other statement. For example, this is perfectly valid (although unusual) C code:

```
#include "stdio.h"

main()
{
  int i;

  {  /* a block statement */
     i = 120;
     printf("%d", i);
  }

  return 0;
}
```

Arrays and Strings

F
O
U
R

An *array* is a collection of variables of the same type that are referenced by a common name. A specific element in an array is accessed by an index. In C, all arrays consist of contiguous memory locations. The lowest address corresponds to the first element, and the highest address to the last element. Arrays may have one or several dimensions. The most common array in C is the *string*, which is simply an array of characters that is terminated by a null. This approach to strings gives C greater power and efficiency than other languages.

Note: In C, arrays and pointers are closely related; a discussion of one usually involves references to the other. This chapter focuses on arrays, and Chapter 5 looks closely at pointers. You will want to read both to fully understand these important C constructs.

Single-Dimension Arrays

The general form used to declare a single-dimension array is

type var-name[size];

Like other variables, arrays must be explicitly declared so that the compiler may allocate space for them in memory. Here, *type* declares the base type of the array, which is the type of each element in the array, and *size* defines how many elements the array will hold. For example, to declare a 100-element array of type **double** called **balance**, use this statement:

```
double balance[100];
```

In C, all arrays have zero as the index of their first element. Therefore, when you write

```
char p[10];
```

you are declaring a character array that has 10 elements, p[0] through [9]. The following program loads an integer array with the numbers zero through 99.

```
main()
{
  int x[100];   /* this reserves 100 integer elements */
  int t;

  for(t=0; t<100; ++t) x[t] = t;

  return 0;
}
```

The amount of storage required to hold an array is directly related to its type and size. For a single-dimension array, the total size of an array in bytes is computed as shown here:

total bytes = sizeof(type) * size of array

C has no boundary checking on arrays: you could overwrite either end of an array and write into some other variable's data, or even into a piece of the program's code. As the programmer, it is your job to provide boundary checking when it is needed. For example, this code will compile without error but is incorrect because the **for** loop causes the array **count** to be overrun.

```
int count[10], i;

 /* this causes count to be overrun */
for(i=0; i<100; i++) count[i] = i;
```

Single-dimension arrays are essentially lists of information of the same type that are stored in contiguous memory locations in index order. For example, assume array **a** is declared as shown here, and starts at memory location 1000:

```
char a[7];
```

This is how it appears in memory:

element	a[0]	a[1]	a[2]	a[3]	a[4]	a[5]	a[6]
address	1000	1001	1002	1003	1004	1005	1006

Generating a Pointer to an Array

You can generate a pointer to the first element of an array simply by specifying its name, without any index. For example, given

```
int sample[10];
```

you can generate a pointer to the first element by simply using the name **sample**, as shown in this fragment, which assigns **p** the address of the first element of **sample**.

```
int *p;
int sample[10];

p = sample;
```

You can also specify the address of the first element of an array by using the & operator. For example, **sample** and **&sample[0]** produce the same results. However, in professionally written C code, you will almost never see something like **&sample[0]** used.

Passing Single-Dimension Arrays to Functions

In C, you cannot pass an entire array as an argument to a function. You can, however, pass a pointer to an array to a function by specifying the array's name without an index. For example, the following fragment passes the address of **i** to **func1( )**.

```
main()
{
  int i[10];

  func1(i);
    .
    .
    .
}
```

If a function will be receiving a single-dimension array, you may declare the formal parameter in one of three ways: as a pointer, as a sized array, or as an unsized array. For example, to receive **i**, you can declare a function called **func1( )** as

```
func1(int *x) /* pointer */
{
    .
    .
    .
}
```

or

```
func1(int x[10]) /* sized array */
{
    .
    .
    .
}
```

or finally, as

```
func1(int x[]) /* unsized array */
{
    .
    .
    .
}
```

All three methods of declaration are identical because each tells the compiler that an integer pointer is going to be received. In the first declaration, a pointer is actually used; in the second, the standard array declaration is employed. In the final version, a modified version of an array declaration simply specifies that a pointer to an array of type **int** of some length is to be received. If you give it a little thought, you can see that as far as the function is concerned, it doesn't matter what the length of the array actually is because C performs no boundary checking. In fact, as far as the compiler is concerned,

```
func1(int x[32])
{
    .
    .
    .
}
```

also works because the C compiler generates code that instructs **func1( )** to receive a pointer; it does not actually create a 32-element array.

Strings

By far the most common use of one-dimensional arrays is the character string. In C, a string is defined as a character array that is terminated by a null. A null is specified as \0 and is zero. Therefore, you must declare character arrays to be one character longer than the largest string that they are to hold. For example, if you wish to declare an array **s** that will hold a ten-character string, you would write

```
char s[11];
```

This makes room for the null at the end of the string.

Although C does not have a string data type, it still allows string constants. A *string constant* is a list of characters enclosed in double quotes. For example:

"hello there"
"this is a test"

It is not necessary to manually add the null onto the end of string constants—the compiler does this automatically.

C supports a wide range of string manipulation functions. The most common are shown in Table 4-1.

These functions use the standard header file **string.h**. (Part Two of this book, "C++-Specific Features," discusses these and other string functions.) The following program illustrates the use of these string functions:

```
#include "stdio.h"
#include "string.h"

main()
{
  char s1[80],s2[80];

  gets(s1); gets(s2);

  printf("lengths: %d %d\n", strlen(s1), strlen(s2));

  if(!strcmp(s1, s2)) printf("The strings are equal\n");

  strcat(s1, s2);
  printf("%s\n",s1);

  strcpy(s1, "This is a test.\n");
  printf(s1);
  if(strchr("hello", 'e')) printf("e is in hello\n");
  if(strstr("hi there", "hi")) printf("found hi");

  return 0;
}
```

Name	Function
strcpy(s1, s2)	Copies **s2** into **s1**
strcat(s1, s2)	Concatenates **s2** onto the end of **s1**
strlen(s1)	Returns the length of **s1**
strcmp(s1, s2)	Returns zero if **s1** and **s2** are the same; less than zero if **s1** < **s2**; greater than zero if **s1** > **s2**
strchr(s1, ch)	Returns a pointer to the first occurrence of **ch** in **s1**
strstr(s1, s2)	Returns a pointer to the first occurrence of **s2** in **s1**

Table 4-1.   C's Most Common String Manipulation Functions

If this program is run and the strings "hello" and "hello" are entered, the output is

```
lengths: 5 5
The strings are equal
hellohello
This is a test.
e is in hello
found hi
```

Remember that **strcmp( )** returns **false** if the strings are equal, so be sure to use the **!** to reverse the condition, as shown in the example, if you are testing for equality.

Two-Dimensional Arrays

C supports multidimensional arrays. The simplest form of the multidimensional array is the two-dimensional array. A *two-dimensional array* is, in essence, an array of one-dimensional arrays. To declare a two-dimensional integer array **d** of size 10,20, you would write

```
int d[10][20];
```

Pay careful attention to the declaration: unlike most other computer languages, which use commas to separate the array dimensions, C places each dimension in its own set of brackets.

Similarly, to access point 1,2 of array **d**, you would use

```
d[1][2]
```

In the following example, a two-dimensional array is loaded with the numbers 1 through 12 and then the array is printed row by row.

```
#include "stdio.h"

main()
{
  int t, i, num[3][4];

  for(t=0; t<3; ++t)
    for(i=0; i<4; ++i)
      num[t][i] = (t*4)+i+1;

  /* now print them out */
```

```
for(t=0; t<3; ++t) {
  for(i=0; i<4; ++i)
    printf("%3d ", num[t][i]);
  printf("\n");
}
return 0;
}
```

Here, **num[0][0]** will have the value **1**, **num[0][1]** the value **2**, **num[0][2]** the value **3**, and so on. The value of **num[2][3]** will be **12**. You can visualize the **num** array as shown here.

	0	1	2	3
0	1	2	3	4
1	5	6	7	8
2	9	10	11	12

Two-dimensional arrays are stored in a row-column matrix, where the first index indicates the row and the second indicates the column. This means that the rightmost index changes more quickly than the leftmost when accessing the elements in the array in the order that they are actually stored in memory. See Figure 4-1 for a graphic representation of a two-dimensional array in memory. You can think of the first index as a "pointer" to the correct row.

In the case of a two-dimensional array, the following formula will find the number of bytes of memory needed for the array.

$$bytes = \text{size of 1st index} * \text{size of 2nd index} * sizeof(\text{base type})$$

Therefore, assuming 2-byte integers, an integer array with dimensions 10,5 would have

$$10 * 5 * 2$$

or 100 bytes allocated.

When a two-dimensional array is used as an argument to a function, only a pointer to the first element is actually passed. However, a function receiving a two-dimensional array as a parameter must minimally define the length of the rightmost dimension. This is because the C compiler needs to know the length of each row if it is to index the array correctly. For example, a function that receives a two-dimensional integer array with dimensions 10,10 is declared like this:

```
func1(int x[][10])
{
    .
    .
    .
}
```

You can specify the first dimension if you like, but it is not necessary. The compiler needs to know the rightmost dimension in order to work on statements such as

```
x[2][4]
```

inside the function. If the length of the rows is not known, then it is impossible to know where the third row begins.

The short program shown here uses a two-dimensional array to store the numeric grade for each student in a teacher's classes. The

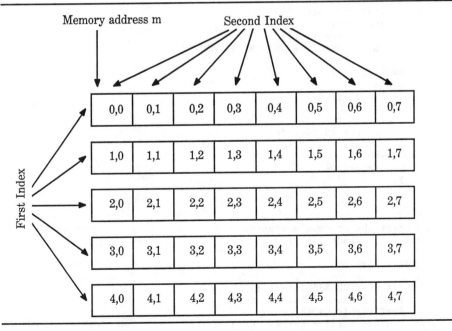

Figure 4-1.   A two-dimensional array in memory

program assumes that the teacher has three classes and a maximum of
30 students per class. Notice the way that the array **grade** is accessed
by each of the functions.

```c
#include "stdio.h"
#include "ctype.h"
#include "stdlib.h"

/* A simple student grades database. */

#define CLASSES  3
#define GRADES   30

int grade[CLASSES][GRADES];

void enter_grades(void);
int get_grade(int num);
void disp_grades(int g[][GRADES]);

main()
{
  char ch, str[80];

  for(;;) {
    do {
      printf("(E)nter grades\n");
      printf("(R)eport grades\n");
      printf("(Q)uit\n");
      gets(str);
      ch = toupper(*str);
    } while(ch!='E' && ch!='R' && ch!='Q');

    switch(ch) {
      case 'E':
        enter_grades();
        break;
      case 'R':
        disp_grades(grade);
        break;
      case 'Q':
        return 0;
    }
  }

}
/* Enter the student's grades. */
void enter_grades(void)
{
  int t, i;

  for(t=0; t<CLASSES; t++) {
    printf("Class # %d:\n", t+1);
    for(i=0; i<GRADES; ++i)
      grade[t][i] = get_grade(i);
  }
}
```

```
/* Read a grade. */
get_grade(int num)
{
  char s[80];

  printf("enter grade for student # %d:\n",num+1);
  gets(s);
  return(atoi(s));
}
/* Display grades. */
void disp_grades(int g[][GRADES])
{
  int t, i;

  for(t=0; t<CLASSES; ++t) {
    printf("Class # %d:\n", t+1);
    for(i=0; i<GRADES; ++i)
      printf("student #%d is %d\n", i+1, g[t][i]);
  }
}
```

Arrays of Strings

It is not uncommon in programming to use an array of strings. For example, the input processor to a database might verify user commands against an array of valid commands. To create an array of strings, use a two-dimensional character array. The size of the left index determines the number of strings and the size of the right index specifies the maximum length of each string. The following code declares an array of 30 strings, each having a maximum length of 80 characters:

```
char str_array[30][80];
```

It is easy to access an individual string: Simply specify only the left index. For example, this statement calls **gets( )** with the third string in **str _ array**:

```
gets(str_array[2]);
```

This is functionally equivalent to

```
gets(&str_array[2][0]);
```

but the previous form is much more common in professionally written code.

To understand better how string arrays work, study the following short program which uses a string array as the basis for a very simple text editor:

```c
#include "stdio.h"

#define MAX 100
#define LEN 80

char text[MAX][LEN];
/* A very simple text editor */
main()
{
  register int t, i, j;

  printf("Enter an empty line to quit.\n");

  for(t=0; t<MAX; t++) {
    printf("%d: ", t);
    gets(text[t]);
    if(!*text[t]) break; /* quit on blank line */
  }

  for(i=0; i<t; i++) {
    for(j=0; text[i][j]; j++) putchar(text[i][j]);
    putchar('\n');
  }

  return 0;
}
```

This program inputs lines of text until a blank line is entered. Then it redisplays each line, one character at a time.

Multidimensional Arrays

C allows arrays of more than two dimensions. The exact limit, if any, is determined by your compiler. The general form of a multidimensional array declaration is

$$type\ name[a][b][c]\ldots[z];$$

Arrays of three or more dimensions are not often used because of the amount of memory required to hold them. For example, a four-dimensional character array with dimensions 10,6,9,4 would require

$$10 * 6 * 9 * 4$$

or 2,160 bytes.

If the array held 2-byte integers, 4320 bytes would be needed. If the array held **double** (assuming 8 bytes per **double**), 34,560 bytes would be required. The storage required increases exponentially with the number of dimensions.

When passing multidimensional arrays into functions, you must declare all but the leftmost dimension. For example, if you declare array **m** as

```
int m[4][3][6][5];
```

a function, **func1( )**, that receives **m** would look like this:

```
func1(int d[][3][6][5])
{
    .
    .
    .
```

Of course, you may include the leftmost dimension if you like.

Pointers Can Be Indexed

In C, pointers and arrays are closely related. As you know, an array name without an index is a pointer to the first element in the array. For example, consider the following array:

```
char p[10];
```

The following statements are identical:

```
p
```

```
&p[0]
```

Put another way,

```
p==&p[0]
```

evaluates true because the address of the first element of an array is the same as the address of the array.

Conversely, any pointer variable can be indexed as if it were declared to be an array. For example, consider this fragment:

```
int *p, i[10];

p = i;
p[5] = 100;    /* assign using index */
*(p+5) = 100;  /* assign using pointer arithmetic */
```

Both of the last two assignment statements place the value **100** in the sixth element of **i**. The first statement indexes **p**; the second uses pointer arithmetic. Either way, the result is the same. (Chapter 5 discusses pointers and pointer arithmetic.)

The same holds true for arrays of two or more dimensions. For example, assuming that **a** is a 10 x 10 integer array, these two statements are equivalent:

```
a
```

```
&a[0][0]
```

Further, the 0,4 element of **a** may be referenced in two ways: either by array indexing, **a[0][4]**, or by the pointer, ***(a+4)**. Similarily, element 1,2 is either **a[1][2]** or ***(a+12)**. In general, for any two-dimensional array,

a[j][k]

is equivalent to

*(a+(j*row__length)+k)

Pointers are sometimes used to access arrays because pointer arithmetic is often a faster process than array indexing.

In a sense, a two-dimensional array is like an array of row pointers to arrays of rows. Therefore, one easy way to use pointers to access elements of a two-dimensional array is to use a separate pointer variable. The following function prints the contents of the specified row for the global integer array **num**.

```
int num[10][10];
   .
   .
   .
void  pr_row(int j)
{
  int *p, t;

  p = &num[j][0]; /* get address of first
                     element in row j */
  for(t=0; t<10; ++t) printf("%d ", *(p+t));
}
```

You can generalize this routine by making the calling arguments be the row, the row length, and a pointer to the first array element, as shown here:

```
void pr_row(int j, int row_dimension, int *p)
{
  int t;

  p = p + (j * row_dimension);
  for(t=0; t<row_dimension; ++t)
    printf("%d ", *(p+t));
}
```

You can think of arrays of more than two dimensions in the same way. For example, a three-dimensional array can be reduced to a pointer to a two-dimensional array, which can be reduced to a pointer to a one-dimensional array. Generally, an n-dimensional array can be reduced to a pointer and an $(n-1)$-dimensional array. This new array can be reduced again by using the same method. The process ends when a single-dimension array is produced.

Array Initialization

C allows the initialization of arrays at the time of declaration. The general form of array initialization is similar to that of other variables, as shown here:

> *type-specifier array _ name[size1] . . . [sizeN]* = { *value-list* };

The *value-list* is a comma-separated list of constants that are type compatible with *type-specifier*. The first constant is placed in the first position of the array, the second constant in the second position, and so on. Note that a semicolon follows the **}**. The following example initializes a ten-element integer array with the numbers 1 through 10.

```
int i[10] = {1, 2, 3, 4, 5, 6, 7, 8, 9, 10};
```

This means that that **i[0]** will have the value **1** and **i[9]** will have the value **10**.

Character arrays that hold strings allow a shorthand initialization that takes the form

> char *array_name[size]* = *"string"*;

For example, this code fragment initializes **str** to the phrase "I like C++":

```
char str[11] = "I like C++";
```

This is the same as writing

```
char str[11] = {'I', ' ', 'l', 'i', 'k', 'e', ' ', 'C',
                '+', '+', '\0'};
```

Because all strings in C end with a null, make sure that the array you declare is long enough to include it. This is why **str** is 11 characters long even though "I like C++" is only 10. When you use the string constant, the compiler automatically supplies the null terminator.

Multidimensional arrays are initialized in the same way as one-dimensional ones. For example, the following initializes **sqrs** with the numbers 1 through 10 and their squares:

```
int sqrs[10][2] = {
  1,1,
  2,4,
  3,9,
  4,16,
  5,25,
  6,36,
  7,49,
  8,64,
  9,81,
  10,100
};
```

Unsized Array Initializations

Imagine that you are using array initialization to build a table of error messages, as shown here:

```
char e1[12] = "read error\n";
char e2[13] = "write error\n";
char e3[18] = "cannot open file\n";
```

As you might guess, manually counting the characters in each message to determine the correct array dimension is very tedious. You can let C automatically dimension the arrays in this example through the use of unsized arrays. In an array initialization statement, if the size of the array is not specified, the compiler automatically creates an array big enough to hold all the initializers present. This is called an *unsized array*. By using this approach, you can rewrite the message table as

```
char e1[] = "read error\n";
char e2[] = "write error\n";
char e3[] = "cannot open file\n";
```

Given these initializations, this statement

```
printf("%s has length %d\n", e2, sizeof e2);
```

prints

```
write error
has length 13
```

The unsized array initialization method also allows you to change any of the messages without manually recounting the length of each message; this avoids possible counting errors.

Unsized array initializations are not restricted to only one-dimensional arrays. For multidimensional arrays, you must specify all but the leftmost dimensions in order to allow the C compiler to index the array properly. In this way, you may build tables of varying lengths with the compiler automatically allocating enough storage for them. For example, the declaration of **sqrs** as an unsized array is shown here:

```
int sqrs[][2] = {
  1,1,
  2,4,
  3,9,
  4,16,
  5,25,
  6,36,
  7,49,
  8,64,
  9,81,
  10,100
};
```

The advantage of this declaration over the sized version is that you may lengthen or shorten the table without changing the array dimensions.

A Tic-Tac-Toe Example

The example that follows illustrates many of the ways that you can manipulate arrays with C. Two-dimensional arrays are commonly used to simulate board game matrices, as in chess and checkers. While it is beyond the scope of this book to present a chess or checkers program, a simple tic-tac-toe program will be developed.

The computer plays a very simple game. When it is the computer's turn to move, it uses **get_computer_move( )** to scan the matrix, looking for an unoccupied cell. When it finds one, it puts an O there. If it cannot find an empty location, it reports a draw game and exits. The **get_player_move( )** function prompts for the location where you want an X placed. The upper-left corner is location 1,1; the lower-right corner is 3,3.

The matrix array is initialized to contain spaces. Each move made by the player and the computer changes a space into either an X or an O. This makes it easy to display the matrix on the screen simply by using the characters stored in the array.

Each time a move is made, the program calls the **check( )** function. It returns a space if there is no winner yet, an X if you have won, or an O if the computer has won. It scans the rows, the columns, and then the diagonals looking for one that contains either all Xs or all Ys.

The **disp_matrix( )** function displays the current state of the game. Notice how initializing the matrix with spaces simplified this function.

The routines in this example all access the array **matrix** differently. Study them to make sure that you understand each array operation.

```c
/* A simple Tic Tac Toe game. */
#include "stdio.h"
#include "stdlib.h"

char matrix[3][3];   /* the tic tac toe matrix */
char check(void);
void init_matrix(void);
void get_player_move(void);
void get_computer_move(void);
void disp_matrix(void);

main()
{

  char done;

  printf("This is the game of Tic Tac Toe.\n");
  printf("You will be playing against the computer.\n");

  done = ' ';

  init_matrix();

  do {
    disp_matrix();
    get_player_move();
    done = check(); /* see if winner */
    if(done!=' ') break; /* winner!*/
    get_computer_move();
    done = check(); /* see if winner */
  } while(done==' ');

  if(done=='X') printf("You won!\n");
  else printf("I won!!!!\n");

  disp_matrix(); /* show final positions */

  return 0;
}

/* Initialize the matrix. */
void init_matrix(void)
{
  int i, j;

  for(i=0; i<3; i++)
    for(j=0; j<3; j++) matrix[i][j] = ' ';
}

/* Get a player's move. */
void get_player_move(void)
```

```
{
  int x, y;
  printf("Enter coordinates for your X: ");
  scanf("%d%d",&x,&y);

  x--; y--;

  if(matrix[x][y]!=' ') {
    printf("Invalid move, try again.\n");
    get_player_move();
  }
  else matrix[x][y] = 'X';
}

/* Get a move from the computer. */
void get_computer_move(void)
{
  int i, j;

  for(i=0; i<3; i++) {
    for(j=0; j<3; j++)
      if(matrix[i][j]==' ') break;
    if(matrix[i][j]==' ') break;
  }

  if(i*j==9)  {
    printf("draw\n");
    exit(0);
  }
  else
    matrix[i][j] = 'O';
}

/* Display the matrix on the screen. */
void disp_matrix(void)
{
  int t;

  for(t=0; t<3; t++) {
    printf(" %c | %c | %c ",matrix[t][0],
           matrix[t][1], matrix [t][2]);
    if(t!=2) printf("\n---|---|---\n");
  }
  printf("\n");
}

/* See if there is a winner. */
char check(void)
{
  int i;

  for(i=0; i<3; i++)  /* check rows */
    if(matrix[i][0]==matrix[i][1] &&
       matrix[i][0]==matrix[i][2]) return matrix[i][0];

  for(i=0; i<3; i++)  /* check columns */
```

```
    if(matrix[0][i]==matrix[1][i] &&
       matrix[0][i]==matrix[2][i]) return matrix[0][i];

  /* test diagonals */
  if(matrix[0][0]==matrix[1][1] && matrix[1][1]==matrix[2][2])
    return matrix[0][0];

  if(matrix[0][2]==matrix[1][1] && matrix[1][1]==matrix[2][0])
    return matrix[0][2];

  return ' ';
}
```

Pointers

The understanding and correct use of pointers is critical to the creation of most successful C (and C++) programs. The reasons for this are threefold. First, pointers provide the means by which functions can modify their calling arguments. Second, pointers are used to support C's dynamic allocation routines. Third, the use of pointers can improve the efficiency of certain routines. As you will see, in C++, pointers take on additional, important roles.

In addition to being one of C's strongest features, pointers are also its most dangerous. For example, uninitialized or wild pointers can cause a system crash. Perhaps worse is that it is very easy to accidentally use a pointer incorrectly and cause a bug that is very difficult to find.

Because of both their importance and the potential for abuse, this chapter examines the subject of pointers in detail.

What Are Pointers?

A pointer is a variable that holds a memory address. Most commonly, this address is the location of another variable in memory. If one variable contains the address of another variable, the first variable is said to *point* to the second. This situation is illustrated in Figure 5-1.

Pointer Variables

If a variable is going to hold a pointer, it must be declared as such. A pointer declaration consists of a base type, an *, and the variable name. The general form for declaring a pointer variable is

    type *name;

where *type* may be any valid type and *name* is the name of the pointer variable.

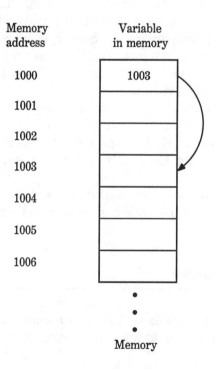

Figure 5-1.   One variable points to another

The base type of the pointer defines what type of variables the pointer can point to. Technically, any type of pointer can point anywhere in memory, but all pointer arithmetic is done relative to its base type, so it is important to declare the pointer correctly. (Pointer arithmetic is discussed a little later in this chapter.)

The Pointer Operators

There are two special pointer operators: * and &. The & is a unary operator that returns the memory address of its operand. (A unary operator requires only one operand.) For example,

```
m = &count;
```

places into **m** the memory address of the variable **count**. This address is the computer's internal location of the variable. It has *nothing* to do with the *value* of **count**. The operation of the & can be remembered as returning "the address of." Therefore, the preceding assignment statement could be verbalized as "**m** receives the address of **count**."

To better understand the preceding assignment, assume that the computer uses memory location 2000 to store the value of the variable **count**. Also assume that **count** has a value of 100. Then, after the preceding assignment, **m** will have the value 2000.

The second operator is *, and it is the complement of the &. It is a unary operator that returns the *value of the variable located at the address that follows*. For example, if **m** contains the memory address of the variable **count**, then

```
q = *m;
```

places the value of **count** into **q**. Following through with this example, **q** will have the value 100 because 100 is stored at location 2000, which is the memory address that was stored in **m**. The operation of the * can be remembered as "at address." In this case, then, the statement could be read as "**q** receives the value at address **m**."

It is sometimes confusing to beginners that the multiplication sign and the "at address" sign are the same and that the bitwise AND and the "address of" sign are the same. These operators have no relationship to each other. Both **&** and ***** have a higher precedence than all other arithmetic operators except the unary minus, with which they are equal.

You must make sure that your pointer variables always point to the correct type of data. For example, when you declare a pointer to be of type **int**, the compiler assumes that any address that it holds will point to an integer variable. Because C allows you to assign any address to a pointer variable, the following code fragment will compile with no error messages (or only warnings, depending upon your compiler) but will not produce the desired result:

```
main()
{
  float x, y;
  int  *p;

  p = &x;
  y = *p;
  return 0;
}
```

This will *not* assign the value of **x** to **y**. Because **p** is declared to be an integer pointer, only 2 bytes of information will be transferred to **y**, not the 4 that normally make up a floating-point number.

Pointer Expressions

In general, expressions involving pointers conform to the same rules as any other C expression. In this section a few special aspects of pointer expressions are examined.

Pointer Assignments

As with any variable, a pointer may be used on the right-hand side of assignment statements to assign its value to another pointer. For example, here, the address in **p1** is assigned to **p2** and the address of **x** is displayed via **p2**:

```
#include "stdio.h"

main()
{
    int x;
    int *p1, *p2;

    p1 = &x;
    p2 = p1;
    printf(" %p", p2); /* print the address of x,
                          not x's value!*/
    return 0;
}
```

The address of **x** is displayed by using the **%p printf( )** format modifier, which causes **printf( )** to display an address in the format used by the host computer.

Pointer Arithmetic

There are only two arithmetic operations that may be used on pointers: addition and subtraction. To understand what occurs in pointer arithmetic, let **p1** be an integer pointer with a current value of 2000. Also, assume that integers are 2 bytes long. After the expression

```
p1++;
```

p1's contents will be 2002, not 2001! Each time **p1** is incremented, it will point to the *next integer*. The same is true of decrements. For example,

```
p1--;
```

causes **p1** to have the value 1998, assuming that it previously was 2000.

Each time a pointer is incremented, it points to the memory location of the next element of its base type. Each time it is decremented, it points to the location of the previous element. In the case of pointers to characters, this often appears as "normal" arithmetic. However, all other pointers will increase or decrease by the length of the data type that they point to. For example, assuming 1-byte characters and 2-byte integers, when a character pointer is incremented, its value increases by one; however, when an integer pointer is incremented, its value increases by two. The reason for this is that each time a pointer is incremented or decremented, it is done relative to the length of its base type so that it will always point to the next element. More generally, all pointer arithmetic is done relative to the base type of the pointer so that the pointer is always pointing to the appropriate element of the base type. Figure 5-2 illustrates this concept.

You are not limited to only the increment and decrement operators, however. You may add or subtract integers to or from pointers. The expression

```
p1 = p1 + 12;
```

makes **p1** point to the twelfth element of **p1**'s type beyond the one it is currently pointing to.

Although you may not add two pointers, you may subtract one pointer from another. Assuming that each pointer is of the same type, the outcome of such a subtraction yields the number of elements of the base type that lie between the two pointers. For example, assuming that

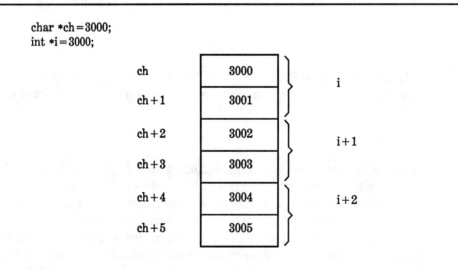

Figure 5-2.   All pointer arithmetic is relative to its base type

p1 and **p2** are integer pointers, that integers are 2 bytes long, and that **p1** contains the address 100 and **p2** contains the address 104, then **p1−p2** equals 2 (because there are two integers between 100 and 104).

Beyond addition and subtraction of a pointer and an integer or subtraction of two pointers, no other arithmetic operations may be performed on pointers. Specifically, you may not multiply or divide pointers; you may not add two pointers; you may not apply the bitwise shift and mask operators to them; and you may not add or subtract type **float** or **double** to pointers.

Pointer Comparisons

It is possible to compare two pointers in a relational expression. For instance, given the two pointers **p** and **q**, the following statement is perfectly valid:

```
if(p<q) printf("p points to lower memory than q\n");
```

Generally, pointer comparisons are used when two pointers are pointing to a common object. For an example, you can construct a pair of stack routines that can store and retrieve integer values. A *stack* is a list that uses first-in, last-out accessing. It is often compared to a stack of plates on a table; the first one set down is the last one to be used. Stacks are used frequently in compilers, interpreters, spreadsheets, and other system-related software. To create a stack, you would need two routines: **push( )** and **pop( )**. The **push( )** function will place values on the stack, and **pop( )** will take them off. These routines are shown here with a simple **main( )** function to drive them. The program simply puts the values you enter into the stack. If you enter zero, a value is popped from the stack.

```
#include "stdio.h"
#include "stdlib.h"

#define STCK_SIZE 50

void push(int i);
int pop(void);

int  *tos, *p1, stack[STCK_SIZE];
```

```
main()
{
  int value;

  tos = stack;  /* let tos hold top of stack */
  p1 = stack; /* initialize p1 */

  do {
    printf("Enter value: ");
    scanf("%d", &value);
    if(value!=0) push(value);
    else printf("value on top is %d\n", pop());
  } while(value!=-1);
  return 0;
}

void push(int i)
{
  p1++;
  if(p1==(tos+STCK_SIZE)) {
    printf("stack overflow");
    exit(1);
  }
  *p1 = i;
}

pop(void)
{
  if(p1==tos) {
    printf("stack underflow");
    exit(1);
  }
  p1--;
  return *(p1+1);
}
```

Looking at this program, you can see that memory for the stack is provided by the array **stack**. The pointer **p1** is set to point to the first byte in **stack**. The **p1** variable is used to actually access the stack. The variable **tos** holds the memory address of the top of the stack. The value of **tos** is used to prevent stack underflows. Once the stack has been initialized, **push( )** and **pop( )** may be used as a stack for integers. Both the **push( )** and **pop( )** functions perform a relational test on the pointer **p1** to detect limit errors. In **push( )**, **p1** is tested against the end of stack by adding STCK_SIZE (the size of the stack) to **tos**. In **pop( )**, **p1** is checked against **tos** to be sure that a stack underflow has not occurred.

In **pop( )**, the parentheses are necessary in the **return** statement. Without them, the statement would look like

```
return *p1 +1;
```

which would return the value at location **p1** plus one, not the value of the location **p1+1**. You must be very careful to use parentheses to ensure the correct order of evaluation when using pointers.

Pointers and Arrays Are Closely Related

There is a close relationship between pointers and arrays. Consider this fragment:

```
char str[80], *p1;

p1 = str;
```

Here, **p1** has been set to the address of the first array element in **str**. If you wished to access the fifth element in **str**, you could write

```
str[4]
```

or

```
*(p1+4)
```

Both statements will return the fifth element. Remember, arrays start at zero, so a four is used to index **str**. You would also add four to the pointer **p1** to get the fifth element because **p1** currently points to the first element of **str**. (Remember: an array name without an index will return the starting address of the array, which is the first element.)

In essence, C allows two methods of accessing array elements. This is important because pointer arithmetic can be faster than array indexing. Since speed is often a consideration in programming, the use of pointers to access array elements is very common in C programs.

To see an example of how you can use pointers in place of array indexing, consider the following two versions of **puts( )** — one with array indexing, one with pointers. The **puts( )** function can be used to write a string to the standard output device.

```
/* Index s as an array. */
void puts(char *s)
{
  register int t;

  for(t=0; s[t]; ++t) putchar(s[t]);
  putchar('\n');
}

/* Access s as a pointer */
void puts(char *s)
{
  while(*s) putchar(*s++);
  putchar('\n');
}
```

Most professional C programmers would find the second version easier to read and understand. In fact, the pointer version is the way that routines of this sort are commonly written in C.

Arrays of Pointers

Pointers may be arrayed like any other data type. The declaration for an **int** pointer array of size 10 is

```
int *x[10];
```

This declaration creates an array of ten integer pointers. (It is *not* a pointer to an array of ten integers!)

To assign the address of an integer variable called **var** to the third element of the pointer array, you would write

```
x[2] = &var;
```

To find the value of **var**, you would write

```
*x[2]
```

If you want to pass an array of pointers into a function, you may use the same method as used for other arrays—simply call the function with the array name without any indexes. For example, a function that will receive array **x** would look like this:

```
void display_array(int *q[])
{
  int t;

  for(t=0; t<10; t++)
    printf("%d ", *q[t]);

}
```

Remember, **q** is not a pointer to integers, but rather a pointer to an array of pointers to integers. Therefore, it is necessary to declare the parameter **q** as an array of integer pointers, as shown here. It may not be declared as simply an integer pointer because that is not what it is.

A common use of pointer arrays is to hold pointers to error messages. You can create a function that will output a message given its code number, as shown in **serror( )** here.

```
void serror(int num)
{
  static char *err[] = {
    "cannot open file\n",
    "read error\n",
    "write error\n",
    "media failure\n"
  };

  printf("%s", err[num]);
}
```

As you can see, **printf( )** inside **serror( )** is called with a character pointer that points to one of the various error messages indexed by the error number passed to the function. For example, if **num** is passed a 2, then the message **write error** is displayed.

It is interesting to note that the command line argument **argv** is an array of character pointers.

Multiple Indirection

It is possible to have a pointer point to another pointer that points to the target value. This situation is referred to as *multiple indirection* or *pointers to pointers*. The concept of arrays of pointers is straightforward because the indexes keep the meaning clear. However, pointers to pointers can be very confusing. The concept of multiple indirection is illustrated in Figure 5-3. As you can see, in the case of a normal pointer, the value of the pointer is the address of the variable that contains the value desired. In the case of a pointer to a pointer, the first pointer contains the address of the second pointer, which points to the variable that contains the value desired.

Multiple indirection can be carried on to whatever extent desired, but there are few cases where more than a pointer to a pointer is needed or, indeed, even wise to use. Excessive indirection is difficult to follow and prone to conceptual errors. (Do not confuse multiple indirection with linked lists, which are used in databases and the like.)

A variable that is a pointer to a pointer must be declared as such. You do this by placing an additional asterisk in front of its name. For example, this declaration tells the compiler that **newbalance** is a pointer to a pointer of type **float**:

```
float **newbalance;
```

It is important to understand that **newbalance** is not a pointer to a floating-point number, but rather a pointer to a **float** pointer.

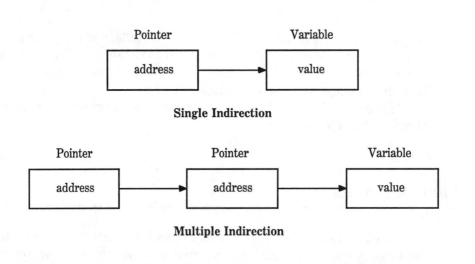

Figure 5-3. Single and multiple indirection

Accessing the target value indirectly pointed to by a pointer to a pointer requires that the asterisk operator be applied twice, as shown in this short example:

```
#include "stdio.h"

main()
{
  int x, *p, **q;

  x = 10;
  p = &x;
  q = &p;

  printf("%d", **q); /* print the value of x */
  return 0;
}
```

Here, **p** is declared as a pointer to an integer and **q** as a pointer to a pointer to an integer. The call to **printf( )** will print the number 10 on the screen.

Initializing Pointers

After a pointer is declared but before it has been assigned a value, it contains an unknown value. (Some compilers automatically initialize pointers to a null value, but you should never count on this.) Should you try to use the pointer prior to giving it a value, you will probably crash not only your program, but even the operating system of your computer — a very nasty type of error!

By convention, a pointer that is pointing nowhere should be given the value null to signify that it points to nothing. However, just because a pointer happens to have a null value does not make it "safe." Should you use a null pointer on the left side of an assignment statement, you still run the risk of crashing your program or operating system.

Because a null pointer is assumed to be unused, you can use the null pointer to make many of your pointer routines easier to code and more efficient. For example, you could use a null pointer to mark the end of a pointer array. If this is done, a routine that accesses that array will know that it has reached the end when the null value is encountered. This approach is illustrated by the **search( )** function shown here:

```
/* look up a name */
search(char *p[], char *name)
{
  register int t;

  for(t=0; p[t]; ++t)
    if(!strcmp(p[t], name)) return t;

    return -1; /* not found */
}
```

The **for** loop inside **search( )** will run until either a match is found or a null pointer is encountered. Because the end of the array is marked with a null, the condition controlling the loop will fail when it is reached.

It is very common practice in professionally written C programs to initialize strings. You saw an example of this in the **serror( )** function in the previous section. Another variation on this theme is the following type of string declaration:

```
char *p = "hello world\n";
```

As you can see, the pointer **p** is not an array. The reason this sort of initialization works has to do with the way the compiler operates. All C compilers create what is called a *string table*, which is used internally by the compiler to store the string constants used by the program. Therefore, this declaration statement places the address of "hello world," as stored in the string table, into the pointer **p**. Throughout the program, **p** can be used like any other string. For example, the following program is perfectly valid:

```
#include "stdio.h"
#include "string.h"

char *p = "hello world";

main()
{
  register int t;

  /* print the string forward and backwards */
```

```
    printf(p);
    for(t=strlen(p)-1; t>-1; t--) printf("%c", p[t]);
    return 0;
}
```

Pointers to Functions

A particularly confusing yet powerful feature of C is the *function pointer*. Even though a function is not a variable, it still has a physical location in memory that can be assigned to a pointer. A function's address is the entry point of the function. Because of this, you can use a function pointer to call a function.

To understand how function pointers work, you must understand a little about how a function is compiled and called in C. First, as each function is compiled, source code is transformed into object code and an entry point is established. When a call is made to a function while your program is running, a machine-language "call" is made to this entry point. Therefore, if a pointer contains the address of a function's entry point, it can be used to call that function.

The address of a function is obtained by using the function's name without any parentheses or arguments. (This is similar to the way an array's address is obtained when only the array name, without indexes, is used.) To see how this is done, study the following program, paying very close attention to the declarations.

```
#include "stdio.h"
#include "string.h"

void check(char *a, char *b, int (*cmp)());

main()
{
  char s1[80],s2[80];
  int (*p)();

  p = strcmp;

  gets(s1);
  gets(s2);

  check(s1, s2, p);
  return 0;
}

void check(char *a, char *b, int (*cmp) ())
```

```
{
  printf("testing for equality\n");
  if(!cmp(a, b)) printf("equal");
  else printf("not equal");
}
```

When the function **check( )** is called, two character pointers and one function pointer are passed as parameters. Inside the function **check( )**, the arguments are declared as character pointers and a function pointer. Notice how the function pointer is declared. You must use a similar form when declaring other function pointers, except that the return type of the function may be different. The parentheses around the ***cmp** are necessary for the compiler to interpret this statement correctly.

Inside **check( )**, the statement

```
cmp(a, b)
```

calls **strcmp( )**, which is pointed to by **cmp** with the arguments **a** and **b**. This also represents the general form of using a function pointer to call the function it points to.

Note that it is possible to call **check( )** by using **strcmp( )** directly, as shown here:

```
check(s1, s2, strcmp);
```

This eliminates the need for an additional pointer variable, **cmp**, which is used for illustration.

You may be asking yourself why anyone would want to write a program this way. Obviously, in this example, nothing is gained and significant confusion is introduced. However, there are times when it is advantageous to pass arbitrary functions into procedures or to keep an array of functions. The following may help to illustrate a use of function pointers. When a compiler is written, it is common for the parser (that part of it that evaluates expressions) to also perform function calls to various support routines, for example, the sine, cosine, and tangent functions. Instead of having a large **switch** statement with all of these functions listed in them, you can use an array of function pointers with the proper function selected by its index. You can get the flavor of this type of use by studying the expanded version of the previous example.

In this program, **check( )** can be made to check for either alphabetical equality or numeric equality simply by calling it with a different comparison function.

```
#include "stdio.h"
#include "ctype.h"
#include "stdlib.h"
#include "string.h"

void check(char *a, char *b, int (*cmp) ());
int numcmp(char *a, char *b);

main()
{
  char s1[80],s2[80];

  gets(s1);
  gets(s2);

  if(isalpha(*s1))
     check(s1, s2, strcmp);
  else
     check(s1, s2, numcmp);
  return 0;
}

void check(char *a, char *b, int (*cmp) ())
{
  printf("testing for equality\n");
  if(!cmp(a, b)) printf("equal");
  else printf("not equal");
}

numcmp(char *a, char *b)
{
  if(atoi(a)==atoi(b)) return 0;
  else return 1;
}
```

C's Dynamic Allocation Functions

Pointers provide necessary support for C's powerful dynamic allocation system. *Dynamic allocation* is the means by which a program can obtain memory while it is running. As you know, global variables are allocated storage at compile time. Local variables use the stack. Neither global nor local variables can be added during the execution of a program. However, there are times when it is necessary for a program to make use of variable amounts of storage. For example, you would want a word processor or a database to take advantage of all the RAM in a system, but because the amount of available RAM varies between computers, neither will be able to do so by using normal variables. Instead, these and other types of programs will allocate memory as they need it by using C's dynamic allocation system.

Memory allocated by C's dynamic allocation functions is obtained from the heap. The *heap* is a region of free memory area that lies between your program and its permanent storage area and the stack. Although the size of the heap is unknown, you can generally expect it to contain a fairly large amount of free memory.

The core of C's allocation system consists of the functions **malloc( )** and **free( )**. (Actually, ANSI C has several other dynamic allocation functions that add flexibility, but these two are the most important.) They work together, using the free memory region to establish and maintain a list of available storage. The **malloc( )** function allocates memory and the **free( )** function releases it. That is, each time a **malloc( )** memory request is made, a portion of the remaining free memory is allocated. Each time a **free( )** memory release call is made, memory is returned to the system. Any program that uses these functions should include the header file **stdlib.h**.

The **malloc( )** function has this prototype:

void *malloc(*size_t number_of_bytes*);

Here, *number_of_bytes* is the number of bytes of memory that you wish to allocate. The type **size_t** is defined by ANSI as (more or less) an **unsigned** integer. The **malloc( )** function returns a pointer of type **void**, which means that you can assign it to any type of pointer. After a successful call, **malloc( )** returns a pointer to the first byte of the region of memory allocated from the heap. If there is not enough available memory to satisfy the **malloc( )** request, an allocation failure occurs and **malloc( )** returns a null.

The **free( )** function is the opposite of **malloc( )** in that it returns previously allocated memory to the system. Once the memory has been freed, it may be reused by a subsequent call to **malloc( )**. The function **free( )** has this prototype:

void free(void **p*);

It is important to remember that you must *never* call **free( )** with an invalid argument because the free list would be destroyed.

The code fragment shown here allocates 1000 bytes of memory:

```
char *p;

p = malloc(1000); /* get 1000 bytes */
```

After the assignment, **p** points to the first of 1000 bytes of free memory. Notice that no cast is needed to assign the return value of **malloc( )** to **p**. In C, a **void *** pointer is automatically converted to the type of the pointer on the left side of an assignment. However, it is important to understand that this automatic conversion does *not* occur in C++. Further, in C++, an implicit type cast is needed when a **void *** pointer is assigned to another type of pointer.

This example allocates space for 50 integers. Notice the use of **sizeof** to ensure portability:

```
int *p;

p = malloc(50*sizeof(int));
```

Because the heap is not infinite, whenever you allocate memory, it is imperative that the value returned by **malloc( )** be checked to make sure that it is not null prior to using the pointer. Using a null pointer will almost certainly crash the computer. The proper way to allocate memory and test for a valid pointer is illustrated in this code fragment:

```
if(!(p=malloc(100)) {
  printf("Out of memory.\n");
  exit(1);
}
```

Of course, you can substitute some other sort of error handler in place of the call to **exit( )**. The point is, however, that you do not want the pointer **p** to be used if it is null.

C's dynamic allocation subsystem is used in conjuction with pointers to support a variety of important programming constructs, such as linked lists and binary trees. You will see some later in this book. Also, C++ includes an improved way to handle dynamic memory allocation.

Problems with Pointers

Nothing will get you into more trouble than a "wild" pointer! Pointers are a mixed blessing. They give you tremendous power and are necessary for many programs. However, when a pointer accidentally contains a wrong value, it can be the most difficult bug to track down.

An erroneous pointer bug is difficult to find because the pointer itself is not the problem; the problem is that each time you perform an operation using it, you are reading or writing to some unknown piece of memory. If you read from it, the worst that can happen is that you get garbage. However, if you write to it, you will be writing over other pieces of your code or data. This, in turn, may not show up until later in the execution of your program and may lead you to look for the bug in the wrong place. There may be little or no evidence to suggest that the pointer is the problem. This type of bug has caused programmers to lose sleep time and time again.

Because pointer errors are such nightmares, you should do your best never to generate one. A few of the more common errors are discussed here. The classic example of a pointer error is the uninitialized pointer. Consider the following:

```
main()  /* this program is wrong */
{
  int x, *p;

  x = 10;
  *p = x;
  return 0;
}
```

This program assigns the value 10 to some unknown memory location. The pointer **p** has never been given a value; therefore, it contains a garbage value. This type of problem often goes unnoticed when your program is very small because the odds are in favor of **p** containing a "safe" address — one that is not in your code, data area, or operating system. However, as your program grows, the probability of **p** pointing into something vital increases. Eventually, your program stops working. The solution to this sort of trouble is to always make sure that a pointer is pointing at something valid before it is used.

A second common error is caused by a simple misunderstanding of how to use a pointer. Consider this:

```
main()  /* this program is wrong */
{
  int x, *p;

  x = 10;
  p = x;
  printf("%d", *p);
  return 0;
}
```

The call to **printf( )** will not print the value of **x**, which is 10, on the screen. It will print some unknown value. The reason is that the assignment

```
p = x;
```

is wrong. That statement has assigned the value 10 to the pointer **p**, which was supposed to contain an address, not a value. To make the program correct, you should write

```
p = &x;
```

Another error that sometimes occurs is caused when incorrect assumptions are made about the placement of variables in memory. You can never know where your data will be placed in memory, or if it will be placed there the same way again, or whether each compiler will treat it in the same way. Therefore, making any comparisons between pointers to two different arrays will yield unexpected results. For example,

```
char s[80], y[80];
char *p1, *p2;

p1 = s;
```

```
p2 = y;

if(p1 < p2) . . .
```

is generally an invalid concept. (In very unusual situations, you might use something like this to determine the relative position of variables.)

A related error assumes that you may index two adjacent arrays as one simply by incrementing a pointer across the array boundaries. For example,

```
int first[10], second[10];
int *p, t;

p = first;
for(t=0; t<20; ++t)  *p++ = t;
```

This is not a good way to initialize arrays **first** and **second** with the numbers 0 through 19. Even though it may work on some compilers under certain circumstances, it assumes that both arrays will be placed back to back in memory with **first** first. This may not always be the case.

The next program illustrates a very dangerous type of bug. See if you can find it.

```
#include "string.h"
#include "stdio.h"

main()  /* this program has a bug */
{
  char *p1;
  char s[80];

  p1 = s;
  do {
    gets(s);  /* read a string */

    /* print the decimal equivalent of each
       character */
    while(*p1) printf(" %d",*p1++);

  } while(strcmp(s, "done"));
  return 0;
}
```

This program uses **p1** to print the ASCII values associated with the characters contained in **s**. The problem is that **p1** is assigned the address of **s** only once. The first time through the loop, **p1** does point to the first character in **s**. However, the second time through, it continues from where it left off because it is not reset to the start of the array s. This next character may be part of the second string, or it may be another variable or a piece of the program! The proper way to write this program is

```
#include "string.h"
#include "stdio.h"

main()  /* this program is correct */
{
  char *p1;
  char s[80];

  do {
    p1 = s;
    gets(s);  /* read a string */

    /* print the decimal equivalent of each
       character */
    while(*p1) printf(" %d",*p1++);

  } while(strcmp(s, "done"));
  return 0;
}
```

Here, each time the loop iterates, **p1** is set to the start of the string. In general, it is important to remember to reinitialize a pointer if it is to be reused.

Just because pointers handled incorrectly can cause very tricky bugs is not a reason to avoid their use. (In fact, pointers are absolutely crucial to successful C++ programming.) When using pointers, simply be careful and make sure that you know where each pointer is pointing before using it.

Functions

Functions are the building blocks of C within which all program activity occurs. They are one of C's most important features and are examined in depth in this chapter.

The General Form of a Function

The general form of a function is

type-specifier function _name(parameter list)
{
    body of the function
}

The *type-specifier* specifies the type of value that the function will return using the **return** statement. It may be any valid type. If no type is specified, the function is assumed to return an integer result. The *parameter list* is a comma-separated list of variable names and their associated types that will receive the values of the arguments when the function is called. A function may be without parameters, in which case the parameter list is empty. However, even if there are no parameters, the parentheses are required.

Unlike variable declarations, in which many variables can be declared to be of a common type by using a comma-separated list of variable names, each function parameter must include both the type and variable name. That is, the parameter declaration list for a function takes this general form:

f(*type varname1, type varname2, . . . , type varnameN*)

For example, here are a correct and an incorrect function parameter declaration:

```
f(int i, int k, float j)   /* correct */

f(int i, k, float j)      /* incorrect */
```

Scope Rules of Functions

The *scope rules* of a language are the rules that govern whether a piece of code knows about, or has access to, another piece of code or data.

In C, each function is a discrete block of code. A function's code is private to that function and cannot be accessed by any statement in any other function except through a call to that function. (It is not possible, for instance, to use the **goto** to jump into the middle of another function.) The code that makes up the body of a function is hidden from the rest of the program, and unless it uses global variables or data, it can neither affect nor be affected by other parts of the program. Stated another way, the code and data that are defined within one function cannot interact with the code or data defined in another function because the two functions have different scopes.

Variables that are defined within a function are called local variables. A local variable comes into existence when the function is entered, and it is destroyed upon exit. Local variables, therefore, cannot hold their values between function calls. The only exception to this rule is when the variable is declared with the **static** storage class specifier. This causes the compiler to treat the variable as if it were a global variable for storage purposes, but still to limit its scope to within the function. (Chapter 2, "Expressions," contains a complete discussion of global and local variables.)

In C, all functions are at the same scope level. That is, it is not possible to define a function within a function. This is why, academically speaking, C is not technically a block-structured language.

Function Arguments

If a function is to use arguments, it must declare variables that will accept the values of the arguments. These variables are called the formal parameters of the function. They behave like other local variables inside the function and are created upon entry into the function and destroyed upon exit. As shown in the following function, the parameter declaration occurs after the function name:

```
/* return 1 if c is part of string s; 0 otherwise */
is_in(char *s,  char c)
{
  while(*s)
    if(*s==c) return 1;
    else s++;

  return 0;
}
```

The function **is_in( )** has two parameters: **s** and **c**. This function returns 1 if the character **c** is part of the string **s**; otherwise, it returns 0.

As with local variables, you may make assignments to a function's formal parameters or use them in any allowable C expression. Even though these variables perform the special task of receiving the value of the arguments passed to the function, you can use them like any other local variable.

Call by Value, Call by Reference

In general, subroutines can be passed arguments in two ways. The first is called *call by value*. This method copies the *value* of an argument into the formal parameter of the subroutine. Thus changes made to the parameters of the subroutine have no effect on the variables used to call it.

Call by reference is the second way a subroutine can have arguments passed to it. In this method, the *address* of an argument is copied into the parameter. Inside the subroutine, the address accesses the actual argument used in the call. This means that changes made to the variable pointed to by the parameter do affect the variable.

C uses call by value to pass arguments. This means, in general, that you cannot alter the variables used to call the function. (You will find out in the next section of this chapter how to coerce a call by reference by using a pointer to allow changes to the calling variables.) Consider the following program:

```
#include "stdio.h"

int sqr(int x);

main()
{
  int t=10;

  printf("%d %d", sqr(t), t);

  return 0;
}

sqr(int x)
{
  x = x*x;
  return(x);
}
```

In this example, the value of the argument to **sqr( )**, 10, is copied into the parameter **x**. When the assignment **x = x*x** takes place, the only thing modified is the local variable **x**. The variable **t**, used to call **sqr( )**, will still have the value 10. Hence, the output will be 100 10. Remember that it is a copy of the value of the argument that is passed into that function. What occurs inside the function will have no effect on the variable used in the call.

Creating a Call by Reference

Even though C's parameter-passing convention is call by value, it is possible to create a call by reference by passing a pointer to the argument. Because this causes the address of the argument to be passed to the function, it is then possible to change the value of the argument outside the function.

Pointers are passed to functions just like any other value. Of course, it is necessary to declare the parameters as pointer types. The following function, **swap( )**, which exchanges the value of its two integer arguments, shows how:

```
void swap(int *x, int *y)
{
  int temp;

  temp = *x;   /* save the value at address x */
  *x = *y;     /* put y into x */
  *y = temp;   /* put x into y */
}
```

The * operator is used to access the variable pointed to by its operand. (See Chapter 2 for a discussion of the * operator.) Hence, the contents of the variables pointed to by **x** and **y** will be swapped.

Remember that **swap( )** (or any other function that uses pointer parameters) must be called with the *addresses of the arguments*. The following program shows the correct way to call **swap( )**:

```
void swap(int *x, int *y);

main()
{
  int x, y;

  x = 10;
  y = 20;
  swap(&x, &y);

  return 0;
}
```

In this example, the variable **x** is assigned the value 10 and **y** the value 20. Then **swap( )** is called with the addresses of **x** and **y**. The unary operator **&** is used to produce the address of the variables. Therefore, the addresses of **x** and **y**, not their values, are passed into the function **swap( )**. (See Chapter 2 for a complete discussion of the **&** operator.)

Calling Functions with Arrays

It is important to understand that when an array is used as a function argument, its address is passed to a function. This is an exception to C's call-by-value parameter-passing convention. This means that the code inside the function will be operating on, and potentially altering, the actual contents of the array used in the call to the function. For example, consider the function **print _ upper( )**, which prints its string argument in uppercase:

```
#include "stdio.h"
#include "ctype.h"

void print_upper(char *string);

main()
{
  char s[80];

  gets(s);
  print_upper(s);

  return 0;
}
/* Print a string in uppercase. */
void print_upper(char *string)
{
  register int t;

  for(t=0; string[t]; ++t)  {
    string[t] = toupper(string[t]);
    putchar(string[t]);
  }
}
```

After the call to **print _ upper( )**, the contents of array **s** in **main( )** are changed to uppercase. If this is not what you want to happen, you could write the program like this:

```
#include "stdio.h"
#include "ctype.h"

void print_upper(char *string);

main()
{
  char s[80];

  gets(s);
  print_upper(s);

  return 0;
}
```

```
void print_upper(char *string)
{
  register int t;

  for(t=0; string[t]; ++t)
    putchar(toupper(string[t]));
}
```

In this version, the contents of array **s** remain unchanged because its values are not altered in function **print_upper( )**.

A classic example of passing arrays into functions is found in the standard library function **gets( )**. Although the **gets( )** in your standard library is more sophisticated, the function shown next will give you an idea of how it works. To avoid confusion with the standard function, this one is called **xgets( )**.

```
/* A very simple version of the standard
   gets() library function */
char *xgets(char *s)
{
  char ch, *p;
  int t;

  p = s;  /* gets returns a pointer to s */

  for(t=0; t<80; ++t) {
    ch = getchar();
    switch(ch) {
      case '\n':
        s[t] = '\0'; /* terminate
                        the string */
        return p;
      case '\b':
        if(t>0) t--;
        break;
      default:
        s[t] = ch;
    }
  }
  s[80] = '\0';
  return p;
}
```

The **xgets( )** function must be called with a character pointer, which can be either a variable that you declared to be a character pointer or the name of a character array, which by definition is a character pointer. Upon entry, **xgets( )** establishes a **for** loop from 0 to 80. This prevents larger strings from being entered at the keyboard. If more than 80 characters are typed, the function will return. Because C has no built-in bounds checking, you should make sure that any variable used to call **xgets( )** can accept at least 80 characters. (The real **gets( )** does not limit input to 80 characters.) As you type characters on the keyboard, they are entered in the string. If you press BACKSPACE, the counter **t** is reduced by 1. When you press ENTER, a null is placed at the end of the string, signaling its termination. Because the actual array used in the call to **xgets( )** is modified, upon return it will contain the characters entered by the user.

argc and argv—Arguments to main( )

Sometimes it is very useful to pass information into a program when you run it. The general method is to pass information into the **main( )** function through the use of command line arguments. A *command-line argument* is the information that follows the program's name on the command line of the operating system. For example, when you compile C programs, you type something like

> cc *program_name*

where *program_name* is the program you wish compiled. The name of the program is passed into the C compiler as an argument.

There are two special built-in arguments, **argc** and **argv**, that are used to receive command-line arguments. The **argc** parameter holds the number of arguments on the command line and is an integer. It is always at least 1 because the name of the program qualifies as the first argument. The **argv** parameter is a pointer to an array of character pointers. Each element in this array points to a command-line argument. All command-line arguments are strings—any numbers will have to be converted by the program into the proper internal format. The simple program shown next illustrates their use. It will print **hello** followed by your name on the screen if you type your name directly after the program name.

```
#include "stdio.h"
#include "stdlib.h"
```

```
main(int argc, char *argv[])
{
  if(argc!=2) {
    printf("You forgot to type your name\n");
    exit(1);
  }
  printf("Hello %s", argv[1]);

  return 0;
}
```

If you titled this program **name** and your name were Tom, you would type **name Tom** to run the program. The output from the program would be **Hello Tom.**

In many environments, command-line arguments must be separated by a space or a tab. Commas, semicolons, and the like are not considered separators. For example,

```
run Spot, run
```

is made up of three strings, while

```
Herb,Rick,Fred
```

is one single string—commas are not legal separators.

Some environments allow you to enclose a string containing spaces with double quotes. This causes the entire string to be treated as a single argument. Check your operating system manual for details on the definition of command-line parameters for your system.

It is important to declare **argv** properly. The most common method for this is

```
char *argv[];
```

The empty brackets indicate that it is an array of undetermined length. You can now access the individual arguments by indexing **argv**. For example, **argv[0]** will point to the first string, which is always the program's name; **argv[1]** will point to the first argument, and so on.

Another short example using command-line arguments is the program called **countdown**, shown next. It counts down from a value specified on the command line and beeps when it reaches zero. Notice that the first argument containing the number is converted into an integer using the standard function **atoi( )**. If the string "display" is present as the second command line argument, the count will also be displayed on the screen.

```c
/* Countdown program. */

#include "stdio.h"
#include "stdlib.h"
#include "ctype.h"
#include "string.h"

main(int argc, char *argv[])
{
  int disp, count;

  if(argc<2) {
    printf("You must enter the length of the count\n");
    printf("on the command line.  Try again.\n");
    exit(1);
  }

  if(argc==3 && !strcmp(argv[2],"display")) disp = 1;
  else disp = 0;

  for(count=atoi(argv[1]); count; --count)
    if(disp) printf("%d\n", count);

  putchar(7);  /* this will ring the bell on most
                  computers */
  printf("done");

  return 0;
}
```

Notice that if no arguments are specified, an error message is printed. It is common for a program that uses command-line arguments to issue instructions if an attempt has been made to run it without the proper information being present.

You access an individual character in one of the command strings by adding a second index to **argv**. For example, the following program displays on the screen, a character at a time, all the arguments with which it was called.

```c
#include "stdio.h"

main(int argc, char *argv[])
{
  int t, i;
```

```
for(t=0; t<argc; ++t) {
  i = 0;
  while(argv[t][i]) {
    putchar(argv[t][i]);
    ++i;
  }
}

return 0;

}
```

Remember, the first index accesses the string and the second index accesses that character of the string.

Usually, you will use **argc** and **argv** to get initial commands into your program. In theory, you can have up to 32,767 arguments, but most operating systems will not allow more than a few. You normally use these arguments to indicate a file name or an option. Using command-line arguments will give your program a very professional appearance and facilitate its use in batch files.

As the programs in this book reflect, it is common practice to declare **main( )** as having no parameters when its command-line parameters are not being used. Some programmers specify **main( )**'s parameters as **void** when not using the command-line parameters. However, in C++, an empty parameter list is the same as one specified as **void**, so there is not much purpose in the explicit use of **void**.

Note: The names **argc** and **argv** are traditional but arbitrary. You may give any names you like to these two parameters to **main( )**. Also, some compilers support additional arguments to **main( )**, so be sure to check your user manual.

The return Statement

The **return** statement has two important uses. First, it causes an immediate exit from the function that it is in. That is, it causes program execution to return back to the calling code. Second, it may be used to return a value. Both of these uses are examined in this section.

Returning from a Function

There are two ways that a function terminates execution and returns to the caller. The first way is when the last statement in the function has executed and, conceptually, the function's ending } is encountered. (Of course, the curly brace isn't actually present in the object code, but you can think of it in this way.) For example, the **pr_reverse( )** function, shown in this program, simply prints the string **I like C** backwards on the screen:

```
#include "string.h"
#include "stdio.h"

void pr_reverse(char *s);

main()
{
  pr_reverse("I like C");

  return 0;
}

void pr_reverse(char *s)
{
  register int t;

  for(t=strlen(s)-1; t>=0; t--) putchar(s[t]);
}
```

Once the string has been displayed, then there is nothing left for **pr_reverse( )** to do, so it returns to the place it was called from.

Remember that a function may have several **return** statements in it. For example, the **find_substr( )** function shown in this program returns either the starting position of a substring within a string or −1 if no match is found:

```
#include "stdio.h"

int find_substr(char *s1, char *s2);

main()
{
  if(find_substr("C is fun", "is")!=-1)
    printf("substring is found");

  return 0;
}
```

```
/* Return index of first match of s2 in s1. * /
find_substr(char *s1, char *s2)
{
  register int t;
  char *p, *p2;

  for(t=0; s1[t]; t++) {
    p = &s1[t];
    p2 = s2;
    while(*p2 && *p2==*p) {
      p++;
      p2++;
    }
    if(!*p2) return t;
  }
  return -1;
}
```

Returning Values

The second way a function returns is when a **return** statement is encountered. All functions, except those of type **void**, return a value. This value is explicitly specified by the **return** statement. If no **return** statement is present, then the return value of the function is technically undefined. This means that as long as a function is not declared as **void**, it may be used as an operand in any valid C expression. Therefore, each of the following expressions is valid in C:

```
x = power(y);

if(max(x,y) > 100) printf("greater");

for(ch=getchar(); isdigit(ch); ) ... ;
```

However, a function cannot be the target of an assignment. A statement such as

```
swap(x,y) = 100; /* incorrect statement */
```

is wrong. The C compiler will flag it as an error and not compile a program that contains a statement like this.

Although all functions not of type **void** have return values, when you write programs your functions generally will be of three types. The first is simply computational. It is specifically designed to perform an operation on its arguments and return a value based on that operation; in essence, it is a "pure" function. Examples of this sort of function are the standard library functions **sqrt( )** and **sin( )**, which compute the square root and sine of their arguments.

The second type of function manipulates information and returns a value that simply indicates the success or failure of that manipulation. An example of this type is the library function **fclose( )**, which closes a file. If the close operation is successful, it returns zero; on failure, it returns non-zero.

The last type of function has no explicit return value. In essence, the function is strictly procedural and produces no value. An example is **exit( )**, which terminates a program. All functions that do not return values should be declared as **void**. By declaring a function as **void**, you prevent its being used in an expression; this helps to avoid accidental misuse.

Sometimes, functions that really don't produce an interesting result will return something anyway. For example, **printf( )** returns the number of characters written, yet it would be unusual to find a program that actually checked this. Therefore, although all functions, except those of type **void**, return values, you don't necessarily have to use them for anything. A very common question concerning function return values is, "Don't I have to assign this value to some variable since a value is being returned?" The answer is no. If there is no assignment specified, then the return value is simply discarded. Consider the following program, which uses **mul( )**:

```
#include "stdio.h"

int mul(int a, int b);

main()
{
  int x, y, z;

  x = 10;   y = 20;
  z = mul(x, y);              /* 1 */
  printf("%d", mul(x,y));     /* 2 */
  mul(x, y);                  /* 3 */

  return 0;
```

```
}

mul(int a, int b)
{
  return a*b;
}
```

In line 1, the return value of **mul( )** is assigned to z. In line 2, the return value is not actually assigned, but it is used by the **printf( )** function. Finally, in line 3, the return value is lost because it is neither assigned to another variable nor used as part of another expression.

Functions Returning Noninteger Values

When the type of a function is not explicitly declared, it is automatically defaulted to **int**. For many C functions, this default is fine. However, when it is necessary to return a different data type, a two-step process is required. First, the function must be given an explicit type specifier; second, the type of the function must be identified prior to the first call made to it. It is only in this way that the compiler can generate correct code for functions returning noninteger values.

Functions may be declared to return any valid C data type. The method of declaration is similar to that of variables: the type specifier precedes the function name. The type specifier tells the compiler what type of data the function is to return. This information is critical if the program is going to run correctly because different data types have different sizes and internal representations.

Before a function returning a noninteger type can be used, its type must be made known to the rest of the program. The reason for this is easy to understand. Unless directed to the contrary, C assumes that a function is going to return an integer value. If your program calls a function that returns a different type prior to that function's declaration, then the compiler will generate the wrong code for the function call. To prevent this, you must use a special form of declaration statement near the top of your program to tell the compiler what value that function is really returning.

There are essentially two ways to declare a function before it is used: the original, pre-ANSI C standard way and the ANSI standard prototype method. This section first examines the older approach. It is outdated, but because thousands of existing programs still use it, you should be familar with it. Also, the prototype method is basically an extension of the traditional concept.

Note: The traditional approach is allowed by the ANSI standard to provide compatibility with older code, but new uses of it are strongly discouraged.

Using the old form to inform the compiler that a function will be returning some type of value other than an integer, you specify its type and its name near the start of your program, as illustrated here:

```
#include "stdio.h"

float sum();  /* identify the function */

float first, second;

main()
{
   first = 123.23;
   second = 99.09;
   printf("%f", sum());

   return 0;
}

float sum()
{
 return first + second;
}
```

The first function type declaration tells the compiler that **sum( )** will return a floating-point data type. This allows the compiler to generate code correctly for calls to **sum( )**. Without the declaration, the compiler will flag a type mismatch error.

The traditional function type declaration statement has the general form

   type _ specifier function _ name( );

Even if the function takes arguments, none are listed in its type declaration when you use the traditional method.

Without the type declaration statement, a mismatch occurs between the type of data the function returns and the type of data the calling routine expects. This produces bizarre and unpredictable results. If both functions are in the same file, the compiler will catch the type mismatch and not compile the program. However, if they are in different files, the compiler will not find the error. Type checking is done only at compile time, not at link time or run time. Therefore, you must make sure that both types are compatible.

Note: When a character is returned from a function declared to be of type **int**, the character value is converted into an integer. Because C handles the conversion from character to integer and back again cleanly, often a function that returns a character value will not be declared as returning a character value; rather, it will simply be allowed to default to returning an integer. In this case, the programmer relies upon the default type conversion of characters into integers and back again. This situation is found frequently in older C code and is not technically considered an error.

Function Prototypes

The ANSI C standard expanded the traditional function declaration by allowing the number and types of the function's arguments to be declared in addition to the function's return type. This expanded definition is called a *function prototype*. Function prototypes were not part of the original C language. They are, however, one of the most important additions by the ANSI committee to the C language. All the examples in this book include full function prototypes. Prototypes enable C to provide stronger type checking, somewhat similar to that provided by languages such as Pascal. Using prototypes allows C to find and report any illegal type conversions between the type of arguments used to call a function and the type definition of its parameters. Also, differences between the number of arguments used to call a function and the number of parameters in the function will be caught.

The general form of a function prototype definition is shown here:

*type func_name(type parm_name1, type parm_name2, . . .,
type parm_nameN);*

The use of the parameter name is optional. However, because its use does let the compiler identify any type mismatches by name when an error occurs, it is a good idea to include it.

For example, the following program causes an error message to be issued because there is an attempt to call **sqr_it( )** with an integer argument instead of the integer pointer required. (It is illegal to transform an integer into a pointer.)

```
/* This program uses a function prototype to
   enforce strong type checking.
*/

void sqr_it(int *i); /* prototype */

main()
{
  int x

  x = 10;
  sqr_it(x);   /* type mismatch */

  return 0;
}

void sqr_it(int *i)
{
  *i = *i * *i;
}
```

Because of the need to maintain compatibility with older versions of C, some special rules apply to function prototypes. First, when a function's return type is declared but no parameter information is included, the compiler simply assumes that no information about the parameters is given. As far as the compiler is concerned, the function could have several parameters or no parameters. How, then, does one prototype a function that does not have any parameters? The answer is this: when a function has no parameters, its prototype uses **void** inside the parentheses. For example, if a function called **f( )** returns a **float** and has no parameters, its prototype looks like this:

```
float f(void);
```

This tells the compiler that the function has no parameters and that any call to that function that has parameters is an error.

Note: In C++, **f( )** and **f(void)** are equivalent and the preceding discussion does not apply.

Another important point about prototyping is the way it affects C's automatic type promotions. In C, when a nonprototyped function is called, all characters are converted to integers and all **float**s to **double**s. These somewhat odd type promotions have to do with the characteristics of the original environment in which C was developed. However, if you prototype a function, the types specified in the prototype are maintained and no type promotions will occur.

Not only does the use of function prototypes for the functions you write help you trap bugs before they occur, but it also helps verify that your program is working correctly by not allowing functions to be called with mismatched arguments.

Keep one fact firmly in mind: Even though the ANSI standard strongly recommends the use of function prototypes, it is not an error if no prototype for a function exists. This is necessary to support C code that was developed before prototypes were invented. However, your code should, in general, include full prototyping information. The traditional function declaration approach is included in this book only for completeness. Remember that although prototypes are optional in C, they are required in C++, so there really is no point in not prototyping all your functions.

Returning Pointers

Pointers to variables are neither integers nor unsigned integers. They are the memory addresses of a certain type of data. The reason for this distinction lies in the fact that when pointer arithmetic is performed, it is relative to the base type. That is, if an integer pointer is incremented, it will contain a value that is 2 greater than its previous value (assuming 2-byte integers). More generally, each time a pointer is incremented, the pointer will point to the next data item of its type. Because each data type may be of different length, the compiler must know what type of data the pointer is pointing to in order to make it point to the next data item. For this reason, you must be careful to specify the correct return type when returning a pointer from a function.

For example, here is a function that returns a pointer to the first occurrence of the character **c** in string **s**:

```
/* Return pointer of first occurrence of c in s. */
char *match(char c, char *s)
{
  while(c!=*s && *s) s++;
  return(s);
}
```

If no match is found, a pointer to the null terminator is returned. A short program that uses **match( )** is shown here:

```
#include "stdio.h"

char *match(char c, char *s);

main()
{
  char s[80], *p, ch;

  gets(s);
  ch = getchar();
  p = match(ch, s);
  if(p)  /* there is a match */
    printf("%s ", p);
  else
    printf("no match found");

  return 0;
}
```

This program reads a string and then a character. If the character is in the string, it then prints the string from the point of the match. Otherwise, it prints **no match found**.

Functions of Type void

One of **void**'s uses is to explicitly declare those functions that do not return values. Doing so prevents their use in any expression and helps head off accidental misuse. For example, the function **print_vertical( )** prints its string argument vertically down the side of the screen. Since it returns no value, it is declared as **void**.

```
void print_vertical(char *str)
{
  while(*str)
    printf("%c\n", *str++);
}
```

Before you can use this or any other **void** function, you must declare its prototype. If you don't, C will assume that it is returning an integer. Thus, when the compiler actually reaches the function, it will declare a type mismatch. The following program shows a proper example. It prints a single command-line argument vertically on the screen.

```
#include "stdio.h"

void print_vertical(char *str);

main(int argc, char *argv[])
{
  if(argc) print_vertical(argv[1]);

  return 0;
}
void print_vertical(char *str)
{
  while(*str)
    printf("%c\n", *str++);
}
```

Before the ANSI C standard defined **void**, functions that did not return values were simply allowed to default to type **int**. Therefore, don't be surprised to see many examples of this in older code.

What Does main( ) Return?

The **main( )** function returns an integer to the calling process, which is generally the operating system. Returning a value from **main( )** is the equivalent of calling **exit( )** with the same value. If **main( )** does not explicitly return a value, the value passed to the calling process is technically undefined. In practice, most C compilers automatically return zero, but you should not rely on this if portability is a concern. Instead, it is better to get into the habit of always explicitly returning a value from **main( )**, as the programs in this book do, so that any calling process receives a known value when your program terminates.

Recursion

In C, functions may call themselves. A function is *recursive* if a statement in the body of the function calls itself. Sometimes called *circular definition*, recursion is the process of defining something in terms of itself.

Examples of recursion abound. A recursive way to define an integer is as one of the digits 0, 1, 2, 3, 4, 5, 6, 7, 8, 9 plus or minus an integer number. For example, the number 15 is the number 7 plus the number 8; 21 is 9 plus 12; and 12 is 9 plus 3.

For a computer language to support recursion, a function must be able to call itself. A simple example is the function **factr( )**, which computes the factorial of an integer. The factorial of a number n is the product of all the whole numbers between 1 and n. For example, 3 factorial is $1 \times 2 \times 3$, or 6. Both **factr( )** and its iterative equivalent are shown here:

```
factr(int n)   /* recursive */
{
  int answer;

  if(n==1) return(1);
  answer = factr(n-1)*n;
  return(answer);
}

fact(int n)     /* non-recursive */
{
  int t, answer;

  answer = 1;
  for(t=1; t<=n; t++)
    answer=answer*(t);

  return(answer);
}
```

The operation of the nonrecursive version of **fact( )** should be clear. It uses a loop running from 1 to n and progressively multiplies each number times the moving product.

The operation of the recursive **factr( )** is a little more complex. When **factr( )** is called with an argument of 1, the function returns 1;

otherwise it returns the product of **factr(n−1)*n.** To evaluate this expression, **factr( )** is called with **n−1.** This happens until *n* equals 1 and the calls to the function begin returning.

In computing the factorial of 2, the first call to **factr( )** causes a second call to be made with the argument of 1. This call returns 1, which is then multiplied by 2 (the original *n* value). The answer is then 2. You might find it interesting to insert **printf( )** statements into **factr( ),** which will show at what level each call is and what the intermediate answers are.

When a function calls itself, new local variables and parameters are allocated storage on the stack, and the function code is executed with these new variables from the start. A recursive call does not make a new copy of the function. Only the arguments are new. As each recursive call returns, the old local variables and parameters are removed from the stack, and execution resumes at the point of the function call inside the function. Recursive functions can be said to "telescope" out and back.

Most recursive routines do not significantly save code size or improve memory utilization. Also, the recursive versions of most routines may execute a bit more slowly than their iterative equivalents because of the added overhead of the repeated function calls. Many recursive calls to a function could cause a stack overrun. Because storage for function parameters and local variables is on the stack and each new call creates a new copy of these variables, it is possible for the stack to overwrite some other data or program memory. However, you probably will not have to worry about this unless a recursive function runs wild.

The main advantage of recursive functions is that they can create clearer and simpler versions of several algorithms than their iterative siblings. For example, the quicksort sorting algorithim is quite difficult to implement in an iterative fashion. Also, some problems, especially AI-related ones, seem to lend themselves to recursive solutions. Finally, some people find it easier to think recursively than iteratively.

When writing recursive functions, you must have an **if** statement somewhere to force the function to return without the recursive call being executed. If you don't do this, once you call the function, it will never return. This is a very common error when recursive functions are written. Use **printf( )** and **getchar( )** liberally during development so that you can watch what is going on and abort execution if you see that you have made a mistake.

Declaring Variable-Length Parameter Lists

It is possible, in C, to specify a function that has a variable number and type of parameters. The most common example is **printf( )**. To tell the compiler that an unknown number and type of parameters may be passed to a function, you must end the declaration of its parameters with three periods. For example, this declaration specifies that **func( )** will have at least two integer parameters and an unknown number (including zero) more parameters after that:

```
func(int a, int b, ...);
```

This form of declaration is also used by a function's prototype.

Any function that uses a variable number of arguments must have at least one actual argument. For example, this is incorrect:

```
func(...);
```

Classic Versus Modern Function Parameter Declarations

C has evolved over the years. One of the most dramatic changes is how function parameters are declared. The older method is sometimes called the *classic* form. By contrast, the declaration approach used in this book is called the *modern* form and was introduced by the ANSI C standard. For reasons of compatibility, both ANSI C and C++ support the classic and modern forms of function declaration. However, the ANSI standard strongly recommends the modern form—advice that is, as expected, also applicable to C++. The old form is, for various technical reasons, inferior to the modern function declaration methods, but it is important for you to know the classic form because there are literally millions of lines of C code in existence that use it! Also, many programs published in books and magazines use this form because it works with all compilers, even old ones. This section examines how the classic form differs from the modern one.

The classic function parameter declaration consists of two parts: a parameter list, which goes inside the parentheses that follow the function name, and the actual parameter declarations, which go between the closing parenthesis and the function's opening curly brace. The general form of the classic parameter definition is shown here:

type func __ name(parm1, parm2, ... parmN)
type parm1;
type parm2;

   .
   .
   .

type parmN;
{
    function code
}

For example, this modern declaration

```
float f(int a, int b, char ch)
{
    .
    .
    .
}
```

looks like this in its classic form:

```
float f(a, b, ch)
int a, b;
char ch;
{
    .
    .
    .
}
```

Notice that in the classic form, more than one parameter can be in a list after the type name.

Keep in mind that there are some very subtle reasons why the modern form is better than the classic form; this is why the modern form is used in this book. When you write new code, you should use the modern form. Bluntly stated, there is no good reason to use the old form of function declaration. However, if you see a program that uses the classic form, remember that your compiler can compile it with no trouble whatsoever.

Implementation Issues

When you create C functions, there are a few important things to remember that affect their efficiency and usability. These issues are the subject of this section.

Parameters and General-Purpose Functions

A general-purpose function is one that will be used in a variety of situations, perhaps by many different programmers. Typically, you should not base general-purpose functions on global data. All of the information a function needs should be passed to it by its parameters. In the few cases where this is not possible, you should use **static** variables.

Besides making your functions general purpose, parameters keep your code readable and less susceptible to bugs that result from side effects.

Efficiency

Functions are the building blocks of C and crucial to the creation of all but the most trivial programs. Let nothing said in this section be construed otherwise. However, in certain specialized applications, you may need to eliminate a function and replace it with in-line code. *In-line code* is the equivalent of a function's statements used without a call to that function. In-line code is used instead of function calls only when execution time is critical.

There are two reasons that in-line code is faster than a function call. First, a CALL instruction takes time to execute. Second, if there are arguments to pass, these have to be placed on the stack, which also takes time. For almost all applications, this very slight increase in execution time is of no significance. But if it is, remember that each function call uses time that would be saved if the code in the function were placed in line. For example, following are two versions of a program that prints the squares of the numbers from 1 to 10. The in-line version runs faster than the other.

```
in line                    function call

                           int sqr(int a);

main()                     main()
{                          {
  int x;                     int x;

  for(x=1; x<11; ++x)        for(x=1; x<11; ++x)
  printf("%d", x*x);         printf("%d", sqr(x));

  return 0;                  return 0;
}                          }

                           sqr(int a)
                           {
                             return a*a;
                           }
```

In C++, the concept of in-line functions is expanded and formalized. In fact, in-line functions are an important component of the C++ language.

Structures, Unions, Enumerations, and User-Defined Types

Structures
Arrays of Structures
Passing Structures to Functions
Structure Pointers
Arrays and Structures Within Structures
Bit-Fields
Unions
Enumerations
Using sizeof to Ensure Portability
typedef

The C language allows you to create custom data types five different ways. The first is the structure, which is a grouping of variables under one name. It is sometimes called a *conglomerate data type*. The second sort of user-defined type is the bit-field, which is a variation on the structure; it allows easy access to the bits within a word. The third is the union, which enables the same piece of memory to be defined as two or more different types of variables. A fourth custom data type is the enumeration, which is a list of symbols. The final user-defined type is created through the use of **typedef**, and it simply creates a new name for an existing type.

Structures

In C, a structure is a collection of variables that are referenced under one name, providing a convenient means of keeping related information together. A *structure definition* forms a template that may be used to create structure variables. The variables that make up the structure are called *structure elements*.

Generally, all the elements in the structure are logically related to each other. For example, the name and address information found in a mailing list would normally be represented in a structure. The following code fragment shows how a structure template that defines the name and address fields can be created. The keyword **struct** tells the compiler that a structure template is being defined.

```
struct addr {
  char name[30];
  char street[40];
  char city[20];
  char state[2];
  unsigned long int zip;
};
```

Notice that the definition is terminated by a semicolon. This is because a structure definition is a statement. Also, the structure tag **addr** identifies this particular data structure and is its type specifier. At this point in the code, no variable has actually been declared; only the form of the data has been defined. To declare an actual variable with this structure, you would write

```
struct addr addr_info;
```

This declares a structure variable of type **addr** called **addr_info**. When you define a structure, you are, in essence, defining a complex variable type. Not until you declare a variable of that type does one actually exist.

The compiler automatically allocates sufficient memory to accommodate all the variables that make up a structure. Figure 7-1 shows how **addr_info** would appear in memory, assuming 1-byte characters and 2-byte integers.

You may also declare one or more variables at the same time that you define a structure. For example,

```
struct addr {
  char name[30];
  char street[40];
  char city[20];
  char state[2];
  unsigned long int zip;
} addr_info, binfo, cinfo;
```

Name	30 bytes	
Street	40 bytes	
City	20 bytes	addr_info
State	3 bytes	
ZIP	4 bytes	

Figure 7-1.   The **addr_info** structure in memory

will define a structure type called **addr** and declare the variables **addr_info**, **binfo**, and **cinfo** of that type.

If you need only one structure variable, the structure tag is not needed. Therefore,

```
struct {
  char name[30];
  char street[40];
  char city[20];
  char state[2];
  unsigned long int zip;
} addr_info;
```

declares one variable named **addr_info**, as defined by the structure preceding it.

The general form of a structure definition is

```
struct tag {
    type variable-name1;
    type variable-name2;
    type variable-name3;
         .
         .
         .
    type variable-nameN;
} struct-vars;
```

Here, *tag* is the name of the structure definition and is effectively the name of a new data type. The *tag* is then used to declare structure variables. The *struct-vars* are the names of actual structure variables. Either the *tag* or the *struct-vars* may be omitted, but not both.

Referencing Structure Elements

Individual structure elements are referenced through the use of the . (sometimes called the "dot") operator. For example, the following code assigns the ZIP code 12345 to the **zip** field of the structure variable **addr_info** declared earlier.

```
addr_info.zip = 12345;
```

The structure variable name followed by a period and the element name will reference that individual structure element. The general form to access a structure element is

structure_name.element_name

Therefore, to print the ZIP code to the screen, you could write

```
printf("%ul", addr_info.zip);
```

This will print the ZIP code contained in the **zip** variable of the structure variable **addr_info**.

In the same fashion, the character array **addr_info.name** can be used to call **gets( )**, as shown here.

```
gets(addr_info.name);
```

This will pass a character pointer to the start of element **name**.

If you wished to access the individual elements of **addr_info.name**, you could index **name**. For example, you could print the contents of **addr_info.name** one character at a time by using this code:

```
register int t;

for(t=0; addr_info.name[t]; ++t)
  putchar(addr_info.name[t]);
```

Structure Assignments

The information contained in one structure may be assigned to another of the same type. That is, instead of having to assign the values of all the elements separately, you can use a single assignment statement. This program illustrates structure assignments:

```
#include "stdio.h"

main()
{
  struct {
    int a;
    int b;
  } x, y;

  x.a = 10;

  y = x;  /* assign one structure to another */

  printf("%d", y.a);

  return 0;
}
```

After the assignment, **y.a** will contain the value 10.

Arrays of Structures

One of the most common uses of structures is in arrays. To declare an array of structures, you must first define a structure, and then declare an array variable of that type. For example, to declare a 100-element array of structures of type **addr**, you would write

```
struct addr addr_info[100];
```

This creates 100 sets of variables that are organized as defined in the structure **addr**.

To access a specific structure, you index the structure name. For example, to print the ZIP code of structure 3, you would write

```
printf("%ul", addr_info[2].zip);
```

Like all array variables, arrays of structures begin their indexing at zero.

Passing Structures to Functions

So far, all structures and arrays of structures used in the examples have been global. In this section, special consideration is given to passing structures and their elements to functions.

Passing a Structure Element to a Function

When you pass an element of a structure variable to a function, you are actually passing the value of that element to the function. Therefore, you are passing a simple variable (unless, of course, that element is complex, such as an array of characters). For example, consider this structure:

```
struct fred {
  char x;
  int y;
  float z;
  char s[10];
} mike;
```

Here are examples of each element being passed to a function.

```
func(mike.x);   /* passes character value of x */

func2(mike.y); /* passes integer value of y */

func3(mike.z); /* passes float value of z */

func4(mike.s); /* passes address of string s */

func(mike.s[2]); /* passes character value of s[2] */
```

However, if you wish to pass the address of individual structure elements, place the **&** operator before the structure name. For example, to pass the address of the elements in the structure **mike**, you would write

```
func(&mike.x);  /* passes address of character x */

func2(&mike.y); /* passes address of integer y */

func3(&mike.z); /* passes address of float z*/

func4(mike.s); /* passes address of string s */

func(&mike.s[2]); /* passes address of character s[2] */
```

Remember that the **&** operator precedes the structure name, not the individual element name. Note also that the string element **s** already signifies an address, so no **&** is required.

Passing an Entire Structure to a Function

When a structure is used as an argument to a function, the entire structure is passed by using the standard call-by-value method. This, of course, means that any changes made to the contents of the structure inside the function to which it is passed do not affect the structure used as an argument.

Note: In some very old versions of C, structures could *not* be passed to functions. Instead, they were treated like arrays, and only a pointer to the structure was passed. If you sometimes use an old C compiler, keep this fact in mind.

The most important consideration when you use a structure as a parameter is that the type of the argument must match the type of the parameter. For example, both the argument **arg** and the parameter **parm** are declared to be of the same type of structure in this program:

```
#include "stdio.h"

/* define a structure type */
struct struct_type {
```

```
  int a, b;
  char ch;
} ;

void fl(struct struct_type parm);

main()
{
  struct struct_type arg;   /* declare arg */

  arg.a = 1000;

  fl(arg);

  return 0;
}

void fl(struct struct_type parm)
{
  printf("%d", parm.a);
}
```

This program, as you can guess, prints the number 1000 on the screen.

Structure Pointers

C allows pointers to structures in the same way that it does to any other type of variable. You declare structure pointers like other pointers by placing the * in front of a structure variable's name. For example, assuming the previously defined structure **addr**, the following declares **addr _ pointer** to be a pointer to data of that type:

```
struct addr *addr_pointer;
```

Using Structure Pointers

There are two primary uses for structure pointers. The first is to generate a call by reference to a function. The second is to create linked lists and other dynamic data structures using C's dynamic allocation system. This chapter is concerned only with the first; later in this book, the use of dynamic allocation is examined.

There is one major drawback to passing all but the simplest structures to functions: the overhead needed to push (and pop) all the structure elements onto the stack. In simple structures with few elements, this overhead is not too important, but if several elements are used, or if some of the elements are arrays, then run-time performance may degrade to unacceptable levels. The solution to this problem is to pass only a pointer to a function.

When a pointer to a structure is passed to a function, only the address of the structure is pushed (and popped) on the stack. This means a very fast function call can be executed. A second advantage, in some cases, is that the function will be referencing the actual structure argument instead of a copy, thus allowing the contents of the actual elements of the structure used in the call to be modified.

To obtain the address of a structure variable, place the & operator before the structure's name. For example, given the following fragment,

```
struct bal {
  float balance;
  char name[80];
} person;

struct bal *p;   /* declare a structure pointer */
```

then

```
p = &person;
```

places the address of the structure **person** into the pointer **p**.

To access the elements of a structure using a pointer to that structure, you must use the −> operator. For example, this references the **balance** field:

```
p->balance
```

The −> is referred to by most C programmers as the *arrow operator*. You form it by using the minus sign followed by a greater-than sign. Use the arrow in place of the dot operator when accessing a structure element, given a pointer to the structure variable.

To see how a structure pointer can be used, examine this simple program, which prints the hours, minutes, and seconds on your screen, using a software delay timer:

```c
/* Display a software timer. */
#include "stdio.h"

struct my_time {
  int hours;
  int minutes;
  int seconds;
} ;

void display(struct my_time *t);
void update(struct my_time *t);
void delay(void);

main()
{
  struct my_time systime;

  systime.hours = 0;
  systime.minutes = 0;
  systime.seconds = 0;

  for(;;) {
    update(&systime);
    display(&systime);
  }

  return 0;
}

void update(struct my_time *t)
{
  t->seconds++;
  if(t->seconds==60) {
    t->seconds = 0;
    t->minutes++;
  }
  if(t->minutes==60) {
    t->minutes = 0;
    t->hours++;
  }
  if(t->hours==24) t->hours = 0;
  delay();
}

void display(struct my_time *t)
{
  printf("%02d:", t->hours);
  printf("%02d:", t->minutes);
  printf("%02d\n", t->seconds);
```

```
}

void delay(void)
{
  long int t;
  for(t=1; t<128000; ++t) ;
}
```

You adjust the timing of this program by varying the loop count in **delay( )**.

As you can see, a global structure called **my＿time** was defined, but no variable was declared. Inside **main( )**, the structure **time** was declared and initialized to 00:00:00. This means that **systime** is known directly only to the **main( )** function.

The functions **update( )**, which changes the time, and **display( )**, which prints the time, are passed the address of **time**. In both functions, the argument is declared to be a pointer to a **my＿time** structure. This is necessary so that the compiler will know how to reference the structure elements.

The actual referencing of each structure element is through the use of a pointer. For example, to set the hours back to zero when 24:00:00 was reached, you would write

```
if(t->hours==24) t->hours = 0;
```

This line of code tells the compiler to take the address of **t** (which is **time** in **main( )**) and assign zero to its element called **hours**.

Remember: Use the dot operator to access structure elements when operating on the structure itself. When using a pointer to a structure, use the arrow operator.

Arrays and Structures Within Structures

A structure element may be either simple or complex. A simple element is any of the built-in data types, such as integer or character. You have already seen one complex element: the character array used in **addr＿info**. Other complex data types are single and multidimensional arrays of the other data types and structures.

A structure element that is an array is treated as you might expect from the earlier examples. For example, consider this structure:

```
struct x {
  int a[10][10]; /* 10 x 10 array of ints */
  float b;
} y;
```

To reference integer 3,7 in **a** of structure **y**, you would write

```
y.a[3][7]
```

When a structure is an element of another structure, it is called a *nested structure*. For example, here the structure **address** is nested inside **emp**:

```
struct emp {
  struct addr address;
  float wage;
} worker;
```

Here, the structure **emp** has been defined as having two elements. The first element is the structure of type **addr**, containing an employee's address, and the second is **wage**, holding the employee's wage. The following code fragment assigns the 93456 to the **zip** element of **address**:

```
worker.address.zip = 93456;
```

The elements of each structure are referenced in order of the outermost to the innermost. The ANSI C standard specifies that structures may be nested to at least 15 levels.

Bit-Fields

Unlike most other computer languages, C has a built-in method to access a single bit within a byte, called a *bit-field*. This can be useful for a number of reasons. First, if storage is limited, you can store several

Boolean (true/false) variables in one byte. Second, certain devices transmit information encoded into bits within one byte. Third, certain encryption routines need to access the bits within a byte. Although all these functions can be performed by using bytes and the bitwise operators, a bit-field can add more structure (and, possibly, efficiency) to your code.

The method C uses to access bits is based on the structure. A bit-field is really just a special type of structure element that defines how long, in bits, the structure is to be. The general form of a bit-field definition is

```
struct tag {
    type name1 : length;
    type name2 : length;
    .
    .
    .
    type name3 : length;
} variable-list;
```

A bit-field must be declared as **int, unsigned,** or **signed.** Bit-fields of length 1 should be declared as **unsigned** because a single bit cannot have a sign. (Some compilers may allow only **unsigned** bit-fields.)

Bit-fields are commonly used when input from a hardware device is being analyzed. For example, the status port of a serial communications adapter might return a status byte organized like this:

bit	Meaning when set
0	Change in clear-to-send line
1	Change in data-set-ready
2	Trailing edge detected
3	Change in receive line
4	Clear-to-send
5	Data-set-ready
6	Telephone ringing
7	Received signal

You can represent the information in a status byte by using the following bit-field:

```
struct status_type {
  unsigned delta_cts: 1;
  unsigned delta_dsr: 1;
  unsigned tr_edge:   1;
  unsigned delta_rec: 1;
  unsigned cts:       1;
  unsigned dsr:       1;
  unsigned ring:      1;
  unsigned rec_line:  1;
} status;
```

You might use a routine similar to the one shown here to enable a program to determine when it can send or receive data:

```
status = get_port_status();

if(status.cts) printf("clear to send");
if(status.dsr) printf("data ready");
```

To assign a value to bit-field, simply use the same form as you would for any other type of structure element. For example, this clears the **ring** field:

```
status.ring = 0;
```

As you can see from these examples, the dot operator is used to access each bit-field. However, if the structure is referenced through a pointer, you must use the −> operator.

You do not have to name each bit-field. This makes it easy to reach the bit you want, passing up unused ones. For example, if you care only about the **cts** and **dsr** bits, you could declare the **status_type** structure like this:

```
struct status_type {
  unsigned :     4;
  unsigned cts:  1;
  unsigned dsr:  1;
} status;
```

Also, notice that the bits after **dsr** do not need to be mentioned in any way.

Bit-field variables have certain restrictions. You cannot take the address of a bit-field variable. Bit-field variables cannot be arrayed. You cannot know, from machine to machine, whether the fields will run from right to left or from left to right; this means that any code that uses bit-fields may have some machine dependencies.

Since a bit-field is simply a special type of structure element, it is valid to mix bit-fields with other types of structure elements. For example,

```
struct emp {
  struct addr address;
  float pay;
  unsigned lay_off:1;   /* lay off or active */
  unsigned hourly:1;    /* hourly pay or wage */
  unsigned deductions:3; /* IRS deductions */
};
```

defines an employee record that uses only 1 byte to hold three pieces of information: the employee's status, whether the employee is salaried, and the number of deductions. Without the use of the bit-field, this information would have taken 3 bytes.

Unions

In C, a **union** is a memory location that is shared by two or more different variables, generally of different types, at different times. The **union** definition is similar to that of a structure. Its general form is

```
union tag {
    type variable-name1;
    type variable-name2;
    type variable-name3;
      .
      .
      .
    type variable-nameN;
} union-variables;
```

Here is an example:

```
union u_type {
  int i;
  char ch;
} ;
```

This definition does not declare any variables. You may declare a variable either by placing its name at the end of the definition or by using a separate declaration statement. To declare a **union** variable **cnvt** of type **u_type**, using the definition just given, you would write

```
union u_type cnvt;
```

In **union cnvt**, integer **i** and character **ch** share the same memory location. (Of course, **i** occupies 2 bytes and **ch** uses only 1.) Figure 7-2 shows how **i** and **ch** share the same address.

At any point, you can refer to the data stored in **cnvt** as either an integer or a character. When a **union** is declared, the compiler automatically creates a variable large enough to hold the largest variable type in the **union**.

To access a **union** element, use the same syntax that you would use for structures: the dot and arrow operators. If you are operating on the **union** directly, use the dot operator. If the **union** variable is accessed through a pointer, use the arrow operator. For example, to assign the integer 10 to element **i** of **cnvt**, you would write

```
cnvt.i = 10;
```

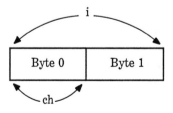

Figure 7-2.   How **i** and **ch** utilize the **union cnvt**

In this example, a pointer to **cnvt** is passed to a function:

```
void func1(union u_type *un)
{
  un->i = 10; /* assign 10 to cnvt using
                    pointer */
}
```

Using a **union** can aid in the production of machine-independent, or portable, code. Because the compiler keeps track of the actual sizes of the variables that make up the **union**, no machine dependencies are produced. You need not worry about the size of an integer, character, **float**, and so on.

Unions are used frequently when type conversions are needed because you can refer to the data held in the union in two or more different ways. For example, using a **union**, you can create your own version of a common library function called **putw( )**, which writes the binary representation of an integer to a disk file. First, you create a **union** made up of one integer and a 2-byte character array:

```
union pw {
  int i;
  char ch[2];
};
```

Now, you can use **pw** to create the version of the **putw( )** function shown in the following program. (To avoid confusion with the library function, this version is called **xputw( )**.)

```
#include <stdio.h>

union pw {
  int i;
  char ch[2];
};

void xputw(int i, FILE *fp);

main()
{
  FILE *fp;

  fp = fopen("test.tmp", "w+");

  xputw(1000, fp);  /* write 1000 as integer to file */
  fclose(fp);
```

```
}

/* Simplified version of putw(). */
void xputw(int i, FILE *fp)
{
  union pw word;

  word.i = i;   /* assign integer */

  /* now, write as two characters */
  putc(word.ch[0], fp); /* write first half */
  putc(word.ch[1], fp); /* write second half */
}
```

Enumerations

Another data type supported by C is the enumeration. An *enumeration* is a set of named integer constants; it specifies all the legal values that a variable of that type may have. Enumerations are not uncommon in everyday life. For example, here is an enumeration of the coins used in the United States:

penny, nickel, dime, quarter, half-dollar, dollar

Enumerations are defined much like structures, with the keyword **enum** used to signal the start of an enumeration type. The general form is

enum *tag* { *enumeration _list* } *variable _ list;*

Here, both the enumeration tag and the variable list are optional. As with structures, the enumeration tag name is used to declare variables of its type. The following fragment defines an enumeration called **coin** and declares **money** to be of that type:

```
enum coin { penny, nickel, dime, quarter,
            half_dollar, dollar};

enum coin money;
```

Given this definition and declaration, the following types of statements are perfectly valid:

```
money = dime;

if(money==quarter) printf("is a quarter\n");
```

The key point about an enumeration is that each of the symbols stands for an integer value. As such, they may be used anywhere that an integer may be used. Each symbol is given a value one greater than the symbol it precedes. The value of the first enumeration symbol is zero. Therefore,

```
printf("%d %d", penny, dime);
```

displays 0 2 on the screen.

You can specify the value of one or more of the symbols by using an initializer. You do this by following the symbol with an equal sign and an integer value. Whenever an initializer is used, symbols that appear after it are assigned values greater than the previous initialization value. For example, the following assigns the value of 100 to **quarter**:

```
enum coin { penny, nickel, dime, quarter=100,
        half_dollar, dollar};
```

Now, the values of these symbols are

penny	0
nickel	1
dime	2
quarter	100
half_dollar	101
dollar	102

One common but erroneous assumption made about enumerations is that the symbols can be input and output directly. This is not the case. For example, the following code fragment will not perform as desired:

```
/* this will not work */

money = dollar;

printf("%s", money);
```

Remember, the symbol **dollar** is simply a name for an integer; it is not a string. For the same reason, it is not possible to use this code to achieve the desired results:

```
/* this code is wrong */

gets(s);

strcpy(money, s);
```

That is, a string that contains the name of a symbol is not automatically converted to that symbol.

Actually, creating code to input and output enumeration symbols is quite tedious (unless you are willing to settle for their integer values). For example, the following code is needed to display, in words, the kind of coin that **money** contains:

```
switch(money) {
  case penny: printf("penny");
    break;
  case nickel: printf("nickel");
    break;
  case dime: printf("dime");
    break;
  case quarter: printf("quarter");
    break;
  case half_dollar: printf("half_dollar");
    break;
  case dollar: printf("dollar");
}
```

Sometimes it is possible to declare an array of strings and use the enumeration value as an index in order to translate an enumeration value into its corresponding string. For example, this code will also output the proper string:

```
char name[][20] = {
  "penny",
  "nickel",
  "dime",
```

```
  "quarter",
  "half_dollar",
  "dollar"
};
  .
  .
  .
printf("%s", name[money]);
```

This method works only if no symbol is initialized. If an initialization is used, incorrect indexes will be generated.

Given that enumeration values must be converted manually to their human-readable string values for console I/O, they find their greatest use in routines that do not make such conversions. It is common to see an enumeration used to define a compiler's symbol table, for example.

Using sizeof to Ensure Portability

You have seen that structures, unions, and enumerations can be used to create variables of varying sizes and that the actual size of these variables may change from machine to machine. The **sizeof** unary operator computes the size of any variable or type and can help eliminate machine-dependent code from your programs.

For example, assume the following sizes for the data types shown here:

Type	Size in bytes
char	1
int	2
long	4
float	4
double	8

The following code will print the numbers 1, 2, and 4 on the screen:

```
char ch;
int i;
float f;
```

```
printf("%d",sizeof(ch));

printf("%d",sizeof(i));

printf("%d",sizeof(f));
```

sizeof is a *compile-time operator:* all the information necessary to compute the size of any variable is known at compile time. For example, consider

```
union x {
  char ch;
  int i;
  float f;
} u_var;
```

The **sizeof(u_var)** will be 4. At run time, it does not matter what the **union u_var** is *actually* holding; all that matters is the size of the largest variable it can hold because the **union** will be as large as its largest element.

typedef

C allows you to define new data type names explicitly by using the **typedef** keyword. You are not actually creating a new data class, but rather defining a new name for an existing type. This process can help make machine-dependent programs more portable; only the **typedef** statements would have to be changed. It also can aid in self-documenting your code by allowing descriptive names for the standard data types. The general form of the **typedef** statement is

典typedef *type name*;

where *type* is any allowable data type and *name* is the new name for this type. The new name you define is in addition to, not a replacement for, the existing type name.

For example, you could create a new name for **float** by using

```
typedef float balance;
```

This statement tells the compiler to recognize **balance** as another name for **float**. Next, you could create a **float** variable using **balance**:

```
balance over_due;
```

Here, **over_due** is a floating-point variable of type **balance**, which is another word for **float**.

Now that **balance** has been defined, it can be used on the right side of another **typedef**. For example,

```
typedef balance overdraft;
```

tells the compiler to recognize **overdraft** as another name for **balance**, which is another name for **float**.

Using **typedef** can help make your code easier to read and easier to port to a new machine. Remember, however, that you are not creating any new data types.

Console I/O

An Important Application Note
Reading and Writing Characters
Reading and Writing Strings
Formatted Console I/O
printf( )
scanf( )

The C I/O system consists of two major categories: console and file I/O. Technically, C makes little distinction between console I/O and file (or disk) I/O. However, from a conceptual point of view, they represent two very different worlds. Also, because the C I/O system is quite large, it seems natural to break the subject into these two convenient pieces. This chapter examines in detail the console I/O functions. Chapter 9 presents the file I/O system and describes how the two systems relate.

With one exception, this chapter covers only those console I/O functions defined by the ANSI C standard. Neither the ANSI C standard nor the traditional K&R standard defines any functions that perform "fancy" text or graphics operations. Instead, the standard C console I/O functions perform only TTY-based output. Most compilers include in their libraries screen control and graphics functions that apply to the specific environment the compiler is designed to run under. However, the implementation of these features varies widely among machines and cannot be generalized. Check your compiler user manual for descriptions of text or graphics manipulation functions as they relate to your compiler.

Note: This chapter refers to the console I/O functions as performing input from the keyboard and output to the screen (by far their most common usage). However, these functions actually have as the target and/or source of their I/O operations the standard input and standard output of the system. Furthermore, standard input and standard output may be redirected to other devices. These concepts are discussed in Chapter 9.

An Important Application Note

Part One of this book uses the I/O system defined by the C language. Although C++ fully supports the C-like I/O functions, it also defines its own object-oriented I/O system. Therefore, if you are writing object-oriented programs, you will want to the use C++-specific I/O system, not the ANSI C system. The C-like I/O system is described in this book for three reasons:

- For the next several years, many C programs will be made into C++ programs. In order to change the C-like I/O functions into C++ object-oriented I/O functions, you will need to know what the C-like functions do.

- An understanding of the basic principles behind the C-like I/O system is crucial to an understanding of the C++ object-oriented I/O system. (Both share the same general concepts and methods.)

- In certain situations (for example, in very short programs), it is not necessary or even helpful to apply object-oriented techniques. In these cases, using the C-like I/O functions may be easier (and more efficient) than using their object-oriented cousins.

In addition, there is an unwritten rule that any C++ programmer must also be a C programmer. If you don't know the C I/O system, you will be limiting your professional horizons.

Reading and Writing Characters

The simplest of the console I/O functions are **getchar( )**, which reads a character from the keyboard, and **putchar( )**, which prints a character to the screen. The **getchar( )** function waits until a key is pressed and then returns its value. The key pressed is also "echoed" to the screen automatically. The **putchar( )** function writes its character argument to the screen at the current cursor position. The prototypes for **getchar( )** and **putchar( )** are shown here:

```
int getchar(void);
int putchar(int c);
```

Don't be disturbed by the fact that **getchar( )** returns an integer; the low-order byte contains the character. Also, you can call **putchar( )** with a character argument. Even though **putchar( )** is declared as using an integer parameter, only the low-order byte is actually output to the screen. The **putchar( )** function returns the character written, or **EOF** if an error occurs. (The **EOF** macro is defined in **stdio.h** and is generally equal to −1.) The header file for these functions is **stdio.h**.

The program that follows inputs characters from the keyboard and displays them in reverse case; that is, uppercase prints as lowercase and lowercase prints as uppercase. To stop the program, enter a period.

```
#include "stdio.h"
#include "ctype.h"

main()
{
  char ch;

  printf("Enter some text (type a period to quit).\n");
  do {
    ch = getchar();
    if(islower(ch)) ch = toupper(ch);
    else ch = tolower(ch);
    putchar(ch);
  } while (ch!='.');

  return 0;
}
```

When using **getchar( )**, remember that any key represents a valid return value. That is, keys like the carriage return, TAB, and ESC may be returned by **getchar( )**.

A Problem with getchar( )

There is a potential problem with **getchar( )**. ANSI has defined **getchar( )** so that it can be implemented in a way that is compatible with the original, UNIX-based version. The trouble is that in its original form under UNIX, **getchar( )** buffers input until ENTER is pressed. This is because the original UNIX systems line-buffered terminal input; you had to enter a carriage return for anything you had just typed to actually be sent to the computer. This leaves one or more characters waiting in the input queue after **getchar( )** returns, which is annoying in interactive environments. Even though the standard specifies that **getchar( )** can be implemented as an interactive function, it seldom is. Therefore, if the preceding program did not behave as you expected, you now know why.

Alternatives to getchar( )

As just explained, **getchar( )** may not be implemented by your compiler in a way that makes it useful in an interactive environment. If this is the case, you will probably want to use a different function to read characters from the keyboard. Although the ANSI standard does not define any function that is guaranteed to provide interactive input, many C compilers include alternative keyboard input functions. These functions are not defined by ANSI, but their use can be recommended on the grounds that **getchar( )** does not fill the needs of the majority of programmers.

Two of the most common alternative functions are **getch( )** and **getche( )**, which have these prototypes:

```
int getch(void);
int getche(void);
```

For most compilers, the prototypes for these functions are found in **conio.h**. The **getch( )** function waits for a keypress and returns immediately when one is received. It does not echo the character to the screen. The **getche( )** function is the same as **getch( )**, but the key is echoed. In Part One of this book, many examples in which a character needs to be read from the keyboard in an interactive program use **getche( )** or **getch( )** instead of **getchar( )**. However, if your compiler does not support this alternative function, or if **getchar( )** is implemented as an interactive function by your compiler, you may substitute **getchar( )** when necessary.

For example, the preceding program is shown here using **getch( )** instead of **getchar( )**:

```
#include "stdio.h"
#include "conio.h"
#include "ctype.h"

main()
{
  char ch;

  printf("Enter some text (type a period to quit).\n");
  do {
    ch = getch();
    if(islower(ch)) ch = toupper(ch);
    else ch = tolower(ch);
    putchar(ch);
  } while (ch!='.');

  return 0;
}
```

Reading and Writing Strings

The next step up in console I/O, in terms of complexity and power, are the functions **gets( )** and **puts( )**. They enable you to read and write strings of characters at the console.

The **gets( )** function reads a string of characters entered at the keyboard and places it at the address pointed to by its character pointer argument. You may type characters at the keyboard until you strike a carriage return. The carriage return does not become part of the string; instead, a null terminator is placed at the end and **gets( )** returns. In fact, it is impossible to use **gets( )** to return a carriage return (although **getchar( )** can do so). You can correct typing mistakes by using the BACKSPACE key prior to pressing ENTER. The prototype for **gets( )** is

    char *gets(char *str);

where *str* is a character array that receives the characters input by the user. It also returns a pointer to *str*. Its prototype is found in **stdio.h**. The following program reads a string into the array **str** and prints its length:

```
#include "stdio.h"
#include "string.h"
```

```
main()
{
  char str[80];

  gets(str);
  printf("length is %d", strlen(str));

  return 0;
}
```

The **puts( )** function writes its string argument to the screen followed by a newline. Its prototype is

   int puts(char *s);

puts( ) recognizes the same backslash codes as **printf( )**, such as '\t' for tab. A call to **puts( )** requires far less overhead than the same call to **printf( )** because **puts( )** can output only a string of characters—it cannot output numbers or do format conversions. Therefore, **puts( )** takes up less space and runs faster than **printf( )** (formatting and conversions take considerable time). Hence, the **puts( )** function is often used when it is important to have highly optimized code. The **puts( )** function returns **EOF** if an error occurs. Otherwise, it returns a nonzero value. However, when writing to the console, it is safe to assume that no error will occur, so the return value of **puts( )** is seldom monitored. The following statement writes **hello** on the screen:

```
puts("hello");
```

The simplest C functions that perform console I/O operations are summarized in Table 8-1.

The following program demonstrates several of the basic console I/O functions. The program is a very simple computerized dictionary. It first prompts the user to enter a word. It then checks its built-in database to see if the word matches one in the database. If a match is found, the program prints the word's meaning. Pay special attention to the indirection used in this program. If you have any trouble understanding it, remember that the **dic** array is an array of pointers to strings.

```
/* A simple dictionary. */

#include "stdio.h"
#include "conio.h"
#include "string.h"
#include "ctype.h"
```

```
/* list of words and meanings */
char  *dic[][40] = {
  "atlas", "a volume of maps",
  "car", "a motorized vehicle",
  "telephone", "a communication device",
  "airplane", "a flying machine",
  "", ""   /* null terminate the list */
};

main()
{
  char word[80], ch;
  char **p;

  do {
    puts("\nEnter word: ");
    gets(word);

    p = (char **)dic;

    /* find matching word and print its meaning */
    do {
      if(!strcmp(*p, word)) {
        puts("meaning:");
        puts(*(p+1));
        break;
      }
      if(!strcmp(*p, word)) break;
      p = p + 2;  /* advance through the list */
    } while(*p);
    if(!*p) puts("word not in dictionary");
    printf("another? (y/n): ");
    ch = getche();
  } while(toupper(ch) != 'N');

  return 0;
}
```

Function	Operation
getchar( )	Reads a character from the keyboard; waits for carriage return in most implementations
getche( )	Reads a character with echo; does not wait for carriage return; not defined by ANSI, but a common extension
getch( )	Reads a character without echo; does not wait for carriage return; not defined by ANSI, but a common extension
putchar( )	Writes a character to the screen
gets( )	Reads a string from the keyboard
puts( )	Writes a string to the screen

Table 8-1.   Console I/O Functions

Formatted Console I/O

In C, the functions **printf( )** and **scanf( )** perform formatted output and input. They can read and write data in various formats under your control. The **printf( )** function writes data to the console; **scanf( )**, its complement, reads data from the keyboard. Both **printf( )** and **scanf( )** can operate on any of the built-in data types, including characters, strings, and numbers.

printf( )

The prototype for **printf( )** is

    int printf(const char *control_string, ...);

The prototype for **printf( )** is in **stdio.h**. The **printf( )** function returns the number of characters written or, if an error occurs, a negative value.

The control string consists of two types of items. The first type is made up of characters that will be printed on the screen. The second type contains format commands that define the way the arguments are displayed. A format command begins with a percent sign and is followed by the format code. There must be exactly the same number of arguments as there are format commands, and the format commands and the arguments are matched in order. For example, this **printf( )** call

```
printf("I like %c %s", 'C', "very much!");
```

displays

```
I like C very much!
```

The **printf( )** function accepts a wide variety of format codes, as shown in Table 8-2.

Code	Format
%c	Character
%d	Signed decimal integers
%i	Signed decimal integers
%e	Scientific notation (lowercase e)
%E	Scientific notation (uppercase E)
%f	Decimal floating point
%g	Uses %e or %f, whichever is shorter (if %e, uses lowercase e)
%G	Uses %E or %f, which ever is shorter (if %e, uses uppercase E)
%o	Unsigned octal
%s	String of characters
%u	Unsigned decimal integers
%x	Unsigned hexadecimal (lowercase letters)
%X	Unsigned hexadecimal (uppercase letters)
%p	Displays a pointer
%n	The associated argument is an integer pointer into which the number of characters written so far is placed
%%	Prints a % sign

Table 8-2.   printf( ) Format Commands

Printing Characters

To print an individual character, use **%c**. This causes its matching argument to be output, unmodified, to the screen.

To print a string, use **%s**.

Printing Numbers

You may use either **%d** or **%i** to print a signed decimal number. These format commands are equivalent; both are supported for historical reasons.

To output an **unsigned** value, use **%u**.

The **%f** format displays floating-point numbers.

The **%e** and **%E** formats tell **printf( )** to display a floating-point argument in scientific notation. Numbers represented in scientific notation take this general form:

$$x.dddddE +/- yy$$

If you want the E to be displayed in uppercase, use the **%E** format; otherwise, use **%e**.

You can tell **printf( )** to use either **%f** or **%e** by using the **%g** or **%G** format code. This causes **printf( )** to select the format specifier that produces the shortest output. Where applicable, if you want the E shown in uppercase, use **%G**; otherwise, use **%g**. The following program demonstrates the effect of the **%g** format code:

```
#include "stdio.h"

main()
{
  double f;

  for(f=1.0; f<1.0e+10; f=f*10)
    printf("%g ", f);

  return 0;
}
```

This program produces the following output:

```
1 10 100 1000 10000 100000 1e+06 1e+07 1e+08 1e+09
```

You can display **unsigned** integers in octal or hexadecimal format by using **%o** and **%x**, respectively. Because the hexadecimal number system uses the letters A through F to represent the numbers 10 through 15, you can display these letters in either upper- or lowercase. For uppercase, use the **%X** format code; for lowercase, use **%x**. The following program illustrates these format codes:

```
#include "stdio.h"

main()
{
  unsigned num;

  for(num=0; num<255; num++) {
```

```
    printf("%o ", num);
    printf("%x ", num);
    printf("%X\n", num);
  }

  return 0;
}
```

Displaying an Address

If you wish to display an address, use **%p**. This format specifier causes **printf( )** to display a machine address in a format compatible with the type of addressing used by the computer. This program displays the address of **sample**:

```
#include "stdio.h"

int sample;

main()
{
  printf("%p", &sample);

  return 0;
}
```

The %n Specifier

The **%n** format code is different from the others. Instead of telling **printf( )** to display something, it causes **printf( )** to load the variable pointed to by its corresponding argument with a value equal to the number of characters that have been output. Put differently, the argument that corresponds to the **%n** format command must be a pointer to a variable. After the call to **printf( )** has returned, this variable will hold the number of characters output up to the point at which the **%n** was encountered. To better understand this somewhat unusual format code, try the following program:

```
#include "stdio.h"

main()
{
  int count;
```

```
   printf("this%n is a test\n", &count);
   printf("%d", count);

   return 0;
}
```

This program displays **this is a test** followed by the number 4. The main application of the **%n** format code is to enable your program to perform dynamic formatting.

Format Code Modifiers

Many format commands may take modifiers that alter their meaning slightly. For example, you can specify a minimum field width, the number of decimal places, and left justification. The format modifier goes between the percent sign and the actual format code.

The Minimum Field Width Specifier

An integer placed between the percent sign and the format code acts as a *minimum field width specifier*. This pads the output with spaces to ensure that it is at least a certain length. If the string or number is greater than that minimum, it will be printed in full even if it overruns the minimum. The default padding is done with spaces. If you wish to pad with zeros, place a zero before the field width specifier. For example, **%05d** will pad a number of less than five digits with zeros so that its total length is five. The following program demonstrates the minimum field width specifier:

```
#include "stdio.h"

main()
{
  double item;

  item = 10.12304;

  printf("%f\n", item);
  printf("%10f\n", item);
```

```
   printf(""%012f\n", item);

   return 0;
}
```

This program produces the following output:

```
10.123040
 10.123040
00010.123040
```

Perhaps the most common use of the minimum field width modifier is in the production of tables in which the columns line up. For example, this program produces a table of squares and cubes for the numbers between 1 and 19:

```
#include "stdio.h"

main()
{
  int i;

  /* display a table of squares and cubes */
  for(i=1; i<20; i++)
    printf("%8d %8d %8d\n", i, i*i, i*i*i);

  return 0;
}
```

A sample of its output is shown here:

```
 1        1        1
 2        4        8
 3        9       27
 4       16       64
 5       25      125
 6       36      216
 7       49      343
 8       64      512
 9       81      729
 0      100     1000
11      121     1331
12      144     1728
13      169     2197
14      196     2744
15      225     3375
16      256     4096
17      289     4913
18      324     5832
19      361     6859
```

The Precision Specifier

The *precision specifier* follows the minimum field width specifier (if one is present). It consists of a period followed by an integer. Its exact meaning depends upon the type of data it is applied to.

When the precision specifier is applied to floating-point data, it determines the number of decimal places displayed. For example, **%10.4f** displays a number at least ten characters wide with four decimal places.

When the precision specifier is applied to strings, it specifies the maximum field length. For example, **%5.7s** displays a string at least five characters long and not exceeding seven. If the string is longer than the maximum field width, the characters are truncated from the end.

When the precision specifier is applied to integer types, it specifies the minimum number of digits that will appear for each number. In this case, leading zeros are added to achieve the minimum number of digits required.

The following program illustrates the precision specifier:

```
#include "stdio.h"

main()
{
  printf("%.4f\n", 123.1234567);
  printf("%3.8d\n", 1000);
  printf("%10.15s\n", "This is a simple test.");

  return 0;
}
```

This program produces the following output:

```
123.1235
00001000
This is a simpl
```

Justifying Output

By default, all output is *right-justified:* if the field width is larger than the data printed, the data is placed on the right edge of the field. You can force the information to be left justified by placing a minus sign directly after the percent sign. For example, %−10.2f left-justifies a floating-point number with two decimal places in a ten-character field.

The following program illustrates left justification:

```
#include "stdio.h"

main()
{
  printf("right-justified:%8d\n", 100);
  printf(" left-justified:%-8d\n", 100);

  return 0;
}
```

Handling Other Data Types

There are two format command modifiers that allow **printf( )** to display **short** and **long** integers. These modifiers may be applied to the **d, i, o, u,** and **x** type specifiers. The l modifier tells **printf( )** that a **long** data type follows. For example, %ld means that a **long int** is to be displayed. The h modifier instructs **printf( )** to display a **short int**. Therefore, %hu indicates that the data is of type **short unsigned int**.

The **L** modifier may also prefix the floating-point commands of **e, f,** and **g**; it indicates that a **long double** follows.

The * and # Modifiers

The **printf( )** function supports two additional modifiers to some of its format codes: the * and the #.

Preceding a **g, f,** or **e** code with a # ensures that the decimal point will be present even if there are no decimal digits. If you precede the **x** format code with a #, the hexadecimal number is printed with a **0x** prefix. The # cannot be applied to any other format specifiers.

The minimum field width and precision specifiers may be provided by arguments to **printf( )** instead of constants. To accomplish this, use an * as a placeholder. When the format string is scanned, **printf( )** will match the * to an argument in the order in which they occur. For example, in Figure 8-1, the minimum field width will be 10, the precision will be 4, and the value to be displayed is 123.3.

The following program illustrates both the # and the *:

```
#include "stdio.h"

main()
{
  printf("%x %#x\n", 10, 10);
  printf("%*.*f", 10, 4, 1234.34);

  return 0;
}
```

scanf( )

The general-purpose console input routine is **scanf( )**. It can read all the built-in data types and automatically convert numbers into the proper internal format. It is much like the reverse of **printf( )**. The prototype for **scanf( )** is

    int scanf(char *control_string,...);

The prototype for **scanf( )** is in **stdio.h**. The **scanf( )** function returns the number of data items successfully assigned a value. If an error occurs, **scanf( )** returns **EOF**.

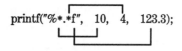

Figure 8-1. How the * is matched to its value

The control string consists of three classifications of characters:

- Format specifiers
- White-space characters
- Non-white-space characters

Format Specifiers

The input format specifiers are preceded by a percent sign and tell **scanf( )** what type of data is to be read next. These codes are listed in Table 8-3.

Inputting Numbers

To read a decimal number, use the **%d** or **%i** specifier. (These specifiers, which do precisely the same thing, are included for compatibility with older versions of C.)

Code	Meaning
%c	Read a single character
%d	Read a decimal integer
%i	Read a decimal integer
%e	Read a floating-point number
%f	Read a floating-point number
%g	Read a floating-point number
%o	Read an octal number
%s	Read a string
%x	Read a hexadecimal number
%p	Read a pointer
%n	Receives an integer value equal to the number of characters read so far
%u	Read an unsigned integer
%[]	Scan for a set of characters

Table 8-3.   scanf( ) Format Codes

To read a floating-point number represented in either standard or scientific notation, use **%e**, **%f**, or **%g**. (These specifiers, which do precisely the same thing, are included for compatibility with older versions of C.)

You can use **scanf( )** to read integers in either octal or hexadecimal form by using the **%o** and **%x** format commands, respectively. The **%x** may be in either upper- or lowercase. Either way, you may enter the letters A through Z in either upper- or lowercase when entering hexadecimal numbers. This program reads an octal and hexadecimal number:

```
#include "stdio.h"

main()
{
  int i, j;

  scanf("%o%x", &i, &j);
  printf("%o %x", i, j);

  return 0;
}
```

Inputting Unsigned Integers

To input an unsigned integer, use the **%u** format specifier. For example, the fragment

```
unsigned num;

scanf("%u", &num);
```

reads an unsigned number and puts its value into **num**.

Reading Individual Characters Using scanf( )

As you learned earlier in this chapter, you can read individual characters by using **getchar( )** or a derivative function. You can also use **scanf( )** for this purpose, using the **%c** format command. However, like most implementations of **getchar( )**, **scanf( )** line-buffers input when the %c specifier is used. This makes it a little troublesome in an interactive environment.

Although spaces, tabs, and newlines are used as field separators when other types of data are read, when a single character is read, white-space characters are read like any other character. For example, with an input stream of "**x y**",

```
scanf("%c%c%c", &a, &b, &c);
```

returns with the character "x" in **a**, a space in **b**, and the character "y" in **c**.

Reading Strings

You can use the **scanf( )** function to read a string from the input stream by using the %s format specifier. Using the %s causes **scanf( )** to read characters until a white-space character is encountered. The characters read are put into the character array pointed to by its corresponding argument, and the result is null terminated. As applied to **scanf( )**, a white-space character is one of the following: a space, a carriage return, or a tab. Unlike **gets( )**, which reads a string until ENTER is pressed, **scanf( )** reads a string until the first white space. This means that you cannot use **scanf( )** to read a string like "this is a test" because the first space terminates the inputting process. To see the effect of the %s command, try this program, using the string "hello there":

```
#include "stdio.h"

main()
{
  char str[80];

  printf("enter a string: ");
  scanf("%s", str);
  printf("here's your string: %s", str);

  return 0;
}
```

The program responds with only the "hello" portion of the string.

Inputting an Address

To input a memory address (pointer), use the **%p** format code. Do not attempt to use an **unsigned** integer or any other format specifier for this purpose because the **%p** makes **scanf( )** read the address in the format used by the CPU. For example, this program inputs a pointer and then displays what is at that memory address:

```
#include "stdio.h"

main()
{
  char *p;

  printf("enter an address: ");
  scanf("%p", &p);
  printf("at location %p is %c\n", p, *p);

  return 0;
}
```

The %n Specifier

The **%n** specifier instructs **scanf( )** to assign to the variable pointed to by the corresponding argument the number of characters read from the input stream at the point at which the **%n** was encountered.

Using a Scanset

The ANSI C standard has added a new feature to **scanf( )**, called a scanset, that was not part of the original K&R version. A *scanset* defines a set of characters that may be read by **scanf( )** and assigned to the corresponding character array. You define a scanset by putting the sequence of characters you want to scan for inside square brackets. The beginning square bracket must be prefixed by a percent sign. For example, this scanset tells **scanf( )** to read only the characters X, Y, and Z:

```
%[XYZ]
```

When you use a scanset, **scanf( )** continues to read characters and put them into the corresponding character array until a character that is not in the scanset is encountered. The corresponding variable must be a pointer to a character array. Upon return from **scanf( )**, the array will contain a null-terminated string made up of the characters read. To see how this works, try this program:

```
#include "stdio.h"

main()
{
  int i;
  char str[80], str2[80];

  scanf("%d%[abcdefg]%s", &i, str, str2);
  printf("%d %s %s", i, str, str2);

  return 0;
}
```

Enter **123abcdtye** followed by ENTER. The program will then display **123 abcd tye**. Because the "t" is not part of the scanset, **scanf( )** stops reading characters into **str** when it encounters the "t."

You can specify an inverted set if the first character in the set is a ^. When the ^ is present, it instructs **scanf( )** to accept any character that is *not* defined by the scanset.

You can specify a range by using a hyphen. For example, this tells **scanf( )** to accept the characters A through Z:

```
%[A-Z]
```

Remember that the scanset is case-sensitive. Therefore, if you want to scan for both upper-and lowercase letters, you must specify them individually.

Discarding Unwanted White Space

A white-space character in the control string causes **scanf( )** to skip over one or more white-space characters in the input stream. A white-space character is a space, a tab, or a newline. In essence, one white-space character in the control string will cause **scanf( )** to read, but not store, any number (including zero) of white-space characters up to the first non-white-space character.

Non-White-Space Characters in the Control String

A non-white-space character in the control string causes **scanf( )** to read and discard a matching character in the input stream. For example, *"%d,%d"* causes **scanf( )** first to read an integer, then to read and discard a comma, and finally to read another integer. If the specified character is not found, **scanf( )** terminates. If you wish to read and discard a percent sign, use %% in the control string.

You Must Pass scanf( ) Addresses

All the variables used to receive values through **scanf( )** must be passed by their addresses. This means that all arguments must be pointers to the variables used as arguments. Remember that this is C's way of creating a call by reference, and it allows a function to alter the contents of an argument. For example, to read an integer into the variable **count**, use the following **scanf( )** call:

```
scanf("%d", &count);
```

Strings will be read into character arrays, and the array name, without any index, is the address of the first element of the array. Therefore, to read a string into the character array **str,** you would use

```
scanf("%s", str);
```

In this case, **str** is already a pointer and need not be preceded by the & operator.

Format Modifiers

As with **printf( )**, **scanf( )** allows a number of its format specifiers to be modified.

The format commands can specify a maximum field length modifier. This is an integer number placed between the percent sign and the format command code that limits the number of characters read for that field. For example, to read no more than 20 characters into **str**, you would write

```
scanf("%20s", str);
```

If the input stream is greater than 20 characters, a subsequent call to input begins where this call leaves off. For example, if

ABCDEFGHIJKLMNOPQRSTUVWXYZ

is entered as the response to the **scanf( )** call in this example, only the first 20 characters, or up to the T, are placed into **str** because of the maximum size specifier. The remaining characters, UVWXYZ, have not yet been used. If another **scanf( )** call is made, such as

```
scanf("%s", str);
```

then the characters UVWXYZ are placed into **str**. Input for a field may terminate before the maximum field length is reached if a white space is encountered. In this case, **scanf( )** moves on to the next field.

To read a long integer, put **l** in front of the format specifier. To read a short integer, put **h** in front of the format specifier. These modifiers can be used with **d**, **i**, **o**, and **x** formats.

By default, the **%f**, **%e**, and **%g** specifiers instruct **scanf( )** to assign data to a **float**. If you put **l** in front of one of these, **scanf( )** assigns the data to a **double**. Using **L** tells **scanf( )** that the variable receiving the data is a **long double**.

Suppressing Input

You can tell **scanf( )** to read a field but to not assign it to any variable if you precede that field's format code with an *****. For example, given

```
scanf("%d%*c%d", &x, &y);
```

you could enter the coordinate pair **10,10**. The comma would be correctly read but would not be assigned to anything. Suppression of assignment is especially useful when you need to process only a part of what is being entered.

NINE

ANSI C Standard File I/O

The ANSI C standard defines a rich set of file functions that can be used to read and write any type of data from or to a file. In fact, C's file system is one of its most elegant, powerful, and flexible features.

This chapter presents an overview of the ANSI C file system and its most commonly used functions. It also discusses the concepts that are central to its use.

A Historical Note

The ANSI C file system is modeled upon what was referred to in early versions of C as the *buffered file system* (sometimes the term *formatted* or *high-level* is used instead). The first versions of C actually contained two distinct file systems, the second being the *UNIX-like file system* (sometimes called either *unformatted* or *unbuffered*). The UNIX-like file system essentially emulated the low-level UNIX file interface. The ANSI C standard does not define the UNIX-like file system for several reasons, including the fact that the two file systems are largely redundant. Also, the UNIX-like file system may not be relevant to certain environments that could otherwise support C. Because all C++ compilers are upwardly compatible with the ANSI C standard, and given that the UNIX-like file system is not particularly relevant to C++ programming, the old, UNIX-like file system is not discussed in this book.

For complete coverage of the UNIX-like file system, see the book *C: The Complete Reference*, 2nd edition, by Herb Schildt (Osborne/McGraw-Hill, 1990). Also, read carefully the section in Chapter 8 entitled "An Important Application Note."

Streams and Files

Before beginning a discussion of the ANSI C file system, it is important to understand the difference between the terms streams and files and how they interact. The C I/O system supplies a consistent interface to the programmer independent of the actual device being accessed. That is, the C I/O system provides a level of abstraction between the programmer and the device being used. This abstraction is called a *stream*, and the actual device a *file*.

Streams

The C file system is designed to work with a wide variety of devices, including terminals, disk drives, and tape drives. Even though each device is very different, the ANSI file system transforms each into a logical device called a stream. All streams are similar in their behavior. Because streams are largely device independent, the same functions that write to a disk file can also write to another device, such as the console. There are two types of streams: text and binary.

Text Streams

A *text stream* is a sequence of characters. The ANSI standard allows (but does not require) a text stream to be organized into lines terminated by a newline character. The newline character is optional on the last line and is determined by the implementation. (Actually, most C compilers do not organize text streams into newline-terminated lines.) In a text stream, certain character translations may occur as required by the host environment. For example, a newline may be converted to a carriage return/linefeed pair. Therefore, there may not be a one-to-one relationship between the characters that are written (or read) and those in the external device. Also, because of possible translations, the number of characters written (or read) may not be the same as those found in the external device.

Binary Streams

A *binary stream* is a sequence comprised of bytes that have a one-to-one correspondence to those found in the external device. That is, no character translations will occur. Also, the number of bytes written (or read) will be the same as the number found in the external device. The standard does specify, however, that a binary stream may have an implementation-defined number of null bytes appended to its end. These null bytes might be used, for example, to pad the information so that it fills a sector on a disk.

Files

In C, a file may be anything from a disk file to a terminal or printer. You associate a stream with a specific file by performing an *open* operation. Once a file is open, information may be exchanged between it and your program.

Not all files have the same capabilities. For example, a disk file can support random access, but a keyboard cannot. This illustrates an important point about the C I/O system: all streams are the same but all files are not.

If the file can support random access (sometimes referred to as *position requests*), opening that file also initializes the *file position indicator* to the start of the file. As each character is read from or written to the file, the position indicator is incremented, thus ensuring progression through the file.

You disassociate a file from a specific stream with a *close* operation. On streams opened for output, closing a stream causes the contents, if any, of its associated stream to be written to the external device. This process is generally referred to as *flushing* the stream, and it guarantees that no information is accidentally left in the disk buffer. All files are closed automatically when your program terminates, normally by **main( )** returning to the operating system or by a call to **exit( )**. Files are not closed when a program terminates by crashing.

Each stream that is associated with a file has a file control structure of type **FILE**. This structure is defined in the header **stdio.h**. You must not modify to this file control structure.

If C's separation of streams and files seems unnecessary or strange, keep in mind its main purpose: consistency of interface. In C's approach, the programmer need think only in terms of streams and use only one file system to accomplish all I/O operations. The C compiler takes care of converting the raw input or output into an easily managed stream.

File System Basics

The ANSI C file system is made up of several interrelated functions. The most common are shown in Table 9-1. These functions require that the header file **stdio.h** be included in any program in which they are used.

The header file **stdio.h**, in addition to providing the prototypes for the I/O functions, defines several types, including **size_t**, **fpos_t**, and **FILE**. The **size_t** type is large enough to hold the result of the subtraction of two pointers and is some variety of **unsigned** integer. **fpos_t** is a type capable of specifying any unique position in a file and is also essentially some variety of **unsigned** integer. The **FILE** type is discussed in the next section.

stdio.h also defines several macros. The ones relevant to this chapter are **EOF**, **SEEK_SET**, **SEEK_CUR**, and **SEEK_END**. The **EOF** macro is generally defined as −1 and is the value returned when an input function tries to read past the end of the file. The others are used with **fseek( )**, which is the function that performs random access on a file. For other macros defined by **stdio.h**, simply examine the file.

Name	Function
fopen( )	Opens a stream
fclose( )	Closes a stream
putc( )	Writes a character to a stream
fputc( )	Same as putc( )
getc( )	Reads a character from a stream
fgetc( )	Same as getc( )
fseek( )	Seeks a specified byte in a stream
fprintf( )	Is to a stream what printf( ) is to the console
fscanf( )	Is to a stream what scanf( ) is to the console
feof( )	Returns true if end-of-file is reached
ferror( )	Returns true if an error has occurred
rewind( )	Resets the file position locator to the beginning of the file
remove( )	Erases a file
fflush( )	Flushes a file

Table 9-1.   The Most Common ANSI C File System Functions

The File Pointer

The common thread that ties the ANSI I/O system together is the file pointer. A *file pointer* is a pointer to information that defines various things about the file, including its name, status, and current position. In essence, the file pointer identifies a specific disk file and is used by the stream associated with it to direct the operation of the ANSI I/O functions. A file pointer is a pointer variable of type **FILE** that is defined in **stdio.h**. To read or write files, your program will need to use file pointers. To obtain a file pointer variable, use a statement like this:

```
FILE *fp;
```

Opening a File

The **fopen( )** function serves two purposes: first, it opens a stream for use and links a file with that stream. Second, it returns the file pointer associated with that file. Most often, and for the rest of this discussion, the file is a disk file. The **fopen( )** function has this prototype:

FILE *fopen(const char *_filename_, const char *_mode_);

where _filename_ is a pointer to a string of characters that make up a valid file name for the operating system and may include a path specification. The string pointed to by _mode_ determines how the file will be opened. The legal values for _mode_ are shown in Table 9-2. Strings like "r + b" may also be represented as "rb + ".

As stated, the **fopen( )** function returns a file pointer. Your program should never alter the value of this pointer. If an error occurs when you try to open the file, **fopen( )** returns a null pointer.

As Table 9-2 shows, a file may be opened in either text or binary mode. In most implementations, in text mode, carriage return/linefeed sequences are translated to newline characters on input. On output, the reverse occurs: newlines are translated to carriage return/linefeeds. No such translations occur on binary files.

If you wished to open a file for output with the name **test**, you could use something like this:

```
FILE *fp;

fp = fopen("test", "w");
```

Mode	Meaning
r	Open a text file for reading
w	Create a text file for writing
a	Append to a text file
rb	Open a binary file for reading
wb	Create a binary file for writing
ab	Append to a binary file
r+	Open a text file for read/write
w+	Create a text file for read/write
a+	Append or create a text file for read/write
r+b	Open a binary file for read/write
w+b	Create a binary file for read/write
a+b	Append a binary file for read/write

Table 9-2.   The Legal Values for Mode

However, you will usually see it written like this:

```
FILE *fp;

if ((fp = fopen("test","w"))==NULL) {
  printf("cannot open file\n");
  exit(1);
}
```

The macro **NULL** is defined in **stdio.h** as '\0'. Opening a file by using this method detects any error in opening a file, such as a write-protected or full disk, before attempting to write to it. A null is used to indicate failure because no file pointer will ever have that value.

If you use **fopen( )** to open a file for writing, any preexisting file by that name will be erased and a new file started. If no file by that name exists, one will be created. If, instead, you want to add to the end of the file, then you must use mode "a." Opening a file for read operations requires that the file exists. If it does not, an error is returned. Finally, if a file is opened for read/write operations, it will not be erased if it exists; however, if it does not exist, it will be created.

The ANSI standard specifies that at least eight files may be open at any one time. However, most C compilers and environments allow more than this.

When you work with a file that is opened in read/write mode, two points are important to understand. First, output may not follow input without a call either to **fflush( )** or to a file-positioning function, such as **fseek( )** or **rewind( )**, occurring between the two operations. (These functions are discussed later in this chapter.) Second, input may not follow output unless the end of the file is encountered or a call to a file-positioning function is made between the two operations.

Closing a File

You use **fclose( )** to close a stream that was opened by a call to **fopen( )**. The **fclose( )** function writes any data still remaining in the disk buffer to the file and does a formal operating-system-level close on the file. Failure to close a stream invites all kinds of trouble, including lost data, destroyed files, and possible intermittent errors in your program. An **fclose( )** also frees the file control block associated with the stream and makes it available for reuse. In most cases, there is an operating system limit to the number of open files you may have at any one time, so it may be necessary to close one file before opening another.

The **fclose( )** function has this prototype:

int fclose(FILE *fp);

where fp is the file pointer returned by the call to **fopen( )**. A return value of zero signifies a successful close operation; any other value indicates an error. You can use the standard function **ferror( )** (discussed later in this chapter) to determine and report any problems. Generally, **fclose( )** will only fail when a disk has been prematurely removed from the drive or when there is no more space on the disk.

Writing a Character

The ANSI C standard defines two equivalent functions that output a character: **putc( )** and **fputc( )**. (Technically, **putc( )** is implemented as a macro.) Having two identical functions preserves compatibility with older versions of C. This book arbitrarily uses **putc( )**, but you can use **fputc( )** if you like.

You use the **putc( )** function to write characters to a stream that was previously opened for output by using the **fopen( )** function. The function is declared as

int putc(int ch, FILE *fp);

where fp is the file pointer returned by **fopen( )** and ch is the character to be output. The file pointer tells **putc( )** which disk file to write to. For historical reasons, ch is defined as an **int**, but only the low-order byte is used.

If a **putc( )** operation is a success, it returns the character written. Upon failure, an **EOF** is returned.

Reading a Character

Like **putc( )** and **fputc( )**, there are two equivalent functions that input a character: **getc( )** and **fgetc( )**. **getc( )** is implemented as a macro.

Again, having two identical functions preserves compatibility with older versions of C. This book arbitrarily uses **getc( )**, but you can use **fgetc( )** if you like.

You use the **getc( )** function to read characters from a stream opened for input by **fopen( )**. The function is declared as

```
int getc(FILE *fp);
```

where *fp* is a file pointer of type **FILE** returned by **fopen( )**. For historical reasons, **getc( )** returns an integer, but the high-order byte is zero.

The **getc( )** function returns an **EOF** mark when the end of the file has been reached. Therefore, to read a text file until the end-of-file mark is read, you could use the following code:

```
do {
  ch = getc(fp);
} while(ch!=EOF);
```

Using fopen( ), getc( ), putc( ), and fclose( )

The functions **fopen( )**, **getc( )**, **putc( )**, and **fclose( )** make up the minimal set of file routines. The following program, **KTOD**, is a simple example of using **putc( )**, **fopen( )**, and **fclose( )**. It simply reads characters from the keyboard and writes them to a disk file until a dollar sign is typed. The file name is specified from the command line. For example, if you call this program **KTOD**, typing **KTOD TEST** will allow you to enter lines of text into the file called "test."

```
/* KTOD: A key to disk program. */

#include "stdio.h"
#include "stdlib.h"
#include "conio.h"

main(int argc, char *argv[])
{
  FILE *fp;
  char ch;

  if(argc!=2) {
    printf("You forgot to enter the filename\n");
    exit(1);
```

```
  }

  if((fp=fopen(argv[1], "w"))==NULL) {
    printf("cannot open file\n");
    exit(1);
  }

  do {
    ch = getche();
    putc(ch, fp);
  } while (ch!='$');

  fclose(fp);

  return 0;
}
```

The complementary program, **DTOS**, will read any ASCII file and display the contents on the screen:

```
/* DTOS: A program that reads files and displays them
        on the screen.
*/

#include "stdio.h"
#include "stdlib.h"

main(int argc, char *argv[])
{
  FILE *fp;
  char ch;

  if(argc!=2) {
    printf("You forgot to enter the filename\n");
    exit(1);
  }

  if((fp=fopen(argv[1], "r"))==NULL) {
    printf("cannot open file\n");
    exit(1);
  }

  ch = getc(fp);    /* read one character */

  while (ch!=EOF) {
    putchar(ch); /* print on screen */
    ch = getc(fp);
  }

  fclose(fp);

  return 0;
}
```

Try these two programs now. First use **KTOD** to create a text file. Then read its contents by using **DTOS**.

Using feof( )

As stated earlier, the ANSI C file system can also operate on binary data. When a file is opened for binary input, it is possible for an integer value equal to the **EOF** mark to be read. This would cause the input routine to indicate an end-of-file condition even though the physical end of the file had not been reached. To solve this problem, C includes the function **feof( )**, which determines when the physical end-of-file has been reached when binary data is being read. The **feof( )** function has this prototype:

int feof(FILE *fp*);

This prototype is in **stdio.h**. It returns true if the end of the file has been reached; otherwise, it returns zero. Therefore, the following routine reads a binary file until end-of-file is encountered:

```
while(!feof(fp)) ch = getc(fp);
```

Of course, this method may be applied to text files as well as binary files.

The **feof( )** function is found in the following program, which copies text or binary files. The files are opened in binary mode, and **feof( )** is used to check for end-of-file.

```
/* Copy a file. */

#include "stdio.h"
#include "stdlib.h"

main(int argc, char *argv[])
{
  FILE *in, *out;
  char ch;

  if(argc!=3) {
    printf("You forgot to enter a filename\n");
    exit(1);
  }
```

```
if((in=fopen(argv[1], "rb"))==NULL) {
  printf("cannot open source file\n");
  exit(1);
}
if((out=fopen(argv[2], "wb")) == NULL) {
  printf("cannot open destination file\n");
  exit(1);
}

/* this code actually copies the file */
while(!feof(in)) {
  ch = getc(in);
  if(!feof(in)) putc(ch, out);
}

fclose(in);
fclose(out);

return 0;
}
```

Working with Strings: fputs( ) and fgets( )

In addition to **putc( )** and **getc( )**, C supports two related functions: **fputs( )** and **fgets( )**. They are used to read and write character strings to and from a disk file. These functions work similarly to **putc( )** and **getc( )**, except that instead of reading or writing a single character, they read or write a string. They have the following prototypes:

int fputs(const char *str*, FILE *fp*);

char *fgets(char *str*, int *length*, FILE *fp*);

The prototypes for **fgets( )** and **fputs( )** are in **stdio.h**.

The function **fputs( )** works exactly like **puts( )**, except that it writes the string to the specified stream. It returns **EOF** if an error occurs.

The **fgets( )** function reads a string from the specified stream until either a newline character is read or *length−1* characters have been read. If a newline is read, it will be part of the string (unlike its relative **gets( )**). The resultant string will be null terminated. The function returns *str* if successful and a null pointer if an error occurs.

The following program demonstrates the **fputs( )** function. It reads strings from the keyboard using **gets( )** and writes them to the file called TEST. To terminate the program, enter a blank line. Because **gets( )** does not store the newline character, one is added before the string is written so you can read the file more easily.

```
#include "stdio.h"
#include "stdlib.h"
#include "string.h"

main()
{
  char str[80];
  FILE *fp;

  if((fp = fopen("TEST", "w"))==NULL) {
    printf("cannot open file\n");
    exit(1);
  }
  do {
    printf("enter a string (CR to quit):\n");
    gets(str);
    strcat(str, "\n");   /* add a newline */
    fputs(str, fp);
  } while(*str!='\n');

  return 0;
}
```

rewind( )

The **rewind( )** function resets the file position indicator to the beginning of the file specified as its argument. That is, it "rewinds" the file. Its prototype is

void rewind(FILE *fp)

where fp is a valid file pointer. The prototype for **rewind( )** is in **stdio.h**.

To see an example of **rewind( )**, you can modify the program shown in the previous section so that it displays the contents of the file just created. To accomplish this, the program rewinds the file after input is complete and then uses **fgets( )** to read back the file. Notice that the file must now be opened in read/write mode using "w+" for the *mode* parameter.

```
#include "stdio.h"
#include "stdlib.h"
#include "string.h"

main()
{
  char str[80];
  FILE *fp;

  if((fp = fopen("TEST", "w+"))==NULL) {
    printf("cannot open file\n");
    exit(1);
  }
  do {
    printf("enter a string (CR to quit):\n");
    gets(str);
    strcat(str, "\n");  /* add a newline */
    fputs(str, fp);
  } while(*str!='\n');

  /* now, read and display the file */
  rewind(fp);  /* reset file position indicator to
                  start of the file. */
  while(!feof(fp)) {
    fgets(str, 79, fp);
    printf(str);
  }

  return 0;
}
```

ferror( )

The **ferror( )** function determines whether a file operation has produced
an error. The function **ferror( )** has the prototype

int ferror(FILE *fp)

where fp is a valid file pointer. It returns true if an error has occurred
during the last file operation; it returns false otherwise. Because each
file operation resets the error condition flag, **ferror( )** should be called
immediately after each file operation; otherwise, an error may be lost.
The prototype for **ferror( )** is in **stdio.h**.

To illustrate how **ferror( )** can be used, the following program
removes tabs from a text file, substituting the appropriate number of

spaces. The tab size is defined by **TAB‗SIZE**. Notice that **ferror( )** is called after each disk operation. To use the program, execute it with the name of the input file and the output file specified on the command line.

```c
/* The program substitutes spaces for tabs
   in a text file and supplies error checking.
*/

#include "stdio.h"
#include "stdlib.h"

#define TAB_SIZE 8
#define IN 0
#define OUT 1

void err(int e);

main(int argc, char *argv[])
{
  FILE *in, *out;
  int tab, i;
  char ch;

  if(argc!=3) {
    printf("usage: detab <in> <out>\n");
    exit(1);
  }

  if((in = fopen(argv[1], "rb"))==NULL) {
    printf("cannot open %s\n", argv[1]);
    exit(1);
  }

  if((out = fopen(argv[2], "wb"))==NULL) {
    printf("cannot open %s\n", argv[2]);
    exit(1);
  }

  tab = 0;
  do {
    ch = getc(in);
    if(ferror(in)) err(IN);

    if(ch=='\t') { /* If tab found, then */
      /* output appropriate number of spaces. */
      for(i=tab; i<8; i++) {
        putc(' ', out);
        if(ferror(out)) err(OUT);
      }
      tab = 0;
    }
    else {
      putc(ch, out);
      if(ferror(out)) err(OUT);
```

```
      tab++;
      if(tab==TAB_SIZE) tab = 0;
      if(ch=='\n' || ch=='\r') tab = 0;
    }
  } while(!feof(in));
  fclose(in);
  if(ferror(in)) err(IN);
  fclose(out);
  if(ferror(out)) err(OUT);

  return 0;
}

void err(int e)
{
  if(e==IN) printf("error on input\n");
  else printf("error on output\n");
  exit(1);
}
```

Erasing Files

The **remove( )** function erases the specified file. Its prototype is

    int remove(char *filename);

It returns zero upon success, nonzero if it fails.

The following program erases the file specified on the command line. However, before it does, it gives the user a chance to change his or her mind. A utility like this might be useful to new computer users.

```
/* Double check before erasing. */

#include "stdio.h"
#include "stdlib.h"
#include "ctype.h"

main(int argc, char *argv[])
{
  char str[80];

  if(argc!=2) {
    printf("usage: xerase <filename>\n");
    exit(1);
  }

  printf("erase %s? (Y/N): ", argv[1]);
  gets(str);

  if(toupper(*str)=='Y')
```

```
    if(remove(argv[l])) {
      printf("cannot erase file\n");
      exit(1);
    }

  return 0;  /* return success to OS */
}
```

Flushing a Stream

To flush the contents of an output stream, use the **fflush( )** function; its prototype is shown here:

int fflush(FILE *fp);

This function will write the contents of any buffered data to the file associated with fp. If you call **fflush( )** with a null, all files opened for output are flushed.

The **fflush( )** function returns zero if successful, **EOF** upon failure.

fread( ) and fwrite( )

To read and write data types that are longer than one byte, the ANSI C file system provides two functions, **fread( )** and **fwrite( )**, that allow the reading and writing of blocks of any type of data. Their prototypes are

size_t fread(void *buffer, size_t num_bytes,
            size_t count, FILE *fp)

size_t fwrite(const void *buffer, size_t num_bytes,
            size_t count, FILE *fp);

In the case of **fread( )**, buffer is a pointer to a region of memory that will receive the data read from the file. For **fwrite( )**, buffer is a pointer to the information that will be written to the file. The number of bytes to be read or written is specified by num_bytes. The argument count determines how many items (each being num_bytes in length) will be read or written. (Remember, the type **size_t** is defined in **stdio.h** and is more or less the same as *unsigned.*) Finally, *fp* is a file pointer to a previously opened stream. Both functions have their prototypes defined in **stdio.h.**

The **fread( )** function returns the number of items read. This value may be less than *count* if the end of the file is reached or an error occurs. The **fwrite( )** function returns the number of items written. This value will equal *count* unless an error occurs.

Using fread( ) and fwrite( )

As long as the file has been opened for binary data, **fread( )** and **fwrite( )** can read and write any type of information. For example, the next program writes and then reads back a **double**, an **int**, and a **long** to and from a disk file. Notice how it uses **sizeof( )** to determine the length of each data type.

```
/* Write some non-character data to a disk file
   and read it back.
*/
#include "stdio.h"
#include "stdlib.h"

main()
{
  FILE *fp;
  double d = 12.23;
  int i = 101;
  long l = 123023L;

  if((fp=fopen("test","wb+"))==NULL) {
    printf("cannot open file\n");
    exit(1);
  }

  fwrite(&d, sizeof(double), 1, fp);
  fwrite(&i, sizeof(int), 1, fp);
  fwrite(&l, sizeof(long), 1, fp);

  rewind(fp);

  fread(&d, sizeof(double), 1, fp);
  fread(&i, sizeof(int), 1, fp);
  fread(&l, sizeof(long), 1, fp);

  printf("%f %d %ld", d, i, l);
  fclose(fp);

  return 0;
}
```

As this program illustrates, the buffer can be, and often is, simply the memory used to hold a variable. In this simple program, the return values of **fread( )** and **fwrite( )** are ignored, but in actual practice, you should check their return values, looking for errors.

One of the most useful applications of **fread( )** and **fwrite( )** involves the reading and writing of user-defined data types, especially structures. For example, given this structure,

```
struct struct_type {
  float balance;
  char name[80];
} cust;
```

the following statement will write the contents of **cust** to the file pointed to by **fp**:

```
fwrite(&cust, sizeof(struct struc_type), 1, fp);
```

fseek( ) and Random Access I/O

You can perform random read and write operations using the ANSI I/O system with the help of **fseek( )**, which sets the file position locator. Its prototype is

int fseek(FILE *fp*, long *numbytes*, int *origin*);

Here, *fp* is a file pointer returned by a call to **fopen( )**; *numbytes*, a **long** integer, is the number of bytes from *origin* to make the current position; and *origin* is one of the following macros defined in **stdio.h**:

Origin	Macro Name
Beginning of file	SEEK_SET
Current position	SEEK_CUR
End of file	SEEK_END

Therefore, to seek *numbytes* from the start of the file, *origin* should be **SEEK_SET**; to seek from the current position, use **SEEK_CUR**; and from the end of the file, use **SEEK_END**. The **fseek( )** function returns zero when successful and nonzero when an error occurs. Remember that *numbytes* must be a **long**. This is required to support files larger than 64K.

The following fragment illustrates **fseek( )**'s usage. It seeks and displays the specified byte in the specified file. Both the file name and the byte to seek are specified from the command line, in the order of the file name followed by the byte.

```
#include "stdio.h"
#include "stdlib.h"

main(int argc, char *argv[])
{
  FILE *fp;

  if(argc!=3) {
    printf("Usage: SEEK filename byte\n");
    exit(1);
  }

  if((fp = fopen(argv[1], "r"))==NULL) {
    printf("cannot open file\n");
    exit(1);
  }

  if(fseek(fp, atol(argv[2]), SEEK_SET)) {
    printf("seek error\n");
    exit(1);
  }
  printf("Byte at %ld is %c\n", atol(argv[2]), getc(fp));
  fclose(fp);

  return 0;
}
```

You can use **fseek( )** to seek in multiples of any type of data simply by multiplying the size of the data by the number of the data item you want to reach. For example, assume that you have a mailing list that uses structures of type **list_type** to hold each address. To seek the tenth address in the file that holds the address, use this command:

```
fseek(fp, 9*sizeof(struct list_type), SEEK_SET);
```

fprintf( ) and fscanf( )

In addition to the basic I/O functions already discussed, the ANSI I/O system includes **fprintf( )** and **fscanf( )**. These functions behave exactly like **printf( )** and **scanf( )** except that they operate with disk files. The prototypes of **fprintf( )** and **fscanf( )** are

> int fprintf(FILE *fp*, const char *control_string, ...);

> int fscanf(FILE *fp*, const char *control_string, ...);

where *fp* is a file pointer returned by a call to **fopen( )**. It is to the file pointed to by *fp* that **fprintf( )** and **fscanf( )** direct their I/O operations.

To illustrate how useful these functions can be, the following program will read a string and an integer from the keyboard, write them to a disk file, and then read and display the information back on the screen.

```
/* fscanf - fprintf example */

#include "stdio.h"
#include "io.h"
#include "stdlib.h"

main()
{
  FILE *fp;
  char s[80];
  int t;

  if((fp=fopen("test", "w")) == NULL) {
    printf("cannot open file\n");
    exit(1);
  }

  printf("enter a string and a number: ");
  fscanf(stdin, "%s%d", s, &t); /* read from keyboard */
  fprintf(fp, "%s %d", s, t); /* write to file */
  fclose(fp);

  if((fp=fopen("test","r")) == NULL) {
```

```
    printf("cannot open file\n");
    exit(1);
}

fscanf(fp, "%s%d", s, &t); /* read from file */
fprintf(stdout, "%s %d", s, t); /* print on screen */

return 0;
}
```

A word of warning: although **fprintf( )** and **fscanf( )** often are the easiest way to write and read assorted data to disk files, they are not always the most efficient. Because formatted ASCII data is being written just as it would appear on the screen instead of in binary, extra overhead is incurred with each call. So, if speed or file size is a concern, you should probably use **fread( )** and **fwrite( )**.

The Standard Streams

Whenever a C program starts execution, three streams are opened automatically. They are standard input (**stdin**), standard output (**stdout**), and standard error (**stderr**). Normally, these refer to the console, but they may be redirected by the operating system to some other device in environments that support redirectable I/O (such as UNIX, OS/2, and DOS).

Because the standard streams are file pointers, they may be used by the ANSI I/O system to perform I/O operations on the console. For example, **putchar( )** could be defined like this:

```
putchar(char c)
{
  putc(c, stdout);
}
```

In general, **stdin** is used to read from the console, **stdout** is used to write to the console, and **stderr** is used to write to the console. You may use **stdin**, **stdout**, and **stderr** as file pointers in any function that uses a variable of type **FILE ***. For example, you can use **fputs( )** to output a string to the console using a call like this:

```
fputs("hello there", stdout);
```

Keep in mind that **stdin, stdout,** and **stderr** are not variables in the normal sense and may not be assigned a value by using **fopen( ).** Also,

just as these file pointers are created automatically at the start of your program, they are closed automatically at the end; you should not try to close them.

The Console I/O Connection

As stated in Chapter 8, C makes little distinction between console I/O and file I/O. The console I/O functions described in Chapter 8 actually direct their I/O operations to either **stdin** or **stdout.** In essence, the console I/O functions are simply special-case versions of their parallel file functions. They exist as a convenience to you, the programmer.

As the preceding section describes, it is possible to perform console I/O by using any of C's file system functions. However, what might surprise you is that it is possible to perform disk file I/O by using a console I/O function, such as **printf( )!** Here's why: because all of the functions described in Chapter 8 and temporarily called "console I/O functions" operate on **stdin** and **stdout,** in environments that allow redirection of I/O, **stdin** and **stdout** could refer to a device other than the keyboard and screen. For example, consider this program:

```
#include "stdio.h"

main()
{
  char str[80];

  printf("enter a string: ");
  gets(str);
  printf(str);

  return 0;
}
```

Assume that this program is called **TEST.** If you execute **TEST** normally, it displays its prompt on the screen, reads a string from the keyboard, and displays that string on the display. However, in an environment that supports redirection of I/O, either **stdin**, **stdout**, or both could be redirected to a file. For example, in a DOS or OS/2 environment, executing **TEST** like this:

```
TEST > OUTPUT
```

causes the output of **TEST** to be written to a file called OUTPUT. Executing **TEST** like this:

```
TEST < INPUT > OUTPUT
```

causes **stdin** to be directed to the file called INPUT and output to be sent to the file called OUTPUT.

When a C program terminates, any redirected streams are reset to their default status.

Using freopen( ) to Redirect the Standard Streams

You can redirect the standard streams by using the **freopen( )** function. This function associates an existing stream with a new file. Hence, you can use it to associate a standard stream with a new file. Its prototype is

FILE *freopen(const char *filename,
                  const char *mode, FILE *stream)

where filename is a pointer to the file name you wish associated with the stream pointed to by stream. The file is opened by using the value of mode, which is the same as the one used with **fopen( )**.

The **freopen( )** function returns stream or, upon failure, a null pointer.

The following program uses **freopen( )** to redirect **stdout** to a file called OUTPUT:

```
#include "stdio.h"

main()
{
  char str[80];
```

```
  freopen("OUTPUT", "w", stdout);

  printf("enter a string: ");
  gets(str);
  printf(str);

  return 0;
}
```

In general, redirecting the standard streams by using **freopen( )** is useful in special situations, such as debugging. However, performing disk I/O by using redirected **stdin** and **stdout** is not as efficient as using functions like **fread( )** or **fwrite( )**.

The C Preprocessor and Comments

The C Preprocessor
#define
#error
#include
Conditional Compilation Directives
#undef
#line
#pragma
The # and ## Preprocessor Operators
Predefined Macro Names
Comments

You can include various instructions to the compiler in the source code of a C program. These are called *preprocessor directives*, and although they are not actually part of the C language, they expand the scope of the C programming environment. This chapter also examines comments, and you will see how to use both to simplify the program development process.

The C Preprocessor

The C preprocessor as defined by the ANSI C standard contains the following directives:

    #if
    #ifdef
    #ifndef
    #else

```
#elif
#include
#define
#undef
#line
#error
#pragma
```

All preprocessor directives begin with a # sign.

Each preprocessing directive must be on its own line. For example,

```
#include "stdio.h"  #include "stdlib.h"
```

will not work.

#define

The **#define** directive is used to define an identifier and a character sequence that will be substituted for the identifier each time it is encountered in the source file. The ANSI C standard refers to the identifier as a *macro name* and to the replacement process as *macro substitution*. The general form of the directive is

#define *macro-name character-sequence*

Notice that there is no semicolon in this statement. There may be any number of spaces between the identifier and the character sequence, but once the character sequence begins, it is terminated only by a newline.

For example, if you wish to use the word TRUE for the value 1 and the word FALSE for the value 0, you would declare two macros:

```
#define TRUE 1
#define FALSE 0
```

This causes the compiler to substitute a 1 or a 0 each time the name TRUE or FALSE is encountered in your source file. For example, the following prints **0 1 2** on the screen:

```
printf("%d %d %d", FALSE, TRUE, TRUE+1);
```

To the compiler, this line looks like this:

```
printf("%d %d %d", 0, 1, 1+1);
```

Once a macro name has been defined, it may be used as part of the definition of other macro names. For example, this code defines the values of ONE, TWO, and THREE:

```
#define ONE    1
#define TWO    ONE+ONE
#define THREE  ONE+TWO
```

Macro substitution is simply the process of replacing an identifier with its associated character sequence. Therefore, if you wished to define a standard error message, you might write something like this:

```
#define E_MS "standard error on input\n"

    .
    .
    .

printf(E_MS);
```

The compiler will actually substitute the string "standard error on input\n" when the identifier **E _ MS** is encountered. To the compiler, the **printf( )** statement will actually appear to be

```
printf("standard error on input\n");
```

No text substitutions will occur if the identifier occurs within a string. For example,

```
#define XYZ this is a test
    .
    .
printf("XYZ");
```

will not print **this is a test**, but rather **XYZ**.

If the character sequence is longer than one line, you may continue it on the next line by placing a backslash at the end of the line, as shown in this example:

```
#define LONG_STRING "this is a very long \
string that is used as an example"
```

Commonly, C programmers use capital letters for defined identifiers. This convention lets anyone reading the program know at a glance that a macro substitution will take place. Also, it is best to put all **#define**s at the start of the file or, perhaps, in a separate include file, rather than sprinkling them throughout the program.

Macro substitution is most frequently used to define names for constants that occur in a program. For example, you may have a program that defines an array and has several routines that access that array. Instead of "hard-coding" the array's size with a constant each time it is needed, it is better to define a size and use that name whenever the size of the array is needed. This method requires a change in only one place, plus a recompilation, to alter the size of the array if it needs to be changed. For example:

```
#define MAX_SIZE 100

float balance[MAX_SIZE];
```

The **#define** directive has another powerful feature: The macro can have arguments. A macro that takes arguments acts much like a function. Each time the macro is encountered, the arguments associated with it are replaced by the actual arguments found in the program. For example:

```
#include "stdio.h"

#define ABS(a)  (a)<0 ? -(a) : (a)

main()
{
  printf("abs of -1 and 1: %d %d", ABS(-1), ABS(1));

  return 0;
}
```

When this program is compiled, **a** in the macro definition will be replaced with the values −1 and 1. The parentheses surrounding **a** ensure proper substitution in all cases. For example, if the parentheses around **a** were removed, the expression

```
ABS(10-20)
```

would be converted to

```
10-20<0 ? -10-20 : 10-20
```

thus yielding the wrong result.

The use of macro substitutions in place of real functions has one major benefit: It increases the speed of the code because no overhead for a function call is incurred. However, this increased speed is paid for with an increase in the size of the program because of duplicated code.

Although parameterized macros are a valuable feature, you will see in Part Two of this book that C++ has a better way of creating in-line code that does not rely upon macros.

#error

The **#error** directive forces the compiler to stop compilation when it is encountered. It is used primarily for debugging. The general form of the directive is

> #error *error-message*

The *error-message* is not enclosed by double quotes. When the **#error** directive is encountered, the error message is displayed, possibly along with other information as defined by the creator of the compiler.

#include

The **#include** directive instructs the compiler to read a source file in addition to the one that contains the **#include** directive. The source file to include must be enclosed by double quotes or angle brackets. For example,

```
#include "stdio.h"
#include <stdio.h>
```

both instruct the C compiler to read and compile the header for the disk file library routines.

It is valid for include files to have **#include** directives in them. This is referred to as *nested includes*. The number of levels of nesting varies among compilers. However, the ANSI standard stipulates that at least eight nested inclusions will be available.

If the file name is enclosed by angle brackets, the file is searched for in a manner defined by the creator of the compiler. Often, this means searching some special directory set aside for include files. If the file name is enclosed by quotes, the file is looked for in another implementation-defined manner. For many implementations, this means searching the current working directory. If the file is not found, the search is repeated as if the file name had been enclosed by angle brackets. Check your compiler's user manual for details on the differences between angle brackets and double quotes.

Conditional Compilation Directives

There are several directives that allow you to compile portions of your program's source code selectively. This process is called *conditional compilation* and is used widely by commercial software houses that provide and maintain many customized versions of one program.

#if, #else, #elif, and #endif

If the constant expression following the **#if** is true, the code that is between it and an **#endif** will be compiled; otherwise, it will be skipped over. The **#endif** directive is used to mark the end of an **#if** block.

The general form of **#if** is

#if *constant-expression*
         statement sequence
#endif

Here is an example:

```
/* simple #if example */
#include "stdio.h"

#define MAX 100

main()
{
#if MAX>99
  printf("compiled for array greater than 99\n");
#endif

  return 0;
}
```

This program displays the message on the screen because, as defined in the program, **MAX** is greater than 99. This example illustrates an important point. The expression that follows the **#if** is *evaluated at compile time.* Therefore, it must contain only identifiers that have been previously defined and constants; no variables may be used.

The **#else** works in much the same way as the **else** that forms part of the C language: It establishes an alternative if the **#if** fails. The previous example can be expanded as shown here:

```
/* simple #if/#else example */
#include "stdio.h"

#define MAX 10
main()
{
#if MAX>99
  printf("compiled for array greater than 99\n");
#else
  printf("compiled for small array\n");
#endif

  return 0;
}
```

In this case, **MAX** is defined to be less than 99, so the **#if** portion of the code is not compiled. The **#else** alternative, however, is compiled. Therefore, the message **compiled for small array** is displayed.

Notice that the **#else** is used to mark both the end of the **#if** block and the beginning of the **#else** block. This is necessary because there can be only one **#endif** associated with any **#if**.

The **#elif** means "else if" and is used to establish an if-else-if chain for multiple compilation options. The **#elif** is followed by a constant expression. If the expression is true, that statement sequence is compiled and no other **#elif** expressions are tested. Otherwise, the next in the series is checked. The general form is

> #if *expression*
>   *statement sequence*
> #elif *expression 1*
>   *statement sequence*
> #elif *expression 2*
>   *statement sequence*
> #elif *expression 3*
>   *statement sequence*
> #elif *expression 4*
>
> .
>
> .
>
> .
>
> #elif *expression N*
>   *statement sequence*
> #endif

For example, this fragment uses the value of **ACTIVE_COUNTRY** to define the currency sign:

```
#define US 0
#define ENGLAND 1
#define FRANCE 2

#define ACTIVE_COUNTRY US

#if ACTIVE_COUNTRY==US
  char currency[]="dollar";
#elif ACTIVE_COUNTRY==ENGLAND
  char currency[]="pound";
#else
  char currency[]="franc";
#endif
```

The **#if**s and **#elif**s may be nested to any level up to some implementation-specific limit with the **#endif**, **#else**, or **#elif** associating with the nearest **#if** or **#elif**. For example, the following is perfectly valid:

```
#if MAX>100
    #if SERIAL_VERSION
        int port=198;
    #elif
        int port=200;
    #endif
#else
    char out_buffer[100];
#endif
```

You can use the **#if** or **#elif** to determine if a macro name is defined by using the **defined** preprocessing operator. It takes this general form:

> #if defined *macro-name*
> *statement sequence*
> #endif

If the *macro-name* is defined, the statement sequence is compiled. Otherwise, it is skipped. For example, this program compiles the conditional code because **DEBUG** is defined by the program:

```
#include "stdio.h"

#define DEBUG

main()
{
  int i=100;
/* ... */
#if defined DEBUG
  printf("value of i is: %d\n", i);
#endif
/*...*/
}
```

You can also precede **defined** with the ! operator to cause conditional compilation when the macro is not defined.

#ifdef and #ifndef

Another method of conditional compilation uses the directives **#ifdef** and **#ifndef**, which mean "if defined" and "if not defined," respectively. The general form of **#ifdef** is

```
#ifdef macro-name
    statement sequence
#endif
```

If the *macro-name* has been previously defined in a **#define** statement, the statement sequence will be compiled.

Note: Using the **#ifdef** is equivalent to using the **#if** with the **defined** operator, as discussed in the previous section.

The general form of **#ifndef** is

```
#ifndef macro-name
    statement sequence
#endif
```

If the *macro-name* is currently undefined by a **#define** statement, the block of code is compiled.

Both the **#ifdef** and **#ifndef** may use an **#else** statement, but not the **#elif**.

For example,

```
#include "stdio.h"

#define TED 10

main()
{
#ifdef TED
  printf("Hi Ted\n");
#else
  printf("Hi anyone\n");
#endif
#ifndef RALPH
  printf("RALPH not defined\n");
#endif

  return 0;
}
```

prints **Hi Ted** and **RALPH not defined**. However, if **TED** were not defined, then **Hi anyone** would be displayed, followed by **RALPH not defined**.

You may nest **#ifdef**s and **#ifndef**s to any level, in the same way as **#if**s.

#undef

The **#undef** directive is used to remove a previously defined definition of the macro name that follows it. The general form is

#undef *macro-name*

Here is an example:

```
#define LEN 100
#define WIDTH 100

char array[LEN][WIDTH];

#undef LEN
#undef WIDTH
/* at this point both LEN and WIDTH are undefined */
```

Both **LEN** and **WIDTH** are defined until the **#undef** statements are encountered.

The **#undef** is principally used to allow macro names to be localized to only those sections of code that need them.

#line

The **#line** directive is used to change the contents of _ _ **LINE** _ _ and _ _ **FILE** _ _, which are predefined identifiers in the compiler. The basic form of the command is

#line *number "filename"*

where *number* is any positive integer and the *filename* is any valid file identifier. The number becomes the number of the current source line, and the file name becomes the name of the source file. The name of the file is optional. The **#line** is primarily used for debugging purposes and special applications.

The _ _**LINE**_ _ identifier is an integer and _ _**FILE**_ _ is a null-terminated string.

For example, the following specifies that the line count will begin with 100 and that the **printf( )** statement will display the number 102 because it is the third line in the program after the **#line 100** statement:

```
#include "stdio.h"

#line 100    /* reset the line counter */
main()       /* line 100 */
{            /* line 101 */
  printf("%d\n",_ _LINE_ _);  /* line 102 */

  return 0;
}
```

#pragma

The **#pragma** directive is an implementation-defined directive that allows various instructions to be given to the compiler. For example, a compiler may have an option to support the tracing of program execution. A trace option would then be specified by a **#pragma** statement. Check the user manual of the compiler for details and options.

The # and ## Preprocessor Operators

ANSI C provides two preprocessor operators: **#** and **##**. These operators are used within a macro **#define**.

The **#** operator causes the argument it precedes to be turned into a quoted string. For example, consider this program:

```
#include "stdio.h"

#define mkstr(s)  # s

main()
{
  printf(mkstr(I like C++));

  return 0;
}
```

The C preprocessor turns the line

```
printf(mkstr(I like C));
```

into

```
printf("I like C");
```

The **##** operator is used to concatenate two tokens, as in this example:

```
#include "stdio.h"

#define concat(a, b)   a ## b

main()
{
  int xy = 10;

  printf("%d", concat(x, y));

  return 0;
}
```

The preprocessor transforms

```
printf("%d", concat(x, y));
```

into

```
printf("%d", xy);
```

If these operators seem strange to you, keep in mind that they are not needed or used in most C programs. They exist primarily to allow the preprocessor to handle some special cases.

Predefined Macro Names

The ANSI C standard specifies five built-in predefined macro names. They are

       _ _LINE_ _
       _ _FILE_ _
       _ _DATE_ _
       _ _TIME_ _
       _ _STDC_ _

If your compiler is nonstandard, some or all of these may be missing. Remember also that your compiler may supply more predefined macros for your use.

The _ _**LINE**_ _ and _ _**FILE**_ _ macros are discussed in the **#line** section of this chapter. The others are examined here.

The _ _**DATE**_ _ macro is a string in the form month/day/year that is the date of the translation of the source file into object code.

The time of the translation of the source code into object code is contained as a string in _ _**TIME**_ _. The form of the string is hour:minute:second.

The macro _ _**STDC**_ _ contains the decimal constant 1. This means that the implementation conforms to the standard. If it is any other number, the implementation must vary from the standard.

Comments

In C, all comments begin with the character pair /* and end with */. There must be no spaces between the characters. Any text that is placed between the beginning and ending comments symbols is ignored by the compiler. For example, this program will print only the word **hello** on the screen:

```
#include "stdio.h"

main()
{
  printf("hello");
  /* printf("there"); */

  return 0;
}
```

Comments may be placed anywhere in a program as long as they do not appear in the middle of any keyword or identifier. That is, the following comment is valid

```
x = 10+ /* add the numbers */5;
```

but

```
swi/*this will not work*/tch(c) { ...
```

is incorrect because a C keyword cannot contain a comment. However, be aware that placing a comment in the middle of an expression often obscures its meaning.

Comments may not be nested. That is, one comment may not contain another comment. For example, this code fragment will cause a compile-time error:

```
/* this is an outer comment
  x = y/a;
  /* this is an inner comment - and causes an error */
*/
```

Include comments whenever they are needed to explain the operation of the code. Minimally, all but the most obvious functions should have a comment at the top that states what the function does, how it is called, and what it returns.

C++-Specific Features

**P
A
R
T

T
W
O**

Part Two of this book examines the C++-specific features of C++. (The C-like features are discussed in Part One.) C++ is essentially a superset of C, so almost everything you already know about C is applicable to C++. Because most of the C++ enhancements to C are to support object-oriented programming (OOP), Part Two also provides a discussion of the theory and merits of object-oriented programming.

Note: This part assumes that you know how to program in C. Knowledge of the C language is a prerequisite to learning C++, so if you don't already know C, you must take some time to learn it.

An Overview of C++

This chapter provides an overview of the key concepts embodied in C++. C++ is an object-oriented programming language, and its object-oriented features are highly interrelated. In Part One, which discusses C++'s C-like features, it was a simple matter to discuss a **for** loop separately from the **printf( )** function, for example. However, the object-oriented features of C++ are, in many places, so intertwined that discussion of one feature implies prior knowledge of one or more other features. To address this problem, this chapter presents a quick overview of the most important C++ features and concepts. The remaining chapters in this part examine C++ in detail.

The Origins of C++

As you know, C++ is an expanded version of C. The C++ extensions to C were first invented by Bjarne Stroustrup in 1980 at Bell Laboratories in Murray Hill, New Jersey. He initially called the new language "C with Classes." However, in 1983 the name was changed to C++.

Although C++'s predecessor, C, is one of the most liked and widely used professional programming languages in the world, the invention of C++ was necessitated by one major programming factor: complexity. In

C, once a program exceeds from 25,000 to 100,000 lines of code, it becomes so complex that it is difficult to grasp as a totality. The purpose of C++ is to allow this barrier to be broken. The essence of C++ is to allow the programmer to comprehend and manage larger, more complex programs.

Most additions made by Stroustrup to C support object-oriented programming, sometimes referred to as OOP. (See the next section for a brief explanation of object-oriented programming.) Stroustrup states that some of C++'s object-oriented features were inspired by another object-oriented language called Simula67. Therefore, C++ represents the blending of two powerful programming methods.

Since the advent of C++, it has gone through two major revisions, one in 1985 and another in 1989. The current version is 2.1, which is the version of C++ discussed here.

When C++ was invented, Stroustrup knew that it was important to maintain the original spirit of C, including its efficiency, its flexibility, and its underlying philosophy that the programmer, not the language, is in charge, while at the same time adding support for object-oriented programming. Happily, his goals were accomplished. C++ still provides the programmer with the freedom and control of C, coupled with the power of objects. The object-oriented features in C++, to use Stroustrup's words, "allow programs to be structured for clarity, extensibility, and ease of maintenance without loss of efficiency."

Although C++ was initially designed to aid in the management of very large programs, it is in no way limited to this use. In fact, the object-oriented attributes of C++ can be effectively applied to virtually any programming task. It is not uncommon to see C++ used for projects such as editors, databases, personal file systems, and communication programs. Also, because C++ shares C's efficiency, much high-performance systems software is constructed using C++.

What Is Object-Oriented Programming?

Object-oriented programming (OOP) is a new way of approaching the job of programming. Approaches to programming have changed dramatically since the invention of the computer, primarily to accommodate the increasing complexity of programs. For example, when computers were first invented, programming was done by toggling in the binary machine instructions using the computer's front panel. As long as programs were just a few hundred instructions long, this approach worked. As programs grew, assembly language was invented so that a programmer could deal with larger, increasingly complex programs, using symbolic representations of the machine instructions. As programs continued to grow, high-level languages were introduced that gave the programmer more tools with which to handle complexity. The first widespread language was, of course, FORTRAN. Although FORTRAN was a very impressive first step, it is hardly a language that encourages clear, easy-to-understand programs.

The 1960s gave birth to structured programming. This is the method encouraged by languages such as C and Pascal. The use of structured languages made it possible to write moderately complex programs fairly easily. However, even using structured programming methods becomes uncontrollable once a project reaches a certain size; its complexity exceeds that which a programmer can manage.

Consider this: At each milestone in the development of programming, methods were created to allow the programmer to deal with increasingly greater complexity. Each step of the way, the new approach took the best elements of the previous methods and moved forward. Today, many projects are near or at the point where the structured approach no longer works. To solve this problem, object-oriented programming was invented.

Object-oriented programming has taken the best ideas of structured programming and combined them with several powerful new concepts that encourage you to approach the task of programming in a new way. In general, when programming in an object-oriented fashion, you decompose a problem into subgroups of related parts that take into account both code and data related to each group. Also, you organize these subgroups into a hierarchical structure. Finally, you translate these subgroups into self-contained units called objects.

All object-oriented programming languages have three things in common: objects, polymorphism, and inheritance.

Objects

The most important feature of an object-oriented language is the object. Put simply, an *object* is a logical entity that contains both data and code that manipulates that data. Within an object, some of the code and/or data may be private to the object and inaccessible to anything outside the object. In this way, an object provides a significant level of protection against some other, unrelated part of the program accidentally modifying or incorrectly using the private parts of the object. This linkage of code and data is often referred to as *encapsulation.*

For all intents and purposes, an object is a variable of a user-defined type. It may seem strange at first to think of an object, which links both code and data, as a variable. However, in object-oriented programming, this is precisely the case. When you define an object, you are implicitly creating a new data type.

Polymorphism

Object-oriented programming languages support *polymorphism,* which is characterized by the phrase "one interface, multiple methods." In very simple terms, this means that one name can be used for several related but slightly different purposes. In essence, polymorphism allows one interface to be used with a general class of actions. The specific action selected is determined by the type of data involved. For example, you might have a program that defines three different types of stacks. One stack is used for integer values, one for floating-point values, and one for **long**s. Because of polymorphism, you can create three sets of functions for both **push( )** and **pop( )** — one set of each type of data — and the compiler will select the correct routine, depending upon what type of data **push( )** or **pop( )** is called with. The general concept (interface) is that of pushing and popping data onto and from a stack. The functions define the specific ways (methods) this is done for each type of data.

The first object-oriented programming languages were interpreters, so polymorphism was, of course, supported at run time. However, C++ is a compiled language. Therefore, in C++, both run-time and compile-time polymorphism are supported.

Inheritance

Inheritance is the process by which one object can acquire the properties of another object. This is important because it supports the concept of classification. If you think about it, most knowledge is made manageable by hierarchical classifications. For example, a Red Delicious apple is part of the classification *apple,* which in turn is part of the *fruit* class, which is under the larger class *food*. Without the use of classifications, each object would have to define explicitly all of its characteristics. However, through the use of classifications, an object need only define those qualities that make it unique within its class. It is the inheritance mechanism that makes it possible for one object to be a specific instance of a more general case.

Programming in C++ Style

Because C++ is a superset of C, you can write C++ programs that look just like C programs. However, doing so prevents you from taking full advantage of C++. (It is something like watching a color TV with the color turned off!) Instead, most C++ programmers use a style and certain features that are unique to C++. Most of the stylistic differences between a C and a C++ program have to do with taking advantage of C++'s object-oriented capabilities. But another advantage to using a programming style unique to C++ is that it helps you begin thinking in C++ rather than in C. (That is, by adopting a different style when writing C++ code, you are telling yourself to stop thinking in C and start thinking in C++.)

Because it is important to learn to write C++ programs that *look* like C++ programs, this section introduces a few of these features. Examine this C++ program:

```
#include "iostream.h"

main()
{
  int i;

  cout << "This is output.\n";  // this is a single line comment
  /* you can still use C style comments */

  // input a number using >>
  cout << "enter a number: ";
  cin >> i;

  // now, output a number using <<
  cout << i << " squared is " << i*i << "\n";

  return 0;
}
```

As you can see, this program looks much different from the average C program. To begin, the header file **iostream.h** is included. This file is defined by C++ and is used to support C++-style I/O operations. (Since C++ is new, some compilers may use slightly different names for the standard header files.)

The first stylistic changes are found in this line:

```
cout << "This is output.\n";   // this is a single line comment
```

This line introduces two new C++ features. First, the statement

```
cout << "This is output.\n";
```

causes **This is output.** to be displayed on the screen followed by a carriage return-linefeed combination. In C++, the << has an expanded role. It is still the left shift operator, but when it is used as shown in this example, it is also an output operator. The word **cout** is an identifier that is linked to the screen. (Actually, like C, C++ supports I/O redirection, but for the sake of discussion, assume that **cout** refers to the screen.) You can use **cout** and the << to output any of the built-in data types, as well as strings of characters.

Note that you can still use **printf( )** or any other of C's I/O functions in a C++ program. (Of course, you must include **stdio.h** if you want to use the C-like I/O functions.) However, many programmers feel that using **cout** << is more in the spirit of C++. Further, while using **printf( )** to output the string is virtually equivalent to using << in this case, the C++ I/O system can be expanded to perform operations automatically on objects that you define (something that you cannot do using **printf( )**).

In general, a C++ program may use any library function supported by ANSI-standard C. However, in cases where C++ provides an alternative approach, such as the << operator, this book will use that alternative instead of a C-like library function (although there is no rule that enforces this).

What follows the output expression is a C++ comment. In C++, comments are defined in two ways. First, you may use a C-like comment, which works the same in C++ as in C. However, in C++ you can also define a *single-line comment* by using **//**. When you start a comment by using **//**, whatever follows is ignored by the compiler until the end of the line is reached. In general, C++ programmers use C-like comments when a multiline comment is being created and use C++ single-line comments when only a single-line comment is needed.

Next, the program prompts the user for a number. The number is read from the keyboard with this statement:

```
cin >> i;
```

In C++, the **>>** operator still retains its right shift meaning. However, when used as shown, it also is C++'s input operator. This statement causes **i** to be given a value read from the keyboard. The identifier **cin** refers to the keyboard. In general, you can use **cin >>** to load a variable of any of the basic data types plus strings.

Note: The line of code just described is not misprinted. Specifically, there is not supposed to be an **&** in front of the **i**. As you know, when inputting information using a function like **scanf( )**, you have to explicitly pass a pointer to the variable that will receive the information. This means preceding the variable name with the "address of" operator, **&**. However, because of the way that the **>>** operator is implemented in C++, you do not need (in fact, must not use) the **&**. In Chapter 13, "Arrays, Pointers, and References," you will learn why this is the case.

Although it is not illustrated by the example, you are free to use any of C's input functions, such as **scanf( )**, instead of using **cin >>**. However, as with **cout**, many programmers feel that **cin >>** is more in the spirit of C++.

Another interesting line in the program is shown here:

```
cout << i << "squared is " << i*i << "\n";
```

As you can probably surmise, this causes the phrase **10 squared is 100** to be displayed (assuming **i** has the value 10), followed by a carriage return-linefeed. As this line illustrates, you can run together several **<<** output operations.

As stated, when used for I/O, the << and >> operators are capable of handling any of C++'s built-in data types. For example, this program inputs a **float**, a **double**, and a string and then outputs them:

```
#include "iostream.h"

main()
{
  float f;
  char str[80];
  double d;

  cout << "Enter two floating point numbers: ";
  cin >> f >> d;

  cout << "Enter a string: ";
  cin >> str;

  cout << f << " " << d << " " << str;

  return 0;
}
```

When you run this program, try entering **This is a test.** when prompted for the string. When the program redisplays the information you entered, only the word "This" will be displayed. The rest of the string is not shown because the >> operator works relative to the strings the same way that the %s specifier works with **scanf( )**. It stops reading input when the first white-space character is encountered. Thus, "is a test" is never read by the program.

This program also illustrates that you can string together several input operations in a single statement.

Another difference between how you may write C and C++ code is where local variables can be declared. In C, you must declare all local variables used within a block at the start of that block. You cannot declare a variable in a block after another statement has occurred. For example, in C, this fragment is incorrect:

```
/* incorrect in C */
f()
{
  int i;

  for(i=0; i<10; i++) {
    int j;  /* won't compile as a C program */
    j = i*2;
      .
      .
      .
  }
}
```

Because the **for** loop intervenes between the declaration of **i** and that of **j**, a C compiler will flag an error and refuse to compile this function. However, in C++, this fragment is perfectly acceptable and will compile without error. The reason is that in C++ you may declare local variables at any point within a block—not just at the beginning.

Here is another version of the preceding program, in which each variable is declared as needed.

```
#include "iostream.h"

main()
{
  float f;
  double d;
  cout << "Enter two floating point numbers: ";
  cin >> f >> d;

  cout << "Enter a string: ";
  char str[80];  // str declared here, just before 1st use
  cin >> str;

  cout << f << " " << d << " " << str;

  return 0;
}
```

Whether you declare all variables at the start of a block or at the point of first use is completely up to you. Since much of the philosophy behind C++ is the encapsulation of code and data, it makes sense that you can declare variables close to where they are used instead of just at the beginning of the block. In the preceding example, the declarations are separated simply for illustration. However, it is easy to imagine more complex examples in which this feature of C++ is more valuable.

Declaring variables close to where they are used can help you avoid accidental side effects. However, the greatest benefit of declaring variables at the point of first use is gained in large functions. Frankly, in short functions (like many of the examples in this book), there is little reason not to simply declare variables at the start of a function. For this reason, this book will declare variables at the point of first use only when it seems warranted by the size or complexity of a function.

There is some debate as to the general wisdom of localizing the declaration of variables. Opponents suggest that sprinkling declarations throughout a block makes it harder, not easier, for someone reading the code to find quickly the declarations of all variables used in that block, making the program harder to maintain. For this reason, some C++

programmers do not make significant use of this feature. This book will not take a stand either way on this issue. However, when applied properly, especially in large functions, declaring variables at the point of their first use can help you create bug-free programs more easily.

Introducing C++ Classes

This section introduces C++'s most important feature: the **class**. In C++, to create an object, you first must define its general form by using the keyword **class**. A **class** is similar syntactically to a structure. The following **class** defines a type called **stack**, which is used to create a stack:

```
#define SIZE 100

// this creates the class stack
class stack {
  int stck[SIZE];
  int tos;
public:
  void init();
  void push(int i);
  int pop(void);
};
```

A **class** may contain private as well as public parts. By default, all items defined in the **class** are private. For example, the variables **stck** and **tos** are private. This means that they cannot be accessed by any function that is not a member of the **class**. This is one way that encapsulation is achieved—access to certain items of data may be tightly controlled by keeping them private. Although it is not shown in this example, you can also define private functions, which then may only be called by other members of the **class**.

To make parts of a **class** public (that is, accessible to other parts of your program), you must declare them after the **public** keyword. All variables or functions defined after **public** can be accessed by all other functions in the program. Essentially, the rest of your program accesses an object through its **public** functions. It should be mentioned at this time that although you can have **public** variables, philosophically you should try to limit or eliminate their use. Instead, you should make all data private and control access to it through **public** functions. One other point: Notice that the **public** keyword is followed by a colon.

The functions **init( )**, **push( )**, and **pop( )** are called *member functions* because they are part of the **class stack**. Remember, an object forms a bond between code and data. Only member functions have access to the private parts of the **class** in which they are declared.

Once you have defined a **class**, you can create an object of that type by using the **class** name. In essence, the **class** name becomes a new data type specifier. For example, this creates an object called **mystack** of type **stack**:

```
stack mystack;
```

You may also create variables when the **class** is defined by putting their names after the closing curly brace, in exactly the same way as you would with a structure.

To review, in C++, a **class** creates a new data type that may be used to create objects of that type. Therefore, an object is an instance of a **class** in just the same way that some other variable is an instance of the **int** data type, for example. Put differently, a **class** is a logical abstraction, an object is real. (That is, an object exists inside the memory of the computer.)

The general form of a **class** declaration is

```
class class-name {
     private data and functions
public:
     public data and functions
} object name list;
```

Of course, the *object name list* may be empty.

Inside the declaration of **stack**, prototypes to the member functions were used. It is important to understand that in C++, when you need to tell the compiler about a function, you must use its full prototype form. (Actually, in C++, all functions must be prototyped. Prototypes are not optional.)

When it comes time to actually code a function that is the member of a **class**, you must tell the compiler which **class** the function belongs to by qualifying the name with the name of the **class** name that it is a member of. For example, here is one way to code the **push( )** function:

```
void stack::push(int i)
{
  if(tos==SIZE) {
    cout << "stack is full";
    return;
  }
  stck[tos] = i;
  tos++;
}
```

The :: is called the *scope resolution operator*. Essentially, it tells the compiler that this version of **push( )** belongs to the **stack class** or, put differently, that this **push( )** is in **stack**'s scope. As you will soon see, in C++, several different **class**es can use the same function name. The compiler knows which function belongs to which **class** because of the scope resolution operator and the **class** name.

To call a member function from a part of your program that is not part of the **class**, you must use the object's name, followed by the dot operator, followed by the name of the function. For example, this calls **init( )** for object **stack1**.

```
stack stack1, stack2;
```

```
stack1.init();
```

At this point, it is very important to understand that **stack1** and **stack2** are two separate objects. This means, for example, that initializing **stack1** does not cause **stack2** to be initialized as well. The only relationship **stack1** has with **stack2** is that they are objects of the same type.

A member function can call another member function directly, without using the dot operator. It is only when a member function is called by code that does not belong to the **class** that the variable name and the dot operator must be used.

The program shown here puts together all the pieces and missing details and illustrates the **stack class**:

```
#include "iostream.h"
```

```
#define SIZE 100
```

```
// this creates the class stack
class stack {
  int stck[SIZE];
  int tos;
public:
  void init();
  void push(int i);
  int pop(void);
};

void stack::init()
{
  tos = 0;
}

void stack::push(int i)
{
  if(tos==SIZE) {
    cout << "stack is full";
    return;
  }
  stck[tos] = i;
  tos++;
}

int stack::pop()
{
  if(tos==0) {
    cout << "stack underflow";
    return 0;
  }
  tos--;
  return stck[tos];
}

main()
{
  stack stack1, stack2;  // create two stack objects

  stack1.init();
  stack2.init();

  stack1.push(1);
  stack2.push(2);

  stack1.push(3);
  stack2.push(4);

  cout << stack1.pop() << " ";
  cout << stack1.pop() << " ";
  cout << stack2.pop() << " ";
  cout << stack2.pop() << "\n";

  return 0;
}
```

Remember: The private parts of an object are accessible only by functions that are members of that object. For example, a statement like

```
stack1.tos = 0; // error
```

could not be in the **main( )** function of the previous program because **tos** is private.

By convention, most C programs have the **main( )** function as the first function in the program. However, in the **stack** program, the member functions of **stack** are defined before the **main( )** function. While there is no rule that dictates this (they could be defined anywhere in the program), it is the most common approach used in writing C++ code. (However, nonmember functions are still typically defined after **main( )**.) This book will follow that convention. Of course, in real applications, the **class**es associated with a program will usually be contained in a header file.

Function Overloading

One way that C++ achieves polymorphism is through the use of function overloading. In C++, two or more functions can share the same name as long as their parameter declarations are different. In this situation, the functions that share the same name are said to be *overloaded,* and the process is referred to as *function overloading.*

To see why function overloading is important, first consider three functions found in the standard library of virtually all C compilers: **abs( )**, **labs( )**, and **fabs( )**. The **abs( )** function returns the absolute value of an integer, **labs( )** returns the absolute value of a **long**, and **fabs( )** returns the absolute value of a **double**. Although these functions perform almost identical actions, in C, three slightly different names must be used to represent these essentially similar tasks. This makes the situation more complex, conceptually, than it actually is. Even though the underlying concept of each function is the same, the programmer has to remember three things, not just one. However, in C++, you can use just one name for all three functions, as this program illustrates:

```
#include "iostream.h"

// abs is overloaded three ways
int abs(int i);
double abs(double d);
long abs(long l);

main()
{
  cout << abs(-10) << "\n";

  cout << abs(-11.0) << "\n";

  cout << abs(-9L) << "\n";

  return 0;
}

int abs(int i)
{
  cout << "using integer abs()\n";

  return i<0 ? -i : i;
}

double abs(double d)
{
  cout << "using double abs()\n";

  return d<0.0 ? -d : d;
}

long abs(long l)
{
  cout << "using long abs()\n";

  return l<0 ? -l : l;
}
```

This program creates three similar but different functions called **abs( )**, each of which returns the absolute value of its argument. The compiler knows which function to call in each situation because of the type of the argument. The value of overloaded functions is that they allow related sets of functions to be accessed with a common name. Thus, the name **abs( )** represents the *general action* that is being performed. It is left to the compiler to choose the right *specific* version for a particular circumstance. The programmer need only remember the general action being performed. Due to polymorphism, three things to remember have been reduced to one. This example is fairly trivial, but if you expand the concept, you can see how polymorphism can help you manage very complex programs.

In general, to overload a function, you simply declare different versions of it. The compiler takes care of the rest. You must observe one important restriction when overloading a function: Two functions may not differ only in their return types. They must differ in the types or number of their arguments. (Return types do not provide sufficient information in all cases for the compiler to decide which function to use.)

Here is another example that uses overloaded functions:

```
#include "iostream.h"
#include "stdio.h"
#include "string.h"

void stradd(char *s1, char *s2);
void stradd(char *s1, int i);

main()
{
  char str[80];

  strcpy(str, "Hello ");
  stradd(str, "there");
  cout << str << "\n";

  stradd(str, 100);
  cout << str << "\n";

  return 0;
}

// concatenate two strings
void stradd(char *s1, char *s2)
{
  strcat(s1, s2);
}

// concatenate a string with a "stringized" integer
void stradd(char *s1, int i)
{
  char temp[80];

  sprintf(temp, "%d", i);
  strcat(s1, temp);
}
```

In this program, the function **stradd( )** is overloaded. One version concatenates two strings (just like **strcat( )** does). The other version "stringizes" an integer and then appends that to a string. Here, overloading is used to create one interface that appends either a string or an integer to another string.

You can use the same name to overload unrelated functions, but you should not. For example, you could use the name **sqr( )** to create functions that return the *square* of an **int** and the *square root* of a **double**. However, these two operations are fundamentally different; applying function overloading in this manner defeats its entire purpose (and, in fact, is considered bad programming style). In practice, you should overload only closely related operations.

Operator Overloading

Polymorphism is also achieved in C++ through operator overloading. As you know, in C++, it is possible to use the ≪ and ≫ operators to perform console I/O operations. They can perform these extra operations because in the **iostream.h** header file, these operators are overloaded. When an operator is overloaded, it takes on an additional meaning relative to a certain **class**. However, it still retains all of its old meanings.

In general, you can overload most of C++'s operators by defining what they mean relative to a specific **class**. For example, think back to the **stack class** developed earlier in this chapter. It is possible to overload the + operator relative to objects of type **stack** so that it appends the contents of one stack to the contents of another. However, the + still retains its original meaning relative to other types of data.

Because operator overloading is, in practice, somewhat more complex than function overloading, examples are deferred until Chapter 14.

Inheritance

As stated earlier in this chapter, inheritance is one of the major traits of an object-oriented programming language. In C++, inheritance is supported by allowing one **class** to incorporate another **class** into its declaration. Inheritance allows a hierarchy of **class**es to be built, moving from most general to most specific. The process involves first defining a *base class*, which defines those qualities common to all objects to be derived from the base. The base **class** represents the most general description. The **class**es derived from the base are usually referred to as *derived classes*. A derived **class** includes all features of the generic base **class** and then adds qualities specific to the derived **class**. To demonstrate how this works, the next example creates **class**es that categorize different types of buildings.

To begin, the **building class** is declared, as shown here. It will serve as the base for two derived **class**es.

```
class building {
  int rooms;
  int floors;
  int area;
public:
  void set_rooms(int num);
  int get_rooms();
  void set_floors(int num);
  int get_floors();
  void set_area(int num);
  int get_area();
};
```

Because (for the sake of this example) all buildings have three common features—one or more rooms, one or more floors, and a total area—the **building class** embodies these components into its declaration. The member functions beginning with **set** set the values of the private data. The functions starting with **get** return those values.

You can now use this broad definition of a building to create derived **class**es that describe specific types of buildings. For example, here is a derived **class** called **house**:

```
// house is derived from building
class house : public building {
  int bedrooms;
  int baths;
public:
  void set_bedrooms(int num);
  int get_bedrooms();
  void set_baths(int num);
  int get_baths();
};
```

Notice how **building** is inherited. The general form for inheritance is

```
class new-class-name : access inherited-class {
  // body of new class
}
```

Here, *access* is optional. However, if present, it must be **public, private,** or **protected.** (These options are further examined in Chapter 12, "Classes and Objects.") For now, all inherited **class**es will use **public.** Using **public** means that all the **public** elements of the base **class** will also be **public** in the derived **class** that inherits it. Therefore, in the example, members of the **class house** have access to the member functions of **building** just as if they had been declared inside **house.** However, **house**'s member functions do *not* have access to the private parts of **building.** This is an important point. Even though **house** inherits **building,** it has access only to the **public** parts of **building.** In this way, inheritance does not circumvent the principles of encapsulation necessary to OOP.

Remember: The derived **class** has direct access to both its member functions and the **public** member functions of the base **class.**

Here is a program illustrating inheritance. It creates two derived **class**es of **building** using inheritance; one is **house,** the other, **school.**

```cpp
#include "iostream.h"

class building {
  int rooms;
  int floors;
  int area;
public:
  void set_rooms(int num);
  int get_rooms();
  void set_floors(int num);
  int get_floors();
  void set_area(int num);
  int get_area();
};

// house is derived from building
class house : public building {
  int bedrooms;
  int baths;
public:
  void set_bedrooms(int num);
  int get_bedrooms();
  void set_baths(int num);
  int get_baths();
};
```

```
// school is also derived from building
class school : public building {
  int classrooms;
  int offices;
public:
  void set_classrooms(int num);
  int get_classrooms();
  void set_offices(int num);
  int get_offices();
};

void building::set_rooms(int num)
{
  rooms = num;
}

void building::set_floors(int num)
{
  floors = num;
}

void building::set_area(int num)
{
  area = num;
}

int building::get_rooms()
{
  return rooms;
}

int building::get_floors()
{
  return floors;
}

int building::get_area()
{
  return area;
}

void house::set_bedrooms(int num)
{
  bedrooms = num;
}

void house::set_baths(int num)
{
  baths = num;
}

int house::get_bedrooms()
{
  return bedrooms;
}

int house::get_baths()
```

```
{
  return baths;
}

void school::set_classrooms(int num)
{
  classrooms = num;
}

void school::set_offices(int num)
{
  offices = num;
}

int school::get_classrooms()
{
  return classrooms;
}

int school::get_offices()
{
  return offices;
}

main()
{
  house h;
  school s;

  h.set_rooms(12);
  h.set_floors(3);
  h.set_area(4500);
  h.set_bedrooms(5);
  h.set_baths(3);

  cout << "house has " << h.get_bedrooms();
  cout << " bedrooms\n";

  s.set_rooms(200);
  s.set_classrooms(180);
  s.set_offices(5);
  s.set_area(25000);

  cout << "school has " << s.get_classrooms();
  cout << " classrooms\n";
  cout << "Its area is " << s.get_area();

  return 0;
}
```

As this program shows, the major advantage of inheritance is that you can create a general classification that can be incorporated into more specific ones. In this way, each object can precisely represent its own classification.

When writing about C++, the terms *base* and *derived* are generally used to describe inheritance. However, you may also see the terms *parent* and *child* used.

Aside from providing the advantages of hierarchical classification, inheritance also provides support for run-time polymorphism through the mechanism of **virtual** functions. (Refer to Chapter 16, "Virtual Functions and Polymorphism," for details.)

Constructors and Destructors

It is very common for some part of an object to require initialization before it can be used. For example, think back to the **stack class** developed earlier in this chapter. Before the stack could be used, **tos** had to be set to zero. This was performed by using the function **init( )**. Because the requirement for initialization is so common, C++ allows objects to initialize themselves when they are created. This automatic initialization is performed through the use of a constructor function.

A *constructor function* is a special function that is a member of the **class** and has the same name as that **class**. For example, here is how the **stack class** looks when converted to use a constructor function for initialization:

```
// this creates the class stack
class stack {
  int stck[SIZE];
  int tos;
public:
  stack();  // constructor
  void push(int i);
  int pop();
};
```

Notice that the constructor **stack( )** has no return type specified. In C++, constructor functions cannot return values.

The **stack( )** function is coded like this:

```
// stack's constructor function
stack::stack()
{
  tos = 0;
  cout << "stack initialized\n";
}
```

Keep in mind that the message **stack initialized** is output as a way to illustrate the constructor. In actual practice, most constructor functions will not output or input anything. They will simply perform various initializations.

An object's constructor is called when the object is created. This means that it is called when the object's declaration is executed. There is an important distinction between a C-like declaration statement and a C++ declaration. In C, variable declarations are, loosely speaking, passive and resolved mostly at compile time. Put differently, in C, variable declarations are not thought of as being executable statments. However, in C++, variable declarations can be active statements that are, in fact, executed at run time. One reason for this is that an object declaration may need to call a constructor, thus making it an executable statement. Although this difference may seem subtle and largely academic at this point, it has some important implications relative to variable initialization, as you will see later.

An object's constructor is called once for global or **static** local objects. For local objects, the constructor is called each time the object declaration is encountered.

The complement of the constructor is the *destructor*. In many circumstances, an object will need to perform some action or actions when it is destroyed. Local objects are created when their block is entered, and destroyed when the block is left. Global objects are destroyed when the program terminates. There are many reasons why a destructor function may be needed. For example, an object may need to deallocate memory that it had previously allocated. In C++, it is the destructor function that handles deactivation. The destructor has the same name as the constructor, but it is preceded by a ~. For example, here are the **stack class** and its constructor and destructor functions. (Keep in mind that the **stack class** does not require a destructor; the one shown here is just for illustration.)

```
// this creates the class stack
class stack {
  int stck[SIZE];
  int tos;
public:
  stack();  // constructor
  ~stack(); // destructor
  void push(int i);
  int pop();
};
```

```
// stack's constructor function
stack::stack()
{
  tos = 0;
  cout << "stack initialized\n";
}

// stack's destructor function
stack::~stack()
{
  cout << "stack destroyed\n";
}
```

Notice that, like constructor functions, destructor functions do not have return values.

To see how constructors and destructors work, here is a new version of the **stack** program examined earlier in this chapter. Notice that **init( )** is no longer needed.

```
#include "iostream.h"

#define SIZE 100

// this creates the class stack
class stack {
  int stck[SIZE];
  int tos;
public:
  stack();  // constructor
  ~stack(); // destructor
  void push(int i);
  int pop();
};

// stack's constructor function
stack::stack()
{
  tos = 0;
  cout << "stack initialized\n";
}

// stack's destructor function
stack::~stack()
{
  cout << "stack destroyed\n";
}

void stack::push(int i)
{
  if(tos==SIZE) {
    cout << "stack is full";
    return;
  }
  stck[tos] = i;
```

```
    tos++;
}

int stack::pop()
{
  if(tos==0) {
    cout << "stack underflow";
    return 0;
  }
  tos--;
  return stck[tos];
}

main()
{
  stack a, b;  // create two stack objects

  a.push(1);
  b.push(2);

  a.push(3);
  b.push(4);

  cout << a.pop() << " ";
  cout << a.pop() << " ";
  cout << b.pop() << " ";
  cout << b.pop() << "\n";

  return 0;
}
```

This program displays the following:

```
stack initialized
stack initialized
3 1 4 2
stack destroyed
stack destroyed
```

The C++ Keywords

In addition to those keywords defined by the C language and those specific to C itself, the C++ extensions to C add the keywords shown in Table 11-1. You cannot use any of them as names for variables or functions. Of these, **catch, try, throw,** and **template** are experimental and reserved for future use. Further, **overload** is obsolete; its use is anachronistic.

asm	private
catch	protected
class	public
delete	template
friend	this
inline	throw
new	try
operator	virtual
overload	

Table 11-1. The C++ keywords

The General Form of a C++ Program

Although individual styles will differ, most C++ programs will have this general form:

```
#includes
base-class declarations
derived class declarations
nonmember function prototypes
main( )
{
      .
      .
      .

}
nonmember function definitions
```

However, keep in mind that, in most large projects, all **class** declarations will be put into a header file and included with each module.

The remaining chapters in this section examine in greater detail the features of C++ discussed in this chapter, as well as other features.

TWELVE

Classes and Objects

The **class** and objects of a **class** form the basis for C++'s implementation of object-oriented programming. This chapter examines in detail these two fundamental features of C++.

Classes

A **class** declaration defines a new type that links code and data. This new type is then used to declare objects of that **class**. A **class** declaration is similar syntactically to a structure. In Chapter 11, "An Overview of C++," a simplified general form of a **class** declaration was shown. Here is the entire general form of a **class** declaration that does not inherit any other **class**.

    class *class-name* {

    private data and functions
  access-specifier:
    data and functions
  access-specifier:
    data and functions
    .
    .
    .
  access-specifier:
    data and functions
  } *object-list;*

The *object-list* is optional. If present, it declares objects of the **class**. Here, *access-specifier* is one of these three C++ keywords:

public
private
protected

By default, functions and data declared within a **class** are private to that **class** and may be accessed only by other members of the **class**. However, by using the **public** access specifier, you allow functions or data to be accessible to other parts of your program. Once an access specifier has been used, it remains in effect until either another access specifier is encountered or the end of the **class** declaration is reached. To switch back to private declarations, you can use the **private** access specifier. The **protected** access specifier is needed only when inheritance is involved (see Chapter 15, "Inheritance").

In **class** declarations, you may change access specification as often as you like within a **class** declaration. That is, you may switch to **public** for some declarations and then switch back to **private** again. The **class** declaration in the following example illustrates this feature:

```
#include "iostream.h"
#include "string.h"

class employee {
  char name[80];
public:
  void putname(char *n);
  void getname(char *n);
```

```
private:
  double wage;
public:
  void putwage(double w);
  double getwage();
} ;

void employee::putname(char *n)
{
  strcpy(name, n);
}

void employee::getname(char *n)
{
  strcpy(n, name);
}

void employee::putwage(double w)
{
  wage = w;
}

double employee::getwage()
{
  return wage;
}

main()
{
  employee ted;
  char name[80];

  ted.putname("Ted Jones");
  ted.putwage(75000);

  ted.getname(name);
  cout << name << " makes $";
  cout << ted.getwage() << " per year.";

  return 0;
}
```

Here, **employee** is a simple **class** that could be used to store an employee's name and wage. Notice that the **public** access specifier is used twice.

Actually, most C++ programmers will code the **employee class** as shown here, with all **private** elements grouped together and all **public** elements grouped together:

```
class employee {
  char name[80];
  double wage;
```

```
public:
  void putname(char *n);
  void getname(char *n);
  void putwage(double w);
  double getwage();
} ;
```

Although you may use the access specifiers as often as you like within a **class** declaration, the only advantage of doing so is that by visually grouping various parts of a **class**, you may make it easier for someone else reading the program to understand it. However, to the compiler, using multiple access specifiers makes no difference. For this reason, this book will not use them in **class** declarations.

Functions that are declared within a **class** are called *member functions*. Member functions may access any element of the **class** they are part of. This includes all **private** elements. Variables that are elements of a **class** are called *member variables* or *data members*. Collectively, any element of a **class** can be referred to as a member of that **class**.

There are a few restrictions on what may be a member of a **class**. No member variable can have an initializer. No member can be an object of the **class** that is being defined. No member can be declared as **extern** or **register**.

In general, you should make all data members of a **class private** to that **class**. This is part of the way that encapsulation is achieved. However, there may be situations in which you will need to make one or more variables **public**. (For example, a heavily used variable may need to be accessible globally in order to achieve faster run times.) When a variable is **public** it may be accessed directly by any other part of your program. The syntax for accessing a **public** member is the same as for effecting a function call: Specify the object's name, the dot operator, and the variable name. This simple program illustrates direct access of a **public** variable:

```
#include "iostream.h"

class myclass {
public:
  int i, j, k; // accessible to entire program
};

main()
{
  myclass a, b;
```

```
   a.i = 100;   // direct access of i, j, and k
   a.j = 4;
   a.k = a.i * a.j;

   b.k = 12;   // remember, a.k and b.k are different
   cout << a.k << " " << b.k;

   return 0;
}
```

Structures and Classes

C++ has elevated the role of the standard C structure to that of an alternative way to specify a **class**. In fact, the only difference between a **class** and a **struct** is that by default all members are **public** in a structure and **private** in a **class**. In all other respects, structures and **classes** are equivalent. For example, consider this short program, which uses a structure to declare a **class** that controls access to a string:

```
#include "iostream.h"
#include "string.h"

struct mystr {
  void buildstr(char *s); // public
  void showstr();
private: // now go private
  char str[255];
} ;

void mystr::buildstr(char *s)
{
  if(!*s) *str = '\0'; // initialize string
  else strcat(str, s);
}

void mystr::showstr()
{
  cout << str << "\n";
}

main()
{
  mystr s;

  s.buildstr(""); // init
  s.buildstr("Hello ");
```

```
    s.buildstr("there!");

    s.showstr();

    return 0;
}
```

This program displays the string **Hello there!**. The class **mystr** could be rewritten by using **class** as shown here:

```
class mystr {
  char str[255];
public:
  void buildstr(char *s); // public
  void showstr();
} ;
```

You might wonder why C++ contains the two virtually equivalent keywords **struct** and **class**. This seeming redundancy is justified for several reasons. First, there is no fundamental reason not to increase the capabilities of a structure. In C, structures already provide a means of grouping data. Therefore, it is a small step to allow them to include member functions. Second, because structures and **class**es are related, it may be easier to transport existing C programs to C++. Finally, although the two are virtually equivalent today, providing two different keywords allows the definition of a **class** to be free to evolve. However, in order for C++ to remain compatible with C, a structure declaration may not be able to evolve in the same way.

Although you can use a **struct** where you use a **class**, generally you shouldn't. For the sake of clarity, you should use a **class** when you want a **class** and a **struct** when you want a C-like structure. This is the style that this book will follow. The advantage to this method is that anyone reading your program will know that structures don't have member functions.

Unions and Classes

Like a structure, a **union** may also be used to define a **class**. In C++, **union**s may contain both member functions and variables. They may also include constructor and destructor functions. A **union** in C++ retains all of its C-like features, the most important being that all data elements share the same location in memory. Like the structure, **union** members are **public** by default. In the next example, a **union** is used to swap the bytes that make up an **unsigned** integer. (This example assumes that integers are 2 bytes long.)

```
#include "iostream.h"

union swap_byte {
  void swap();
  void set_byte(unsigned i);
  void show_word();

  unsigned u;
  unsigned char c[2];
};

void swap_byte::swap()
{
  unsigned char t;

  t = c[0];
  c[0] = c[1];
  c[1] = t;
}

void swap_byte::show_word()
{
  cout << u;
}

void swap_byte::set_byte(unsigned i)
{
  u = i;
}

main()
{
  swap_byte b;

  b.set_byte(49034);
  b.swap();
  b.show_word();

  return 0;
}
```

It is important to understand that like a structure, a **union** declaration in C++ defines a special type of **class**. This means that the principles of encapsulation are preserved.

There are several restrictions that must be observed when you use C++ **unions**. First, a **union** cannot inherit any other **classes** of any type. Further, a **union** cannot be a base **class**. A **union** cannot have virtual member functions. (Virtual functions are discussed in Chapter 16, "Virtual Functions and Polymorphism.") No **static** variables can be members of a **union**. A **union** cannot have as a member any object that overloads the = operator. Finally, no object can be a member of a **union** if the object has a constructor or destructor function.

Unlike structures, there can be compelling reasons to define a **class** by using **union** rather than **class**. If the object that you want to create needs its data elements to share the same memory location, you will need to create that **class** by using a **union**.

There is a special type of **union** in C++ called an anonymous **union**. An *anonymous union* does not contain a type name, and no variables may be declared of this sort of **union**. Instead, an anonymous **union** tells the compiler that member variables of the **union** are to share the same location. However, the variables themselves are referenced directly, without the normal dot operator syntax. For example, consider this program:

```
#include "iostream.h"
#include "string.h"

main()
{
  // define anonymous union
  union {
    long l;
    double d;
    char s[4];
  } ;

  // now, reference union elements directly
  l = 100000;
  cout << l << " ";
  d = 123.2342;
  cout << d << " ";
  strcpy(s, "hi");
  cout << s;

  return 0;
}
```

As you can see, the elements of the **union** are referenced as if they had been declared as normal local variables. In fact, relative to programs, that is exactly how you will use them. Further, even though they are defined within a **union** declaration, they are at the same scope level as any other local variable within the same block. Indeed, the members of an anonymous **union** may not have the same name as any other identifier known to the current scope. This implies that the names of the members of an anonymous **union** must not conflict with other identifiers known within the scope of the **union**.

All restrictions involving **unions** apply to anonymous ones, with several additions. First, the only elements contained within an anonymous **union** must be data. No member functions are allowed. Anonymous **unions** cannot contain **private** or **protected** elements. Finally, global anonymous **unions** must be specified as **static**.

Friend Functions

It is possible to grant a nonmember function access to the private elements of a **class** by using a **friend**. A **friend** function has access to all **private** and **protected** members of the **class** for which it is a **friend**. To declare a **friend** function within a **class**, simply put the keyword **friend** in front of the function declaration. Consider this program:

```
#include "iostream.h"

class myclass {
  int a, b;
public:
  friend int sum(myclass x);
  void set_ab(int i, int j);
};

void myclass::set_ab(int i, int j)
{
  a = i;
  b = j;
}

// Note: sum() is not a member function of any class.
int sum(myclass x)
{
  /* Because sum() is a friend of myclass, it can
     directly access a and b. */

  return x.a + x.b;
```

```
}

main()
{
  myclass n;

  n.set_ab(3, 4);

  cout << sum(n);

  return 0;
}
```

In this example, the **sum( )** function is not a member of **myclass**. However, it still has full access to its **private** members. Also, notice that **sum( )** is called normally. Because it is not a member function, it does not have to be (indeed, may not be) qualified with an object's name.

Although there is nothing gained by making **sum( )** a **friend** rather than a member function of **myclass**, there are some circumstances in which **friend** functions are quite valuable. First, **friend**s can be useful when you are overloading certain types of operators (see Chapter 14, "Function and Operator Overloading"). Second, **friend** functions make the creation of some types of I/O functions easier (see Chapter 18, "C++ File I/O"). The third reason that **friend** functions may be desirable is that in some cases, two or more **class**es may contain members that are interrelated relative to other parts of your program.

For example, imagine two different classes, each of which displays a pop-up message on the screen when error conditions occur. Other parts of your program may wish to know if a pop-up message is currently being displayed before writing to the screen so that no message is accidentally overwritten. Although you can create member functions in each **class** that return a value indicating whether a message is active, this means additional overhead when the condition is checked (that is, two function calls, not just one). If the condition needs to be checked frequently, this additional overhead may not be acceptable. However, using a **friend** function makes it possible to check the status of each object directly by calling only one function that has access to each **class**. Thus, in situations like this, a **friend** function allows you to generate more efficient code. The following program illustrates this concept:

```
#include "iostream.h"

#define IDLE 0
#define INUSE 1

class C2;  // forward reference
```

```
class C1 {
  int status;  // IDLE if off, INUSE if on screen
  // ...
public:
  void set_status(int state);
  friend int idle(C1 a, C2 b);
};

class C2 {
  int status; // IDLE if off, INUSE if on screen
  // ...
public:
  void set_status(int state);
  friend int idle(C1 a, C2 b);
};

void C1::set_status(int state)
{
  status = state;
}

void C2::set_status(int state)
{
  status = state;
}

int idle(C1 a, C2 b)
{
  if(a.status || b.status) return 0;
  else return 1;
}

main()
{
  C1 x;
  C2 y;

  x.set_status(IDLE);
  y.set_status(IDLE);

  if(idle(x, y)) cout << "screen can be used\n";
  else cout << "in use\n";

  x.set_status(INUSE);

  if(idle(x, y)) cout << "screen can be used\n";
  else cout << "in use\n";

  return 0;
}
```

Notice that this program uses a forward reference for the **class C2**. This is necessary because the declaration of **idle( )** inside **C1** references **C2** before it is declared. To create a forward reference to a class, simply use the form shown in this program.

A **friend** of one **class** may be a member of another. For example, here is the preceding program rewritten so that **idle( )** is a member of **C1**:

```
#include "iostream.h"

#define IDLE 0
#define INUSE 1

class C2;  // forward reference

class C1 {
  int status;  // IDLE if off, INUSE if on screen
  // ...
public:
  void set_status(int state);
  int idle(C2 b);  // now a member of C1
};

class C2 {
  int status;  // IDLE if off, INUSE if on screen
  // ...
public:
  void set_status(int state);
  friend int C1::idle(C1 a, C2 b);
};

void C1::set_status(int state)
{
  status = state;
}

void C2::set_status(int state)
{
  status = state;
}

// idle() is member of C1, but friend of C2
int C1::idle(C2 b)
{
  if(status ¦¦ b.status) return 0;
  else return 1;
}

main()
{
  C1 x;
  C2 y;

  x.set_status(IDLE);
  y.set_status(IDLE);

  if(x.idle(y)) cout << "screen can be used\n";
  else cout << "in use\n";
```

```
    x.set_status(INUSE);

    if(x.idle(y)) cout << "screen can be used\n";
    else cout << "in use\n";

    return 0;
}
```

Because **idle( )** is a member of **C1**, it can access the **status** variable of objects of type **C1** directly. Thus, only objects of type **C2** need be passed to **idle( )**.

One final note: A derived class does not inherit **friend** functions.

Inline Functions

In C++, you can create short functions that are not actually called; rather, their code is expanded in line at the point of each invocation. This process is similar to using a C-like parameterized macro. To cause a function to be expanded in line rather than called, precede its definition with the **inline** keyword. For example, in this program, the function **max( )** is expanded in line instead of called:

```
#include "iostream.h"

inline int max(int a, int b)
{
  return a>b ? a : b;
}

main()
{
  cout << max(10, 20);
  cout << " " << max(99, 88);

  return 0;
}
```

As far as the compiler is concerned, the preceding program is equivalent to this one:

```
#include "iostream.h"

main()
{

  cout << 10>20 ? 10 : 20;
  cout << " " << 99>88 ? 99 : 88;

  return 0;
}
```

The reason that **inline** functions are an important addition to C++ is that they allow you to create very efficient code. As you probably know, each time a function is called, a significant amount of overhead is generated by the calling and return mechanism. Typically, arguments are pushed onto the stack and various registers are saved when a function is called and then restored when the function returns. The trouble is that these instructions take time. However, when a function is expanded in line, none of those operations occur. Although expanding function calls in line can produce faster run times, it also often results in larger code size because of the duplicated code. For this reason, it is best to **inline** only very small functions. Further, it is also a good idea to only **inline** those functions that will have significant impact on the performance of your program.

Like the **register** specifier, **inline** is actually simply a *request*, not a command, to the compiler. The compiler can choose to ignore it.

A number of restrictions apply to using **inline**. First, an **inline** function cannot contain any **static** data. An **inline** function cannot use any loop statement, a **switch**, or a **goto**. **Inline** functions cannot be recursive. Array declarations are not allowed in **inline** functions. Finally, if a function's return type is **void**, no **return** statement is allowed.

Inline functions may be **class** member functions. For example, this is a perfectly valid C++ program:

```
#include "iostream.h"

class myclass {
  int a, b;
public:
  void init(int i, int j);
  void show();
};

inline void myclass::init(int i, int j)
{
```

```
   a=i;
   b=j;
}

inline void myclass::show()
{
  cout << a << " " << b << "\n";
}

main()
{
  myclass x;

  x.init(10, 20);
  x.show();

  return 0;
}
```

Defining Inline Functions Within a Class

It is possible to define short functions within a **class** declaration. When a function is defined inside a **class** declaration, it is automatically made into an **inline** function (if possible). It is not necessary (but not an error) to precede its declaration with the **inline** keyword. For example, the preceding program is rewritten here with the definitions of **init( )** and **show( )** contained within the declaration of **myclass**:

```
#include "iostream.h"

class myclass {
  int a, b;
public:
  // automatic inline
  void init(int i, int j) {a=i; b=j;}
  void show() {cout << a << " " << b << "\n";}
};

main()
{
  myclass x;

  x.init(10, 20);
  x.show();

  return 0;
}
```

Notice the format of the function code within **myclass**. Because **inline** functions are short, this style of coding within a **class** is fairly typical. However, you are free to use any format you like. For example, this is a perfectly valid way to rewrite the **class** declaration:

```
#include "iostream.h"

class myclass {
  int a, b;
public:
  // automatic inline
  void init(int i, int j)
  {
    a=i;
    b=j;
  }

  void show()
  {
    cout << a << " " << b << "\n";
  }
};
```

Technically, the inlining of the **show( )** function is pointless because (in general) the amount of time the I/O statement will take far exceeds the overhead of a function call. However, it is extremely common to see all short member functions defined inside their **class** in C++ programs. This type of automatic inlining probably does no harm.

Keep in mind that constructor and destructor functions may also be inlined—either by default, if defined within their **class**, or explicitly.

Parameterized Constructors

It is possible to pass arguments to constructor functions. Typically, these arguments are used to help initialize an object when it is created. To create a parameterized constructor, simply add parameters to it the way you would to any other function. When you define the constructor's body, use the parameters to initialize the object. For example, here is a simple **class** that includes a parameterized constructor:

```
#include "iostream.h"

class myclass {
  int a, b;
public:
  myclass(int i, int j) {a=i; b=j;}
  void show() {cout << a << " " << b;}
};

main()
{
  myclass ob(3, 5);

  ob.show();

  return 0;
}
```

Notice that in the definition of **myclass( )**, the parameters **i** and **j** are used to give initial values to **a** and **b**.

The program illustrates the most common way to specify arguments when you declare an object that uses a parameterized constructor function. Specifically, this statement

```
myclass ob(3, 4);
```

causes an object called **ob** to be created and passes the arguments **3** and **4** to the **i** and **j** parameters of **myclass( )**. You may also pass arguments using this type declaration statement:

```
myclass ob = myclass(3, 4);
```

However, the first method is the one generally used.

Here is another example that uses a parameterized constructor function. It creates a **class** that keeps information about library books.

```
#include "iostream.h"
#include "string.h"

#define IN 1
#define CHECKED_OUT 0

class book {
  char author[40];
  char title[40];
  int status;
public:
```

```
  book(char *n, char *t, int s);
  int get_status() {return status;}
  void set_status(int s) {status = s;}
  void show();
};

book::book(char *n, char *t, int s)
{
  strcpy(author, n);
  strcpy(title, t);
  status = s;
}

void book::show()
{
  cout << title << " by " << author;
  cout << " is ";
  if(status==IN) cout << "in.\n";
  else cout << "out.\n";
}

main()
{
  book b1("Twain", "Tom Sawyer", IN);
  book b2("Melville", "Moby Dick", CHECKED_OUT);

  b1.show();
  b2.show();

  return 0;
}
```

Parameterized constructor functions are very useful because they
allow you to avoid having to make an additional function call simply to
initialize one or more variables in an object. Each function call you can
avoid makes your program more efficient. Also, notice that the short
get_status() and **set_status()** are defined within the **book** class. This
is a very common practice when writing C++ programs.

Static Class Members

Both function and data members of a class can be made **static**. This
section explains what this means relative to each type of member.

Static Data Members

When you precede a member variable's declaration with **static**, you are
telling the compiler that only one copy of that variable will exist and

that all objects of the **class** will share that variable. Unlike regular data members, individual copies of a **static** member variable are not made for each object. No matter how many objects of a **class** are created, only one copy of a **static** data member exists. Thus, all objects of that **class** use that same variable.

All **static** variables are initialized to zero when the first object is created. No other initializations are allowed.

To understand the effect of **static** data, consider this program:

```
#include "iostream.h"

class shared {
  static int a;
  int b;
public:
  void set(int i, int j) {a=i; b=j;}
  void show();
} ;

void shared::show()
{
  cout << "This is static a: " << a;
  cout << "\nThis is non-static b: " << b;
  cout << "\n";
}

main()
{
  shared x, y;

  x.set(1, 1); // set a to 1
  x.show();

  y.set(2, 2); // change a to 2
  y.show();

  x.show(); /* Here, a has been changed for both x and y
               because a is shared by both objects. */

  return 0;
}
```

This program displays the following output when run.

```
This is static a: 1
This is non-static b: 1
This is static a: 2
This is non-static b: 2
This is static a: 2
This is non-static b: 1
```

A **static** member variable exists *before* any object of its class is created. For example, in the following short program, **a** is both **public** and **static**. Thus it may be directly accessed in **main( )**. Further, since **a** exists before an object of **shared** is created, **a** can be given a value at any time. As this program illustrates, the value of **a** is unchanged by the creation of object **x**. For this reason, both output statements display the same value: 99.

```
#include "iostream.h"

class shared {
public:
  static int a;
} ;

main()
{
  // init a before creating any objects
  shared::a = 99;
  cout << "this is initial value of a: " << shared::a;
  cout << "\n";

  shared x;

  cout << "this is x.a: " << x.a;

  return 0;
}
```

Notice how **a** is referenced through the use of the class name and the scope resolution operator. In general, when your program references a **static** member independently of an object, you must qualify it by using the name of the **class** of which it is a member.

One of the most common uses of **static** member variables is to provide access control to some shared resource. For example, you might create several objects, each of which needs to write to a specific disk file. Clearly, however, only one object can be allowed to write to the file at a time. In this case, you will want to declare a **static** variable that indicates when the file is in use and when it is free. Each object then interrogates this variable before writing to the file. The following program shows how you might use a **static** variable of this type to control access to a scarce resource:

```
#include "iostream.h"

class cl {
```

```
    static int resource;
public:
  int get_resource();
  void free_resource() {resource = 0;}
};

int cl::get_resource()
{
  if(resource) return 0; // resource already in use
  else {
    resource = 1;
    return 1;  // resource allocated to this object
  }
}

main()
{
  cl ob1, ob2;

  if(ob1.get_resource()) cout << "ob1 has resource\n";

  if(!ob2.get_resource()) cout << "ob2 denied resource\n";

  ob1.free_resource();  // let someone else use it

  if(ob2.get_resource())
    cout << "ob2 can now use resource\n";

  return 0;
}
```

By using **static** member variables, you should be able to virtually eliminate any need for global variables. The trouble with global variables relative to OOP is that they almost always violate the principle of encapsulation.

Static Member Functions

Member functions may also be declared as **static**. There are several restrictions placed on **static** member functions. First, they may only access other **static** members of the class. (Of course, global functions and data may be accessed by **static** member functions.) Second, **static** member functions do not have a **this** pointer. (See Chapter 13, "Arrays, Pointers, and References," for information on **this**.) In fact, it is the absence of a **this** pointer that prevents a **static** member function from accessing other non-**static** elements of a **class**. To understand why, assume that there are two objects of some class that contains the **static** function called **f( )**. If **f( )** attempts to access a non-**static** member variable called **x**, which object will be the recipient of that access and which **x** will be referenced? The point is that each object will have its own copy of **x**, and **f( )** has no way of knowing which one to use. Therefore, **static** functions may not access non-**static** members of the class of which they are members.

Following is a slightly reworked version of the program that concluded the previous section. Notice that **get_resource( )** is now declared as **static**. As the program illustrates, **get_resource( )** may be accessed either by itself, independent of any object using the **class** name and the scope resolution operator, or in connection with an object.

```
#include "iostream.h"

class cl {
  static int resource;
public:
  static int get_resource();
  void free_resource() {resource = 0;}
};

int cl::get_resource()
{
  if(resource) return 0; // resource already in use
  else {
    resource = 1;
    return 1;  // resource allocated to this object
  }
}

main()
{
  cl ob1, ob2;

  /* get_resource() is static so may be called independent
     of any object. */
  if(cl::get_resource()) cout << "ob1 has resource\n";

  if(!cl::get_resource()) cout << "ob2 denied resource\n";

  ob1.free_resource();

  if(ob2.get_resource()) // can still call using object syntax
    cout << "ob2 can now use resource\n";

  return 0;
}
```

Actually, **static** member functions have limited applications, but one good use for them is that they can "preinitialize" **private static** data before any object is actually created. For example, this is a perfectly valid C++ program:

```
#include "iostream.h"

class static_type {
  static int i;
public:
  static void init(int x) {i = x;}
  void show() {cout << i;}
};

main()
{
  // init static data before object creation
  static_type::init(100);

  static_type x;
  x.show(); // displays 100

  return 0;
}
```

When Constructors and Destructors Are Executed

When an object's constructor function is executed depends upon whether it is a local object or a global object. A local object's constructor function is executed when the object declaration statement is encountered. Further, a local object's constructors are called in the order in which they are encountered, from left to right, top to bottom. The destructor functions for local objects are executed in reverse order from the constructor functions.

Global objects have their constructor functions execute *before* **main( )** begins execution. Global constructors are executed in order of left to right, top to bottom, within the same file. You cannot know the order of execution of global constructors spread among several files. Global destructors execute in reverse order *after* **main( )** has terminated.

This program illustrates when constructors and destructors are executed:

```
#include "iostream.h"

class myclass {
public:
  int who;
  myclass(int id);
  ~myclass();
```

```
} glob_ob1(1), glob_ob2(2);

myclass::myclass(int id)
{
  cout << "Initializing " << id << "\n";
  who = id;
}

myclass::~myclass()
{
  cout << "Destructing " << who << "\n";
}

main()
{
  myclass local_ob1(3);

  cout << "This will not be first line displayed\n";

  myclass local_ob2(4);

  return 0;
}
```

It displays this output:

```
Initializing 1
Initializing 2
Initializing 3
This will not be first line displayed
Initializing 4
Destructing 4
Destructing 3
Destructing 2
Destructing 1
```

Nested Classes

It is possible to define one **class** within another. In versions of C++ prior to 2.1, there was no reason to nest one class inside another because the nested class was at the same scope level as the enclosing class. Put differently, in versions of C++ prior to 2.1, a **class** did not define a scope, so a nested class was at the same scope level as the enclosing class. However, beginning with C++ version 2.1, a **class** declaration does, in fact, define a scope, and a nested class is valid only within the scope of the enclosing class.

The Scope Resolution Operator

As you know, the :: operator is used to link a **class** name with a member name in order to tell the compiler what **class** the member is part of. However, the scope resolution operator has another related use: it can allow access to a name in an enclosing scope that is "hidden" by a local declaration of the same name. For example, consider this fragment:

```
   .
   .
   .
int i;  // global i

void f()
{
   int i; // local i

   i = 10; // uses local i
   .
   .
   .
}

   .
   .
   .
```

However, what if function **f( )** needs to access the global version of **i**? It may do so if the **i** is preceded by the :: operator, as shown here.

```
   .
   .
   .
int i;  // global i

void f()
{
   int i; // local i

   ::i = 10; // now refers to global i
   .
   .
   .
}

   .
   .
   .
```

Local Classes

A **class** may be defined within a function. For example, this is a valid C++ program:

```
#include "iostream.h"

void f();

main()
{
  f();
  // myclass not known here
  return 0;
}

void f()
{
  class myclass {
    int i;
  public:
    void put_i(int n) {i=n;}
    int get_i() {return i;}
  } ob;

  ob.put_i(10);
  cout << ob.get_i();
}
```

When a **class** is declared within a function, it is known only to that function and unknown outside of it.

Several restrictions apply to local **class**es. First, all member functions must be defined in line. The local **class** may not use any local variables of the function in which it is declared. (Some implementations may allow a local **class** to use **static** local variables, however.) No **static** variables may be declared inside a local class. Because of these restrictions, local classes are not common in C++ programming.

Passing Objects to Functions

Objects may be passed to functions in just the same way that any other type of variable can. Objects are passed to functions through the use of the standard call-by-value mechanism. This means that a copy of an object is made when it is passed to a function. However, the fact that a copy is created means, in essence, that another object is created. This raises the question of whether the object's constructor function is executed when the copy is made and whether the destructor function is executed when the copy is destroyed. The answer to these two questions may surprise you. To begin, here is an example:

```
#include "iostream.h"

class myclass {
  int i;
public:
  myclass(int n);
  ~myclass();
  void set_i(int n) {i=n;}
  int get_i() {return i;}
};

myclass::myclass(int n)
{
  i = n;
  cout << "Constructing " << i << "\n";
}

myclass::~myclass()
{
  cout << "Destroying " << i << "\n";
}

void f(myclass ob);

main()
{
  myclass o(1);

  f(o);
  cout << "This is i in main: ";
  cout << o.get_i() << "\n";

  return 0;
}

void f(myclass ob)
{
  ob.set_i(2);

  cout << "This is local i: " << ob.get_i();
  cout << "\n";
}
```

This program produces this output:

```
Constructing 1
This is local i: 2
Destroying 2
This is i in main: 1
Destroying 1
```

Notice that only one call is made to the constructor function. However, two calls are made to the destructor function. The reason that the constructor function is not called when the copy of the object is made is easy to understand. When you pass an object to a function, you want the current state of that object. If the constructor is called when the copy is created, initialization will occur, possibly changing the object. Thus, the constructor function cannot be executed when the copy of an object is generated in a function call.

Although the constructor function is not called when an object is passed to a function, it is necessary to call the destructor when the copy is destroyed. (The copy is destroyed like any other local variable, when the function terminates.) Remember, the copy of the object does exist as long as the function is executing. This means that the copy could be performing operations that will require a destructor function to be called when the copy is destroyed. For example, it is perfectly valid for the copy to allocate memory that must be freed when it is destroyed. For this reason, the destructor function must be executed when the copy is destroyed.

To summarize: When a copy of an object is generated because it is passed to a function, the object's constructor function is not called. However, when the copy of the object inside the function is destroyed, its destructor function is called.

Returning Objects

A function may return an object to the caller. For example, this is a valid C++ program:

```
#include "iostream.h"

class myclass {
  int i;
public:
```

```
  void set_i(int n) {i=n;}
  int get_i() {return i;}
};

myclass f();   // return object of type myclass

main()
{
  myclass o;

  o = f();

  cout << o.get_i() << "\n";

  return 0;
}

myclass f()
{
  myclass x;

  x.set_i(1);
  return x;
}
```

Object Assignment

Assuming that both objects are of the same type, you can assign one object to another. This causes the data of the object on the right side to be copied into the data of the object on the left. For example, this program displays **99**:

```
#include "iostream.h"

class myclass {
  int i;
public:
  void set_i(int n) {i=n;}
  int get_i() {return i;}
};

main()
{
  myclass ob1, ob2;

  ob1.set_i(99);
  ob2 = ob1; // assign data from ob1 to ob2
```

```
  cout << "this is ob2's i: " << ob2.get_i();

  return 0;
}
```

By default, all data from one object is assigned to the other by use of a bit-by-bit copy. However, it is possible to overload the assignment operator and define some other assignment procedure (see Chapter 14, "Function and Operator Overloading").

Arrays, Pointers, and References

As you know, pointers and their relatives, arrays, are very important to the C language. Therefore, it should be no surprise that they are also important to the enhanced features provided by C++. In fact, pointers are so important to C++ that a new form of pointer, called a *reference*, has been added. This chapter examines arrays, pointers, and references as they relate to objects.

Arrays of Objects

In C++, it is possible to have arrays of objects. The syntax for declaring and using an object array is exactly the same as it is for any other type of variable. For example, this program uses a three-element array of objects:

```
#include "iostream.h"

class cl {
  int i;
public:
  void set_i(int j) {i=j;}
  int get_i() {return i;}
};

main()
{
  cl ob[3];
  int i;
```

```
for(i=0; i<3; i++) ob[i].set_i(i+1);

for(i=0; i<3; i++)
  cout << ob[i].get_i() << "\n";

return 0;
}
```

The program displays the numbers **1, 2,** and **3** on the screen.

You may initialize each object in an array by specifying an initialization list like you do for other types of arrays. Each value in the list is simply passed to the constructor function as each element in the array is created. For example, here is a slightly different version of the preceding program that uses an initialization:

```
#include "iostream.h"

class cl {
  int i;
public:
  cl(int j) {i=j;}  // constructor
  int get_i() {return i;}
};

main()
{
  cl ob[3] = {1, 2, 3};  // initializer
  int i;

  for(i=0; i<3; i++)
    cout << ob[i].get_i() << "\n";

  return 0;
}
```

This program raises an important issue relative to creating arrays of objects. The constructor function defined in **cl** requires a parameter. This implies that any array declared of this type will be initialized. That is, it precludes this array declaration:

```
cl a[9]; // error, constructor requires initializers
```

The reason that this statement isn't valid (as **cl** is currently defined) is that it implies that **cl** has a parameterless constructor because no parameters are specified. However, **cl** does not. Because there is no valid constructor to cover this declaration, the compiler will report an error. To solve this problem, you need to overload the constructor function with one that takes no parameters. In this way, arrays that are initialized and those that are not initialized are allowed. (Overloading is discussed in Chapter 14, "Function and Operator Overloading.") For example, here is an improved version of **cl**:

```
class cl {
  int i;
public:
  cl() {i=0;}  // called for non-initialized arrays
  cl(int j) {i=j;}  // called for initialized arrays
  int get_i() {return i;}
};
```

Given this **class**, both of the following statements are permissible:

```
cl al[3] = {3, 5, 6};
```

```
cl a2[34];
```

Pointers to Objects

Just as you can have pointers to other types of variables, you can have pointers to objects. When accessing members of a **class** given a pointer to an object, use the arrow ($->$) operator instead of the dot operator. The next program illustrates how to access an object given a pointer to it:

```
#include "iostream.h"

class cl {
  int i;
public:
  cl(int j) {i=j;}
  int get_i() {return i;}
};

main()
{
  cl ob(88), *p;

  p = &ob;  // get address of ob
```

```
  cout << p->get_i(); // use -> to call get_i()

  return 0;
}
```

As you know, when a pointer is incremented, it points to the next element of its type. For example, an integer pointer will point to the next integer. In general, all pointer arithmetic is relative to the type of data that the pointer is declared as pointing to. The same is true of pointers to objects. For example, this program uses a pointer to access all three elements of array **ob** after being assigned **ob**'s starting address:

```
#include "iostream.h"

class cl {
  int i;
public:
  cl() {i=0;}
  cl(int j) {i=j;}
  int get_i() {return i;}
};

main()
{
  cl ob[3] = {1, 2, 3};
  cl *p;
  int i;

  p = ob;  // get start of array
  for(i=0; i<3; i++) {
    cout << p->get_i() << "\n";
    p++;
  }

  return 0;
}
```

You can assign the address of a **public** member of an object to a pointer and then access that member by using the pointer. For example, this is a valid C++ program that displays the number **1** on the screen:

```
#include "iostream.h"

class cl {
public:
  int i;
```

```
  cl(int j) {i=j;}
};

main()
{
  cl ob(1);
  int *p;

  p = &ob.i;  // get address of ob.i

  cout << *p; // access ob.i via p

  return 0;
}
```

Because **p** is pointing to an integer, it is declared as an integer pointer. It is irrelevant that **i** is a member of object **ob** in this situation.

The this Pointer

When a member function is called, it is automatically passed an argument that is a pointer to the object that generated the call (that is, the object that invoked it). This pointer is called **this**. To understand **this**, first consider a program that creates a **class** called **pwr** that computes the result of a number raised to some power:

```
#include "iostream.h"

class pwr {
  double b;
  int e;
  double val;
public:
  pwr(double base, int exp);
  double get_pwr() {return val;}
};

pwr::pwr(double base, int exp)
{
  b = base;
  e = exp;
  val = 1;
  if(exp==0) return;
  for( ; exp>0; exp--) val = val * b;
}
```

```
main()
{
  pwr x(4.0, 2), y(2.5, 1), z(5.7, 0);

  cout << x.get_pwr() << " ";
  cout << y.get_pwr() << " ";
  cout << z.get_pwr() << "\n";

  return 0;
}
```

Within a member function, the members of a **class** can be accessed directly, without any object or **class** qualification. Thus, inside **pwr( )**, the statement

```
b = base;
```

means that the copy of **b** associated with the object that generated the call will be assigned the value contained in **base**. However, the same statement can also be written like this:

```
this->b = base;
```

Remember, the **this** pointer points to the object that invoked **pwr( )**. Thus, **this** −>**b** refers to that object's copy of **b**. In fact, writing the statement without using **this** is really just a shorthand approach. Here is the entire **pwr( )** function written using the **this** pointer:

```
pwr::pwr(double base, int exp)
{
  this->b = base;
  this->e = exp;
  this->val = 1;
  if(exp==0) return;
  for( ; exp>0; exp--)
    this->val = this->val * this->b;
}
```

Actually, no C++ programmer would write **pwr( )** as just shown because nothing is gained, and the shorthand form is easier. However, the **this** pointer is very important when operators are overloaded (see Chapter 14) and can aid in the management of certain types of linked lists.

Keep in mind that **friend** functions are not members of a **class** and are not passed a **this** pointer, and that **static** member functions do not have a **this** pointer either.

Pointers to Derived Types

Assume two **class**es called **B** and **D**. Further, assume that **D** is derived from the base **class B**. In this situation, a pointer of type **B** * may also point to an object of type **D**. More generally, a pointer of a base **class** can also be used as a pointer to any derived **class**. However, the opposite is not true. A pointer of type **D** * may not point to an object of type **B**. Further, although you can use a base pointer to point to a derived object, you can access only the members of the derived type that were imported from the base. That is, you won't be able to access any members added by the derived **class**. (You can cast a base pointer into a derived pointer and access the entire derived **class**, however.)

Here is a short program that illustrates this feature of C++:

```
#include "iostream.h"

class base {
  int i;
public:
  void set_i(int num) {i=num;}
  int get_i() {return i;}
};

class derived: public base {
  int j;
public:
  void set_j(int num) {j=num;}
  int get_j() {return j;}
};

main()
{
  base *bp;
  derived d;

  bp = &d; // base pointer points to derived object

  // access derived object using base pointer
  bp->set_i(10);
  cout << bp->get_i() << " ";
```

```
/* This won't work.  You can't access element of
   a derived class using a base class pointer.

   bp->set_j(88);  // error
   cout << bp->get_j();  // error
*/
   return 0;
}
```

As you can see, a base pointer is used to access an object of a derived **class.**

Although considered poor form by most C++ programmers, it is possible to cast a base pointer into a pointer of the derived type to access a member of the derived class using the base pointer. For example, this is valid C++ code:

```
// access now allowed because of cast
((derived *)bp)->set_j(88);
cout << ((derived *)bp)->get_j();
```

It is important to remember that pointer arithmetic is relative to the type the pointer is declared as pointing to. For this reason, when a base pointer is pointing to a derived object, incrementing the pointer does not cause it to point to the next object of the derived type. Instead, it will point to what it thinks is the next object of the base type. For example, this program, while syntactically correct, contains this error:

```
#include "iostream.h"

class base {
  int i;
public:
  void set_i(int num) {i=num;}
  int get_i() {return i;}
};

class derived: public base {
  int j;
public:
  void set_j(int num) {j=num;}
  int get_j() {return j;}
};

main()
{
  base *bp;
```

```
    derived d[2];

    bp = d;

    d[0].set_i(1);
    d[1].set_i(2);

    cout << bp->get_i() << " ";
    bp++;  // relative to base, not derived
    cout << bp->get_i();  // garbage value displayed

    return 0;
}
```

The use of base pointers to derived types is most useful when creating run-time polymorphism through the mechanism of virtual functions (see Chapter 16, "Virtual Functions and Polymorphism").

Pointers to Class Members

C++ allows you to generate a very special type of pointer that "points" generically to a **public** member of a **class**, not to a specific instance of that member in an object. This sort of pointer is called a pointer to a **class** member or, for short, a *pointer to a member*. A pointer to a member is not the same as a normal C++ pointer. Instead, a pointer to a member provides only an offset into an object of the member's **class** at which that member can be found. Since member pointers are not true pointers, the . and −> cannot be applied to them. To access a member of a **class** given a pointer to it, you must use the special pointer-to-member operators .* and −>*. Their job is to allow you to access a member of a **class** given a pointer to that member.

Here is an example:

```
#include "iostream.h"

class cl {
public:
  cl(int i) {val=i;}
  int val;
  int double_val() {return val+val;}
};

main()
```

```
{
  int cl::*data; // data member pointer
  int (cl::*func)(); // function member pointer
  cl ob1(1), ob2(2); // create objects

  data = &cl::val; // get offset of val
  func = &cl::double_val;  // get offset of double_val()

  cout << "Here are values: ";
  cout << ob1.*data << " " << ob1.*data << "\n";

  cout << "Here they are doubled: ";
  cout << (ob1.*func)() << " ";
  cout << (ob2.*func)() << "\n";

  return 0;
}
```

In **main( )**, this program creates two member pointers: **data** and **func**. Note carefully the syntax of each declaration. When declaring pointers to members, you must specify the **class** and use the scope resolution operator. The program also creates objects of **cl** called **ob1** and **ob2**. As the program illustrates, member pointers may point to either functions or data. Next, the program obtains the addresses of **val** and **double_val( )**. As stated earlier, these "addresses" are really just offsets into an object of type **cl**, at which point **val** and **double_val( )** will be found. Next, to display the values of each object's **val**, each is accessed through **data**. Finally, the program uses **func** to call the **double_val( )** function. The extra parentheses are necessary in order to correctly associate the .* operator.

When you are accessing a member of an object by using an object or a reference (discussed later in this chapter), you must use the .* operator. However, if you are using a pointer to the object, you need to use the −>* operator, as illustrated in this version of the preceding program:

```
#include "iostream.h"

class cl {
public:
  cl(int i) {val=i;}
  int val;
  int double_val() {return val+val;}
};

main()
{
```

```
int cl::*data; // data member pointer
int (cl::*func)(); // function member pointer
cl ob1(1), ob2(2); // create objects
cl *p1, *p2;

p1 = &ob1;
p2 = &ob2;

data = &cl::val; // get offset of val
func = &cl::double_val;  // get offset of double_val()

cout << "Here are values: ";
cout << p1->*data << " " << p1->*data << "\n";

cout << "Here they are doubled: ";
cout << (p1->*func)() << " ";
cout << (p2->*func)() << "\n";

return 0;
}
```

In this version, **p1** and **p2** are pointers to objects of type **cl**. Therefore, the $->*$ operator is used to access **val** and **double_val( )**.

Remember, pointers to members are different from pointers to specific instances of elements of an object. For example, consider this fragment (assume that **cl** is declared as shown in the preceding programs):

```
int cl::*d;
int *p;
cl o;

p = &o.val // this is address of a specific val

d = &cl::val // this is offset of generic val
```

Here, **p** is a pointer to an integer inside a *specific* object. However, **d** is simply an offset that indicates where **val** will be found in any object of type **cl**.

References

C++ contains a feature that is related to the pointer. This feature is called a reference. A *reference* is essentially an implicit pointer that acts as another name for an object.

Reference Parameters

One important use for a reference is to allow you to create functions that automatically use call-by-reference parameter passing rather than C++'s default call-by-value method.

As you know, in C, to create a call-by-reference you must explicitly pass the address of an argument to the function. For example, consider this short program that uses this approach in a function called **neg( )**, which reverses the sign of the integer variable pointed to by its argument.

```
#include "iostream.h"

void neg(int *i);

main()
{
  int x;

  x = 10;
  cout << x << " negated is ";

  neg(&x);
  cout << x << "\n";

  return 0;
}

void neg(int *i)
{
  *i = -*i;
}
```

In this program, **neg( )** takes as a parameter a pointer to the integer whose sign it will reverse. Therefore, **neg( )** is explicitly called with the address of **x**. Further, inside **neg( )** the * operator must be used to access the variable pointed to by **i**. As you know, this is how you generate a "manual" call-by-reference in C. However, in C++, you can automate this feature completely by using a reference parameter.

To create a reference parameter, precede the parameter's name with an **&**. Here is how **neg( )** is declared using a reference:

```
void neg(int &i);
```

This tells the compiler to make **i** another name for whatever argument **neg( )** is called with. Once **i** has been made into a reference, it is no longer necessary (or even legal) to apply the * operator. Instead, each time **i** is used, it is implicitly a reference to the variable that **neg( )** was called with. Further, when calling **neg( )**, it is no longer necessary (or legal) to precede the argument's name with the & operator. Instead, the compiler does this automatically. Here is the reference version of the preceding program:

```
#include "iostream.h"

void neg(int &i);   // i now a reference

main()
{
  int x;

  x = 10;
  cout << x << " negated is ";

  neg(x);  // no longer need the & operator
  cout << x << "\n";

  return 0;
}

void neg(int &i)
{
  i = -i;  // i is now a reference, don't need *
}
```

To review: When you create a reference parameter, that parameter automatically refers to (implicitly points to) the argument used to call the function. Therefore, the statement **i = −i** actually operates on **x**, not on a copy of **x**. There is no need to apply the & operator to an argument. Also, inside the function, the reference parameter is used directly without the need to apply the * operator.

It is important to understand that when you assign a value to a reference, you are actually assigning that value to the variable that the reference refers to. In the case of function parameters, this will be the variable used in the call to the function.

Inside the function, it is not possible to change what the reference parameter is "pointing" to. That is, a statement like

```
i++:
```

inside **neg( )** increments the value of the variable used in the call. It does not cause **i** to point to some new location.

Here is another example. This program uses reference parameters to swap the values of the variables it is called with. (The **swap( )** function is the classic example of call-by-reference parameter passing.)

```
#include "iostream.h"

void swap(int &i, int &j);

main()
{
  int a, b, c, d;

  a = 1;
  b = 2;
  c = 3;
  d = 4;

  cout << "a and b: " << a << " " << b << "\n";
  swap(a, b);  // no & operator needed
  cout << "a and b: " << a << " " << b << "\n";

  cout << "c and d: " << c << " " << d << "\n";
  swap(c, d);
  cout << "c and d: " << c << " " << d << "\n";

  return 0;
}

void swap(int &i, int &j)
{
  int t;

  t = i;   // no * operator needed
  i = j;
  j = t;
}
```

This program displays the following:

```
a and b: 1 2
a and b: 2 1
c and d: 3 4
c and d: 4 3
```

Passing References to Objects

In Chapter 12, "Classes and Objects," it was explained that when an object is passed as an argument to a function, a copy of that object is made. Further, when the copy is made, that object's constructor function is *not* called. However, when the function terminates, the copy's destructor *is* called. If for some reason you do not want the destructor function to be called, simply pass the object by reference. (Later in this book you will see examples where this is the case.) When you pass by reference, no copy of the object is made. This means that no object used as a parameter is destroyed when the function terminates, and the parameter's destructor is not called. For example, try this program:

```
#include "iostream.h"

class cl {
  int id;
public:
  int i;
  cl(int i);
  ~cl();
  void neg(cl &o) {o.i = -o.i;} // no temporary created
};

cl::cl(int num)
{
  cout << "Constructing " << num << "\n";
  id = num;
}

cl::~cl()
{
  cout << "Destructing " << id << "\n";
}

main()
{
  cl o(1);

  o.i = 10;
  o.neg(o);

  cout << o.i << "\n";

  return 0;
}
```

Here is the output of this program:

```
Constructing 1
-10
Destructing 1
```

As you can see, only one call is made to **cl**'s destructor function. Had **o** been passed by value, a second object would have been created inside

neg( ), and the destructor would have been called a second time when that object was destroyed at the time **neg( )** terminated.

When passing parameters by reference, remember that changes to the object inside the function affect the calling object.

Returning References

A function may return a reference. This has the rather startling effect of allowing a function to be used on the left side of an assignment statement! For example, consider this simple program:

```
#include "iostream.h"

char &replace(int i);  // return a reference

char s[80] = "Hello There";

main()
{
  replace(5) = 'X'; // assign X to space after Hello

  cout << s;

  return 0;
}

char &replace(int i)
{
  return s[i];
}
```

This program replaces the space between **Hello** and **There** with an **X**. That is, the program displays **HelloXthere**. Take a look at how this is accomplished.

As shown, **replace( )** is declared as returning a reference to a character array. As **replace( )** is coded, it returns a reference to the element of **s** that is specified by its argument **i**. The reference returned by **replace( )** is then used in **main( )** to assign to that element the character **X**.

Independent References

By far the most common uses for references are to pass an argument using call-by-reference and to act as a return value from a function.

However, you can declare a reference that is simply a variable. This type of reference is called an *independent reference.*

When you create an independent reference, all you are creating is another name for a variable. All independent reference variables must be initialized when they are created. The reason for this is easy to understand. Aside from initialization, you cannot change what object a reference variable points to. Therefore, it must be initialized when it is declared. (Relative to references, initialization is a wholly separate operation from assignment.)

The following program illustrates an independent reference:

```
#include "iostream.h"

main()
{
  int a;
  int &ref = a; // independent reference

  a = 10;
  cout << a << " " << ref << "\n";

  ref = 100;
  cout << a << " " << ref << "\n";

  int b = 19;
  ref = b; // this puts b's value into a
  cout << a << " " << ref << "\n";

  ref--;  // this decrements a
          // it does not affect what ref refers to

  cout << a << " " << ref << "\n";

  return 0;
}
```

The program displays this output:

```
10 10
100 100
19 19
18 18
```

You can use an independent reference to refer to a constant. For example,

```
int &count = 9;
```

causes **count** to point to the location in your program's constant table where the value 9 is stored.

Actually, independent references are of little real value because each one is, literally, just another name for another variable. Having two names to describe the same object is likely to confuse, not organize, your program.

Restrictions to References

There are a number of restrictions that apply to references. You cannot reference another reference. Put differently, you cannot obtain the address of a reference. You cannot create arrays of references. You cannot create a pointer to a reference. You cannot reference a bit-field.

A reference variable must be initialized when it is declared unless it is a member of a **class**, a function parameter, or a return value.

A Matter of Style

When declaring pointer and reference variables some C++ programmers use a unique coding style that associates the * or the & with the type name and not the variable. For example, here are two functionally equivalent declarations.

```
int& p; // & associated with type

int &p; // & associated with variable
```

Associating the * or & with the type name reflects the desire of some programmers for C++ to contain a separate pointer type. However, the trouble with associating the & or * with the type rather than the variable is that, according to the formal C++ syntax, neither the & nor the * is distributive over a list of variables. Thus, misleading declarations are easily created. For example, the following declaration creates *one, not two*, integer pointers. Here, **b** is declared as an integer (not an integer pointer) because, as specified by the C++ syntax, when used in a declaration the * (or &) is linked to the individual variable that it precedes, not to the type that it follows.

```
int* a, b;
```

The trouble with this declaration is that the visual message suggests that both **a** and **b** are pointer types, even though, in fact, only **a** is a pointer. This visual confusion not only misleads novice C++ programmers, but occasionally old pros, too.

It is important to understand that, as far as the C++ compiler is concerned, it doesn't matter whether you write **int *p** or **int* p**. Thus, if you prefer to associate the * or & with the type rather than the variable, feel free to do so. However, to avoid confusion, this book will continue to associate the * and the & with the variables that they modify rather than the types.

C++'s Dynamic Allocation Operators

In C, dynamic memory allocation is achieved by using (among others) the functions **malloc( )** and **free( )**. For the sake of compatibility, the old C dynamic allocation functions are still available in C++. However, C++ provides its own alternative dynamic allocation system based upon two new operators: **new** and **delete**. As you will see, there are substantial advantages to C++'s approach to dynamic memory allocation.

The **new** operator returns a pointer to allocated memory. Like **malloc( )**, **new** allocates memory from the heap. It returns a null pointer if there is insufficient memory to fulfill the allocation request. The **delete** operator frees memory previously allocated using **new**. The general forms of **new** and **delete** are shown here:

p_var = new *type*;
delete p_var;

Here, *p_var* is a pointer variable that receives a pointer to memory that is large enough to hold an item of type *type*. For example, here is a program that allocates memory to hold an integer:

```
#include "iostream.h"
#include "stdlib.h"

main()
{
  int *p;

  p = new int;  // allocate space for an int

  if(!p) {
    cout << "Allocation error\n";
    exit(1);
  }

  *p = 100;

  cout << "At " << p << " ";
  cout << "is the value " << *p << "\n";

  delete p;

  return 0;
}
```

The **delete** operator must be used only with a valid pointer previously allocated by using **new**. Using any other type of pointer with **delete** is undefined and will almost certainly cause serious problems, such as a system crash.

Although **new** and **delete** perform similar functions to **malloc( )** and **free( )**, they have several advantages. First, **new** automatically allocates enough memory to hold an object of the specified type. You do not need to use the **sizeof** operator. Because the size is computed automatically, it eliminates any possibility for error in this regard. Second, **new** automatically returns a pointer of the specified type. You don't need to use an explicit type cast as you do when allocating memory by using **malloc( )**. Finally, both **new** and **delete** can be overloaded, allowing you to create customized allocation systems.

You can initialize the allocated memory to some known value by putting an initializer after the type name in the **new** statement. For example, this program gives the allocated integer an initial value of 87:

```
#include "iostream.h"
#include "stdlib.h"
```

```
main()
{
  int *p;

  p = new int (87);  // initialize to 87

  if(!p) {
    cout << "Allocation error\n";
    exit(1);
  }

  cout << "At " << p << " ";
  cout << "is the value " << *p << "\n";

  delete p;

  return 0;
}
```

Here is the general form of **new** when an initialization is included:

p_var = new *var_type* (*initializer*);

You can allocate arrays using **new** by using this general form:

p_var = new *array_type* [*size*][*size*]...[*size*];

For example, the next program allocates a ten-element integer array.

```
#include "iostream.h"
#include "stdlib.h"

main()
{
  int *p, i;

  p = new int [10];  // allocate 10 integer array

  if(!p) {
    cout << "Allocation error\n";
    exit(1);
  }

  for(i=0; i<10; i++ )
    p[i] = i;

  for(i=0; i<10; i++)
    cout << p[i] << " ";

  delete [10] p; // release 10 elements

  return 0;
}
```

Notice the **delete** statement. When an array allocated by using **new** is released, **delete** must be told how many elements there are in the array. (As you will see in the next section, this is especially important when you are allocating arrays of objects.)

One restriction applies to allocating arrays: They may not be given initial values. That is, you may not specify an initializer when allocating arrays.

Allocating Objects

You can allocate objects dynamically by using **new**. When you do this, an object is created and a pointer is returned to it. The dynamically created object acts just like any other object. When it is created, its constructor function (if it has one) is called. When the object is freed, its destructor function is executed.

Here is a short program that creates a **class** called **balance** that links a person's name with his or her account balance. Inside **main( )**, an object of type **balance** is created dynamically.

```
#include "iostream.h"
#include "stdlib.h"
#include "string.h"

class balance {
  double cur_bal;
  char name[80];
public:
  void set(double n, char *s) {
    cur_bal = n;
    strcpy(name, s);
  }
  void get_bal(double &n, char *s) {
    n = cur_bal;
    strcpy(s, name);
  }
};

main()
{
  balance *p;
  char s[80];
  double n;

  p = new balance;
  if(!p) {
```

```
    cout << "Allocation error\n";
    exit(1);
  }

  p->set(12387.87, "Ralph Wilson");

  p->get_bal(n, s);

  cout << s << "'s balance is: " << n;
  cout << "\n";

  delete p;

  return 0;
}
```

Because **p** contains a pointer to an object, the arrow operator is used to access members of the object.

As stated, dynamically allocated objects may have constructors and destructors. Also, the constructor functions can be parameterized. Examine this version of the previous program:

```
#include "iostream.h"
#include "stdlib.h"
#include "string.h"

class balance {
  double cur_bal;
  char name[80];
public:
  balance(double n, char *s) {
    cur_bal = n;
    strcpy(name, s);
  }
  ~balance() {
    cout << "Destructing ";
    cout << name << "\n";
  }
  void get_bal(double &n, char *s) {
    n = cur_bal;
    strcpy(s, name);
  }
};

main()
{
  balance *p;
  char s[80];
  double n;

  // this version uses an initializer
  p = new balance (12387.87, "Ralph Wilson");
  if(!p) {
```

```
      cout << "Allocation error\n";
      exit(l);
   }

   p->get_bal(n, s);

   cout << s << "'s balance is: " << n;
   cout << "\n";

   delete p;

   return 0;
}
```

The parameters to the object's constructor function are after the type name, just as in other sorts of initialization.

You can allocate arrays of objects, but there is one catch. Since no array allocated by using **new** can have an initializer, you must make sure that if the **class** contains constructor functions, one will be parameterless. If you don't, the C++ compiler will not find a matching constructor when you declare an array and will not compile your program.

In this version of the preceding program, an array of **balance** objects is allocated, and the parameterless constructor is called.

```
#include "iostream.h"
#include "stdlib.h"
#include "string.h"

class balance {
  double cur_bal;
  char name[80];
public:
  balance(double n, char *s) {
    cur_bal = n;
    strcpy(name, s);
  }
  balance() {} // parameterless constructor
  ~balance() {
    cout << "Destructing ";
    cout << name << "\n";
  }
  void set(double n, char *s) {
    cur_bal = n;
    strcpy(name, s);
  }
  void get_bal(double &n, char *s) {
    n = cur_bal;
    strcpy(s, name);
  }
};
```

```
main()
{
  balance *p;
  char s[80];
  double n;
  int i;

  p = new balance [3]; // allocate entire array
  if(!p) {
    cout << "Allocation error\n";
    exit(1);
  }

  // note use of dot, not arrow operators
  p[0].set(12387.87, "Ralph Wilson");
  p[1].set(144.00, "A. C. Conners");
  p[2].set(-11.23, "I. M. Overdrawn");

  for(i=0; i<3; i++) {
    p[i].get_bal(n, s);

    cout << s << "'s balance is: " << n;
    cout << "\n";
  }

  delete [3] p;
  return 0;
}
```

One reason that you need to specify the number of elements in the array to the **delete** operator is so that the proper number of destructor functions can be called (that is, one for each object in the array). Be sure that this number is actually the same as the number of objects in the array. C++ does not check this for you, so if you specify too many or too few, run-time errors will result.

One final point about **new** and **delete**: Although there is no formal rule that states this, it is best not to mix **new** and **delete** with **malloc( )** and **free( )** in the same program. There is no guarantee that they are mutually compatible.

Function and Operator Overloading

Function and operator overloading are very important to C++ programming. Not only do these two features provide most of the support for compile-time polymorphism, they also add great flexibility and extensibility to the language. For example, the overloading of the << and >> operators forms the basis of C++'s approach to I/O.

This chapter begins with function overloading and concludes by examining operator overloading. Although similar to function overloading, operator overloading introduces several nuances to the process. Therefore, before attempting to overload an operator, you should thoroughly understand function overloading.

Function Overloading

As discussed in Chapter 11, "An Overview of C++," function overloading is simply the process of using the same name for two or more functions. The central point is, however, that each redefinition of the function must use either different types of parameters or a different number of parameters. It is only through these differences that the compiler knows which function to call in any given situation. For example, this program overloads **myfunc( )** by using different types of parameters.

```
#include "iostream.h"

int myfunc(int i); // these differ in types of parameters
double myfunc(double i);

main()
{
  cout << myfunc(10) << " "; // calls myfunc(int i)
  cout << myfunc(5.4); // calls myfunc(double i)

  return 0;
}

double myfunc(double i)
{
  return i;
}

int myfunc(int i)
{
  return i;
}
```

The next program overloads **myfunc( )** using a different number of parameters:

```
#include "iostream.h"

int myfunc(int i);  // these differ in number of parameters
int myfunc(int i, int j);

main()
{
  cout << myfunc(10) << " "; // calls myfunc(int i)
  cout << myfunc(4, 5); // calls myfunc(int i, int j)

  return 0;
}

int myfunc(int i)
{
  return i;
}

int myfunc(int i, int j)
{
  return i*j;
}
```

As mentioned, the key point about function overloading is that the functions must differ in regard to the types or number of parameters.

Two functions differing only in their return types cannot be overloaded. For example, this is an invalid attempt to overload **myfunc( )**:

```
int myfunc(int i);    // Error: differing return types are
float myfunc(int i);  // insufficient when overloading.
```

Function Overloading and Ambiguity

You can create a situation in which the compiler is unable to choose between two (or more) overloaded functions. When this happens, the situation is said to be *ambiguous*. Ambiguous statements are errors, and programs containing ambiguity will not compile.

By far the main cause of ambiguity involves C++'s automatic type conversions. As you know, C++ automatically attempts to convert the arguments used to call a function into the type of arguments expected by the function. For example, consider this fragment:

```
int myfunc(double d);
   .
   .
   .
cout << myfunc('c');  // not an error, conversion applied
```

As the comment indicates, this is not an error because C++ automatically converts the character **c** into its **double** equivalent. In C++, very few type conversions of this sort are actually disallowed. Although automatic type conversions are convenient, they are also a prime cause of ambiguity. For example, consider the following program:

```
#include "iostream.h"

float myfunc(float i);
double myfunc(double i);

main()
{
  cout << myfunc(10.1) << " "; // unambiguous, calls myfunc(double)
  cout << myfunc(10); // ambiguous

  return 0;
}

float myfunc(float i)
{
```

```
  return i;
}

double myfunc(double i)
{
  return -i;
}
```

Here, **myfunc( )** is overloaded so that it can take arguments of either type **float** or type **double**. In the unambiguous line, **myfunc(double)** is called because, unless explicitly specified as **float**, all floating-point constants in C++ are automatically of type **double**. Hence, that call is unambiguous. However, when **myfunc( )** is called by using the integer 10, ambiguity is introduced because the compiler has no way of knowing whether it should be converted to a **float** or to a **double**. This causes an error message to be displayed, and the program will not compile.

The preceding example illustrates that it is not the overloading of **myfunc( )** relative to **double** and **float** that causes the ambiguity. Rather, it is the specific call to **myfunc( )** by using an indeterminate type of argument that causes the confusion. Put differently, it is not the overloading of **myfunc( )** that is in error, but the specific invocation.

Here is another example of ambiguity caused by C++'s automatic type conversions:

```
#include "iostream.h"

char myfunc(unsigned char ch);
char myfunc(char ch);

main()
{
  cout << myfunc('c');  // this calls myfunc(char)
  cout << myfunc(88) << " ";  // ambiguous

  return 0;
}

char myfunc(unsigned char ch)
{
  return ch-1;
}

char myfunc(char ch)
{
  return ch+1;
}
```

In C++, **unsigned char** and **char** are *not* inherently ambiguous. However, when **myfunc( )** is called by using the integer 88, the compiler does not know which function to call. That is, should 88 be converted into a **char** or an **unsigned char**?

Another way you can cause ambiguity is by using default arguments in overloaded functions. To see how, examine this program:

```
#include "iostream.h"

int myfunc(int i);
int myfunc(int i, int j=1);

main()
{
  cout << myfunc(4, 5) << " ";  // unambiguous
  cout << myfunc(10);  // ambiguous

  return 0;
}

int myfunc(int i)
{
  return i;
}

int myfunc(int i, int j)
{
  return i*j;
}
```

Here, in the first call to **myfunc( )**, two arguments are specified; therefore, no ambiguity is introduced and **myfunc(int i, int j)** is called. However, when the second call to **myfunc( )** is made, ambiguity occurs because the compiler does not know whether to call the version of **myfunc( )** that takes one argument or to apply the default to the version that takes two arguments.

The overload Anachronism

When C++ was created, the keyword **overload** was needed to create an overloaded function. Although it is no longer needed and is considered obsolete, it is still accepted by C++ compilers for the sake of compatibility with older C++ programs. Because you might encounter older programs or perhaps find yourself in a situation where only an old C++ compiler is available, it is a good idea to know how **overload** was used. Here is its general form:

overload *func-name*

where *func-name* is the name of the function that you will be overloading. This statement must precede the overloaded declarations. For example, this tells an old-style compiler that you will be overloading a function called **test( )**:

```
overload test;
```

Because **overload** is an anachronism, you should avoid its use in C++ programs that you create.

Overloading Constructor Functions

Aside from performing the special role of initialization, constructor functions are no different from other types of functions. This includes overloading. In fact, it is very common to find overloaded constructor functions. For example, consider this program that creates a **class** called **date**, which holds a calender date. Notice that the constructor is overloaded two ways:

```
#include "iostream.h"
#include "stdio.h"

class date {
  int day, month, year;
public:
  date(char *d);
  date(int m, int d, int y);
  void show_date();
};

// Initialize using string.
date::date(char *d)
```

```
{
  sscanf(d, "%d%*c%d%*c%d", &month, &day, &year);
}

// Initialize using integers.
date::date(int m, int d, int y)
{
  day = d;
  month = m;
  year = y;
}

void date::show_date()
{
  cout << month << "/" << day;
  cout << "/" << year << "\n";
}

main()
{
  date ob1(12, 4, 92), ob2("10/22/94");

  ob1.show_date();
  ob2.show_date();

  return 0;
}
```

In this program, you can initialize an object of type **date**, either by specifying the date using three digits to represent the month, day, and year, or by using a string that contains the date in this general form:

mm/dd/yy

The most common reason to overload a constructor is to allow an object to be created by using the most appropriate and natural means for each particular circumstance. For example, in the following **main( )**, the user is prompted for the date, which is input to array **s**. This string can then be used directly to create **d**. There is no need for it to be converted to any other form. However, if **date( )** were not overloaded to accept the string form, you would have to manually convert it into three integers each time you created an object.

```
main()
{
  char s[80];

  cout << "Enter new date: ";
```

```
cin >> s;

date d(s);
d.show_date();

return 0;
}
```

In another situation, initializing an object of type **date** by using three integers may be more convenient. For example, if the date is generated by using some sort of computational method, then creating a **date** object using **date(int, int, int)** is the most natural and appropriate constructor to employ. The point here is that by overloading **date**'s constructor, you have made it more flexible and easier to use. This increased flexibility and ease of use are especially important if you are creating class libraries that will be used by other programmers.

Finding the Address of an Overloaded Function

As you know, in C you can assign the address of a function to a pointer and then call that function by using the pointer. The same feature also exists in C++. However, because of function overloading, this process is a little more complex. To understand why, first consider this statement, which assigns the address of some function called **myfunc( )** to a pointer called **p**:

```
p = myfunc;
```

If this is part of a C program, then there is one and only one function called **myfunc( )**, and the compiler has no difficulty assigning its address to **p**. However, if this statement is part of a C++ program, then **myfunc( )** might be overloaded. Assuming that it is, how does the compiler know which function's address to assign to **p**? The answer is that it depends upon how **p** is declared. For example, consider this program:

```
#include "iostream.h"

int myfunc(int a);
int myfunc(int a, int b);
```

```
main()
{
  int (*fp)(int a);   // pointer to int xxx(int)

  fp = myfunc;   // points to myfunc(int)

  cout << fp(5);

  return 0;
}

int myfunc(int a)
{
  return a;
}

int myfunc(int a, int b)
{
  return a*b;
}
```

As the program illustrates, **fp** is declared as a pointer to a function that returns an integer and that takes one integer argument. C++ uses this information to select the **myfunc(int a)** version of **myfunc( )**. Had **fp** been declared like this:

```
int (*fp)(int a, int b);
```

then **fp** would have been assigned the address of the **myfunc(int a, int b)** version of **myfunc( )**.

To review: When you assign the address of an overloaded function to a function pointer, it is the declaration of the pointer that determines which function's address is assigned. Further, the declaration of the function pointer must exactly match one and only one of the overloaded function's declarations.

Operator Overloading

Closely related to function overloading is operator overloading. In C++, you can overload most operators so that they perform special operations relative to **classes** that you create. For example, a **class** that maintains a stack might overload **+** to perform a push operation and **−** to perform a pop. When an operator is overloaded, none of its original meanings are lost. Instead, the type of objects it can be applied to is expanded.

You overload operators by creating **operator** functions. An **operator** function defines the specific operations that the overloaded operator will perform relative to the **class** it is designed to work on. **operator** functions can be either members or nonmembers of the **class** that they will operate on. Nonmember **operator** functions are almost always **friend** functions of the **class**, however. The way **operator** functions are written differs between member and **friend** functions. Therefore, each will be examined separately, beginning with member **operator** functions.

Creating a Member operator Function

Member **operator** functions take this general form:

> *ret-type class-name*::operator#(*arg-list*)
> {
>   // operations
> }

Often, **operator** functions return an object of the **class** they operate on, but *ret-type* can be any valid type. The **#** is a placeholder. When you create an **operator** function, substitute the operator for the **#**. For example, if you are overloading the **/** operator, use **operator/**. When you are overloading a unary operator, *arg-list* will be empty. When you are overloading binary operators, *arg-list* will contain one parameter. (The reasons for this seemingly unusual situation will be made clear in a moment.)

Here is a simple first example of operator overloading. This program creates a **class** called **loc**, which stores longitude and latitude values. It overloads the **+** operator relative to this **class**. Examine this program carefully, paying special attention to the definition of **operator+( )**:

```
#include "iostream.h"

class loc {
```

```
    int longitude, latitude;
public:
  loc() {};
  loc(int lg, int lt) {
    longitude = lg;
    latitude = lt;
  }

  void show() {
    cout << longitude << " ";
    cout << latitude << "\n";
  }

  loc operator+(loc op2);
};

loc loc::operator+(loc op2)
{
  loc temp;

  temp.longitude = op2.longitude + longitude;
  temp.latitude = op2.latitude + latitude;
  return temp;
}

main()
{
  loc ob1(10, 20), ob2( 5, 30);

  ob1.show(); // displays 10 20
  ob2.show(); // displays 5 30

  ob1 = ob1 + ob2;
  ob1.show(); // displays 15 50

  return 0;
}
```

As you can see, **operator+( )** has only one parameter even though it overloads the binary + operator. (You might expect two parameters corresponding to the two operands of a binary operator.) The reason that **operator+( )** takes only one parameter is that the operand on the left side of the + is passed implicitly to the function using the **this** pointer. The operand on the right is passed in the parameter **op2**. The fact that the left operand is passed using **this** also implies one important point: When binary operators are overloaded, it is the object on the left that generates the call to the **operator** function.

As mentioned, it is common for an overloaded **operator** function to return an object of the **class** it operates upon. By doing so, it allows the operator to be used in larger C++ expressions. For example, if the **operator+( )** function returned some other type, this expression would not have been valid:

```
ob1 = ob1 + ob2;
```

In order for the sum of **ob1** and **ob2** to be assigned to **ob1**, the outcome of that operation must be an object of type **loc**.

Further, having **operator+( )** return an object of type **loc** makes possible the following statement:

```
(ob1+ob2).show();   // displays outcome of ob1+ob2
```

In this situation, **ob1+ob2** generates a temporary object that ceases to exist after the call to **show( )** terminates.

It is important to understand that an **operator** function can return any type and that the type returned depends solely upon your specific application. It is just that, often, an **operator** function will return an object of the **class** upon which it operates.

One last point about the **operator+( )** function: It does not modify either operand. Because the traditional use of the + operator does not modify either operand, it makes sense for the overloaded version not to do so either. (For example, 5+7 yields 12, but neither 5 nor 7 is changed.) Also, relative to how it is used by the **loc class**, **operator+( )** should not alter either operand. Although you are free to perform any operation you want inside an **operator** function, it is usually best to stay within the context of the normal use of the operator.

The next program adds three additional overloaded operators to the **loc class**: the −, the =, and the unary ++. Pay special attention to how these functions are defined.

```
#include "iostream.h"

class loc {
  int longitude, latitude;
public:
  loc() {}; // needed to construct temporaries
  loc(int lg, int lt) {
    longitude = lg;
    latitude = lt;
  }
```

```
  void show() {
    cout << longitude << " ";
    cout << latitude << "\n";
  }

  loc operator+(loc op2);
  loc operator-(loc op2);
  loc operator=(loc op2);
  loc operator++();
};

loc loc::operator+(loc op2)
{
  loc temp;

  temp.longitude = op2.longitude + longitude;
  temp.latitude = op2.latitude + latitude;
  return temp;
}

loc loc::operator-(loc op2)
{
  loc temp;

  // notice order of operands
  temp.longitude = longitude - op2.longitude;
  temp.latitude = latitude - op2.latitude;
  return temp;
}

loc loc::operator=(loc op2)
{
  longitude = op2.longitude;
  latitude = op2.latitude;
  return *this; // i.e., return object that generated call
}

loc loc::operator++()
{
  longitude++;
  latitude++;
  return *this;
}

main()
{
  loc ob1(10, 20), ob2( 5, 30), ob3(90, 90);

  ob1.show();
  ob2.show();

  ob1++;
  ob1.show();  // displays 11 21
```

```
ob2 = ob1++;
ob1.show(); // displays 12 22
ob2.show(); // displays 12 22

ob1 = ob2 = ob3;  // multiple assignment
ob1.show(); // displays 90 90
ob2.show(); // displays 90 90

return 0;
}
```

First, examine the **operator−( )** function. Notice the order of the operands in the subtraction. In keeping with the meaning of subtraction, the operand on the right side of the minus sign is subtracted from the operand on the left. Because it is the object on the left that generates the call to the **operator−( )** function, **op2**'s data must be subtracted from the data pointed to by **this**. It is important to remember which operand generates the call to the function.

In C++, if the = is not overloaded, a default assignment operation is created automatically for any **class** you define. The default assignment is simply a member-by-member copy. However, by overloading the =, you can define explicitly what the assignment does relative to a **class**. In this example, the overloaded = does exactly the same thing as the default, but in other situations, it could perform other operations. Notice that the **operator=( )** function returns ***this**, which is the object that generated the call. This arrangement is necessary if you want to be able to use multiple assignment statements such as this:

```
ob1 = ob2 = ob3;  // multiple assignment
```

Finally, look at the definition of **operator+ +( )**. As you can see, it takes no parameters. Since **+ +** is a unary operator, its only operand is implicitly passed by using the **this** pointer.

Notice that both **operator=( )** and **operator+ +( )** alter the value of an operand. In the case of assignment, the operand on the left (the one generating the call to the **operator+( )** function) is assigned a new value. In the case of the **+ +**, the operand is incremented. As stated previously, although you are free to make these functions do anything you please, it is almost always wisest to stay consistent with their original meanings.

In versions of C++ prior to specification 2.1, it was not possible to determine whether an overloaded **+ +** or **− −** preceded or followed its operand. For example, assuming some object called **O**, these two statements were identical:

```
O++;

++O;
```

However, beginning with specification 2.1, a means was created for determining whether an increment or decrement prefixes or postfixes its operand. To accomplish this, define two versions of the **operator+ +( )** function. One is defined as shown in the foregoing program. The other is declared like this:

```
loc operator++(int x);
```

If the **+ +** precedes its operand, the **operator+ +( )** function is called. If the **+ +** follows its operand, the **operator+ +(int x)** is called and **x** has the value zero.

You can overload any of C++'s "shorthand" operators, such as **+ =**, **− =**, and the like. For example, this function overloads **+ =** relative to **loc**:

```
loc loc::operator+=(loc op2)
{
  longitude = op2.longitude + longitude;
  latitude = op2.latitude + latitude;
  return *this;
}
```

When overloading one of these operators, keep in mind that you are simply combining an assignment with another type of operation.

Except for the **=** operator, **operator** functions are inherited by any derived **class**. However, a derived **class** is free to overload any operator (including those overloaded by the base **class**) it chooses relative to itself.

There are some restrictions that apply to operator overloading. You cannot alter the precedence of an operator. You cannot change the number of operands that an operator takes. (You can choose to ignore an operand, however.) Finally, these operators cannot be overloaded:

. : .* ?

As stated, technically you are free to perform any activity inside an **operator** function. For example, if you want to overload the + operator in such a way that it writes **I like C++** ten times to a disk file, you can do so. However, when you stray significantly from the default meaning of an operator, you run the risk of dangerously destructuring your program. For example, when someone reading your program sees a statement like **Ob1 + Ob2**, he or she expects something resembling addition to be taking place—not a disk access, for example. Therefore, before decoupling an overloaded operator from its default meaning, be sure that you have sufficient reason to do so. One good example where decoupling is successful is found in the way C++ overloads the **<<** and **>>** operators for I/O. Although the I/O operations have no relationship to bit shifting, these operators provide a visual "clue" as to their meaning relative to both I/O and bit shifting, and this decoupling works. In general, however, it is best to stay within the context of the default meaning of an operator when overloading it.

Before looking at some examples of overloading more exotic operators, such as the [] or **new** and **delete**, a short diversion that examines operator overloading using a **friend** function is in order.

Operator Overloading Using a friend

You can overload an operator relative to a **class** by using a **friend** function. Since a **friend** is not a member of the **class**, it does not have a **this** pointer. Therefore, an overloaded **friend operator** function is passed the operands explicitly. This means that a **friend** that overloads a binary operator has two parameters, and a **friend** that overloads a unary operator has one parameter.

In this program, the **operator+( )** function is made into a **friend:**

```cpp
#include "iostream.h"

class loc {
  int longitude, latitude;
public:
  loc() {}; // needed to construct temporaries
  loc(int lg, int lt) {
    longitude = lg;
    latitude = lt;
  }

  void show() {
    cout << longitude << " ";
    cout << latitude << "\n";
  }

  friend loc operator+(loc op1, loc op2);  // now a friend
  loc operator-(loc op2);
  loc operator=(loc op2);
  loc operator++();
};

// now, + is overloaded using friend function
loc operator+(loc op1, loc op2)
{
  loc temp;

  temp.longitude = op1.longitude + op2.longitude;
  temp.latitude = op1.latitude + op2.latitude;
  return temp;
}

loc loc::operator-(loc op2)
{
  loc temp;

  // notice order of operands
  temp.longitude = longitude - op2.longitude;
  temp.latitude = latitude - op2.latitude;
  return temp;
}

loc loc::operator=(loc op2)
{
  longitude = op2.longitude;
  latitude = op2.latitude;
  return *this; // i.e., return object that generated call
}

loc loc::operator++()
{
  longitude++;
```

```
    latitude++;
    return *this;
}

main()
{
    loc obl(10, 20), ob2( 5, 30);

    obl = obl + ob2;
    obl.show();

    return 0;
}
```

There are some restrictions that apply to **friend operator** functions. First, you may not overload the =, ( ), [], or −> operators by using a **friend** function. Second, as explained in the next section, when overloading the increment or decrement operators, you will need to use a reference parameter when using a **friend** function.

Using a friend to Overload + + or − −

If you want to use a **friend** function to overload the increment or decrement operators, you must pass the operand as a reference parameter. This is because **friend** functions do not have **this** pointers. Assuming that you stay true to the original meaning of the + + and − − operators, these operations imply the modification of the operand they operate upon. However, if you overload these operators by using a **friend**, then the operand is passed by value as a parameter. This means that a **friend operator** function has no way to modify the operand. Since the **friend operator** function is not passed a **this** pointer to the operand, but rather a copy of the operand, no changes made to that parameter affect the operand that generated the call. However, you can remedy this situation by specifying the parameter to the **friend operator** function as a reference parameter. This causes any changes made to the parameter inside the function to affect the operand that generated the call. For example, this program uses **friend** functions to overload the + + and − − operators relative to the **loc class**:

```
#include "iostream.h"

class loc {
    int longitude, latitude;
public:
    loc() {};
```

```
  loc(int lg, int lt) {
    longitude = lg;
    latitude = lt;
  }

  void show() {
    cout << longitude << " ";
    cout << latitude << "\n";
  }

  loc operator=(loc op2);
  friend loc operator++(loc &op);
  friend loc operator--(loc &op);
};

loc loc::operator=(loc op2)
{
  longitude = op2.longitude;
  latitude = op2.latitude;
  return *this; // i.e., return object that generated call
}

// now a friend - use a reference parameter
loc operator++(loc &op)
{
  op.longitude++;
  op.latitude++;
  return op;
}

// make op-- a friend - use reference
loc operator--(loc &op)
{
  op.longitude--;
  op.latitude--;
  return op;
}

main()
{
  loc ob1(10, 20), ob2;

  ob1.show();
  ob1++;
  ob1.show(); // displays 11 21

  ob2 = ob1++;
  ob2.show(); // displays 12 22

  ob2--;
  ob2.show(); // displays 11 21
  return 0;
}
```

friend operator Functions Add Flexibility

In many cases, whether you overload an operator by using a **friend** or a member function makes no functional difference. In those cases, to preserve the greatest degree of encapsulation, it is best to overload by using member functions. However, there is one situation in which overloading by using a **friend** increases the flexibility of an overloaded operator. Let's examine this case now.

As you know, when you overload a binary operator by using a member function, the object on the left side of the operator generates the call to the overloaded **operator** function. Further, a pointer to that object is passed in the **this** pointer. Now, assume some **class** called **C** that has addition of an object of that class to an integer defined via an overloaded member **operator** function. Given an object of that **class** called **Ob**, the following expression is valid:

Ob + 100 // valid

In this case, **Ob** generates the call to the overloaded + function, and the addition is performed. But what happens if the expression is written like this?

100 + Ob // invalid

In this case, it is the integer that appears on the left. Since an integer is a built-in type, no operation between an integer and an object of **Ob**'s type is defined. Therefore, the compiler will not compile this expression. As you can imagine, in some applications, having to always position the object on the left could be a significant burden and cause of frustration.

The solution to the preceding problem is to overload objects of type **C** for addition by using a **friend**, not a member, function. When this is done, both arguments are explicitly passed to the **operator** function. Therefore, to allow both *object + integer* and *integer + object*, simply overload the function twice — one version for each situation. Thus, when you overload an operator by using two **friend** functions, the object may appear on either the left or right side of the operator.

This program illustrates how **friend** functions are used to define an operation that involves an object and built-in type:

```
#include "iostream.h"

class loc {
  int longitude, latitude;
public:
  loc() {};
  loc(int lg, int lt) {
    longitude = lg;
    latitude = lt;
  }

  void show() {
    cout << longitude << " ";
    cout << latitude << "\n";
  }

  loc operator+(loc op2);
  friend loc operator+(loc op1, int op2);
  friend loc operator+(int op1, loc op2);
};

loc loc::operator+(loc op2)
{
  loc temp;

  temp.longitude = op2.longitude + longitude;
  temp.latitude = op2.latitude + latitude;
  return temp;
}

// + is overloaded for loc + int
loc operator+(loc op1, int op2)
{
  loc temp;

  temp.longitude = op1.longitude + op2;
  temp.latitude = op1.latitude + op2;
  return temp;
}
// + is overloaded for int + loc
loc operator+(int op1, loc op2)
{
  loc temp;

  temp.longitude = op1 + op2.longitude;
  temp.latitude = op1 + op2.latitude;
  return temp;
```

```
}

main()
{
  loc ob1(10, 20), ob2( 5, 30), ob3(7, 14);

  ob1.show();
  ob2.show();
  ob3.show();

  ob1 = ob2 + 10;  // both of these
  ob3 = 10 + ob2;  // are valid

  ob1.show();
  ob3.show();

  return 0;
}
```

Overloading new and delete

It is possible to overload **new** and **delete**. You might choose to do this if you want to use some special allocation method. For example, you may want allocation routines that automatically begin using a disk file as virtual memory when the heap has been exhausted. Whatever the reason, it is a very simple matter to overload these operators.

The skeletons for the functions that overload **new** and **delete** are shown here:

```
void *operator new(size_t size)
{
  // perform allocation
  return pointer_to_memory;
}

void operator delete(void *p)
{
  // free memory pointed to by p
}
```

The type **size_t** is defined as a type capable of containing the largest single piece of memory that can be allocated. **size_t** is an unsigned integer type. The parameter **size** will contain the number of bytes needed to hold the object being allocated. The overloaded **new** function must return a pointer to the memory that it allocates, or zero if an allocation error occurs. Beyond these constraints, the overloaded **new** function can do anything else you require.

The **delete** function receives a pointer to the region of memory to free. It then releases the previously allocated memory back to the system.

The **new** and **delete** operators may be overloaded globally so that all uses of these operators call your custom versions, or are relative to one or more **class**es. Let's begin with an example of overloading **new** and **delete** relative to a **class**. For the sake of simplicity, no new allocation scheme will be used. Instead, the overloaded functions will simply invoke **malloc( )** and **free( )**. (In your own application, you may, of course, implement any alternative allocation scheme you like.)

To overload the **new** and **delete** operators relative to a **class**, simply make the overloaded operator functions **class** members. For example, here the **new** and **delete** operators are overloaded relative to the **loc class**:

```
#include "iostream.h"
#include "stdlib.h"

class loc {
  int longitude, latitude;
public:
  loc() {};
  loc(int lg, int lt) {
    longitude = lg;
    latitude = lt;
  }

  void show() {
    cout << longitude << " ";
    cout << latitude << "\n";
  }

  void *operator new(size_t size);
  void operator delete(void *p);
};

// new overloaded relative to loc
void *loc::operator new(size_t size)
{
  cout << "In my new\n";
  return malloc(size);
}

// delete overloaded relative to loc
void loc::operator delete(void *p)
{
```

```
  cout << "In my delete\n";
  free(p);
}

main()
{
  loc *p1, *p2;

  p1 = new loc (10, 20);
  if(!p1) {
    cout << "Allocation error\n";
    exit(1);
  }
  p2 = new loc (-10, -20);
  if(!p2) {
    cout << "Allocation error\n";
    exit(1);
  }

  p1->show();
  p2->show();

  delete p1;
  delete p2;

  return 0;
}
```

You may overload **new** two or more different ways, but the first parameter must always be **size**. Other parameters may be used by you for other purposes relative to your application. However, **delete** may not be overloaded more than once for each class, and it is automatically a **static** member of any **class** that it is a part of. You may, however, add a second parameter to **delete** when it is overloaded relative to a **class**. The second parameter is of type **size_t** and indicates the size of the object to be freed. Most of the time, however, there is no need to do this.

When **new** and **delete** are overloaded relative to a specific **class**, the use of these operators on any other type of data causes the original **new** or **delete** to be employed. The overloaded operators are only applied to the types for which they are defined. This means that if you add this line to the **main( )**, the default **new** will be executed:

```
int *f = new float;  // uses default new
```

You can overload **new** and **delete** globally by overloading these operators outside of any **class** declaration. When **new** and **delete** are overloaded globally, C++'s default **new** and **delete** are ignored and the new operators are used for all allocation requests. Of course, if you have defined any versions of **new** and **delete** relative to one or more **classes**, then the **class**-specific versions are used when allocating objects of the **class** for which they are defined. In other words, when either **new** or **delete** is encountered, the compiler first checks to see whether they are defined relative to the **class** they are operating on. If so, those specific versions are used. If not, C++ uses the globally defined **new** and **delete**. If these have been overloaded, then the overloaded versions are used.

To see an example of overloading **new** and **delete** globally, examine this program:

```
#include "iostream.h"
#include "stdlib.h"

class loc {
  int longitude, latitude;
public:
  loc() {};
  loc(int lg, int lt) {
    longitude = lg;
    latitude = lt;
  }

  void show() {
    cout << longitude << " ";
    cout << latitude << "\n";
  }
};

void *operator new(size_t size)
{
  cout << "In my new\n";
  return malloc(size);
}

void operator delete(void *p)
{
  cout << "In my delete\n";
  free(p);
}

main()
{
  loc *p1, *p2;

  p1 = new loc (10, 20);
  if(!p1) {
    cout << "Allocation error\n";
    exit(1);
  }
  p2 = new loc (-10, -20);
```

```
if(!p2) {
  cout << "Allocation error\n";
  exit(1);
}

float *f = new float; // uses overloaded new, too
if(!f) {
  cout << "Allocation error\n";
  exit(1);
}

*f = 10.10;
cout << *f << "\n";

p1->show();
p2->show();

delete p1;
delete p2;
delete f;   // uses overloaded delete

return 0;
}
```

Run this program to prove to yourself that the built-in **new** and **delete** operators have, indeed, been overloaded.

When **delete** is overloaded globally, it has only one argument. Unlike **delete** overloaded as a **class** member, which can optionally take two arguments, the global **delete** may take only one.

Note: For Turbo C++ users, in version 1.0, when overloading **delete** globally, you must specify a second parameter of type **size_t**, which is completely ignored. For example, in the preceding program, the global **delete** should be declared like this:

```
void operator delete(void *p, size_t)
```

It is possible that this anomaly will be corrected in future versions of Turbo C++. The second parameter is not needed when overloading **delete** by using a member function.

Overloading Some Special Operators

C++ (and its predecessor, C) defines array subscripting, function calling, and dereferencing as operations. The operators that perform these functions are the [], ( ), and −>, respectively. These rather exotic operators may be overloaded in C++, opening up some very interesting uses.

One important restriction applies to overloading these three operators: They must be non-static member functions. They cannot be **friend**s.

Overloading [ ]

In C++, the [] is considered a binary operator when you are overloading it. Therefore, the general form of a member **operator[]( )** function is as shown here:

```
type class-name::operator[](int i)
{
    // ...
}
```

Technically, the parameter does not have to be of type **int**, but an **operator[]( )** function is typically used to provide array subscripting, and as such, an integer value is generally used.

Given an object called **O**, the expression

```
O[3]
```

translates into this call to the **operator[]( )** function:

```
operator[](3)
```

That is, the value of the expression within the subscripting operators is passed to the **operator[]( )** function in its explicit parameter. The **this** pointer will point to **O**, the object that generated the call.

In the following program, **atype** declares an array of three integers. Its constructor function initializes each member of the array to the specified values. The overloaded **operator[]( )** function returns the value of the array as indexed by the value of its parameter.

```
#include "iostream.h"

class atype {
  int a[3];
public:
  atype(int i, int j, int k) {
    a[0] = i;
    a[1] = j;
    a[2] = k;
  }
  int operator[](int i) {return a[i];}
};

main()
{
  atype ob(1, 2, 3);

  cout << ob[1];  // displays 2

  return 0;
}
```

You can design the **operator[]( )** function in such a way that the [] can be used on both the left and right sides of an assignment statement. To do this, simply specify the return value of **operator[]( )** to be a reference. The following program makes this change and shows its use:

```
#include "iostream.h"

class atype {
  int a[3];
public:
  atype(int i, int j, int k) {
    a[0] = i;
    a[1] = j;
    a[2] = k;
  }
  int &operator[](int i) {return a[i];}
};

main()
{
  atype ob(1, 2, 3);

  cout << ob[1];  // displays 2
  cout << " ";

  ob[1] = 25;  // [] on left of =

  cout << ob[1];  // now displays 25

  return 0;
}
```

Because **operator[]( )** now returns a reference to the array element indexed by **i**, it can be used on the left side of an assignment to modify an element of the array. (Of course, it may still be used on the right side as well.)

One advantage of being able to overload the [] operator is that it allows a means of implementing safe array indexing in C++. As you know, in C++, it is possible to overrun (or underrun) an array boundary at run time without generating a run-time error message.

However, if you create a **class** that contains the array, and allow access to that array only through the overloaded [] subscripting operator, then you can intercept an out-of-range index. For example, this program adds a range check to the preceding program and proves that it works:

```
// A safe array example.
#include "iostream.h"
#include "stdlib.h"

class atype {
  int a[3];
public:
  atype(int i, int j, int k) {
    a[0] = i;
    a[1] = j;
    a[2] = k;
  }
  int &operator[](int i);
};

// Provide range checking for atype.
int &atype::operator[](int i)
{
  if(i<0 || i> 2) {
    cout << "boundary error\n";
    exit(1);
  }
  return a[i];
}

main()
{
  atype ob(1, 2, 3);

  cout << ob[1];  // displays 2
  cout << " ";

  ob[1] = 25;  // [] appears on left
```

```
cout << ob[1];  // displays 25

ob[3] = 44; // generates runtime error, 3 out-of-range
return 0;
}
```

In this program, when the statement

```
ob[3] = 44;
```

executes, the boundary error is intercepted by **operator[]( )**, and the program is terminated before any damage can be done. (In actual practice, some sort of error-handling function would be called to deal with the out-of-range condition; the program would not have to terminate.)

Overloading ( )

When you overload the ( ) function call operator, you are not, per se, creating a new way to call a function. Rather, you are creating an **operator** function that can be passed an arbitrary number of parameters. Let's begin with an example. Given the overloaded **operator** function declaration

```
double operator(int a, float f, char *s);
```

and an object **O** of its **class,** then the statement

```
O(10, 23.34, "hi");
```

translates into this call to the **operator( )** function.

```
operator()(10, 23.34, "hi");
```

In general, when you overload the ( ) operator, you define the parameters that you want to pass to that function. When you use the ( ) operator in your program, the arguments you specify are copied to those parameters. As always, the object that generates the call (**O** in this example) is pointed to by the **this** pointer.

Here is an example of overloading ( ) relative to the **loc class**. It assigns the value of its two arguments to the longitude and latitude of the object it is applied to.

```
#include "iostream.h"

class loc {
  int longitude, latitude;
public:
  loc() {};
  loc(int lg, int lt) {
    longitude = lg;
    latitude = lt;
  }

  void show() {
    cout << longitude << " ";
    cout << latitude << "\n";
  }

  loc operator+(loc op2);
  loc operator()(int i, int j);
};

loc loc::operator()(int i, int j)
{
  longitude = i;
  latitude = j;
  return *this;
}

loc loc::operator+(loc op2)
{
  loc temp;

  temp.longitude = op2.longitude + longitude;
  temp.latitude = op2.latitude + latitude;
  return temp;
}

main()
{
  loc ob1(10, 20), ob2(1, 1);

  ob1.show();
  ob1(7, 8);  // can be executed by itself
  ob1.show();

  ob1 = ob2 + ob1(10, 10);  // can be used in expressions
  ob1.show();

  return 0;
}
```

Remember, like overloading any other **operator** function, when overloading ( ), you can use any type of parameters and return any type of value. These types will be dictated by the demands of your programs.

Overloading −>

The −> pointer operator is considered a unary operator when overloading. Its general usage is shown here:

> *object* − > *element*;

Here, *object* is the object that activates the call. The **operator−>( )** function must return a pointer or reference to an object of the **class** that **operator−>( )** operates upon. The *element* must be some element accessible within the object pointed to.

The following program illustrates overloading the −> by showing the equivalence between **ob.i** and **ob−>i** when **operator−>( )** returns the **this** pointer:

```
#include "iostream.h"

class myclass {
public:
  int i;
  myclass *operator->() {return this;}
};

main()
{
  myclass ob;

  ob->i = 10;   // same as ob.i

  cout << ob.i << " " << ob->i;
}
```

Overloading the Comma Operator

You can overload C++'s comma operator. The comma is a binary operator, and like all overloaded operators, you may make an overloaded comma perform any operation you want. However, if you want the overloaded comma to perform in a fashion similar to its normal operation, the overloaded comma must discard the value of the left-hand operand and make the right-hand operand the value of the comma operation. In a comma-separated list, all but the rightmost operand must be discarded. As you know, this is the way the comma works by default in C++.

Here is a program that illustrates the effect of overloading the comma operator in its default manner of operation:

```cpp
#include "iostream.h"

class loc {
  int longitude, latitude;
public:
  loc() {};
  loc(int lg, int lt) {
    longitude = lg;
    latitude = lt;
  }

  void show() {
    cout << longitude << " ";
    cout << latitude << "\n";
  }

  loc operator+(loc op2);
  loc operator,(loc op2);
};

loc loc::operator,(loc op2)
{
  loc temp;

  temp.longitude = op2.longitude;
  temp.latitude = op2.latitude;
  cout << op2.longitude << " " << op2.latitude << "\n";
  return temp;
}

loc loc::operator+(loc op2)
{
  loc temp;

  temp.longitude = op2.longitude + longitude;
  temp.latitude = op2.latitude + latitude;
  return temp;
}

main()
{
```

```
loc ob1(10, 20), ob2( 5, 30), ob3(1, 1);

ob1.show();
ob2.show();
ob3.show();
cout << "\n";

ob1 = (ob1, ob2+ob2, ob3);

ob1.show();  // displays 1 1, the value of ob3
return 0;
}
```

This program displays the following output:

```
10 20
5 30
1 1

10 60
1 1
1 1
```

Notice that although the values of the left-hand operands are discarded, each expression is still executed by the compiler so that any desired side effects will be performed.

Remember, the left-hand operand is passed via **this**, and its value is discarded by the **operator,( )** function. The value of the right-hand operation is returned by the function. This causes the overloaded comma to behave similarly to its default operation. If you want the overloaded comma to do something else, you will have to change these two features.

Inheritance

Inheritance is one of the cornerstones of OOP because it allows the creation of hierarchical classifications. Using inheritance, you can create a general class that defines traits common to a set of related items. This class may then be inherited by other more specific classes, each adding only those things that are unique to the inheriting class.

In keeping with standard C++ terminology, a class that is inherited is referred to as a *base class*. The class that does the inheriting is called the *derived class*. Further, a derived class can be used as a base class for another derived class. In this way, multiple inheritance is achieved.

C++'s support of inheritance is both rich and flexible. Inheritance was introduced in Chapter 11, "An Overview of C++." It is examined in detail here.

Base Class Access Control

As you know, when a **class** inherits another, it uses this general form:

```
class derived-class-name : access base-class-name {
    // body of class
};
```

When one **class** inherits another, the members of the base class become members of the derived class. The access status of the base class members inside the derived class is determined by *access*. The base class access-specifier must be either **public** or **private**. If neither is specified, the access-specifier is **private** by default if the derived class is a **class**. If the derived class is a **struct**, then **public** is the default in the absence of an explicit access-specifier. Let's examine the ramifications of using **public** or **private** access.

When the access-specifier for a base class is **public**, all **public** members of the base become **public** members of the derived class, and all **protected** members of the base become **protected** members of the derived class. In all cases, the base's **private** elements remain private to the base and are not accessible by members of the derived class. For example, as illustrated in this program, objects of type **derived** can directly access the **public** members of **base**:

```
#include "iostream.h"

class base {
  int i, j;
public:
  void set(int a, int b) {i=a; j=b;}
  void show() { cout << i << " " << j << "\n";}
};

class derived : public base {
  int k;
public:
  derived(int x) {k=x;}
  void showk() {cout << k << "\n";}
};

main()
{
  derived ob(3);

  ob.set(1, 2); // access member of base
  ob.show();  // access member of base

  ob.showk(); // uses member of derived class

  return 0;
}
```

When the base class is inherited by using the **private** access-specifier, all **public** and **protected** members of the base class become **private** members of the derived class. For example, this program will not even compile because both **set( )** and **show( )** are now **private** elements of **derived**:

```
// This program won't compile.
#include "iostream.h"

class base {
  int i, j;
public:
  void set(int a, int b) {i=a; j=b;}
  void show() { cout << i << " " << j << "\n";}
};

// Public elements of base are private in derived.
class derived : private base {
  int k;
public:
  derived(int x) {k=x;}
  void showk() {cout << k << "\n";}
};

main()
{
  derived ob(3);

  ob.set(1, 2); // error, can't access set()
  ob.show(); // error, can't access show()

  return 0;
}
```

Remember that when a base class' access specifier is **private, public** and **protected** members of the base become **private** members of the derived class. This means that they are still accessible by members of the derived class but cannot be accessed by parts of your program that are not members of either the base or derived class.

Inheritance and protected Members

The **protected** keyword is included in C++ to provide greater flexibility to the inheritance mechanism. In this section you will see why.

When a member of a class is declared as **protected**, that member is not accessible by other, nonmember, elements of the program. With one important exception, access to a **protected** member is the same as access to a **private** member—it can be accessed only by other members of the class that it is a part of. The sole exception to this is when a **protected** member is inherited. In this case, a **protected** member differs substantially from a **private** one.

As you know from the preceding section, a **private** member of a base class is inaccessible by any derived **class**. However, if the base class is inherited as **public**, then the base class' **protected** members remain **protected** members of the derived class and *are* accessible by the derived class. Therefore, by using **protected**, you can create class members that are private to their class but that can still be inherited and accessed by a derived class. Here is an example:

```
#include "iostream.h"

class base {
protected:
  int i, j; // private to base, but accessible by derived
public:
  void set(int a, int b) {i=a; j=b;}
  void show() { cout << i << " " << j << "\n";}
};

class derived : public base {
  int k;
public:
  // derived may access bases i and j
  void setk() {k=i*j;}

  void showk() {cout << k << "\n";}
};

main()
{
  derived ob;

  ob.set(2, 3);  // OK, known to derived
  ob.show(); // OK, known to derived

  ob.setk();
  ob.showk();
  return 0;
}
```

In this example, because **base** is inherited by **derived** as **public** and because **i** and **j** are declared as **protected**, **derived**'s function **setk( )** may access them. If **i** and **j** had been declared as **private** by **base**, then **derived** would not have access to them, and the program would not compile.

When a derived class is used as a base class for another derived class, then any **protected** member of the initial base class that is inherited (as **public**) by the first derived class may also be inherited as **protected** again by a second derived class. For example, this program is correct, and **derived2** does, indeed, have access to **i** and **j**.

```
#include "iostream.h"

class base {
protected:
  int i, j;
public:
  void set(int a, int b) {i=a; j=b;}
  void show() { cout << i << " " << j << "\n";}
};

// i and j inherited as protected
class derived1 : public base {
  int k;
public:
  void setk() {k = i*j;} // legal
  void showk() {cout << k << "\n";}
};

// i and j inherited indirectly through derived1
class derived2 : public derived1 {
  int m;
public:
  void setm() {m = i-j;} // legal
  void showm() {cout << m << "\n";}
};

main()
{
  derived1 ob1;
  derived2 ob2;

  ob1.set(2, 3);
  ob1.show();
  ob1.setk();
  ob1.showk();

  ob2.set(3, 4);
  ob2.show();
  ob2.setk();
  ob2.setm();
  ob2.showk();
  ob2.showm();

  return 0;
}
```

If, however, **base** was inherited as **private**, then all members of **base** become **private** members of **derived1**, which means that they would not be accessible by **derived2**. (However, **i** and **j** would still be accessible by **derived1**). This situation is illustrated by the following program, which is in error (and won't compile). The comments describe each error:

```
// This program won't compile.

#include "iostream.h"

class base {
protected:
  int i, j;
public:
  void set(int a, int b) {i=a; j=b;}
  void show() { cout << i << " " << j << "\n";}
};

// Now, all elements of base are private in derived1.
class derived1 : private base {
  int k;
public:
  // this is legal because i and j are private to derived1
  void setk() {k = i*j;}   // OK
  void showk() {cout << k << "\n";}
};

// Access to i, j, set(), and show() not inherited.
class derived2 : public derived1 {
  int m;
public:
  // illegal because i and j are private to derived1
  void setm() {m = i-j;}   // error
  void showm() {cout << m << "\n";}
};

main()
{
  derived1 ob1;
  derived2 ob2;

  ob1.set(1, 2);  // error, can't use set()
  ob1.show();  // error, can't use show()

  ob2.set(3, 4);  // error, can't use set()
  ob2.show();  // error, can't use show()

  return 0;
}
```

Note: Even though **base** is inherited as **private** by **derived1**, **derived1** still has access to **base**'s **public** and **protected** elements. However, it cannot pass along this privilege.

Inheriting Multiple Base Classes

It is possible for a derived class to inherit two or more base classes. For example, in this short example, **derived** inherits both **base1** and **base2**.

```
// An example of multiple base classes.

#include "iostream.h"

class base1 {
protected:
  int x;
public:
  void showx() {cout << x << "\n";}
};

class base2 {
protected:
  int y;
public:
  void showy() {cout << y << "\n";}
};

// Inherit multiple base classes.
class derived: public base1, public base2 {
public:
  void set(int i, int j) {x=i; y=j;}
};

main()
{
  derived ob;

  ob.set(10, 20); // provided by derived
  ob.showx();  // from base1
  ob.showy();  // from base2

  return 0;
}
```

As the example illustrates, to inherit more than one base class, use a comma-separated list. Further, be sure to use an access-specifier for each base inherited.

Constructors, Destructors, and Inheritance

There are two major questions that arise relative to constructors and destructors when inheritance is involved. First, when are base class and derived class constructor and destructor functions called? Second, how can parameters be passed to base class constructor functions? This section examines these two important topics.

When Constructor and Destructor Functions Are Executed

It is possible for a base class, a derived class, or both to contain constructor and/or destructor functions. It is important to understand the order in which these functions are executed when an object of a derived class comes into existence and when it goes out of existence. To begin, examine this short program:

```
#include "iostream.h"

class base {
public:
  base() {cout << "Constructing base\n";}
  ~base() {cout << "Destructing base\n";}
};

class derived: public base {
public:
  derived() {cout << "Constructing derived\n";}
  ~derived() {cout << "Destructing derived\n";}
};

main()
{
  derived ob;

  // do nothing but construct and destruct ob

  return 0;
}
```

As the comment in **main( )** indicates, this program simply constructs and then destroys an object called **ob** that is of class **derived**. When executed, this program displays

```
Constructing base
Constructing derived
Destructing derived
Destructing base
```

As you can see, first **base**'s constructor is executed followed by **derived**'s. Next (because **ob** is immediately destroyed in this program), **derived**'s destructor is called, followed by **base**'s.

The results of the foregoing experiment can be generalized. When an object of a derived class is created, if the base class contains a constructor, it will be called first, followed by the derived class' constructor. When a derived object is destroyed, its destructor is called first, followed by the base class' destructor, if it exists. Put differently, constructor functions are executed in their order of derivation. Destructor functions are executed in reverse order of derivation.

If you think about it, it makes sense that constructor functions are executed in order of derivation. Because a base class has no knowledge of any derived class, any initialization it needs to perform is separate from and possibly prerequisite to any initialization performed by the derived class. Therefore, it must be executed first.

Likewise, it is quite sensible that destructors be executed in reverse order of derivation. Because the base class underlies a derived class, the destruction of the base class implies the destruction of the derived class. Therefore, the derived destruction must be called before the object is fully destroyed.

In cases of multiple inheritance (that is, where a derived class becomes the base class for another derived class), the general rule applies: Constructors are called in order of derivation, destructors in reverse order. For example, this program

```
#include "iostream.h"

class base {
public:
  base() {cout << "Constructing base\n";}
  ~base() {cout << "Destructing base\n";}
};

class derived1 : public base {
public:
  derived1() {cout << "Constructing derived1\n";}
  ~derived1() {cout << "Destructing derived1\n";}
};

class derived2: public derived1 {
public:
  derived2() {cout << "Constructing derived2\n";}
  ~derived2() {cout << "Destructing derived2\n";}
};
```

```
main()
{
  derived2 ob;

  // construct and destruct ob

  return 0;
}
```

displays this output:

```
Constructing base
Constructing derived1
Constructing derived2
Destructing derived2
Destructing derived1
Destructing base
```

The same general rule applies in situations involving multiple base classes. For example, this program

```
#include "iostream.h"

class base1 {
public:
  base1() {cout << "Constructing base1\n";}
  ~base1() {cout << "Destructing base1\n";}
};

class base2 {
public:
  base2() {cout << "Constructing base2\n";}
  ~base2() {cout << "Destructing base2\n";}
};

class derived: public base1, public base2 {
public:
  derived() {cout << "Constructing derived\n";}
  ~derived() {cout << "Destructing derived\n";}
};

main()
{
  derived ob;

  // construct and destruct ob

  return 0;
}
```

produces this output:

```
Constructing base1
Constructing base2
Constructing derived
Destructing derived
Destructing base2
Destructing base1
```

As you can see, constructors are called in order of derivation—left to right—as specified in **derived**'s inheritance list. Destructors are called in reverse order—right to left. This means that had **base2** been specified before **base1** in **derived**'s list, as shown here:

```
class derived: public base2, public base1 {
```

then the output of this program would have looked like this:

```
Constructing base2
Constructing base1
Constructing derived
Destructing derived
Destructing base1
Destructing base2
```

Passing Parameters to Base Class Constructors

So far, none of the preceding examples have included constructor functions that require arguments. In cases where only the derived class's constructor requires one or more parameters, you simply use the standard parameterized constructor syntax (see Chapter 12, "Classes and Objects"). However, how do you pass arguments to a constructor function in a base class? The answer is to use an expanded form of the derived class's constructor declaration that passes along arguments to one or more base class constructors. The general form of this expanded derived class construction declaration is shown here:

$$derived\text{-}constructor(arg\text{-}list) : base1(arg\text{-}list),$$
$$base2(arg\text{-}list),$$

.

.

.

$$baseN(arg\text{-}list);$$

```
  {
    // body of derived constructor
  }
```

Here, *base1* through *baseN* are the names of the base classes inherited by the derived class. Notice that a colon separates the derived class's constructor function declaration from the base classes and that the base classes are separated from each other by commas, in the case of multiple base classes. Consider this program:

```
#include "iostream.h"

class base {
protected:
  int i;
public:
  base(int x) {i=x; cout << "Constructing base\n";}
  ~base() {cout << "Destructing base\n";}
};

class derived: public base {
  int j;
public:
  // derived uses x; y is passed along to base.
  derived(int x, int y): base(y)
    {j=x; cout << "Constructing derived\n";}

  ~derived() {cout << "Destructing derived\n";}
  void show() {cout << i << " " << j << "\n";}
};

main()
{
  derived ob(3, 4);

  ob.show();   // displays 4 3

  return 0;
}
```

Here, **derived**'s constructor is declared as taking two parameters, **x** and **y**. However, **derived( )** uses only **x**; **y** is passed along to **base( )**. In general, the derived class' constructor must declare both the parameter(s) that it requires as well as any required by the base class. As the example illustrates, any parameters required by the base class are passed to it in the base class' argument list specified after the colon.

Here is an example that uses multiple base classes:

```
#include "iostream.h"

class base1 {
protected:
  int i;
public:
  base1(int x) {i=x; cout << "Constructing base1\n";}
  ~base1() {cout << "Destructing base1\n";}
};

class base2 {
protected:
  int k;
public:
  base2(int x) {k=x; cout << "Constructing base2\n";}
  ~base2() {cout << "Destructing base1\n";}
};

class derived: public base1, public base2 {
  int j;
public:
  derived(int x, int y, int z): base1(y), base2(z)
    {j=x; cout << "Constructing derived\n";}

  ~derived() {cout << "Destructing derived\n";}
  void show() {cout << i << " " << j << " " << k << "\n";}
};

main()
{
  derived ob(3, 4, 5);

  ob.show();  // displays 4 3 5

  return 0;
}
```

It is important to understand that arguments to a base class constructor are passed via arguments to the derived class' constructor. Therefore, even if a derived class' constructor does not use any arguments, it will still need to declare one or more if the base class takes one or more arguments. In this situation, the arguments passed to the derived class are simply passed along to the base. For example, in this program, the derived class' constructor takes no arguments, but **base1( )** and **base2( )** do:

```
#include "iostream.h"

class base1 {
protected:
  int i;
```

```
public:
  base1(int x) {i=x; cout << "Constructing base1\n";}
  ~base1() {cout << "Destructing base1\n";}
};

class base2 {
protected:
  int k;
public:
  base2(int x) {k=x; cout << "Constructing base2\n";}
  ~base2() {cout << "Destructing base2\n";}
};

class derived: public base1, public base2 {
public:
  /* Derived constructor uses no parameter,
     but still must be declared as taking them to
     pass them along to base classes.
  */
  derived(int x, int y): base1(x), base2(y)
    {cout << "Constructing derived\n";}

  ~derived() {cout << "Destructing derived\n";}
  void show() {cout << i << " " << k << "\n";}
};

main()
{
  derived ob(3, 4);

  ob.show();  // displays 3 4

  return 0;
}
```

A derived class' constructor function is free to make use of any and all parameters that it is declared as taking even if one or more are passed along to a base class. Put differently, an argument that is passed along to a base class does not preclude its use by the derived class as well. For example, this fragment is perfectly valid:

```
class derived: public base {
  int j;
public:
  // derived uses both x and y and then passes them to base.
  derived(int x, int y): base(x, y)
    {j = x*y; cout << "Constructing derived\n";}
```

One final point to keep in mind when passing arguments to base class constructors: The argument can consist of any expression valid at the time. This includes function calls and variables. This is in keeping with the fact that C++ allows dynamic initialization.

Granting Access

When a base class is inherited as **private**, all members of that class (**public, protected,** or **private**) become private members of the derived class. However, in certain circumstances, you may want to restore one or more inherited members to their original access specification. For example, you might want to grant certain **public** members of the base class **public** status in the derived class even though the base class is inherited as **private**. To do this, you must use an *access declaration* within the derived class. An access declaration takes this general form:

base-class::member;

The access declaration is put under the appropriate access heading in the derived class. Notice that no type declaration is required (or, indeed, allowed) in an access declaration.

To see how an access declaration works, let's begin with this short fragment:

```
class base {
public:
  int j;  // public in base
};

// Inherit base as private.
class derived: private base {
public:

  // here is access declaration
  base::j; // make j public again
  .
  .
  .
};
```

As you know, because **base** is inherited as **private** by **derived**, the public variable **j** is made a private variable of **derived** by default. However, if

```
base::j;
```

is included as the access declaration under **derived**'s **public** heading, **j** is restored to its **public** status.

You can use an access declaration to restore the access rights of **public** and **protected** members. However, you cannot use an access declaration to raise or lower a member's access status. For example, a member declared as **private** to a base class cannot be made **public** by a derived class. (If C++ allowed this to occur, it would destroy its encapsulation mechanism!)

The following program illustrates the access declaration:

```
#include "iostream.h"

class base {
  int i; // private to base
public:
  int j, k;
  void seti(int x) {i = x;}
  int geti() {return i;}
};

// Inherit base as private.
class derived: private base {
public:
  // The next three statements override
  // base's inheritance as private
  // and restore j, seti(), and geti() to public access.
  base::j; // make j public again - but not k
  base::seti; // make seti() public
  base::geti; // make geti() public

// base::i;  // illegal, you cannot elevate access

  int a; // public
};

main()
{
  derived ob;

//ob.i = 10;  // illegal because i is private in derived

  ob.j = 20;  // legal because j is made public in derived
//ob.k = 30;  // illegal because k is private in derived

  ob.a = 40;  // legal because a is public in derived
  ob.seti(10);

  cout << ob.geti() << " " << ob.j << " " << ob.a;

  return 0;
}
```

Notice how this program uses access declarations to restore **j**, **seti( )**, and **geti( )** to **public** status.

Access declarations are supported in C++ to accommodate those situations in which most of an inherited class is intended to be made **private,** but a few members are to retain their **public** or **protected** status.

Virtual Base Classes

An element of ambiguity can be introduced into a C++ program when multiple base classes are inherited. For example, consider this incorrect program:

```
// This program contains an error and will not compile.
#include <iostream.h>

class base {
public:
  int i;
};

// derived1 inherits base.
class derived1 : public base {
public:
  int j;
};

// derived2 inherits base.
class derived2 : public base {
public:
  int k;
};

// derived3 inherits both derived1 and derived2.  This
// means that there are two copies of base in derived3!
class derived3 : public derived1, public derived2 {
public:
  int sum;
};

main(void)
{
  derived3 ob;

  ob.i = 10;   // this is ambiguous, which i???
  ob.j = 20;
```

```
  ob.k = 30;

  // i ambiguous here, too
  ob.sum = ob.i + ob.j + ob.k;

  // also ambiguous, which i?
  cout << ob.i << " ";

  cout << ob.j << " " << ob.k << " ";
  cout << ob.sum;

  return 0;
}
```

As the comments in the program indicate, both **derived1** and **derived2** inherit **base**. However, **derived3** inherits both **derived1** and **derived2**. This means that there are two copies of **base** present in an object of type **derived3**. Therefore, in an expression like

```
ob.i = 20;
```

which **i** is being referred to—the one in **derived1** or the one in **derived2**? Because there are two copies of **base** present in object **ob**, there are two **ob.i**'s! As you can see, the statement is inherently ambiguous.

There are two ways to remedy the preceding program. The first is to apply the scope resolution operator to **i** and manually select one **i**. For example, this version of the program does compile and run as expected:

```
// This program uses explicit scope resolution to select i.
#include <iostream.h>

class base {
public:
  int i;
};

// derived1 inherits base.
class derived1 : public base {
public:
  int j;
};

// derived2 inherits base.
class derived2 : public base {
public:
  int k;
};
```

```
// derived3 inherits both derived1 and derived2.  This means
// that there are two copies of base in derived3!
class derived3 : public derived1, public derived2 {
public:
  int sum;
};

main(void)
{
  derived3 ob;

  ob.derived1::i = 10;   // scope resolved, use derived1's i
  ob.j = 20;
  ob.k = 30;

  // scope resolved
  ob.sum = ob.derived1::i + ob.j + ob.k;

  // also resolved here
  cout << ob.derived1::i << " ";

  cout << ob.j << " " << ob.k << " ";
  cout << ob.sum;

  return 0;
}
```

As you can see, because the :: was applied, the program has manually selected **derived2**'s version of **base**. However, this solution raises a deeper issue: What if only one copy of **base** is actually required? Is there some way to prevent two copies from being included in **derived3**? The answer, as you probably have guessed, is yes. This solution is achieved using **virtual** base **class**es.

When two or more objects are derived from a common base **class**, you can prevent multiple copies of the base **class** from being present in an object derived from those objects by declaring the base **class** as **virtual** when it is inherited. You accomplish this by preceding the base class' name with the keyword **virtual** when it is inherited. For example, here is another version of the example program in which **derived3** contains only one copy of **base**:

```
// This program uses virtual base classes.
#include <iostream.h>

class base {
public:
  int i;
};
```

```
// derived1 inherits base as virtual.
class derived1 : virtual public base {
public:
  int j;
};

// derived2 inherits base as virtual.
class derived2 : virtual public base {
public:
  int k;
};

// derived3 inherits both derived1 and derived2.
// This time, there is only one copy of base class.
class derived3 : public derived1, public derived2 {
public:
  int sum;
};

main(void)
{
  derived3 ob;

  ob.i = 10;   // now unambiguous
  ob.j = 20;
  ob.k = 30;

  // unambiguous
  ob.sum = ob.i + ob.j + ob.k;

  // unambiguous
  cout << ob.i << " ";

  cout << ob.j << " " << ob.k << " ";
  cout << ob.sum;

  return 0;
}
```

As you can see, the keyword **virtual** precedes the rest of the inherited **class'** specification. Now that both **derived1** and **derived2** have inherited **base** as **virtual**, any multiple inheritance involving them will cause only one copy of **base** to be present. Therefore, in **derived3**, there is only one copy of **base**; therefore **ob.i = 10** is perfectly valid and unambiguous.

One further point to keep in mind: Even though both **derived1** and **derived2** specify **base** as **virtual, base** is still present in any objects of either type. For example, the following sequence is perfectly valid:

```
// define a class of type derived1
derived1 myclass;

myclass.i = 88;
```

The only difference between a normal base **class** and a **virtual** one is when an object inherits the base more than once. If **virtual** base **classes** are used, then only one base **class** is present in the object. Otherwise, multiple copies will be found.

Virtual Functions and Polymorphism

Virtual Functions
Pure Virtual Functions
Using Virtual Functions
Early Versus Late Binding

Polymorphism (one interface, multiple methods) is supported by C++ both at compile time and at run time. Compile-time polymorphism, supported by overloaded functions and operators, was discussed in Chapter 11. Run-time polymorphism is accomplished by using inheritance and virtual functions, and these are the topics of this chapter.

Virtual Functions

A *virtual function* is a function that is declared as **virtual** in a base class and redefined by a derived class. To declare a function as virtual, its declaration is preceded by the keyword **virtual**. The redefinition of the function in the derived class overrides the definition of the function in the base class. In essence, the virtual function declared in the base class acts to a large extent as a placeholder that specifies a general class of action and stipulates the interface. The redefinition of the virtual function by a derived class specifies the actual operations performed by the function (the method).

When accessed "normally," virtual functions behave just like any other type of class member function. However, what makes virtual functions important and capable of supporting run-time polymorphism is how they behave when accessed via a pointer. As you know, a base class pointer can be used to point to any class derived from that base. When a base pointer points to a derived object that contains a virtual function, C++ determines which version of that function to call based upon *the type of object pointed to* by the pointer. Thus, when different objects are pointed to, different versions of the virtual function are executed.

Before discussing any more theory, examine this short example:

```cpp
#include "iostream.h"

class base {
public:
  virtual void vfunc() {
    cout << "This is base's vfunc()\n";
  }
};

class derived1 : public base {
public:
  void vfunc() {
    cout << "This is derived1's vfunc()\n";
  }
};

class derived2 : public base {
public:
  void vfunc() {
    cout << "This is derived2's vfunc()\n";
  }
};

main()
{
  base *p, b;
  derived1 d1;
  derived2 d2;

  // point to base
  p = &b;
  p->vfunc(); // access base's vfunc()

  // point to derived1
  p = &d1;
  p->vfunc(); // access derived1's vfunc()

  // point to derived2
  p = &d2;
  p->vfunc(); // access derived2's vfunc()

  return 0;
}
```

This programs displays the following.

```
This is base's vfunc( )
This is derived1's vfunc( )
This is derived2's vfunc( )
```

As the program illustrates, inside **base**, the virtual function **vfunc( )** is declared. Notice that the keyword **virtual** precedes the rest of the function declaration. When **vfunc( )** is redefined by **derived1** and **derived2**, the keyword **virtual** is not needed. (However, it is not an error to include it when redefining a virtual function inside a derived class.)

In this program, **base** is inherited by both **derived1** and **derived2**. Inside each class definition, **vfunc( )** is redefined relative to that class. Inside **main( )**, four variables are declared:

Name	Type
p	base class pointer
b	object of base
d1	object of derived1
d2	object of derived2

Next, **p** is assigned the address of **b** and **vfunc( )** is called via **p**. Since **p** is pointing to an object of type **base**, that version of **vfunc( )** is executed. Next, **p** is set to the address of **d1**, and again **vfunc( )** is called by using **p**. This time **p** points to an object of type **derived1**. This causes **derived1::vfunc( )** to be executed. Finally, **p** is assigned the address of **d2** and **p−>vfunc( )** causes the version of **vfunc( )** redefined inside **derived2** to be executed. The key point here is that the kind of object to which **p** points determines which version of **vfunc( )** is executed. Further, this determination is made at run time, and this process forms the basis for run-time polymorphism.

Note: Although you can call a virtual function in the "normal" manner by using an object's name and the dot operator, it is only when access is through a base class pointer that run-time polymorphism is achieved. For example, assuming the preceding example, this is syntactically valid:

```
d2.vfunc(); // calls derived2's vfunc()
```

Although calling a virtual function in this manner is not wrong, it simply does not take advantage of the virtual nature of **vfunc( )**.

The redefinition of a virtual function by a derived class is similar to function overloading. However, this term is not applied to virtual function redefinition because several differences exist. Perhaps the most important is that the prototype for a redefined virtual function must match exactly the prototype specified in the base class. This differs from overloading a normal function, in which return types and the number and type of parameters may differ. (In fact, when you overload a function, either the number or the type of the parameters *must* differ! It is through these differences that C++ can select the correct version of an overloaded function.) However, when a virtual function is redefined, all aspects of its prototype must be the same. If you change the prototype when you attempt to redefine a virtual function, the function will simply be considered overloaded by the C++ compiler, and its virtual nature will be lost. Another important restriction is that virtual functions must be members of classes they are part of. They cannot be **friend**s. Finally, constructor functions cannot be virtual, but destructor functions can.

Because of the restrictions and differences between function over-loading and virtual function redefinition, the term *overriding* is used to describe virtual function redefinition by a derived class.

The Virtual Attribute Is Inherited

When a virtual function is inherited, its virtual nature is also inherited. This means that when a derived class that inherits a virtual function from a base class is, itself, used as a base class for another derived class, the virtual function can still be overridden. Put differently, no matter how many times a virtual function is inherited, it remains virtual. For example, consider this variation on the preceding program:

```
#include "iostream.h"

class base {
public:
  virtual void vfunc() {
    cout << "This is base's vfunc()\n";
  }
};

class derived1 : public base {
public:
  void vfunc() {
    cout << "This is derived1's vfunc()\n";
  }
};

// derived2 inherits virtual function vfunc()
// from derived1.
```

```
class derived2 : public derived1 {
public:
  // vfunc() is still virtual
  void vfunc() {
    cout << "This is derived2's vfunc()\n";
  }
};

main()
{
  base *p, b;
  derived1 d1;
  derived2 d2;

  // point to base
  p = &b;
  p->vfunc(); // access base's vfunc()

  // point to derived1
  p = &d1;
  p->vfunc(); // access derived1's vfunc()

  // point to derived2
  p = &d2;
  p->vfunc(); // access derived2's vfunc()

  return 0;
}
```

As expected, the preceding program displays this output:

```
This is base's vfunc( )
This is derived1's vfunc( )
This is derived2's vfunc( )
```

Virtual Functions Are Hierarchical

As you know, when a function is declared as **virtual** by a base class, it may be overridden by a derived class. However, the function does not have to be overridden. When a derived class fails to override a virtual function, then when an object of that derived class accesses that function, the function defined by the base class is used. For example, consider this program:

```
#include "iostream.h"

class base {
public:
```

```
   virtual void vfunc() {
     cout << "This is base's vfunc()\n";
   }
};

class derived1 : public base {
public:
   void vfunc() {
     cout << "This is derived1's vfunc()\n";
   }
};

class derived2 : public base {
public:
// vfunc() not overridden by derived2, base's is used
};

main()
{
  base *p, b;
  derived1 d1;
  derived2 d2;

  // point to base
  p = &b;
  p->vfunc(); // access base's vfunc()

  // point to derived1
  p = &d1;
  p->vfunc(); // access derived1's vfunc()

  // point to derived2
  p = &d2;
  p->vfunc(); // use base's vfunc()

  return 0;
}
```

The preceding program produces this output:

> This is base's vfunc( )
> This is derived1's vfunc( )
> This is base's vfunc( )

Because **derived2** does not override **vfunc( )**, the function defined by
base is used when **vfunc( )** is referenced relative to objects of type
derived2.

The preceding program illustrates a special case of a more general
rule. Because inheritance is hierarchical in C++, it makes sense that

virtual functions are also hierarchical. This means that when a derived class fails to override a virtual function, then the one used will be the first one found in reverse order of derivation. For example, in the following program, **derived2** is derived from **derived1**, which is derived from **base**. However, **derived2** does not override **vfunc( )**. Because, relative to **derived2**, the closest version of **vfunc( )** is in **derived1**, this version of the function is used when an object of **derived2** attempts to access **vfunc( )**.

```
#include "iostream.h"

class base {
public:
  virtual void vfunc() {
    cout << "This is base's vfunc()\n";
  }
};

class derived1 : public base {
public:
  void vfunc() {
    cout << "This is derived1's vfunc()\n";
  }
};

class derived2 : public derived1 {
public:
/* vfunc() not overridden by derived2.
   In this case, since derived2 is derived from
   derived1, derived1's vfunc() is used.
*/
};

main()
{
  base *p, b;
  derived1 d1;
  derived2 d2;

  // point to base
  p = &b;
  p->vfunc(); // access base's vfunc()

  // point to derived1
  p = &d1;
  p->vfunc(); // access derived1's vfunc()

  // point to derived2
  p = &d2;
  p->vfunc(); // use derived1's vfunc()

  return 0;
}
```

The preceding program displays the following:

This is base's vfunc( )
This is derived1's vfunc( )
This is derived1's vfunc( )

Pure Virtual Functions

As the examples in the preceding section illustrate, when a virtual function is not redefined by a derived class, the version defined in the base class will be used. However, in many situations there can be no meaningful definition of a virtual function within a base class. For example, a base class may not be able to define an object sufficiently to allow a base class virtual function to be created. Further, in some situations you will want to ensure that all derived classes override a virtual function. To handle these two cases, C++ supports the pure virtual function.

A *pure virtual function* is a virtual function that has no definition within the base class. To declare a pure virtual function, use this general form:

virtual type func _ name(parameter-list) = 0;

When a virtual function is made pure, any derived class must provide its own definition. If the derived class fails to override the pure virtual function, a compile-time error will result.

The following program contains a simple example of a pure virtual function. The base type, **number,** contains an integer called **val,** the function **setval( ),** and the pure virtual function **show( ).** The derived classes **hextype, dectype,** and **octtype** inherit **number** and redefine **show( )** so that it outputs the value of **val** in each respective number base (that is, hexadecimal, decimal, or octal).

```
#include "iostream.h"

class number {
protected:
```

```
   int val;
public:
   void setval(int i) {val = i;}

   // show() is a pure virtual function
   virtual void show() = 0;
};

class hextype : public number {
public:
   void show() {
      cout << hex << val << "\n";
   }
};

class dectype : public number {
public:
   void show() {
      cout << val << "\n";
   }
};

class octtype : public number {
public:
   void show() {
      cout << oct << val << "\n";
   }
};

main()
{
   dectype d;
   hextype h;
   octtype o;

   d.setval(20);
   d.show();  // displays 20 - decimal

   h.setval(20);
   h.show();  // displays 14 - hexadecimal

   o.setval(20);
   o.show();  // displays 24 - octal

   return 0;
}
```

Although this example is quite simple, it illustrates how a base class may not be able to meaningfully define a virtual function. In this case, **number** simply provides the common interface for the derived types to use. However, relative to this example, there is no reason to define **show( )** inside **number** because the point of the derived classes is to display a number in various number bases. Of course, you can always create an arbitrary definition of a virtual function. However, making **show( )** pure also ensures that all derived classes will, indeed, redefine it relative to their own needs.

Keep in mind that when a virtual function is declared as pure, all derived classes must override it. If a derived class fails to do this, a compile-time error will result.

Abstract Classes

A class that contains at lease one pure virtual function is said to be *abstract*. Because an abstract class contains one or more functions for which there is no definition (that is, a pure virtual function), no objects may be created by using an abstract class. Instead, an abstract class constitutes an incomplete type that is used as a foundation for derived classes.

Although you cannot create objects of an abstract class, you can create pointers to an abstract class. This allows abstract classes to support run-time polymorphism, which relies upon base class pointers to select the proper virtual function.

Using Virtual Functions

As has been mentioned, one of the central aspects of object-oriented programming is the principle of "one interface, multiple methods." This means that a general class of actions can be defined, the interface to which is constant, with each specific instance of that general class defining the actual operations relative to each specific situation. In concrete C++ terms, a base class can be used to define the nature of the interface to a general class. Each derived class then implements the specific operations as they relate to the type of data used by the derived type.

One of the most powerful and flexible ways to implement the "one interface, multiple methods" approach is to use virtual functions, abstract classes, and run-time polymorphism. Using these features, you create a class hierarchy that moves from general to specific (base to derived). Following this philosophy, you define all common features and interfaces in a base class. In cases where certain actions can be implemented only by the derived class, you use a virtual function to define the interface that will be used by the derived class or classes. In essence, in the base class you create and define everything you can that relates to the general case. The derived class fills in the specific details.

Following is a simple example that illustrates the value of the "one interface, multiple methods" philosophy. A class hierarchy is created that performs conversions from one type of unit to another. The base class **convert** declares two variables, **val1** and **val2**, which hold the initial and converted values, respectively. It also defines the functions **getinit( )** and **getconv( )**, which return the initial value and the converted value. These elements of **convert** are fixed and applicable to all derived classes that will inherit **convert**. However, the function that will actually perform the conversion is a pure virtual function because it can be defined only by classes derived from **convert**.

```
// Virtual function practical example.
#include "iostream.h"

class convert {
protected:
  double val1;   // initial value
  double val2;   // converted value
public:
  convert(double i) {
    val1 = i;
  }
  double getconv() {return val2;}
  double getinit() {return val1;}

  virtual void compute() = 0;
};

// Liters to gallons.
class l_to_g : public convert {
public:
  l_to_g(double i) : convert(i) { }
```

```
  void compute() {
    val2 = val1 / 3.7854;
  }
};

// Fahrenheit to Celsius
class f_to_c : public convert {
public:
  f_to_c(double i) : convert(i) { }
  void compute() {
    val2 = (val1-32) / 1.8;
  }
};

main()
{
  convert *p;  // pointer to base class

  l_to_g lgob(4);
  f_to_c fcob(70);

  // use virtual function mechanism to convert
  p = &lgob;
  cout << p->getinit() << " liters is ";
  p->compute();
  cout << p->getconv() << " gallons\n";  // l_to_g

  p = &fcob;
  cout << p->getinit() << " in Fahrenheit is ";
  p->compute();
  cout << p->getconv() << " Celsius\n";  // f_to_c

  return 0;
}
```

The preceding program creates two derived classes from **convert**, called **l_to_g** and **f_to_c**. These classes perform the conversions of liters to gallons and Fahrenheit to Celsius, respectively. As you can see, each derived class overrides **compute( )** in its own way to perform the desired conversion. However, even though the actual conversion (that is, method) differs between **l_to_g** and **f_to_c**, the interface remains constant.

One of the values of derived classes and virtual functions is that adding a new specific class is a very easy matter. For example, assuming the preceding program, you can add a conversion from feet to meters by including this class:

```
// Feet to meters
class f_to_m : public convert {
public:
```

```
  f_to_m(double i) : convert(i) { }
  void compute() {
    val2 = val1 / 3.28;
  }
};
```

An important use of abstract classes and virtual functions is in *class libraries.* You can create a generic, extensible class library that will be used by other programmers. Another programmer will inherit your general class, which defines the interface and all elements common to all classes derived from it, and will simply define those functions specific to the derived class. By creating class libraries, you are able to create and control the interface of a general class while still letting other programmers adapt it to their specific situations.

One final point: The base class **convert** is an example of an incomplete type. The virtual function **compute( )** is not defined within **convert** because no meaningful definition can be provided. The class **convert** simply does not contain sufficient information for **compute( )** to be defined. It is only when **convert** is inherited by a derived class that a complete type is created.

Early Versus Late Binding

Before concluding this chapter on virtual functions and run-time polymorphism, there are two terms that need to be defined because they are used frequently in discussions of C++ and object-oriented programming. The terms are *early binding* and *late binding.*

Early binding refers to events that occur at compile time. In essence, early binding means that all information needed to call a function is known at compile time. (Put differently, early binding means that an object and a function call are bound during compilation.) Examples of early binding include normal function calls (including standard library functions), overloaded function calls, and overloaded operators. The main advantage to early binding is efficiency. Because all information necessary to call a function is determined at compile time, these types of function calls are very fast.

The opposite of early binding is *late binding*. As it relates to C++, late binding refers to function calls that are not resolved until run time. Virtual functions are used to achieve late binding. As you know, when access is via a base pointer, the actual virtual function called is determined by the type of object pointed to by the pointer. Because in most cases this cannot be determined at compile time, the object and the function are not linked until run time. The main advantage to late binding is flexibility. Unlike early binding, late binding allows you to create programs that can respond to events occurring while the program executes without having to create a large amount of "contingency code." Keep in mind that because a function call is not resolved until run time, late binding can make for somewhat slower execution times.

SEVENTEEN

The C++ I/O System Basics

C++ Streams
The Basic Stream Classes
Formatted I/O
Overloading << and >>
Creating Your Own Manipulator Functions
A Short Note About the Old Stream Class Library

In addition to supporting all of C's I/O system, C++ defines its own, object-oriented I/O system. Also like C's I/O system, C++'s I/O system is fully integrated. That is, the different aspects of C++'s I/O system, such as console I/O and disk I/O, are actually just different perspectives on the same mechanism. This chapter discusses the foundations of the C++ object-oriented I/O system. Although the examples in this chapter use "console" I/O, the information is applicable to other devices, including disk files (discussed in Chapter 18, "C++ File I/O").

As you know, C's I/O system is extremely rich, flexible, and powerful. You might be wondering why C++ defines yet another system. The answer is that C's I/O system knows nothing about objects. Therefore, for C++ to provide complete support for object-oriented programming, it was necessary to create an object-oriented I/O system that could operate on user-defined objects. In addition to support for objects, there are some side benefits to using C++'s I/O system even in programs that don't make extensive (or any) use of user-defined objects. You will see some examples later in this chapter.

In this chapter you will learn how to format data. You will learn how to overload C++'s << and >> I/O operators so they can be used with classes that you create. You will also see how to create special I/O functions called manipulators that can make your programs more efficient.

C++ Streams

Like C's I/O system, the C++ I/O system operates through streams. Streams were discussed in detail in Chapter 9, "ANSI C Standard File I/O"; that discussion will not be repeated here. However, to summarize: A stream is a logical device that either produces or consumes information. A stream is linked to a physical device by the C++ I/O system. All streams behave in the same way even though the actual physical devices they are connected to may differ substantially. Because all streams behave the same, the same C++ I/O functions can operate on virtually any type of physical device. For example, you can use the same function that writes to a file to write to the printer or to the screen. The advantage to this approach is that you need learn only one interface.

The Basic Stream Classes

C++ provides support for its I/O in the header file **iostream.h**. In this file, a class hierarchy is defined that supports I/O operations. The lowest-level class is called **streambuf**. This class provides the basic input and output operations. It is used primarily as a base class for other classes. (Unless you are deriving your own I/O classes, you will not use **streambuf** directly.) The class **ios** is next in the hierarchy. It provides formatting, error-checking, and status information. From **ios** are derived the classes **istream**, **ostream**, and **iostream**. These classes are used to create streams capable of input, output, and input/output, respectively. As you will see in subsequent chapters, other classes are derived from **ios** to support disk files and in-RAM formatting.

The **ios** class contains many member functions and variables that control or monitor the fundamental operation of a stream. In the course of this and the next chapter, many references will be made to its members. Just keep in mind that if you are using the C++ I/O system in a normal fashion, the members of **ios** will be available for use with any stream.

C++'s Predefined Streams

When a C++ program begins execution, four built-in streams are automatically opened. They are

Stream	Meaning	Default Device
Cin	Standard input	Keyboard
Cout	Standard output	Screen
Cerr	Standard error output	Screen
Clog	Buffered version of cerr	Screen

Streams **cin**, **cout**, and **cerr** correspond to C's **stdin**, **stdout**, and **stderr**.

By default, the standard streams are used to communicate with the console. However, in environments that support I/O redirection (such as DOS, UNIX, and OS/2), the standard streams can be redirected to other devices or files. However, for sake of simplicity, the examples in this chapter assume that no I/O redirection has occurred.

Formatted I/O

The C++ I/O system allows you to format I/O operations. For example, you can set a field width, specify a number base, or determine how many digits after the decimal point will be displayed. In essence, any format that you can output or input by using C's **printf( )** and **scanf( )** functions can also be output or input by using C++'s << and >> I/O operators.

There are two related but conceptually different ways that you can format data. First, you can directly access various members of the **ios** class. Specifically, you can set various format status flags defined inside the **ios** class or call various **ios** member functions. Second, you can use special functions called *manipulators* that can be included as part of an I/O expression.

We will begin the discussion of formatted I/O by using the **ios** member functions and flags.

Formatting Using the ios Members

Associated with each stream is a set of format flags that control some of the ways information is formatted by a stream. In **ios** is defined the following enumeration; the values defined by this enumeration are used to set or clear format flags:

```
// formatting flags
enum {
  skipws = 0x0001,
  left = 0x0002,
  right = 0x0004,
  internal = 0x0008,
  dec = 0x0010,
  oct = 0x0020,
  hex = 0x0040,
  showbase = 0x0080,
  showpoint = 0x0100,
  uppercase = 0x0200,
  showpos = 0x0400,
  scientific = 0x0800,
  fixed = 0x1000,
  unitbuf = 0x2000,
  stdio = 0x4000
};
```

When the **skipws** flag is set, leading white-space characters (spaces, tabs, and newlines) are discarded when input is performed on a stream. When **skipws** is cleared, white-space characters are not discarded.

When the **left** flag is set, output is left justified. When **right** is set, output is right justified. When the **internal** flag is set, a numeric value is padded to fill a field with spaces inserted between any sign or base character. (You will learn how to specify a field width shortly.) If none of these flags is set, output is right justified by default.

Also by default, numeric values are output in decimal. However, you can change the number base. Setting the **oct** flag causes output to be displayed in octal. Setting the **hex** flag causes output to be displayed in hexadecimal. To return output to decimal, set the **dec** flag.

Setting **showbase** causes the base of numeric values to be shown. For example, if the conversion base is hexadecimal, the value 1F will be displayed as 0x1F.

By default, when scientific notation is displayed, the "e" is in lower-case. Also, when a hexadecimal value is displayed, the "x" is in lowercase. When **uppercase** is set, these characters are displayed in uppercase.

Setting **showpos** causes a leading plus sign to be displayed before positive values.

Setting **showpoint** causes a decimal point and trailing zeroes to be displayed for all floating-point output—whether needed or not.

Setting the **scientific** flag causes floating-point numeric values to be displayed in scientific notation. When **fixed** is set, floating-point values are displayed in normal notation. By default, when **fixed** is set, six decimal places are displayed. When neither flag is set, the compiler chooses an appropriate method.

When **unitbuf** is set, the C++ I/O system performance is improved because output is partially buffered. When set, the buffer is flushed after each insertion operation.

When **stdio** is set, each stream is flushed after each output. Flushing a stream causes output to actually be written to the physical device linked to the stream.

The format flags are stored in a **long** integer.

Setting the Format Flags

To set a format flag, use the **setf( )** function. This function is a member of **ios**. Its most common form is shown here:

long setf(long *flags*);

This function returns the previous settings of the format flags and turns on those flags specified by *flags*. (All other flags are unaffected.) For example, to turn on the **showpos** flag, you can use this statement:

```
stream.setf(ios::showpos);
```

Here, *stream* is the stream you wish to affect. For example, the following program displays the value 100 in hexadecimal and indicates its base.

```
#include "iostream.h"

main()
{
  cout.setf(ios::hex);
  cout.setf(ios::showbase);

  cout << 100;   // displays 0x64

}
```

It is important to understand that **setf( )** is a member function of the **ios** class and affects streams created by that class. Therefore, any call to **setf( )** is done relative to a specific stream. There is no concept of calling **setf( )** by itself. Put differently, there is no concept in C++ of global format status. Each stream maintains its own format status information individually.

Although there is nothing technically wrong with the preceding program, there is a more efficient way to write it. Instead of making multiple calls to **setf( )**, you can simply OR together the values of the flags you want set. For example, this single call accomplishes the same thing:

```
// You can OR together two or more flags,
cout.setf(ios::showbase | ios::hex);
```

Remember: Because the format flags are defined within the **ios** class, you must access their values by using **ios** and the scope resolution operator. For example, **showbase** by itself will not be recognized. You must specify **ios::showbase**.

Clearing Format Flags

The complement of **setf( )** is **unsetf( )**. This member function of **ios** is used to clear one or more format flags. Its general form is

long unsetf(long *flags*);

The flags specified by *flags* are cleared. (All other flags are unaffected.) The previous flag settings are returned.

The following program illustrates **unsetf( )**. It first sets both the **uppercase** and **scientific** flags. It then outputs 100.12 in scientific notation. In this case, the E used in the scientific notation is in uppercase. Next, it clears the **uppercase** flag and again outputs 100.12 in scientific notation, using a lowercase "e".

```
#include "iostream.h"

main()
{
  cout.setf(ios::uppercase | ios::scientific);

  cout << 100.12;  // displays 1.0012E+02

  cout.unsetf(ios::uppercase); // clear uppercase

  cout << " \n" << 100; // displays 1.0012e+02

  return 0;
}
```

An Overloaded Form of setf( )

There is an overloaded form of **setf( )** that takes this general form:

long setf(long *flags1*, long *flags2*);

In this version, only the flags specified by *flags2* are affected. They are first reset and then set according to the flags specified by *flags1*. Note that even if *flags1* contains other flags not specified by *flags2*, only those specified by *flags2* will be affected. The previous flags setting is returned. For example, the following program sets **showpos** and **showpoint**. It then resets both flags and sets **showpoint** again.

```
#include "iostream.h"

main( )
{
  cout.setf(ios::showpos | ios::showpoint);

  cout << 10.00 << " \n" // displays +10.000000

  cout.setf(ios::showpoint, ios::showpos | ios::showpoint);

  cout << 10.00; // showpos reset, this displays 10.00000
```

```
    return 0;
}
```

Remember, only the flags specified in *flags2* can be affected by flags specified by *flags1*. For example, this program will not work:

```
// This program will not work.
#include "iostream.h"

main( )
{
  cout.setf(ios::showbase | ios::hex);

  cout << 100;  // displays 0x64

  cout.setf(ios::oct, ios::hex);  // error, oct not set

  cout << " \n" << 100; // displays 100 - not 0144

  return 0;
}
```

Here, in the call to **setf( )**, *flags2* specifies that only **hex** can be affected. Because the value of *flags1* is **oct**, **hex** is turned off, but **oct** is not turned on. The following program shows a corrected version:

```
// This is now correct.
#include "iostream.h"

main()
{
  // you can OR together two or more flags
  cout.setf(ios::showbase | ios::hex);

  cout << 100;  // displays 0x64

  // now oct can be affected
  cout.setf(ios::oct, ios::hex | ios::oct);

  cout << " \n" << 100; // displays 0144

  return 0;
}
```

References to the **oct**, **dec**, and **hex** fields can collectively be referred to as **ios::basefield**. Similarly, the **left**, **right**, and **internal** fields can be referred to as **ios::adjustfield**.

Finally, the **scientific** and **fixed** fields can be referenced as **ios::floatfield**. For example, the preceding program could have been written this way:

```
#include "iostream.h"

main()
{
  // you can OR together two or more flags
  cout.setf(ios::showbase | ios::hex);

  cout << 100;  // displays 0x64

  // use ios::basefield
  cout.setf(ios::oct, ios::basefield);

  cout << " \n" << 100; // displays 0144

  return 0;
}
```

Keep in mind that most of the time you will want to use **unsetf( )** to clear flags and the single parameter version of **setf( )** (described earlier) to set flags. The **setf(long** *flags1*, **long** *flags2*) version of **setf( )** is used in specialized situations. For example, you may have a flag template that specifies the state of all format flags but wish to alter only one or two. In this case, you could specify the template in *flags1* and use *flags2* to specify which of those flags will be affected.

Examining the Formatting Flags

There will be times when you want only to know the current format settings but not alter any. Because both **setf( )** and **unsetf( )** alter the setting of one or more flags, **ios** also includes the member function **flags( )**, which simply returns the current setting of each format flag encoded into a **long int**. Its prototype is shown here:

long flags( );

The following program uses **flags( )** to display the setting of the format flags relative to **cout**. Pay special attention to the **showflags( )** function. You might find it useful in programs you write.

```
#include "iostream.h"

void showflags() ;

main()
{
  // show default condition of format flags
  showflags();

  cout.setf(ios::right | ios::showpoint | ios::fixed);

  showflags();

  return 0;
}

// This function displays the status of the format flags.
void showflags()
{
  long f, i;
  int j;

  char flgs[15][12] = {
    "skipws",
    "left",
    "right",
    "internal",
    "dec",
    "oct",
    "hex",
    "showbase",
    "showpoint",
    "uppercase",
    "showpos",
    "scientific",
    "fixed",
    "unitbuf",
    "stdio"
  };

  f = cout.flags();  // get flag settings

  // check each flag
  for(i=1, j=0; i<=0x4000; i = i<<1, j++)
    if(i & f) cout << flgs[j] << " is on \n";
    else cout << flgs[j] << " is off \n";

  cout << " \n";
}
```

The output from the program is shown here:

```
skipws is on
left is off
right is off
```

```
internal is off
dec is off
oct is off
hex is off
showbase is off
showpoint is off
uppercase is off
showpos is off
scientific is off
fixed is off
unitbuf is off
stdio is off

skipws is on
left is off
right is on
internal is off
dec is off
oct is off
hex is off
showbase is off
showpoint is on
uppercase is off
showpos is off
scientific is off
fixed is on
unitbuf is off
stdio is off
```

Setting All Flags

The **flags( )** function has a second form that allows you to set all format flags associated with a stream to those specified in the argument to **flags( )**. The prototype for this version of **flags( )** is shown here:

long flags(long f);

When you use this version, the bit pattern found in f is copied to the variable used to hold the format flags associated with the stream. The function returns the previous settings.

The next program illustrates this version of **flags( )**. It first constructs a flag mask that turns on **showpos**, **showbase**, **oct**, and **right**. These flags have the values 0x0400, 0x0080, 0x0020, and 0x0004. When added together, they produce the value used in the program, 0x04A4. All other flags are turned off. It then uses **flags( )** to set the flag variable associated with **cout** to these settings. The function **showflags( )** verifies that the flags are set as indicated. (It is the same as used in the previous program.)

```
#include "iostream.h"

void showflags() ;

main()

{

  // show default condition of format flags
  showflags();

  // showpos, showbase, oct, right are on, others off
  long f = 0x04A4;
  cout.flags(f);  // set all flags

  showflags();

  return 0;
}
```

Using width( ), precision( ), and fill( )

In addition to the formatting flags, there are three member functions defined by **ios** that set these format parameters: the field width, the precision, and the fill character. The functions that do these things are **width( )**, **precision( )**, and **fill( )**, repectively. Each is examined in turn.

By default, when a value is output, it occupies only as much space as the number of characters it takes to display it. However, you can specify a minimum field width by using the **width( )** function. Its prototype is shown here:

int width(int *w*);

Here, *w* becomes the field width, and the previous field width is returned.

After you set a minimum field width, when a value uses less than the specified width, the field will be padded with the current fill character (space, by default) to reach the field width. However, keep in mind that if the size of the value output exceeds the minimum field width, then the field will be overrun. No values are truncated.

By default, six digits are displayed after the decimal point when floating-point values are output. However, you can set this number by using the **precision( )** function. Its prototype is shown here:

int precision(int p);

Here, the precision is set to p, and the old value is returned.

Also by default, when a field needs to be filled, it is filled with spaces. However, you can specify the fill character by using the **fill( )** function. Its prototype is

char fill(char ch);

After a call to **fill( )**, ch becomes the new fill character, and the old one is returned.

Here is a program that illustrates these functions:

```
#include "iostream.h"

main()
{
  cout.precision(d2) ;
  cout.width(10);

  cout << 10.12345 << "\n";   // displays 10.12

  cout.fill('*');

  cout.width(10);
  cout << 10.12345 << "\n"; // displays ****10.12

  // field width applies to strings, too
  cout.width(10);
  cout << "Hi!" << "\n"; // displays *******Hi!
  cout.width(10);
  cout.setf(ios::left); // left justify
  cout << 10.12345; // displays 10.12*****

  return 0;
}
```

This program's output is shown here:

```
     10.12
****10.12
*******Hi!
10.12*****
```

Manipulator	Purpose	Input/Output
dec	Format numeric data in decimal	Output
endl	Output a newline character and flush the stream	Output
ends	Output a null	Output
flush	Flush a stream	Output
hex	Format numeric data in hexadecimal	Output
oct	Format numeric data in octal	Output
resetiosflags(long f)	Turn off the flags specified in f	Input and output
setbase(int base)	Set the number base to base	Output
setfill(int ch)	Set the fill character to ch	Output
setiosflags(long f)	Turn on the flags specified in f	Input and output
setprecision(int p)	Set the number of digits displayed after a decimal point	Output
setw(int w)	Set the field width to w	Output
ws	Skip leading white space	Input

Table 17-1.   The C++ Manipulators

Using Manipulators to Format I/O

The second way you may alter the format parameters of a stream is through the use of special functions called *manipulators* that can be included in an I/O expression. The standard manipulators are shown in Table 17-1. As you can see by examining the table, many of the I/O manipulators parallel member functions of the **ios** class.

To access manipulators that take parameters (such as **setw( )**), you must include **iomanip.h** in your program.

Here is an example that uses some manipulators:

```
#include "iostream.h"
#include "iomanip.h"

main()
{
```

```
  cout << hex << 100 << endl;

  cout << setfill('?') << setw(10) << 2343.0;

  return 0;
}
```

This displays

```
64
???????2342
```

Notice how the manipulators occur in the chain of I/O operations. Also notice that when a manipulator does not take an argument, such as **endl( )** in the example, it is not followed by parentheses. This is because it is the address of the function that is passed to the overloaded **<<** operator.

As a comparison, here is a functionally equivalent version of the preceding program that uses **ios** member functions to achieve the same results:

```
#include "iostream.h"
#include "iomanip.h"

main()
{
  cout.setf(ios::hex);
  cout << 100 << "\n";   // 100 in hex

  cout.fill('?');
  cout.width(10);
  cout << 2343.0;

  return 0;
}
```

As the examples suggest, the main advantage of using manipulators instead of the **ios** member functions is that they commonly allow more compact code to be written.

You can use the **setiosflags( )** manipulator to directly set the various format flags related to a stream. For example, this program uses **setiosflags( )** to set the **showbase** and **showpos** flags:

```
#include "iostream.h"
#include "iomanip.h"

main(void)
{
```

```
cout << setiosflags(ios::showpos);
cout << setiosflags(ios::showbase);
cout << 123 << " " << hex << 123;

return 0;
}
```

The manipulator **setiosflags( )** performs the same function as the member function **setf( )**.

Overloading << and >>

As you know, the << and the >> operators are overloaded in C++ to perform I/O operations on C++'s built-in types. You can also overload these operators so that they perform I/O operations on types that you create.

In the language of C++, the << output operator is referred to as the *insertion operator* because it inserts characters into a stream. Likewise, the >> input operator is called the *extraction operator* because it extracts characters from a stream. The operator functions that overload the insertion and extraction operators are generally called *inserters* and *extractors*, respectively.

Creating Your Own Inserters

It is quite simple to create an inserter for a class that you create. All inserter functions have this general form:

ostream &operator << (ostream &*stream*, *class_type obj*)
{
  // body of inserter
  return *stream*;
}

Notice that the function returns a reference to a stream of type **ostream**. (Remember, **ostream** is a class derived from **ios** that supports output.) Further, the first parameter to the function is a reference to the output stream. The second parameter is the object being inserted. The last thing the inserter must do before exiting is return *stream*. This allows the inserter to be used in a chain of insertions.

Within an inserter function, you may put any type of procedures or operations that you want. That is, precisely what an inserter does is completely up to you. However, for the inserter to be in keeping with good programming practices, you should limit the operations performed by an inserter to outputting information to a stream. For example, having an inserter compute pi to 30 decimal places as a side effect to an insertion operation is probably not a very good idea.

To see an example, let's create an inserter for objects of type **phonebook:**

```
class phonebook {
public:
  char name[80];
  int areacode;
  int prefix;
  int num;
  phonebook(char *n, int a, int p, int nm)
  {
    strcpy(name, n);
    areacode = a;
    prefix = p;
    num = nm;
  }
};
```

This class holds a person's name and telephone number. Here is one way to create an inserter function for objects of type **phonebook**.

```
// Display name and phone number
ostream &operator<<(ostream &stream, phonebook o)
{
  stream << o.name << " ";
  stream << "(" << o.areacode << ") ";
  stream << o.prefix << "-" << o.num << "\n";
  return stream; // must return stream
}
```

Here is a short program that illustrates the **phonebook** inserter function.

```
#include "iostream.h"
#include "string.h"
```

```
class phonebook {
public:
  char name[80];
  int areacode;
  int prefix;
  int num;
  phonebook(char *n, int a, int p, int nm)
  {
    strcpy(name, n);
    areacode = a;
    prefix = p;
    num = nm;
  }
};

// Display name and phone number.
ostream &operator<<(ostream &stream, phonebook o)
{
  stream << o.name << " ";
  stream << "(" << o.areacode << ") ";
  stream << o.prefix << "-" << o.num << "\n";
  return stream; // must return stream
}

main()
{
  phonebook a("Ted", 111, 555, 1234);
  phonebook b("Alice", 312, 555, 5768);
  phonebook c("Tom", 212, 555, 9991);

  cout << a << b << c;

  return 0;
}
```

The program produces this output:

```
Ted (111) 555-1234
Alice (312) 555-5768
Tom (212) 555-9991
```

In the preceding program, notice that the **phonebook** inserter is *not* a member of **phonebook**. Although this may seem weird at first, the reason is easy to understand. When an operator function of any type is a member of a class, the left operand (passed implicitly through *this*) is the object that generates the call to the operator function. Further, this object is an *object of the class* for which the operator function is a member. There is no way to change this. If an overloaded operator function is a member of a class, the left operand must be an object of that class. However, when you overload inserters, the left operand is a *stream* and the right operand is an object of the class. Therefore, overloaded inserters cannot be members of the class for which they are overloaded. The variables **name, areacode, prefix**, and **num** are **public** in the preceding program so that they can be accessed by the inserter.

The fact that inserters cannot be members of the class for which they are defined seems to be a serious flaw in C++. Since overloaded inserters are not members, how can they access the private elements of a class? In the foregoing program, all members were made **public**. However, encapsulation is an essential component of object-oriented programming. Requiring all data to be output by using an inserter to be made **public** conflicts with this principle. Fortunately, there is a solution to this dilemma: Make the inserter a **friend** of the class. This preserves the requirement that the first argument to the overloaded inserter be a stream and still grants the function access to **private** parts of the class for which it is overloaded. Here is the same program modified to make the inserter into a **friend** function:

```
#include "iostream.h"
#include "string.h"

class phonebook {
  // now private
  char name[80];
  int areacode;
  int prefix;
  int num;
public:
  phonebook(char *n, int a, int p, int nm)
  {
    strcpy(name, n);
    areacode = a;
    prefix = p;
    num = nm;
  }
  friend ostream &operator<<(ostream &stream, phonebook o);
};

// Display name and phone number.
ostream &operator<<(ostream &stream, phonebook o)
{
  stream << o.name << " ";
  stream << "(" << o.areacode << ") ";
  stream << o.prefix << "-" << o.num << "\n";
  return stream; // must return stream
}
main()
{
```

```
phonebook a("Ted", 111, 555, 1234);
phonebook b("Alice", 312, 555, 5768);
phonebook c("Tom", 212, 555, 9991);

cout << a << b << c;

return 0;
}
```

When you define the body of an inserter function, remember to keep it as general as possible. For example, the inserter shown in the preceding example can be used with any stream because the body of the function directs its output to **stream**, which is the stream that invoked the inserter. While it would not be wrong to have written

```
stream << o.name << " ";
```

as

```
cout << o.name << " ";
```

this would have the effect of hard-coding **cout** as the output stream. The original version will work with any stream, including those linked to disk files. Although in some situations, especially where special output devices are involved, you will want to hard-code the output stream, in most cases you will not. In general, the more flexible your inserters are, the more valuable they are.

Note: The inserter for the **phonebook** class works fine unless the value of **num** is something like 0034, in which case the preceding zeroes will not be displayed. To fix this, you can either make **num** into a string or you can set the fill character to zero and use the **width( )** format function to generate the leading zeroes. The solution is left to the reader as an exercise.

Before moving on to extractors, let's look at one more example of an inserter function. An inserter need not be limited to handling only straight text. An inserter can be used to output data in any form that makes sense. For example, an inserter for some class that is part of a CAD system may output plotter instructions. Another inserter might generate graphics images. To taste the flavor of outputting things other than text, examine the following program, which draws boxes on the screen. (Because neither C nor C++ defines graphics, the program uses characters to draw a box, but feel free to substitute graphics if your system supports them.)

```cpp
#include "iostream.h"

class box {
  int x, y;
public:

  box(int i, int j) {x=i; y=j;}

  friend ostream &operator<<(ostream &stream, box o);
};

// Output a box.
ostream &operator<<(ostream &stream, box o)
{
  register int i, j;

  for(i=0; i<o.x; i++)
     stream << "*";

  stream << "\n";

  for(j=1; j<o.y-1; j++) {
    for(i=0; i<o.x; i++)
      if(i==0 || i==o.x-1) stream << "*";
      else stream << " ";
    stream << "\n";
  }

  for(i=0; i<o.x; i++)
     stream << "*";

  stream << "/n";
  return stream;
}

main()
{
  box a(14, 6), b(30, 7), c(40, 5);

  cout << "Here are some boxes:/n";
  cout << a << b << c;

return 0;
}
```

The program displays the following:

```
Here are some boxes:
**************
*            *
*            *
*            *
*            *
**************
******************************
*                            *
*                            *
*                            *
*                            *
*                            *
******************************
****************************************
*                                      *
*                                      *
*                                      *
****************************************
```

Creating Your Own Extractors

Extractors are the complement of inserters. The general form of an extractor function is

```
istream &operator >> (istream &stream, class_type &obj)
{
    // body of extra
    return stream;
}
```

Extractors return a reference to a stream of type **istream**, which is an input stream. The first parameter must also be a reference to a stream of type **istream**. Notice that the second parameter must be a reference to an object of the class for which the extractor is overloaded. This is so the object will modified by the input (extraction) operation.

Continuing with the **phonebook** class, here is one way to write an extraction function:

```
istream &operator>>(istream &stream, phonebook &o)
{
    cout << "Enter name: ";
```

```
    stream >> o.name;
    cout << "Enter area code: ";
    stream >> o.areacode;
    cout << "Enter prefix: ";
    stream >> o.prefix;
    cout << "Enter number: ";
    stream >> o.num;
    cout << "\n";
    return stream;
}
```

Notice that although this is an input function, it performs output by prompting the user. The point is that although the main purpose of an extractor is input, it can perform any operations necessary to achieve that end. However, as with inserters, it is best to keep the actions performed by an extractor directly related to input. If you don't, you run the risk of losing much in terms of structure and clarity.

Here is a program that illustrates the **phonebook** extractor:

```
#include "iostream.h"
#include "string.h"

class phonebook {
  char name[80];
  int areacode;
  int prefix;
  int num;
public:
  phonebook() { };
  phonebook(char *n, int a, int p, int nm)
  {
    strcpy(name, n);
    areacode = a;
    prefix = p;
    num = nm;
  }
  friend ostream &operator<<(ostream &stream, phonebook o);
  friend istream &operator>>(istream &stream, phonebook &o);
};

// Display name and phone number.
ostream &operator<<(ostream &stream, phonebook o)
{
  stream << o.name << " ";
  stream << "(" << o.areacode << ") ";
  stream << o.prefix << "-" << o.num << "\n";
  return stream; // must return stream
}
```

```
// Input name and telephone number.
istream &operator>>(istream &stream, phonebook &o)
{
  cout << "Enter name: ";
  stream >> o.name;
  cout << "Enter area code: ";
  stream >> o.areacode;
  cout << "Enter prefix: ";
  stream >> o.prefix;
  cout << "Enter number: ";
  stream >> o.num;
  cout << "\n";
  return stream;
}

main()
{
  phonebook a;

  cin >> a;

  cout << a;

  return 0;
}
```

Creating Your Own Manipulator Functions

In addition to overloading the insertion and extraction operators, you can further customize C++'s I/O system by creating your own manipulator functions. Custom manipulators are important for two main reasons. First, you can consolidate a sequence of several separate I/O operations into one manipulator. For example, it is not uncommon to have situations in which the same sequence of I/O operations occurs frequently within a program. In these cases you can use a custom manipulator to perform these actions, thus simplifying your source code and preventing accidental errors. A custom manipulator can also be important when you need to perform I/O operations on a nonstandard device. For example, you might use a manipulator to send control codes to a special type of printer or to an optical recognition system.

Custom manipulators are a feature of C++ that supports OOP, but that also can benefit programs that aren't object oriented. As you will see, custom manipulators can help make any I/O-intensive program clearer and more efficient.

As you know, there are two basic types of manipulators: those that operate on input streams and those that operate on output streams. However, in addition to these two broad categories, there is a secondary division: those manipulators that take an argument and those that don't. There are some significant differences between the way a parameterless manipulator and a parameterized manipulator are created. This section discusses how to create each type, beginning with creating parameterless manipulators.

Creating Parameterless Manipulators

All parameterless manipulator output functions have this skeleton:

```
ostream &manip-name(ostream &stream)
{
   // your code here
   return stream;
}
```

Here, *manip-name* is the name of the manipulator. Notice that a reference to a stream of type **ostream** is returned. This is necessary if a manipulator is used as part of a larger I/O expression. It is important to note that even though the manipulator has as its single argument a reference to the stream upon which it is operating, no argument is used when the manipulator is inserted in an output operation.

As a simple first example, the following program creates a manipulator called **sethex( )**, which turns on the **showbase** flag and sets output to hexadecimal.

```
#include "iostream.h"
#include "iomanip.h"

// A simple output manipulator.
ostream &sethex(ostream &stream)
{
  stream.setf(ios::showbase);
  stream.setf(ios::hex);
  return stream;
}
```

```
main(void)
{
  cout << 256 << " " << sethex << 256;

  return 0;
}
```

This program displays **256 0x100**. As you can see, **sethex** is used as part of an I/O expression in the same way as any of the built-in manipulators.

Custom manipulators need not be complex to be useful. For example, the simple manipulators **la( )** and **ra( )** display a left and right arrow, respectively, for emphasis, as shown here:

```
#include "iostream.h"
#include "iomanip.h"

// Right Arrow
ostream &ra(ostream &stream)
{
  stream << "-------> ";
  return stream;
}

// Left Arrow
ostream &la(ostream &stream)
{
  stream << " <-------";
  return stream;
}

main(void)
{
  cout << "High balance " << ra << 1233.23 << "\n";
  cout << "Over draft " << ra << 567.66 << la;

  return 0;
}
```

This program displays:

```
High balance -------> 1233.23
Over draft -------> 567.66 <-------
```

If used frequently, these simple manipulators save you from some tedious typing.

Using an output manipulator is particularly useful for sending special codes to a device. For example, a printer may be able to accept various codes that change the type size or font, or that position the print head in a special location. If these adjustments are going to be made frequently, then they are perfect candidates for a manipulator.

All parameterless input manipulator functions have this skeleton:

istream &*manip-name*(istream &*stream*)
{
   // your code here

   return *stream*;
}

An input manipulator receives a reference to the stream for which it was invoked. This stream must be returned by the manipulator.

The following program creates the **getpass( )** input manipulator, which rings the bell and then prompts for a password:

```
#include "iostream.h"
#include "string.h"

// A simple input manipulator
istream &getpass(istream &stream)
{
  cout << '\a';  // sound bell
  cout << "Enter password: ";

  return stream;
}

main(void)
{
  char pw[80];

  do {
    cin >> getpass >> pw;
  } while (strcmp(pw, "password"));

  cout << "Logon complete\n";

  return 0;
}
```

It is crucial that your manipulator return **stream**. If this is not done, your manipulator cannot be used in a series of input or output operations.

Creating Parameterized Manipulators

Creating a manipulator function that takes an argument is less straight-forward than creating manipulators that don't. First, to create a parameterized manipulator you must include **iomanip.h**. In **iomanip.h** is defined the class **OMANIP**, which is used to create output manipulators that take an argument. **iomanip.h** also defines the class **IMANIP**, which is used to create parameterized input manipulators. In general, whenever you need to create a manipulator that takes an argument, you will need to create two overloaded manipulator functions. In one, you need to define two parameters. The first parameter is a reference to the stream, and the second is the parameter that will be passed to the function. The second version of the manipulator defines only one parameter—the one specified when the manipulator is used in an I/O expression. This second version generates a call to the first version. In general, for output manipulators, you will use these general forms for creating parameterized manipulators:

```
ostream &manip-name(ostream &stream, type param)
{
  // your code here
  return stream;
}
  // Overload
OMANIP (type) manip-name(type param) {
  return OMANIP (type) (manip-name, param);
}
```

Here, *type* specifies the type of parameter used by the manipulator. By default, you may only use types **int** and **long** for *type*. In a moment you will see how to use other types.

The following program creates a parameterized manipulator called **indent( )**, which indents the specified number of spaces.

```
#include "iostream.h"
#include "iomanip.h"

// Indent length number of spaces.
ostream &indent(ostream &stream, int length)
{
  register int i;
```

```
      for(i=0; i<length; i++) cout << " ";
      return stream;
}

// Overload.
OMANIP (int) indent(int length) {
    return OMANIP (int) (indent, length);
}

main(void)
{
    cout << indent(10) << "This is a test\n";
    cout << indent(20) << "of the indent manipulator.\n";
    cout << indent(5) << "It works!\n";

    return 0;
}
```

As you can see, **indent( )** is overloaded as previously described. When **indent(10)** is encountered in the output expression, the second version of **indent( )** is executed, with value 10 passed to the **length** parameter. This version then executes the first version with the value 10 again passed in **length**. This process repeats itself for each **indent( )** call.

In **iomanip.h**, **OMANIP** and **IMANIP** are overloaded to accept either integer or long integer parameters. If you want to use a different type of parameter, you must first tell the compiler about it by using the **IOMANIPdeclare** macro (defined in **iomanip.h**), as shown here:

IOMANIPdeclare(*type*);

Here, *type* is the type of the parameter you want your manipulator to have. For example, the next program shows how to pass a **double** value to a manipulator function. It then outputs the value by using a dollars-and-cents format.

```
#include "iostream.h"
#include "iomanip.h"

IOMANIPdeclare(double);  // specify double parameter

ostream &dollars(ostream &stream, double amount)
{
    stream.setf(ios::showpoint);
    stream << "$" << setw(10) << setprecision(2)  << amount;
    return stream;
}
```

```
OMANIP (double) dollars(double amount) {
  return OMANIP (double) (dollars, amount);
}

main(void)
{
  cout << dollars(123.123456);
  cout << "\n" << dollars(10.0);
  cout << "\n" << dollars(1234.23);
  cout << "\n" << dollars(0.0);

  return 0;
}
```

This program displays the following:

```
$     123.12
$      10.00
$   1.23e+03
$       0.00
```

You can use parameters of any valid type, including classes that you define. However, the parameter to **IOMANIPdeclare** must be a single identifier. Therefore, if you need to use a pointer or reference type, you will need to define a new type name by using **typedef**. For example, to tell the compiler about a character pointer parameter to a manipulator, you must use this statement sequence:

```
typedef char * charptr;

IOMANIPdeclare(charptr);
```

Input manipulators may also take a parameter. The following program improves the **getpass( )** manipulator developed earlier. This version takes an argument that specifies how many tries the user has to enter the password correctly.

```
// This program uses a manipulator to input a password.
#include "iostream.h"
#include "iomanip.h"
#include "string.h"
#include "stdlib.h"

char *password="IlikeC++";
char pw[80];
```

```
// Input a password
istream &getpass(istream &stream, int tries)
{
  do {
    cout << "Enter password: ";
    stream >> pw;
    if(!strcmp(password, pw)) return stream;
    cout << "\a"; // bell
    tries--;
  } while(tries>0);

  cout << "All tries failed!\n";
  exit(1) ; // didn't enter password
}

// Overloaded.
IMANIP(int) getpass(int tries) {
  return IMANIP(int)(getpass, tries);
}

main(void)
{
  // give 3 tries to enter password
  cin >> getpass(3);
  cout << "Login Complete!\n";

  return 0;
}
```

Notice that the format is the same as for output manipulators, with two exceptions: The input stream **istream** must be used, and the **class IMANIP** is specified.

As you work with C++, you will find that custom manipulators can help streamline your I/O statements.

A Short Note About the Old Stream Class Library

When C++ was invented, a smaller and slightly different I/O **class** library was created. This library is defined in the file **stream.h**. However, when C++ version 2.0 was released by AT&T, the I/O library was enhanced and was put in the file **iostream.h**. Most C++ compilers still support the old stream library for the sake of compatibility with older C++ programs. However, you should use the IOSTREAM library when writing new programs.

C++ File I/O

E
I
G
H
T
E
E
N

Although the C++ approach to I/O forms an integrated system, file I/O (specifically, disk file I/O) is sufficiently specialized that it is generally thought of as a special case, subject to its own constraints and quirks. In part, this is because the most common file is a disk file, and disk files have capabilities and features that most other devices don't. Keep in mind, however, that disk file I/O is simply a special case of a general I/O system and that most of the material discussed in this chapter also applies to streams connected to other types of devices.

Note: The C++ I/O system discussed in this chapter reflects specification 2 of C++. If you have an older, nonconforming version, its I/O system will not have all the capabilities described here.

fstream.h and the File Classes

To perform file I/O, you must include the header file **fstream.h** in your program. It defines several classes, including **ifstream**, **ofstream**, and

fstream. These classes are derived from **istream** and **ostream**, respectively. Remember, **istream** and **ostream** are derived from **ios**, so **ifstream**, **ofstream**, and **fstream** also have access to all operations defined by **ios** (discussed in the preceding chapter).

Opening and Closing a File

In C++, you open a file by linking it to a stream. Before you can open a file, you must first obtain a stream. There are three types of streams: input, output, and input/output. To create an input stream, you must declare the stream to be of class **ifstream**. To create an output stream, you must declare it as class **ofstream**. Streams that will be performing both input and output operations must be declared as class **fstream**. For example, this fragment creates one input stream, one output stream, and one stream capable of both input and output:

```
ifstream in; // input

ofstream out; // output

fstream io; // input and output
```

Once you have created a stream, one way to associate it with a file is by using the function **open( )**. This function is a member of each of the three stream classes. Its prototype is

void open(char *filename, int mode, int access);

Here, filename is the name of the file, which may include a path specifier. The value of mode determines how the file is opened. It must be one (or more) of these values (inherited by **fstream.h**):

ios::app
ios::ate
ios::in

ios::nocreate
ios::noreplace
ios::out
ios::trunc

You can combine two or more of these values by ORing them together. Let's see what each of these values means.

Including **ios::app** causes all output to that file to be appended to the end. This value can be used only with files capable of output. Including **ios::ate** causes a seek to end-of-file to occur when the file is opened. Although **ios::ate** causes a seek to end-of-file, I/O operations can still occur anywhere within the file.

The **ios::in** value specifies that the file is capable of input. The **ios::out** value specifies that the file is capable of output. However, creating a stream by using **ifstream** implies input and creating a stream using **ofstream** implies output, so in these cases, it is unnecessary to supply these values.

Including **ios::nocreate** causes the **open( )** function to fail if the file does not already exist. The **ios::noreplace** value causes the **open( )** function to fail if the file does already exist.

The **ios::trunc** value causes the contents of a preexisting file by the same name to be destroyed and truncates the file to zero length.

The value of *access* determines how the file can be accessed. Its default value is **filebuf::openprot** (**filebuf** is a parent class of the stream classes), which is 0x644 for UNIX environments; it means a normal file. In DOS environments, the *access* value generally corresponds to DOS's file attribute codes. They are

Attribute	Meaning
0	Normal file—open access
1	Read-only file
2	Hidden file
4	System file
8	Archive bit set

You can OR two or more of these together. For DOS, a normal file has an *access* value of zero. For other operating systems, check your compiler user manual for the valid values of *access*.

The following fragment opens a normal output file in a DOS environment:

```
ofstream out;

out.open("test", ios::out, 0);
```

However, you will seldom (if ever) see **open( )** called as shown, because both the *mode* and *access* parameters have default values. For **ifstream**, *mode* is **ios::in,** and for **ofstream** it is **ios::out.** By default, *access* has a value that creates a normal file. Therefore, the preceding statement will usually look like this:

```
out.open("test");  // defaults to output and normal file
```

To open a stream for input and output, you must specify both the **ios::in** and the **ios::out** *mode* values, as shown in the next example. (No default value for *mode* is supplied.)

```
fstream mystream;

mystream.open("test", ios::in | ios::out);
```

If **open( )** fails, **mystream** will be zero. Therefore, before using a file, you should test to make sure that the open operation succeeded. You can do so by using a statement like this:

```
if(!mystream) {
  cout << "Cannot open file\n";
  // handle error
}
```

Although it is entirely proper to open a file by using the **open( )** function, most of the time you will not do so because the **ifstream,** **ofstream,** and **fstream** classes have constructor functions that automatically open the file. The constructor functions have the same parameters and defaults as the **open( )** function. Therefore, you will most commonly see a file opened as shown here:

```
ifstream  mystream("myfile"); // open file for input
```

As stated, if for some reason the file cannot be opened, the value of the associated stream variable will be zero. Therefore, whether you use a constructor function to open the file or an explicit call to **open( )**, you will want to confirm that the file has actually been opened by testing the value of the stream.

To close a file, use the member function **close( )**. For example, to close the file linked to a stream called **mystream,** use this statement:

```
mystream.close();
```

The **close( )** function takes no parameters and returns no value.

Reading and Writing Text Files

It is very easy to read from or write to a text file. Simply use the << and >> operators the same way you do when performing console I/O, except that instead of using **cin** and **cout,** you substitute a stream that is linked to a file. For example, this program creates a short inventory file that contains each item's name and its cost:

```
#include "iostream.h"
#include "fstream.h"

main()
{
  ofstream out("INVNTRY"); // output, normal file

  if(!out) {
    cout << "Cannot open INVENTORY file.\n";
    return 1;
  }

  out << "Radios " << 39.95 << endl;
  out << "Toasters " << 19.95 << endl;
  out << "Mixers " << 24.80 << endl;

  out.close();
  return 0;
}
```

The following program reads the inventory file created by the previous program and displays its contents on the screen:

```
#include "iostream.h"
#include "fstream.h"

main()
{
  ifstream in("INVNTRY"); // input

  if(!in) {
    cout << "Cannot open INVENTORY file.\n";
    return 1;
  }

  char item[20];
  float cost;

  cout.precision(2);

  in >> item >>  cost;
  cout << item << " " << cost << "\n";
  in >> item >> cost;
  cout << item << " " << cost << "\n";
  in >> item >> cost;
  cout << item << " " << cost << "\n";

  in.close();
  return 0;
}
```

In a way, reading and writing files by using >> and << are like using C's **fprintf( )** and **fscanf( )** functions. All information is stored in the file in the same format as it would be displayed on the screen.

Following is another example of disk I/O. This program reads strings entered at the keyboard and writes them to disk. The program stops when the user enters a blank line. To use the program, specify the name of the output file on the command line.

```
#include "iostream.h"
#include "fstream.h"
#include "stdio.h"

main(int argc, char *argv[])
{
  if(argc!=2) {
    cout << "Usage: output <filename>\n";
    return 1;
  }

  ofstream out(argv[1]); // output, normal file

  if(!out) {
    cout << "Cannot open output file.\n";
```

```
    return 1;
  }

  char str[80];
  cout << "Write strings to disk, RETURN to stop\n";

  do {
    cout << ": ";
    gets(str);
    out << str << endl;
  } while (*str);

  out.close();
  return 0;
}
```

When reading text files using the **>>** operator, keep in mind that certain character translations will occur. For example, white-space characters are omitted. If you want to prevent any character translations, you must use C++'s binary I/O functions, discussed in the next section.

When inputting, if end-of-file is encountered, the stream linked to that file will be a zero. (The next section illustrates this fact.)

Binary I/O

There are two ways to write and read binary data to or from a file. These two methods are explained here.

put( ) and get( )

First, you may write a byte by using the member function **put( )** and read a byte by using the member function **get( )**. The **get( )** function has many forms, but the most commonly used version is shown here along with **put( )**:

istream &get(char &*ch*);
ostream &put(char *ch*);

The **get( )** function reads a single character from the associated stream and puts that value in *ch*. It returns a reference to the stream. The **put( )** function writes *ch* to the stream and returns the stream.

The following program displays the contents of any file on the screen. It uses the **get( )** function.

```
#include "iostream.h"
#include "fstream.h"

main(int argc, char *argv[])
{
  char ch;

  if(argc!=2) {
    cout << "Usage: PR <filename>\n";
    return 1;
  }

  ifstream in(argv[1]);
  if(!in) {
    cout << "Cannot open file";
    return 1;
  }

  while(in) { // in will be 0 when eof is reached
    in.get(ch);
    cout << ch;
  }

  return 0;
}
```

As stated in the preceding section, when the end-of-file is reached, the stream associated with the file becomes zero. Therefore, when **in** reaches the end of the file, it will be zero, causing the **while** loop to stop.

There is actually a more compact way to code the loop that reads and displays a file, as shown here:

```
while(in.get(ch))
  cout << ch;
```

This works because **get( )** returns a reference to the stream **in**, and **in** will be zero when the end of the file is encountered.

The next program uses **put( )** to write all characters from zero to 255 to a file called CHARS. As you probably know, the ASCII characters occupy only about half the available values that can be held by a **char**. The other values are generally called the *extended character set* and include such things as a foreign language and mathematical symbols. (Not all systems support the extended character set, but most do.)

```
#include "iostream.h"
#include "fstream.h"

main()
{
```

```
  ofstream out("CHARS");

  if(!out) {
    cout << "Cannot open output file.\n";
    return 1;
  }

  int i;
  // write all characters to disk
  for(i=0; i<256; i++) out.put(i);

  out.close();
  return 0;
}
```

You might find it interesting to examine the contents of the CHARS file to see what extended characters your computer has.

read( ) and write( )

The second way to read and write blocks of binary data is to use C++'s **read( )** and **write( )** functions. Their prototypes are

> istream &read(unsigned char *buf*, int *num*);
> ostream &write(const unsigned char *buf*, int *num*);

The **read( )** function reads *num* bytes from the associated stream and puts them in the buffer pointed to by *buf*. The **write( )** function writes *num* bytes to the associated stream from the buffer pointed to by *buf*.

The next program writes a structure to disk; then reads it back in:

```
#include "iostream.h"
#include "fstream.h"
#include "string.h"

struct status {
  char name[80];
  float balance;
  unsigned long account_num;
};

main()
{
  struct status acc;

  strcpy(acc.name, "Ralph Trantor");
  acc.balance = 1123.23;
  acc.account_num = 34235678;
```

```
ofstream outbal("balance");

if(!outbal) {
  cout << "Cannot open file\n";
  return 1;
}

outbal.write((unsigned char *) &acc, sizeof(struct status));
outbal.close();

// now, read back;

ifstream inbal("balance");

if(!inbal) {
  cout << "Cannot open file\n";
  return 1;
}

inbal.read((unsigned char *) &acc, sizeof(struct status));

cout << acc.name << endl;
cout << "Account # " << acc.account_num;
cout.precision(2);
cout.setf(ios::fixed);
cout << endl << "Balance: $" << acc.balance;

inbal.close();
return 0;
}
```

As you can see, only a single call to **read( )** or **write( )** is necessary to read or write the entire structure. Each individual field need not be read or written separately. As this example illustrates, the buffer can be any type of object.

Note: The type casts inside the calls to **read( )** and **write( )** are necessary when operating on a buffer that is not defined as a character array. Because of C++'s strong type checking, a pointer of one type will not automatically be converted into a pointer of another type.

If the end of the file is reached before *num* characters have been read, then **read( )** simply stops, and the buffer contains as many characters as were available. You can find out how many characters have been read by using another member function, called **gcount( )**, which has this prototype:

int gcount();

It returns the number of characters read by the last binary input operation. The following program shows another example of **read( )** and **write( )** and illustrates the use of **gcount( )**:

```
#include "iostream.h"
#include "fstream.h"

main(void)
{
  float fnum[4] = {99.75, -34.4, 1776.0, 200.1};
  int i;

  ofstream out("numbers");
  if(!out) {
    cout << "Cannot open file";
    return 1;
   }

  out.write((unsigned char *) &fnum, sizeof fnum);

  out.close();

  for(i=0; i<4; i++) // clear array
    fnum[i] = 0.0;

  ifstream in("numbers");
  in.read((unsigned char *) &fnum, sizeof fnum);

  // see how many bytes have been read
  cout << in.gcount() << " bytes read\n";

  for(i=0; i<4; i++) // show values read from file
    cout << fnum[i] << " ";

  in.close();

  return 0;
}
```

The preceding program writes an array of floating-point values to disk and then reads them back. After the call to **read( )**, **gcount( )** is used to determine how many bytes were just read.

More get( ) Functions

In addition to the form shown earlier, the **get( )** function is overloaded in several different ways. The prototypes for the two most commonly used overloaded forms are shown here:

```
istream &get(char *buf, int num, char delim = '\n');
int get()
```

The first overloaded form reads characters into the array pointed to by *buf* until either *num* characters have been read or the character specified by *delim* has been encountered. The array pointed to by *buf* will be null terminated by **get( )**. If no *delim* parameter is specified, by default a newline character acts as a delimiter. If the delimiter character is encountered in the input stream, it is *not* extracted. Instead, it remains in the stream until the next input operation.

The second overloaded form of **get( )** returns the next character from the stream. It returns EOF if the end of the file is encountered. This form of **get( )** is similar to C's **getc( )** function.

getline( )

Another member function that performs input is **getline( )**. Its prototype is

```
istream &getline(char *buf, int num, char delim = '\n');
```

As you can see, this function is virtually identical to the **get(buf, num, delim)** version of **get( )**. It reads characters from input and puts them into the array pointed to by *buf* until either *num* characters have been read or the character specified by *delim* is encountered. If not specified, *delim* defaults to the newline character. The array pointed to by *buf* is null terminated. The difference between **get(buf, num, delim)** and **getline( )** is that **getline( )** reads and removes the delimiter from the input stream.

Here is a program that demonstrates the **getline( )** function. It reads the contents of a text file one line at a time and displays it on the screen.

```
// Read and display a text file line by line.

#include "iostream.h"
#include "fstream.h"

main(int argc, char *argv[])
{
```

```
if(argc!=2) {
  cout << "Usage: Display <filename>\n";
  return 1;
}

ifstream in(argv[1]); // input

if(!in) {
  cout << "Cannot open input file.\n";
  return 1;
}

char str[255];

while(in) {
  in.getline(str, 255);  // delim defaults to '\n'
  cout << str << endl
}

in.close();

return 0;
}
```

Detecting EOF

You can detect when the end of the file is reached by using the member function **eof( )**, which has this prototype:

```
int eof();
```

It returns nonzero when the end of the file has been reached; otherwise it returns zero.

The following program uses **eof( )** to display the contents of a file in both hexadecimal and ASCII. (Its output is similar to that used by the DOS DEBUG command.)

```
/* Display contents of specified file
   in both ASCII and in hex.
*/
#include "iostream.h"
#include "fstream.h"
#include "ctype.h"
#include "iomanip.h"
#include "stdio.h"
```

```
main(int argc, char *argv[])
{
  if(argc!=2) {
    cout << "Usage: Display <filename>\n";
    return 1;
  }

  ifstream in(argv[1]); // input, normal file

  if(!in) {
    cout << "Cannot open input file.\n";
    return 1;
  }

  register int i, j;
  int count = 0;
  char c[16];

  cout.setf(ios::uppercase);
  while(!in.eof()) {
    for(i=0; i<16 && !in.eof(); i++) {
      in.get(c[i]);
    }
    if(i<16) i--; // get rid of eof

    for(j=0; j<i; j++)
      cout << setw(3) << hex << (int) c[j];
    for(; j<16; j++) cout << "   ";

    cout << "\t";
    for(j=0; j<i; j++)
      if(isprint(c[j])) cout << c[j];
      else cout << ".";

    cout << endl;

    count++;
    if(count==16) {
      count = 0;
      cout << "Press ENTER to continue: ";
      cin.get();
      cout << endl;
    }
  }

  in.close();

  return 0;
}
```

When this program is used to display itself, the first screen looks like this:

```
2F 2A 20 44 69 73 70 6C 61 79 20 63 6F 6E 74 65 /* Display conte
6E 74 73 20 6F 66 20 73 70 65 63 69 66 69 65 64 nts of specified
20 69 6E 20 62 6F 74 68 20 41 53 43 49 49 20 61 in both ASCII a
```

```
6E 64  A 20 20 20 69 6E 20 68 65 78 2E  A 2A 2F  nd.   in hex..*/
 A 23 69 6E 63 6C 75 64 65 20 22 69 6F 73 74 72  .#include "iostr
65 61 6D 2E 68 22  A 23 69 6E 63 6C 75 64 65 20  eam.h".#include
22 66 73 74 72 65 61 6D 2E 68 22  A 23 69 6E 63  "fstream.h".#inc
6C 75 64 65 20 22 63 74 79 70 65 2E 68 22  A 23  lude "ctype.h".#
69 6E 63 6C 75 64 65 20 22 69 6F 6D 61 6E 69 70  include "iomanip
2E 68 22  A 23 69 6E 63 6C 75 64 65 20 22 73 74  .h".#include "st
64 69 6F 2E 68 22  A  A 6D 61 69 6E 28 69 6E 74  dio.h"..main(int
20 61 72 67 63 2C 20 63 68 61 72 20 2A 61 72 67   argc, char *arg
76 5B 5D 29  A 7B  A 20 20 69 66 28 61 72 67 63  v[]).{.  if(argc
21 3D 32 29 20 7B  A 20 20 20 20 63 6F 75 74 20  !=2) {.    cout
3C 3C 20 22 55 73 61 67 65 3A 20 44 69 73 70 6C  << "Usage: Displ
61 79 20 3C 66 69 6C 65 6E 61 6D 65 3E 5C 6E 22  ay <filename>\n"
Press ENTER to continue:
```

The ignore( ) Function

You can use the **ignore( )** member function to read and discard characters from the input stream. It has this prototype:

istream &ignore(int *num* = 1, int *delim* = EOF);

It reads and discards characters until either *num* characters have been ignored (1 by default) or until the character specified by *delim* is encountered (EOF by default). If the delimiting character is encountered, it is not removed from the input stream.

The next program reads a file called TEST. It ignores characters until either a space is encountered or 10 characters have been read. It then displays the rest of the file.

```
#include "iostream.h"
#include "fstream.h"

main()
{
  ifstream in("test");

  if(!in) {
    cout << "Cannot open file\n";
    return 1;
  }

  // Ignore up to 10 characters or until first
  // space is found.
  in.ignore(10, ' ');
```

```
char c;
while(in) {
  in.get(c);
  cout << c;
}

in.close();
return 0;
}
```

peek( ) and putback( )

You can obtain the next character in the input stream without removing it from that stream by using **peek( )**. It has this prototype:

   int peek();

It returns the next character in the stream or EOF if the end of the file is encountered.

You can return the last character read from a stream to that stream by using **putback( )**. Its prototype is

   istream &putback(char *c*);

where *c* is the last character read.

flush( )

When output is performed, data is not immediately written to the physical device linked to the stream. Instead, information is stored in an internal buffer until the buffer is full. Only then are the contents of that buffer written to disk. However, you can force the information to be physically written to disk before the buffer is full by calling **flush( )**. Its prototype is

   ostream &flush();

Calls to **flush( )** might be warranted when a program is going to be used in adverse environments (for example, in situations where power outages occur frequently).

Random Access

In C++'s I/O system, you perform random access by using the **seekg( )** and **seekp( )** functions. Their most common forms are

istream &seekg(streamoff *offset*, seek_dir *origin*);
ostream &seekp(streamoff *offset*, seek_dir *origin*);

Here, **streamoff** is a type defined in **iostream.h** that is capable of containing the largest valid value that *offset* can have. Also, **seek_dir** is an enumeration that has these values:

```
ios::beg
ios::cur
ios::end
```

The C++ I/O system manages two pointers associated with a file. One is the *get pointer*, which specifies where in the file the next input operation will occur. The other is the *put pointer*, which specifies where in the file the next output operation will occur. Each time an input or output operation takes place, the appropriate pointer is automatically sequentially advanced. However, using the **seekg( )** and **seekp( )** functions allows you to access the file in a nonsequential fashion.

The **seekg( )** function moves the associated file's current get pointer *offset* number of bytes from the specified *origin*, which must be one of these three values:

ios::beg	Beginning-of-file
ios::cur	Current location
ios::end	End-of-file

The **seekp( )** function moves the associated file's current put pointer *offset* number of bytes from the specified *origin*, which must be one of the values just shown.

The following program demonstrates the **seekp( )** function. It allows you to change a specific character in a file. Specify a file name on the command line, followed by the number of the byte in the file you want to change, followed by the new character. Notice that the file is opened for read/write operations.

```
#include "iostream.h"
#include "fstream.h"
#include "stdlib.h"

main(int argc, char *argv[])
{
  if(argc!=4) {
    cout << "Usage: CHANGE <filename> <byte> <char>\n";
    return 1;
  }

  fstream out(argv[1], ios::in|ios::out);
  if(!out) {
    cout << "Cannot open file";
    return 1;
  }

  out.seekp(atoi(argv[2]), ios::beg);

  out.put(*argv[3]);
  out.close();

  return 0;
}
```

For example, to use this program to change the 12th byte of a file called TEST to a Z, use this command line:

    change test 12 Z

The next program uses **seekg( )**. It displays the contents of a file beginning with the location you specify on the command line.

```
#include "iostream.h"
#include "fstream.h"
#include "stdlib.h"

main(int argc, char *argv[])
```

```
{
  char ch;

  if(argc!=3) {
    cout << "Usage: SHOW <filename> <starting location>\n";
    return 1;
  }

  ifstream in(argv[1]);
  if(!in) {
    cout << "Cannot open file";
    return 1;
  }

  in.seekg(atoi(argv[2]), ios::beg);

  while(in.get(ch))
    cout << ch;

  return 0;
}
```

The following program uses both **seekp( )** and **seekg( )** to reverse the first <num> characters in a file:

```
#include "iostream.h"
#include "fstream.h"
#include "stdlib.h"

main(int argc, char *argv[])
{
  if(argc!=3) {
    cout << "Usage: Reverse <filename> <num>\n";
    return 1;
  }

  fstream inout(argv[1], ios::in|ios::out);

  if(!inout) {
    cout << "Cannot open input file.\n";
    return 1;
  }

  long e, i, j;
  char c1, c2;
  e = atol(argv[2]);

  for(i=0, j=e; i<j; i++, j--) {
    inout.seekg(i, ios::beg);
    inout.get(c1);
    inout.seekg(j, ios::beg);
    inout.get(c2);

    inout.seekp(i, ios::beg);
```

```
   inout.put(c2);
   inout.seekp(j, ios::beg);
   inout.put(cl);
  }

  inout.close();
  return 0;
}
```

To use the program, specify the name of the file that you want to reverse, followed by the number of characters to reverse. For example, to reverse the first ten characters of a file called TEST, use this command line:

reverse test 10

If the file had contained this:

This is a test.

the file will contain the following after the program executes:

a si sihTtest.

You can determine the current position of each file pointer by using these functions:

streampos tellg( );
streampos tellp( );

Here, **streampos** is a type defined in **iostream.h** that is capable of holding the largest value that either function can return.

I/O Status

The C++ I/O system maintains status information about the outcome of each I/O operation. The current state of the I/O system is held in an integer, in which the following flags are encoded:

Name	Meaning
goodbit	0 when no errors occur
	1 when an error has occurred
eofbit	1 when end-of-file is encountered
	0 otherwise
failbit	1 when a nonfatal I/O error has occurred
	0 otherwise
badbit	1 when a fatal I/O error has occurred
	0 otherwise

These flags are enumerated inside **ios**.

There are two ways in which you can obtain I/O status information. First, you can call the **rdstate( )** member function. It has this prototype:

```
int rdstate();
```

It returns the current status of the error flags encoded into an integer. As you can probably guess from looking at the preceding list of flags, **rdstate( )** returns zero when no error has occurred. Otherwise, an error bit is turned on.

The following program illustrates **rdstate( )**. It displays the contents of a text file. If an error occurs, the program reports it, using **checkstatus( )**.

```
#include "iostream.h"
#include "fstream.h"

void checkstatus(ifstream &in);

main(int argc, char *argv[])
{
  if(argc!=2) {
    cout << "Usage: Display <filename>\n";
    return 1;
  }

  ifstream in(argv[1]);

  if(!in) {
    cout << "Cannot open input file.\n";
    return 1;
  }
```

```
   char c;
   while(in.get(c)) {
     cout << c;
     checkstatus(in);
   }

   checkstatus(in);   // check final status
   in.close();
   return 0;
}

void checkstatus(ifstream &in)
{
   int i;

   i = in.rdstate();

   if(i & ios::eofbit)
     cout << "EOF encountered\n";
   else if(i & ios::failbit)
     cout << "Non-Fatal I/O error\n";
   else if(i & ios::badbit)
     cout << "Fatal I/O error\n";
}
```

This program will always report one "error." After the **while** loop ends, the final call to **checkstatus( )** reports, as expected, that an EOF has been encountered. You might find the **checkstatus( )** function useful in programs that you write.

The other way that you can determine if an error has occurred is by using one or more of these functions:

    int bad( );
    int eof( );
    int fail( );
    int good( );

The **eof( )** function was discussed earlier. The **bad( )** function returns true if **badbit** is set. The **fail( )** returns true if **failbit** is set. The **good( )** function returns true if there are no errors. Otherwise, it returns false.

Once an error has occurred, it may need to be cleared before your program continues. To do this, use the **clear( )** function, which has this prototype:

    void clear(int *flags* = 0);

If *flags* is zero (as it is by default), all error flags are cleared (reset to zero). Otherwise, set *flags* to the flags or values you want to clear.

Customized I/O and Files

In Chapter 17, "The C++ I/O System Basics," you learned how to overload the insertion and extraction operators relative to your own classes. In that chapter, only console I/O was performed. However, because all C++ streams are the same, you can use the same overloaded inserter function to output to the screen or to a file with no changes whatsoever. As an example, the following program reworks the phone book example in Chapter 17 so that it stores a list on disk. The program is very simple: It allows you to add names to the list or to display the list on the screen. However, as an exercise, you might find it interesting to enhance the program so that it will find a specific number and delete unwanted numbers.

```cpp
#include "iostream.h"
#include "fstream.h"
#include "string.h"

class phonebook {
  char name[80];
  char areacode[4];
  char prefix[4];
  char num[5];
public:
  phonebook() { };
  phonebook(char *n, char *a, char *p, char *nm)
  {
    strcpy(name, n);
    strcpy(areacode, a);
    strcpy(prefix, p);
    strcpy(num, nm);
  }
  friend ostream &operator<<(ostream &stream, phonebook o);
  friend istream &operator>>(istream &stream, phonebook &o);
};

// Display name and phone number.
ostream &operator<<(ostream &stream, phonebook o)
{
  stream << o.name << " ";
  stream << "(" << o.areacode << ") ";
```

```
    stream << o.prefix << "-";
    stream <<  o.num << "\n";
    return stream; // must return stream
}

// Input name and telephone number.
istream &operator>>(istream &stream, phonebook &o)
{
    cout << "Enter name: ";
    stream >> o.name;
    cout << "Enter area code: ";
    stream >> o.areacode;
    cout << "Enter prefix: ";
    stream >> o.prefix;
    cout << "Enter number: ";
    stream >> o.num;
    cout << "\n";
    return stream;
}

main()
{
    phonebook a;

    fstream pb("phone", ios::in | ios::out | ios::app);

    if(!pb) {
        cout << "Cannot open phone book file\n";
        return 1;
    }

    for(;;) {

        char c;
        do {
            cout << "1. Enter numbers\n";
            cout << "2. Display numbers\n";
            cout << "3. Quit\n";
            cout << "\nEnter a choice: ";
            cin >> c;
        } while(c<'1' || c>'3');

        switch(c) {
            case '1':
                cin >> a;
                cout << "Entry is: ";
                cout << a;  // show on screen
                pb << a;  // write to disk
                break;
            case '2':
                char ch;
                pb.seekg(0, ios::beg);
                while(!pb.eof()) {
                    pb.get(ch);
                    cout << ch;
                }
```

```
      pb.clear();  // reset eof
      cout << endl;
      break;
    case '3':
      pb.close();
      return 0;
  }
 }
}
```

Notice that the overloaded ≪ operator can be used to write to a disk file or to the screen without any changes. This is one of the most important and useful features of C++'s approach to I/O.

Array-Based I/O

In addition to console and file I/O, C++'s stream-based I/O system allows *array-based I/O*. *Array-based I/O* uses RAM as the input device, the output device, or both. Array-based I/O is performed through normal C++ streams. In fact, all the information presented in the two preceding chapters is applicable to array-based I/O. What makes array-based I/O unique is that the device linked to the stream is memory.

In some C++ literature, array-based I/O is referred to as *in-RAM I/O*. Also, because the streams are, like all C++ streams, capable of handling formatted information, array-based I/O is sometimes called *in-RAM formatting*. (Sometimes the archaic term *incore formatting* is also used. However, because core memory is largely a thing of the past, this book uses the terms *in-RAM* and *array-based*.)

C++'s array-based I/O is similar in effect to C's **sprintf( )** and **sscanf( )** functions. Both approaches use memory as an input or output device.

To use array-based I/O in your programs you must include **strstream.h**.

The Array-Based Classes

The array-based I/O classes are **istrstream**, **ostrstream**, and **strstream**. These classes are used to create input, output, and input/output streams, respectively. All of these classes have **strstreambuf** as one of their base classes. This class defines several low-level details that are used by the derived classes. In addition to **strstreambuf**, the **istrstream** class also has **istream** as a base. The **ostrstream** class is also derived from **ostream**, and the **strstream** calls also contain the **iostream** classes. Therefore, all array-based classes have access to the same member functions that the "normal" I/O classes do.

Creating an Array-Based Output Stream

To link an output stream to an array, use this **ostrstream** constructor:

ostrstream ostr(char *buf, int size, int mode = ios::out)

Here, *buf* is a pointer to the array that will be used to collect characters written to the stream. The size of the array is passed in the *size* parameter. By default, the stream is opened for normal output, but you can OR various other options with it to create the mode that you need. (For example, you might include the **ios::app** to cause output to be written at the end of any information already contained in the array.) For most purposes, *mode* will be allowed to default.

Once you have opened an array-based output stream, all output to that stream is put into the array. However, no output will be written outside the bounds of the array. An attempt to do so results in an error.

Here is a simple program that demonstrates an array-based output stream:

```
#include "strstream.h"
#include "iostream.h"

main()
{
```

```
char str[80];

ostrstream outs(str, sizeof(str));

outs << "Hello ";
outs << 99-14 << hex << " ";
outs.setf(ios::showbase);
outs << 100 << ends;
cout << str;   // display string on console

return 0;
}
```

This program displays **Hello 85 0x64**. Keep in mind that **outs** is a stream like any other stream; it has the same capabilities as any of the other types of streams that have been described. The only difference is that the device it is linked to is memory. Because **outs** is a stream, manipulators such as **hex** and **ends** are perfectly valid. Also, **ostream** member functions such as **setf( )** are also available for use.

If you want the output array to be null terminated, you must explicitly write a null. In the preceding program, the **ends** manipulator was used to null terminate the string, but you could also have used '**\0**'.

If you're not quite sure what is really happening in the preceding program, compare it to the following C program. This program is functionally equivalent to the C++ version. However, it uses **sprintf( )** to construct an output array.

```
#include "stdio.h"

main()
{
  char str[80];
  sprintf(str, "Hello %d %#x", 99-14, 100);
  printf(str);
  return 0;
}
```

You can determine how many characters are in the output array by calling the **pcount( )** member function. It has this prototype:

   int pcount( );

The number returned by **pcount( )** also includes the null terminator, if it exists.

The next program illustrates **pcount( )**. It reports that 17 characters are in **outs** — 16 characters plus the null terminator.

```
#include "strstream.h"
#include "iostream.h"

main()
{
  char str[80];

  ostrstream outs(str, sizeof(str));

  outs << "Hello ";
  outs << 34 << " " << 1234.23;
  outs << ends;  // null terminate

  cout << outs.pcount(); // display how many chars in outs

  cout << " " << str;

  return 0;
}
```

Using an Array as Input

To link an input stream to an array, use this **istrstream** constructor:

istrstream istr(const char *buf);

Here, buf is a pointer to the array that will be used as a source of characters each time input is performed on the stream. The contents of the array pointed to by buf must be null terminated. However, the null terminator is never read from the array.

Here is an example that uses a string as input:

```
#include "iostream.h"
#include "strstream.h"

main()
{
  char s[] = "10 Hello 0x88 12.23 done";

  istrstream ins(s);

  int i;
```

```
    char str[80];
    float f;

    // reading: 10 Hello
    ins >> i;
    ins >> str;
    cout << i << " " << str << endl;

    // reading 0x88 12.23 done
    ins >> i;

    ins >> f;
    ins >> str;

    cout << hex << i << " " << f << " " << str;

    return 0;
}
```

If you want only part of a string to be used for input, use this form of the **istrstream** constructor:

istrstream istr(const char *buf, int size);

Here, only the first size elements of the array pointed to by buf will be used. This string need not be null terminated because it is the value of size that determines the size of the string.

Streams linked to memory behave just like those linked to other devices. For example, the following program illustrates how contents of any text array may be read. When the end of the array (same as end-of-file) is reached, **ins** will be zero.

```
// This program shows how to read the contents of any
// array that contains text.
#include "iostream.h"
#include "strstream.h"

main()
{
    char s[] = "10.23 this is a test !@#$\n";

    istrstream ins(s);

    char ch;

    // This will read and display the contents
    // of any text array.
    ins.unsetf(ios::skipws); // don't skip spaces
    while (ins) {  // 0 when end of array is reached
```

```
   ins >> ch;
   cout << ch;
 }

 return 0;
}
```

Using Binary I/O

Arrays linked to array-based streams may also contain binary information. When reading binary information, you may need to use the **eof( )**
function to determine when the end of the array has been reached. For
example, this program shows how to read the contents of any array—
binary or text—by using the binary input function **get( )**:

```
#include "iostream.h"
#include "strstream.h"

main()
{
  char s[] = "abcdefghijklmnop\23\22\21";

  istrstream ins(s);

  char ch;

  // This will read the contents of any type of array.
  while (!ins.eof()) {
    ins.get(ch);
    cout << ch;
  }

  return 0;
}
```

In this example, the values formed by \23\22\21 are the nontext control characters CTRL-W, CTRL-V, and CTRL-U. However, any type of
binary data could have been read.

   To output binary characters, use the **put( )** function. If you need to
read buffers of binary data, you can use the **read( )** member function. To
write buffers of binary data, use the **write( )** function.

Input/Output Array-Based Streams

To create an array-based stream that can perform both input and output, use this **strstream** constructor function:

strstream iostr(char *buf*, int *size*, int *mode*);

Here, *buf* points to the string that will be used for I/O operations. The value of *size* specifies the size of the array. The value of *mode* determines how the stream operates. For normal input/output operations, *mode* will be **ios::in | ios::out**. For input, the array must be null terminated.

Here is a program that uses an array to perform both input and output:

```
// Perform both input and output.
#include "iostream.h"
#include "strstream.h"

main()
{
  char iostr[80];

  strstream ios(iostr, sizeof(iostr), ios::in | ios::out);

  int a, b;
  char str[80];

  ios << "10 20 testing";
  ios >> a >> b >> str;
  cout << a << " " << b << " " << str << endl;
}
```

It first writes **10 20 testing** to **iostr** and reads this information from **iostr**.

Random Access Within Arrays

Remember that all normal I/O operations apply to array-based I/O. This includes random access using **seekg( )** and **seekp( )**. For example, the next program seeks the eighth character inside **iostr** and displays it. (It outputs **h**.)

```
#include "iostream.h"
#include "strstream.h"

main()
{
  char iostr[80];

  strstream ios(iostr, sizeof(iostr), ios::in | ios::out);

  char ch;

  ios << "abcdefghijklmnopqrstuvwxyz";
  ios.seekg(7, ios::beg);
  ios >> ch;
  cout << "Character at 7: " << ch;

}
```

You can seek anywhere *inside* the I/O array. However, you are not allowed to seek past an array boundary.

You can also apply functions like **tellg( )** and **tellp( )** to array-based streams.

Using Dynamic Arrays

In the first part of this chapter, when you linked a stream to an output array, the array and its size were passed to the **ostrstream** constructor. This approach is fine as long as you know the maximum number of characters that you will be outputting to that array. However, what if you don't know how large the output array needs to be? The solution to this problem is to use a second form of the **ostrstream** constructor, shown here:

    ostrstream( );

When this constructor is used, **ostrstream** creates and maintains a dynamically allocated array. This array is allowed to grow in length to accommodate the output that it must store.

Notice that the **ostrstream** constructor does *not* return a pointer to the allocated array. To access the dynamically allocated array, you must use a second function, called **str( )**. This function "freezes" the array and returns a pointer to it. Once a dynamic array is frozen, it may not be used for output again. Therefore, wait to freeze the array until you are through outputting characters to it.

Here is a program that uses a dynamic output array:

```
#include "strstream.h"
#include "iostream.h"

main()
{

  char *p;

  ostrstream outs;  // dynamically allocate array

  outs << "I like C++ ";
  outs << -10 << hex << " ";
  outs.setf(ios::showbase);
  outs << 100 << ends;

  p = outs.str(); // Freeze dynamic buffer and return
                  // pointer to it.

  cout << p;

  delete p;  // Free dynamic buffer created by ostrstream().
  return 0;
}
```

As this program illustrates, once a dynamic array has been frozen, it is your responsibility to release its memory back to the system when you are through with it. However, if you never freeze the array, the memory is automatically freed when the stream is destroyed.

You can also use dynamic I/O arrays with the **strstream** class, which may perform both input and output on an array.

Manipulators and Array-Based I/O

Because array-based streams are the same as any other stream, manipulators that you create for I/O in general can be used with array-based I/O with no changes whatsoever. For example, in Chapter 17, the output manipulators **ra( )** and **la( )** (right arrow and left arrow, respectively) were created for console I/O. This program shows that they are just as effective on array-based I/O:

```
// This program uses custom manipulators with
// array-based I/O.

#include "strstream.h"
#include "iostream.h"

// Right Arrow
ostream &ra(ostream &stream)
{
  stream << "-------> ";
  return stream;
}

// Left Arrow
ostream &la(ostream &stream)
{
  stream << " <-------";
  return stream;
}

main()
{
  char str[80];

  ostrstream outs(str, sizeof(str));

  outs << ra << "Look at this number: ";
  outs << 1000000 << la << ends; // null terminate

  cout << " " << str;

  return 0;
}
```

This program displays this output:

```
-------> Look at this number: 1000000 <-------
```

Custom Extractors and Inserters

Because array-based streams are just like other streams, you can create your own extractor and inserter functions the same way you create them for other types of streams. For example, the following program creates a class called **plot**, which maintains the x,y coordinates of a point in two-dimensional space. The overloaded inserter for this class displays a small coordinate plane and plots the location of the point. For simplicity, the range of the x,y coordinates is restricted to 0 through 5.

```cpp
#include "iostream.h"
#include "strstream.h"

const int size=5;

class plot {
  int x, y;
public:
  plot(int i, int j) {
    // for sake of example, restrict x and y to 0 through size
    if(i>size) i = size;  if (i<0) i=0;
    if(j>size) j = size;  if (j<0) j=0;
    x=i; y=j;
  }
  // An inserter for plot.
  friend ostream &operator<<(ostream &stream, plot o);
};

ostream &operator<<(ostream &stream, plot o)
{
  register int i, j;

  for(j=size; j>=0; j--) {
    stream << j;
    if(j == o.y) {
      for(i=0; i<o.x; i++) stream << "   ";
      stream << '*';
    }
    stream << "\n";
  }

  for(i=0; i<=size; i++) stream << " " << i;
  stream << "\n";

  return stream;
}

main()
{
  plot a(2, 3), b(1, 1);

  // output first using cout
  cout << "Output using cout:\n";
  cout << a << "\n" << b << "\n\n";

  char str[200];  // now use RAM-based I/O
  ostrstream outs(str, sizeof(str));
```

```
// now output using outs and in-RAM formatting
outs << a << b << ends;

cout << "Output using in-RAM formatting:\n";
cout << str;
}
```

This program produces the following output:

```
Output using cout:
5
4
3     *
2
1
0
 0 1 2 3 4 5

5
4
3
2
1  *
0
 0 1 2 3 4 5

Output using in-RAM formatting:
5
4
3     *
2
1
0
 0 1 2 3 4 5
5
4
3
2
1  *
0
 0 1 2 3 4 5
```

Uses for Array-Based Formatting

In C, the in-RAM I/O functions **sprintf( )** and **sscanf( )** were particularly useful for preparing output or reading input from nonstandard
devices. However, because of C++'s ability to overload inserters and

extractors relative to a class and to create custom manipulators, many exotic devices can be handled easily by using these features, making the need for in-RAM formatting less important. Still, there are many uses for array-based I/O.

One common use of array-based formatting is to construct a string to be used as input by either a standard library or third-party function. For example, you may need to construct a string that will be parsed by the **strtok( )** standard library function. (The **strtok( )** function "tokenizes"—that is, decomposes to its elements—a string.) Another place where array-based I/O can be used is in text editors that perform complex formatting operations. Often it is easier to use C++'s array-based formatted I/O to construct a complex string than it is to do so by "manual" means.

Perhaps the most important use of RAM-based I/O is that it allows you to fully construct and maintain a complete screen image in memory. This is useful in multitasking environments in which you need to restore a screen that has been overwritten by another task.

TWENTY

Issues and Advanced Topics

Default Function Arguments
Creating Conversion Functions
Copy Constructors
Dynamic Initialization
const and volatile Member Functions
Using the asm Keyword
Linkage Specification
The overload Anachronism
Differences Between C and C++
Future C++ Directions

This chapter discusses several C++ topics not examined elsewhere in this book. Topics include conversion functions, copy constructors, default function arguments, the **asm** keyword, linkage specification, and differences between C and C++.

Default Function Arguments

C++ allows a function to assign a parameter a default value when no argument corresponding to that parameter is specified in a call to that function. The default value is specified in a manner syntactically similar to a variable initialization. For example, this declares **myfunc( )** as taking one **double** argument with a default value of 0.0:

```
void myfunc(double d = 0.0)
{
  .
  .
  .
}
```

Now, **myfunc( )** can be called one of two ways, as the following examples show:

```
myfunc(198.234);  // pass an explicit value

myfunc();    // let function use default
```

The first call passes the value 198.234 to **d**. The second call automatically gives **i** the default value zero.

Default arguments are included in C++ because they provide another method for the programmer to manage greater complexity. To handle the widest variety of situations, quite frequently a function contains more parameters than are required for its most common usage. Thus, when the default arguments apply, you need only remember and specify the arguments that are meaningful to the most common situation, not to the most general case.

A simple illustration of how useful a default function argument can be is shown by the **clrscr( )** function in the following program. The **clrscr( )** function clears the screen by outputting a series of linefeeds (not the most efficient way, but sufficient for this example). Because a very common video mode displays 25 lines of text, the default argument of 25 is provided. However, because some terminals can display more or less than 25 lines (often depending upon what type of video mode is used), you can override the default argument by specifying one explicitly.

```
#include "iostream.h"

void clrscr(int size=25);

main()
{
  register int i;

  for(i=0; i<30; i++ ) cout << i << endl;
  cin.get();
  clrscr(); // clears 25 lines

  for(i=0; i<30; i++ ) cout << i << endl;
  cin.get();
  clrscr(10); // clears 10 lines

  return 0;
}

void clrscr(int size)
{
    for(; size; size--) cout << endl;
}
```

As this program illustrates, when the default value is appropriate to the situation, no argument need be specified when **clrscr( )** is called. However, it is still possible to override the default and give **size** a different value.

A default argument can also be used as a flag telling the function to reuse a previous argument. To illustrate this type of default argument usage a simple function called **iputs( )** is developed here that automatically indents a string by a specified amount. To begin, here is a version of this function that does *not* use a default argument:

```
void iputs(char *str, int indent)
{
  if(indent < 0) indent = 0;

  for( ; indent; indent--) cout << " ";

  cout << str << "\n";
}
```

This version of **iputs( )** is called with the string to output as the first argument and the amount to indent as the second. Although there is nothing wrong with writing **iputs( )** this way, you can improve its usability by providing a default argument for the **indent** parameter that tells **iputs( )** to indent to the previously specified level. It is quite common to display a block of text with each line indented the same amount. In this situation, instead of having to supply the same **indent** argument over and over, you can give **indent** a default value that tells **iputs( )** to indent to the previously specified level. This approach is illustrated in the following program:

```
#include "iostream.h"

// Default indent to -1.  This value tells the function
// to reuse the previous value.
void iputs(char *str, int indent = -1);

main()
{
  iputs("Hello there", 10);
  iputs("This will be indented 10 spaces by default");
  iputs("This will be indented 5 spaces", 5);
  iputs("This is not indented", 0);
}
```

```
void iputs(char *str, int indent)
{
  static i = 0;  // holds previous indent value

  if(indent>=0)
    i = indent;
  else    // reuse old indent value
    indent = i;

  for( ; indent; indent--) cout << " ";

  cout << str << "\n";
}
```

This program displays this output:

```
        Hello there
        This will be indented 10 spaces by default
    This will be indented 5 spaces
This is not indented
```

When you are creating functions that have default argument values, it is important to remember that the default values must be specified only once, and this must be the first time the function is declared within the file. In the preceding example, the default argument was specified in **iputs( )**'s prototype. If you try to specify new (or even the same) default values in **iputs( )**'s definition, the compiler will display an error and not compile your program. Even though default arguments may not be redefined within a program, you can specify different default arguments for each version of an overloaded function.

All parameters that take default values must appear to the right of those that do not. For example, it is incorrect to define **iputs( )** like this:

```
// wrong!
void iputs(int indent = -1, char *str);
```

Once you begin to define parameters that take default values, you may not specify a nondefaulting parameter. That is, a declaration like this is also wrong and will not compile:

```
int myfunc(float f, char *str, int i=10, int j);
```

Because **i** has been given a default value, **j** must be given one too.

You can also use default parameters in an object's constructor function. For example, the **cube** class shown here maintains the integer dimensions of a cube. Its constructor function defaults all dimensions to zero if no other arguments are supplied, as shown here:

```
#include "iostream.h"

class cube {
  int x, y, z;
public:
  cube(int i=0, int j=0, int k=0) {
    x=i;
    y=j;
    z=k;
  }

  int volume() {
    return x*y*z;
  }
};

main()
{
  cube a(2,3,4), b;

  cout << a.volume() << endl;
  cout << b.volume();

  return 0;
}
```

There are two advantages to including default arguments, when appropriate, in a class's constructor function. First, they prevent you from having to provide a parameterless constructor. For example, if the parameters to **cube( )** were not given defaults, the second constructor shown here would be needed to handle the declaration of **b** (which specified no arguments).

```
cube() {x=0; y=0; z=0}
```

Second, defaulting common initial values is more convenient than specifying them each time an object is declared.

Using Default Arguments Correctly

Although default arguments can be very powerful tools when used correctly, they can be misused. The point of default arguments is to allow a function to perform its job in an efficient, easy-to-use manner while still allowing considerable flexibility. Toward this end, all default arguments should represent the way the function is used most of the time. For example, a default argument makes sense if the default value will be used 90 percent of the time. However, if a common value will occur in only 10 percent of the calls and the rest of the time the arguments corresponding to that parameter vary widely, it is probably not a good idea to provide a default argument. The point of default arguments is that their values are those that the programmer will normally associate with a given function. When there is no single value that is normally associated with a parameter, there is no reason for a default argument. In fact, declaring default arguments when there is an insufficient basis destructures your code—it misleads and confuses anyone reading your program. Where, between 10% and 90%, you should elect to use a default argument is, of course, subjective, but 51 percent would seem a reasonable break point.

Creating Conversion Functions

In some situations, you will want to use an object of a class in an expression involving other types of data. Sometimes, overloaded operator functions can provide the means of doing this. However, in other cases, what you want is a simple type conversion from the class type to the target type. Also, the target type is frequently a basic type, such as **float** or **int**. To handle these cases, C++ allows you to create custom *conversion functions*. A conversion function converts your class into a type compatible with that of the rest of the expression. The general format of a type conversion function is

    operator (*type*)( ) {return *value*;}

Here, *type* is the target type that you are converting your class to, and *value* is the value of the class after conversion. Conversion functions return the data of type *type*, and no other return type specifier is allowed. Also, no parameters may be included. A conversion function must be a member of the class for which it is defined.

The following illustration of how to create a conversion function uses the **stack** class developed in Chapter 11. Suppose that you want to be able to mix objects of type **stack** with an integer expression. Further, suppose that the value of a **stack** object used in an integer expression is the number of values currently on the stack. (You might want to do something like this if, for example, you are using **stack** objects in a simulation and are monitoring how quickly the stacks fill up.) One way to approach this is to convert an object of type **stack** into an integer that represents the number of items on the stack. To accomplish this, you use a conversion function that looks like this:

```
operator int() {return tos;}
```

Here is a program that illustrates how the conversion function works:

```
#include "iostream.h"

#define SIZE 100

// this creates the class stack
class stack {
  int stck[SIZE];
  int tos;
public:
  void init();
  void push(int i);
  int pop(void);
  operator int() {return tos;} // conversion of stack to int
};

void stack::init()
{
  tos = 0;
}

void stack::push(int i)
{
  if(tos==SIZE) {
    cout << "stack is full";
    return;
  }
  stck[tos] = i;
  tos++;
}

int stack::pop()
{
  if(tos==0) {
```

```
      cout << "stack underflow";
      return 0;
    }
    tos--;
    return stck[tos];
  }

main()
{
  stack stck;
  int i, j;
  stck.init();

  for(i=0; i<20; i++)  stck.push(i);

  j = stck; // convert to integer

  cout << j << " items on stack\n";

  cout << SIZE - stck << " spaces open\n";
  return 0;
}
```

This program displays this output:

```
20 items on stack
80 spaces open
```

As the program illustrates, when a **stack** object is used in an integer expression, such as **j = stck,** the conversion function is applied to the object. In this specific case, the conversion function returns the value 20. Also, when **stck** is subtracted from **SIZE,** the conversion function is also called.

Here is another example of a conversion function. This program creates a class called **pwr( )** that stores and computes the outcome of some number raised to some power. It stores the result as a **double.** By supplying a conversion function to type **double** and returning the result, you can use objects of type **pwr** in expressions involving other **double** values.

```
#include "iostream.h"

class pwr {
  double b;
  int e;
  double val;
public:
  pwr(double base, int exp);
  pwr operator+(pwr o) {
    double base;
    int exp;
```

```
      base = b + o.b;
      exp = e + o.e;

      pwr temp(base, exp);
      return temp;
   }
   operator double() {return val;}   // convert to double
};

pwr::pwr(double base, int exp)
{
   b = base;
   e = exp;
   val = 1;
   if(exp==0) return;
   for( ; exp>0; exp--) val = val * b;
}

main()
{
   pwr x(4.0, 2);
   double a;

   a = x; // convert to double
   cout << x + 100.2; // convert x to double and add 100.2
   cout << "\n";

   pwr y(3.3, 3), z(0, 0);

   z = x + y;  // no conversion
   a = z;  // convert to double
   cout << a;

   return 0;
}
```

As you can see, when **x** is used in the expression **x + 100.2**, the conversion function is used to produce the **double** value. Notice also that in the expression **x + y**, no conversion is applied because the expression involves only objects of type **pwr**.

As you can infer from the foregoing examples, there are many situations in which it is benificial to create a conversion function for a class. Often, conversion functions provide a more natural syntax to be used when class objects are mixed with the built-in types. Specifically, in the case of the **pwr** class, the availability of the conversion to **double** makes objects of that class used in "normal" mathematical expressions both easier to program and easier to understand.

One final point: You can create different conversion functions to meet different needs. You could define one that converts to **double** or **long**, for example. Each will be applied automatically as determined by the type of each expression.

Copy Constructors

By default, when one object is used to initialize another, C++ performs a bitwise copy. That is, an identical copy of the initializing object is created in the target object. Although it is perfectly adequate for many cases—and generally exactly what you want to happen—there are situations in which a bitwise copy cannot be used. One of the most common situations in which to avoid a bitwise copy is when an object allocates memory when it is created. For example, assume two objects, A and B, of the same class, and assume that A is already in existence. Further, assume that when an object is created, it allocates memory for some internal purpose. Finally, assume that A is used to initialize B. If a simple bitwise copy is performed, then B will be using the same piece of allocated memory that A is using, instead of allocating its own. Clearly, this is not the desired outcome.

To solve the type of problem just described, C++ allows you to create a *copy constructor*, which the compiler uses when one object is used to initialize another. When a copy constructor exists, the bitwise copy is bypassed. The general form of a copy constructor is

```
classname (const classname &o) {
  // body of constructor
}
```

Here, *o* is a reference to the object on the right side of the initialization. For example,

```
// assume some class called myclass

myclass x = y; // explicit use of =

// or

myclass x(y); // more "C++-like" initialization form
```

In either case, a reference to y would be passed to *o*.

Following is an example where an explicit copy constructor function is needed. This program creates a (very) limited "safe" integer array type that prevents array boundaries from being overrun. Storage for each array is allocated by the use of **new**, and a pointer to the memory is maintained within each array object.

```
/* This program creates a "safe" array class.  Since space
   for the array is allocated using new, a copy constructor
   is provided to allocate memory when one array object is
   used to initialize another.
*/
#include "iostream.h"
#include "stdlib.h"

class array {
  int *p;
  int size;
public:
  array(int sz) {
    p = new int[sz];
    if(!p) exit(1);
    size = sz;
  }
  ~array() {delete p;}

  // copy constructor
  array(const array &a);

  void put(int i, int j) {
    if(i>=0 && i<size) p[i] = j;
  }
  int get(int i) {
    return p[i];
  }
};

// copy constructor
array::array(const array &a) {
  int i;

  p = new int[a.size];
  if(!p) exit(1);
  for(i=0; i<a.size; i++) p[i] = a.p[i];
}

main()
{
  array num(10);
  int i;

  for(i=0; i<10; i++) num.put(i, i);
  for(i=9; i>=0; i--) cout << num.get(i);
  cout << "\n";

  // create another array and initialize with num
  array x(num);   // invokes copy constructor
  for(i=0; i<10; i++) cout << x.get(i);

  return 0;
}
```

When **num** is used to initialize **x**, the copy constructor is called, memory
for the new array is allocated and stored in **x.p**, and the contents of

num are copied to **x**'s array. In this way, **x** and **num** have arrays that have the same values, but each array is separate and distinct. (That is, **num.p** and **x.p** do not point to the same piece of memory.) If the copy constructor had not been created, the default bitwise initialization would have resulted in **x** and **num** sharing the same memory for their arrays. (That is, **num.p** and **x.p** would have, indeed, pointed to the same location.)

The copy constructor is called only for initializations. For example, this sequence does not call the copy constructor defined in the preceding program:

```
array a(10);

    .
    .
    .

array b(10);

b = a; // does not call copy constructor
```

In this case, **b** = **a** performs the assignment operation. If = is not overloaded (as it is not here), a bitwise copy will be made. Therefore, in some cases, you may need to overload the = operator as well as create a copy constructor to avoid problems.

Dynamic Initialization

Dynamic initialization is the process by which variables are initialized at run time rather than at compile time. Further, dynamic initialization allows a variable to be initialized through the use of any expression valid at the point of that initialization, including other variables and function calls. Both C and C++ allow local variables to be dynamically initialized. However, in C++, you may also dynamically initialize global variables. For example, this program is perfectly valid:

```
#include "iostream.h"
#include "stdlib.h"
```

```
int i = atoi("1233");  // valid in C++, not C
int x = i * 2;  // valid in C++, not C

main()
{
  cout << "value of i is " << i << endl;
  cout << "value of x is " << x << endl;
  return 0;
}
```

As expected, this programs displays this output:

```
value of i is 1233
value of x is 2466
```

Stated formally, in C++, all global variables are initialized *before* each variable is first used. Generally, most C++ compilers initialize global variables before program execution begins.

const and volatile Member Functions

Class member functions may be declared as **const**, **volatile**, or both. A few rules apply. First, objects declared as **volatile** may call only member functions also declared as **volatile**. A **const** object may not invoke a non-**const** member function. However, a **const** member function can be called by either **const** or non-**const** objects. The rules combine for functions that are both **const** and **volatile**.

Using the asm Keyword

You can embed assembly language directly into your C++ program by using the **asm** keyword. The **asm** keyword has this syntax:

asm (*"string"*);

Here, *string* is passed, untouched, to the assembler.

Turbo C++ and Borland C++ accept three slightly different general forms of the **asm** statement, which are shown here:

asm *instruction* ;
asm *instruction* newline
asm {
   instruction sequence
}

Here, *instruction* is any valid 80x86 assembly language instruction. Unlike any other Turbo C++ statement, an **asm** statement does not have to end with a semicolon. It may end with either a semicolon or a newline.

As a simple (and fairly "safe") example, this program uses **asm** to execute an **INT 5** instruction, which invokes the PC's print-screen function:

```
// Print the screen.
#include <iostream.h>

main(void)
{
  asm (int 5);   // use asm int 5 for Turbo C
  return 0;
}
```

Caution: You must have a thorough working knowledge of assembly language programming to use the **asm** statement. If you are not proficient at assembly language, it is best to avoid using it, because very nasty errors may result.

Linkage Specification

In C++, you may specify how a function is linked. For example, you can tell the compiler to link a function as a C function, as a C++ function, or, depending upon the implementation of your C++ compiler, as a function produced by another language altogether, such as FORTRAN. By default, functions are linked as C++ functions. However, by using a *linkage specification,* you can cause a function to be linked as a different type of language function. The general form of a linkage specifier is

> extern *"language" function-prototype*

where *language* denotes the desired language. All C++ compilers will support C and C++ linkage. Some will support additional languages.

This program causes **myCfunc( )** to be linked as a C function:

```
#include <iostream.h>

extern "C" void myCfunc(void);

main(void)
{
  myCfunc();

  return 0;
}
// This will link as a C function.
void myCfunc(void)
{
  cout << "This links as a C function.\n";
}
```

Note: The **extern** keyword is a necessary part of the linkage specification. Further, the linkage specification must be global; it cannot be used inside a function.

You can specify more than one function at a time by using this form of the linkage specification:

> extern *"language"* {
>   prototypes
> }

The use of a linkage specification is rare, and you will probably not need to use one.

The overload Anachronism

In the first versions of C++ created by Bjarne Stroustrup, overloaded functions had to be explicitly declared as such by use of the **overload** keyword. For example, if **myfunc( )** were to be overloaded, you would need to put this line of code in your program:

```
overload myfunc;
```

However, beginning with the 2.0 specification for C++, the **overload** keyword is no longer needed. For compatibility with older C++ programs, it is still allowed in C++ programs, but its use is now considered anachronistic.

Differences Between C and C++

For the most part, C++ is a superset of ANSI standard C, and virtually all C programs are also C++ programs. However, a few differences do exist, the most important of which are discussed here.

One of the most important yet subtle differences between C and C++ is that in C, a function declared like this:

```
int f();
```

says *nothing* about any parameters to that function. That is, when there is nothing specified between the parentheses following the function's name, in C this means that nothing is being stated, one way or the other, about any parameters to that function. It might have parameters, it might not have parameters. However, in C++, a function declaration like this means that the function does *not* have parameters. That is, in C++, these two declarations are equivalent:

```
int f();

int f(void);
```

In C++, **void** is optional. Many C++ programmers include **void** as a means of making it completely clear to anyone reading the program that a function does not have any parameters, but this is technically unnecessary.

In C++, all functions must be prototyped. This is an option in C (although good programming practice suggests full prototyping be used in a C program).

A small but potentially important difference between C and C++ is that in C, a character constant is automatically elevated to an integer. In C++, it is not.

In C, it is not an error to declare a global variable several times, even though this is bad programming practice. In C++, it is an error.

In C, an identifier may be up to 31 characters long. In C++, no such limit exists. However, from a practical point of view, extremely long identifiers are unwieldy and seldom needed.

In C, although it is unusual, you can call **main( )** from within your program. This is not allowed by C++.

In C, you cannot take the address of a **register** variable. In C++, this is allowed.

Future C++ Directions

At the time of this writing there are two experimental features that will probably be added to C++. They are templates and exception handling. Although it is premature to discuss these experimental features at length, a brief description is provided to pique your interest.

A *template* is used to construct a general family of classes or functions that describe a generic set of operations. However, the type of the data that the classes and functions will be operating on is not defined by the classes or functions. Rather, it is specified as a parameter. In the future, templates will allow generic subsystems to be built that can operate on virtually any type of data. For example, it will be possible to define a bounded array class with the actual type of the elements held by the array specified by a parameter. You won't need to build separate array classes for each new data type.

In the future, you will be able to cause program execution to jump to a predetermined point when an exceptional condition has occurred. This is referred to as *exception handling*. The general mechanism works like this: when an exception occurs, the exception is *thrown* by use of the **throw** keyword. The exception is *caught* elsewhere in your program where an appropriate **catch** statement is found.

As C++ continues to evolve, these two experimental features are expected to be incorporated into commercially available compilers.

Some C++ Applications

A String Class
A Pop-up Window Class
A Linked List Class

Part Three of this book provides a sampling of applications written using C++. The purpose of this section is twofold. First, the examples help illustrate the benefits of object-oriented programming, including the advantages of polymorphism, encapsulation, and inheritance, as they relate to C++ specifically. Second, the examples show how C++ is also an enhanced and expanded version of C that gives the programmer more power independent of object-oriented methodologies—in other words, a "better C."

A few words are in order about a programming philosophy that fits very well with OOP in general and C++ in particular and that is used extensively in the applications presented here. This programming philosophy is based upon the concept of *messages*. In a message-based approach, all (or at least most) data is held privately inside a **class**. To retrieve or alter an item of data, you send the object a message to this effect. The object processes the message and, if it is correct and possible, performs the actions that the message requests. Code outside the **class** never operates directly on any data privately held by the **class**. This approach reduces the possibility of accidental side effects. It also lets you govern precisely what values the private data of an object may have, because the message handler never allows incorrect actions to be performed on the private data.

In C++, to send an object a message means to call a member (or **friend**) function. The member function then accesses the private data. To better understand this concept, think about a **class** that manages access to a database. In normal C code, to modify an entry in the database, you would simply write a line of code something like the following. (Assume that **database** is an array of some C-like structures.)

```
database[record].balance = 100.75;
```

However, using a message-based approach and C++, you would call a member function with the record number and new value as arguments.

For example, you would use a statement something like the following. (Here, **database** is an object.)

```
database.newbalance(record, 100.75);
```

In this case, no other code actually "touches" the data protected within the object.

The message-based approach is central to preserving encapsulation. Without it, most data would have to be public.

A String Class

As you know, in C++, strings are implemented as null-terminated character arrays and not as a separate data type. This approach makes C++ strings powerful, elegant, and efficient. Also, the close relationship between arrays and pointers allows you to write many "lean and mean" string operations. However, there are many times when you need to use a string but don't need an extremely high level of efficiency and power. In these cases, working with C++ strings can become a tiresome chore. Fortunately, using C++, it is possible to create a string type that trades a little efficiency for a big gain in ease of use.

In this chapter, a string class is developed that makes creating, using, and changing strings much easier.

Defining a String Type

First, it is important to define what is meant by a string type and what sorts of operations can be performed on it. Fortunately, other languages have defined string types that can be looked to as models on which to base the string type discussed here. It may seem strange at first, but one very good model for a string type is BASIC. Although most C and C++ programmers are unenthusiastic about BASIC as a programming language in general, the way that it handles strings is intuitive and easy to use. BASIC is also a good model because virtually all programmers know it.

The string class developed in this chapter does not "clone" BASIC's approach, but it does borrow its most important features, which are examined here.

In BASIC, to give a string a value, you simply assign it a quoted string by using BASIC's assignment operator, the =. For example, this is a valid BASIC string assignment:

```
A$ = "This is a string"
```

(All string variables in BASIC must end with a dollar sign. Of course, the string class developed in this chapter does not have this restriction.) This statement assigns to **A$** the string "This is a string".

You may also assign one string variable to another. For example, this copies into **B$** the string contained in **A$**:

```
B$ = A$
```

As you can see, the main difference between BASIC and C in terms of assigning a string variable a string is that BASIC uses an operator, whereas C uses a call to the **strcpy( )** function (although C allows character arrays to be *initialized* using the = operator).

The **+** operator is used to concatenate two strings in BASIC. For example, this sequence causes **C$** to contain the value "Hi there":

```
A$ = "Hi "
B$ = "there"
C$ = A$ + B$
```

Actually, the preceding sequence could have been simplified like this:

```
A$ = "Hi "
C$ = A$ + "there"
```

Here, a string variable is concatenated with a quoted string. Thus BASIC allows string variables to be concatenated with other string variables or with quoted strings.

One difference between BASIC string concatenation and the standard **strcat( )** function is that the **strcat( )** function modifies one of the strings it is called with so that it contains the result. However, when you add two strings in BASIC, a temporary string containing their concatenation is produced, and the original strings are left unchanged.

String comparisons in BASIC are straightforward because they use the same relational operators used when comparing other data types. All string comparisons are performed using dictionary order. For example, this determines if **A$** is greater than **B$**:

```
IF A$ > B$ THEN PRINT "A$ is greater than B$"
```

As the preceding examples show, the major advantage of BASIC's approach to strings is that it allows all major string operations to be performed using the same operators used by other data types. In a sense, BASIC overloads its assignment, addition, and relational operators so that they also work strings. It is this basic concept that will be implemented by the string class in this chapter. The string type developed here will substitute overloaded operators for calls to library functions.

With BASIC's approach to strings as a backdrop, we are now ready to develop a string class for C++.

The string Class

The string class defined here will meet the following requirements:

- Strings may be assigned by using the assignment operator.

- String objects may be assigned other string objects or quoted strings.

- Concatenation of two string objects is accomplished with the **+** operator.

- String comparisons are performed with the relational operators.

- String objects may be initialized by using either a quoted string or another string object.

- Strings must be able to be of arbitrary and variable lengths. This implies that storage for each string is dynamically allocated.

- A method of converting string objects to C-like strings will be provided.

The **class** that will manage strings is called **string**. Its declaration is shown here:

```
class string {
  char *p;
  int size;
public:
  string(char *str);
  string();
  string(const string &o);  // copy constructor

  ~string() {delete p;}

  friend ostream &operator<<(ostream &stream, string &o);
  friend istream &operator>>(istream &stream, string &o);

  string operator=(string &o);  // assign a string object
  string operator=(char *s);  // assign a quoted string

  string operator+(string &o); // concatenate a string
  string operator+(char *s); // concatenate a quoted string
  friend string operator+(char *s, string &o); /*  concatenate
          a quoted string with a string object */

  string operator-(string &o); // subtract a substring
  string operator-(char *s);  // subtract a quoted substring

  // relational operations between string objects
  int operator==(string &o) {return !strcmp(p, o.p);}
  int operator!=(string &o) {return strcmp(p, o.p);}
  int operator<(string &o) {return strcmp(p, o.p) < 0;}
  int operator>(string &o) {return strcmp(p, o.p) > 0;}
  int operator<=(string &o) {return strcmp(p, o.p) <= 0;}
  int operator>=(string &o) {return strcmp(p, o.p) >= 0;}

  // operations between string objects and quoted strings
  int operator==(char *s) {return !strcmp(p, s);}
  int operator!=(char *s) {return strcmp(p, s);}
  int operator<(char *s) {return strcmp(p, s) < 0;}
```

```
int operator>(char *s) {return strcmp(p, s) > 0;}
int operator<=(char *s) {return strcmp(p, s) <= 0;}
int operator>=(char *s) {return strcmp(p, s) >= 0;}

int strsize() {return strlen(p);} // return size of string
void makestr(char *s) {strcpy(s, p);} // make quoted string

operator char *() {return p;}  // conversion to char *
};
```

The **private** part of **string** contains only two items: **p** and **size**. When a string object is created, memory to hold the string is dynamically allocated by using **new**, and a pointer to that memory is put in **p**. The string pointed to by **p** will be a normal, null-terminated, C-like string. Although it is not technically necessary, the size of the string is held in **size**. Because the string pointed to by **p** is a normal C-like string, it would be possible to compute the size of the string each time it is needed. However, as you will see, this value is used so often by the **string** member functions that the repeated calls to **strlen( )** cannot be justified.

The next several sections detail how the **string** class works.

The Constructor and Destructor Functions

A **string** object may be declared in three different ways. It may be declared without any initialization, and it may be declared with a quoted string as an initializer or with a **string** object as an initializer. The constructors that support these three operations are shown here:

```
// No explicit initialization.
string::string() {
  size = 1; // make room for null terminator
  p = new char[size];
  if(!p) {
    cout << "Allocation error\n";
    exit(1);
  }
  *p = '\0';
}

// Initialize using a C-like quoted string.
string::string(char *str) {
  size = strlen(str) + 1;  // make room for null terminator
```

```
  p = new char[size];
  if(!p) {
    cout << "Allocation error\n";
    exit(1);
  }
  strcpy(p, str);
}

// Initialize using a string object.
string::string(const string &o) {
  size = o.size;
  p = new char[size];
  if(!p) {
    cout << "Allocation error\n";
    exit(1);
  }
  strcpy(p, o.p);
}
```

When a **string** is created with no initializer, it is assigned a null-string. Although the string could have been left undefined, knowing that all **string** objects contain a valid, null-terminated string simplifies several other member functions.

When a **string** is initialized by a quoted string, first its size is determined. This value is stored in **size**. Next, sufficient memory is allocated by **new**. After the safety check that confirms that **p** is not null, the initializing string is copied into the memory pointed to by **p**.

When a **string** object is used to initialize another, the process is similar to using a quoted string. The only difference is that the size of the string is known and does not have to be computed.

You might think that the parameterless constructor could have been avoided by providing a default for the parameter of one of the other constructors. However, a parameterless constructor is required when an array of objects is declared.

Given the three preceding constructors, the following declarations are allowed:

```
string x("my string"); // use quoted string
string y(x); // use another object
string z; // no explicit initializaion
```

The **string** destructor function simply frees the memory pointed to by **p**.

I/O on Strings

Because it is very common to want to input or output strings, the **string** class overloads the **<<** and **>>** operators, as shown here:

```
// Output a string.
ostream &operator<<(ostream &stream, string &o)
{
  stream << o.p;
  return stream;
}

// Input a string.
istream &operator>>(istream &stream, string &o)
{
  char t[255];  // arbitrary size - change if necessary
  int len;

  for(len=0; len<255; len++) {
    stream.get(t[len]);
    if(t[len]=='\n') break;
    if(t[len]=='\b')
      if(len) {
        len--;
        cout << "'\b'";
      }
  }
  t[len] = '\0';
  len++;

  if(len > o.size) {
    delete o.p;
    o.p = new char[len];
    if(!o.p) {
      cout << "Allocation error\n";
      exit(1);
    }
    o.size = len;
  }
  strcpy(o.p, t);
  return stream;
}
```

As you can see, output is very simple. However, notice that the parameter **o** is passed by reference. The reason for this may not be apparent at first glance. Remember that the **string** destructor function frees the memory pointed to by **p**. If **o** were a normal, call-by-value parameter, a copy of the argument would be made and assigned to **o**. This means that the copy's **p** would contain the same value and point to the same memory as the **p** contained within the original object used as the argument. However, when that copy is destroyed at the time the function exits, the memory pointed to by **p** is freed—but the memory freed is the same memory that the original argument's **p** is still using! Thus, passing a **string** object by value causes the memory pointed to by the argument to be prematurely freed. However, if a reference parameter is used, no new object is created and the premature releasing of the memory pointed to by **p** is avoided. For this reason, all **string** parameters are passed by reference. (Any function you create that takes **string** parameters should do the same.)

Inputting a **string** proves to be a little more difficult than outputting one. The reason is that a statement like this cannot be used to read input:

```
stream >> t;
```

This is because the version of **>>** overloaded for reading C-like strings stops reading input when the first white-space character is encountered. Therefore, it is necessary to read a string by inputting a character at a time. The version overloaded for the **string** type reads characters until a newline is encountered.

Once the string has been read, if the size of the new string exceeds that of the one currently held by **o**, that memory is released and a larger amount is allocated. The new string is then copied into it.

The Assignment Functions

You can assign a **string** object a string in two ways. First, you can assign another **string** object to it. Second, you can assign it a quoted string. The two overloaded **operator=( )** functions that accomplish these operations are shown here:

```
// Assign a string object to a string object.
string string::operator=(string &o)
{
  string temp(o.p);

  if(o.size > size) {
    delete p;  // free old memory
    p = new char[o.size];
    if(!p) {
      cout << "Allocation error\n";
      exit(1);
    }
  }

  strcpy(p, o.p);
  strcpy(temp.p, o.p);

  return temp;
}

// Assign a quoted string to a string object.
string string::operator=(char *s)
{
  int len = strlen(s) + 1;
  if(size < len) {
    delete p;
    p = new char[len];
    size = len;
    if(!p) {
      cout << "Allocation error\n";
      exit(1);
    }
  }
  strcpy(p, s);
  return *this;
}
```

These two functions work by first checking to see if the memory currently pointed to by **p** of the target **string** object is sufficiently large to hold what will be copied to it. If not, the old memory is released and new memory is allocated. Then the string is copied into the object and the result is returned. These functions allow the following types of assignments:

```
string x("test"), y;

y = x; // string object to string object

x = "new string for x"; // quoted string to string object
```

Each assignment function must return the value assigned (that is, the right-hand value) so that multiple assignments like this can be supported:

```
string x, y, z;

x = y = z = "test";
```

Concatenation

Concatenation of two strings is accomplished by using the **+** operator. The **string** class allows for the following three distinct concatenation situations.

- Concatenation of a string object with another string object
- Concatenation of a string object with a quoted string
- Concatenation of a quoted string with a string object

When used in these situations, the **+** operator produces as its outcome a **string** object that is the concatenation of its two operands. It does not actually modify either operand. (This approach differs from the **strcat( )** function, which modifies its first argument.)

The overloaded **operator+( )** functions are shown here:

```
// Concatenate two string objects.
string string::operator+(string &o)
{
  int len;
  string temp;

  delete temp.p;
  len = strlen(o.p) + strlen(p) + 1;
  temp.p = new char[len];
  temp.size = len;
  if(!temp.p) {
    cout << "Allocation error\n";
    exit(1);
  }
  strcpy(temp.p, p);

  strcat(temp.p, o.p);
```

```
    return temp;
}

// Concatenate a string object and a quoted string.
string string::operator+(char *s)
{
  int len;
  string temp;

  delete temp.p;

  len = strlen(s) + strlen(p) + 1;
  temp.p = new char[len];
  temp.size = len;
  if(!temp.p) {
    cout << "Allocation error\n";
    exit(1);
  }
  strcpy(temp.p, p);

  strcat(temp.p, s);

  return temp;
}

// Concatenate a quoted string and a string object.
string operator+(char *s, string &o)
{
  int len;
  string temp;

  delete temp.p;

  len = strlen(s) + strlen(o.p) + 1;
  temp.p = new char[len];
  temp.size = len;
  if(!temp.p) {
    cout << "Allocation error\n";
    exit(1);
  }
  strcpy(temp.p, s);

  strcat(temp.p, o.p);

  return temp;
}
```

All three functions work basically in the same way. First, a temporary **string** object called **temp** is created. This object will contain the outcome of the concatenation, and it is the object returned by the functions. Next, the memory pointed to by **temp.p** is freed. The reason for this is that when **temp** is created, only 1 byte of memory is allocated (as a placeholder) because there is no explicit initialization. Next, enough memory is allocated to hold the concatenation of the two strings. Finally, the two strings are copied into the memory pointed to by **temp.p**, and **temp** is returned.

Substring Subtraction

A useful string function not found in many other computer languages is substring subtraction. As implemented by the **string** class, *substring subtraction* removes all occurrences of a specified substring from another string. Substring subtraction is accomplished by using the – operator.

The **string** class supports two cases of substring subtraction. One allows a **string** object to be subtracted from another **string** object. The other allows a quoted string to be removed from a **string** object. The two **operator –( )** functions are shown here:

```
// Subtract a substring from a string.
string string::operator-(string &substr)
{
  string temp(p);
  char *s1;
  int i, j;

  s1 = p;
  for(i=0; *s1; i++) {
    if(*s1!=*substr.p) { // if not first letter of substring
      temp.p[i] = *s1;    // then copy into temp
      s1++;
    }
    else { // might be substring
      for(j=0; substr.p[j]==s1[j] && substr.p[j]; j++) ;
      if(!substr.p[j]) {  // is substring, so remove it
        s1 += j;
        i--;
      }
      else {  // is not substring, continue copying
        temp.p[i] = *s1;
        s1++;
      }
    }
  }
  temp.p[i] = '\0';
  return temp;
}

// Subtract quoted string from a string object.
string string::operator-(char *substr)
{
```

```
  string temp(p);
  char *sl;
  int i, j;

  sl = p;
  for(i=0; *sl; i++) {
    if(*sl!=*substr) { // if not first letter of substring
      temp.p[i] = *sl; // then copy into temp
      sl++;
    }
    else {
      for(j=0; substr[j]==sl[j] && substr[j]; j++) ;
      if(!substr[j]) { // is substring, so remove it
        sl += j;
        i--;
      }
      else { // is not substring, continue copying
        temp.p[i] = *sl;
        sl++;
      }
    }
  }
  temp.p[i] = '\0';
  return temp;
}
```

These functions work by copying the contents of the left-hand operand
into **temp**, removing any occurrences of the substring specified by the
right-hand operand during the process. The resulting **string** is returned.
Understand that neither operand is modified by the process.

The **string** class allows substring subtractions like these:

```
string x("I like C++"), y("like");
string z;

z = x - y;  // z will contain "I  C++"

z = x - "C++"  // z will contain "I like "

// multiple occurrences are removed
z = "ABCDABCD";
x = z -"A" // x contains "BCDBCD"
```

The Relational Operators

The **string** class supports the full range of relational operations to be
applied to strings. The overloaded relational operators are defined

within the **string class** declaration. They are repeated here for your convenience:

```
// relational operations between string objects
int operator==(string &o) {return !strcmp(p, o.p);}
int operator!=(string &o) {return strcmp(p, o.p);}
int operator<(string &o) {return strcmp(p, o.p) < 0;}
int operator>(string &o) {return strcmp(p, o.p) > 0;}
int operator<=(string &o) {return strcmp(p, o.p) <= 0;}
int operator>=(string &o) {return strcmp(p, o.p) >= 0;}

// operations between string objects and quoted strings
int operator==(char *s) {return !strcmp(p, s);}
int operator!=(char *s) {return strcmp(p, s);}
int operator<(char *s) {return strcmp(p, s) < 0;}
int operator>(char *s) {return strcmp(p, s) > 0;}
int operator<=(char *s) {return strcmp(p, s) <= 0;}
int operator>=(char *s) {return strcmp(p, s) >= 0;}
```

The relational operations are very straightforward; you should have no trouble understanding their implementation. However, keep in mind that the **string** class implements comparisons between two **string** objects or comparisons that have a **string** object as the left operand and a quoted string as the right operand. If you want to be able to put the quoted string on the left and a **string** object on the right, you will need to add additional relational functions.

Given the overloaded relational operator functions defined by **string,** the following types of string comparisons are allowed:

```
string x("one"), y("two"), z("three");

if(x < y) cout << "x less than y";

if(z=="three")  cout "z equals three";

y = "o";
z = "ne";
if(z==(y+z)) cout "x equals y+z";
```

Miscellaneous String Functions

The **string** class defines three functions that make **string** objects integrate more completely with normal C-like strings. They are **strsize( ),**

makestr( ), and the conversion function **operator char** *( ). These functions are defined within the **string** declaration and are shown here:

```
int strsize() {return strlen(p);} // return size of string
void makestr(char *s) {strcpy(s, p);} // make quoted string

operator char *() {return p;}  // conversion to char *
```

The first two functions are easy to understand. As you can see, the **strsize( )** function returns the length of the string pointed to by **p**. The **makestr( )** function copies into a character array the string pointed to by **p**. This function is useful when you want to obtain a C-like string given a **string** object.

The conversion function **operator char** *( ) returns **p**, which is, of course, a pointer to the string contained within the object. This function allows a **string** object to be used anywhere that a C-like string can be used. For example, this is valid code:

```
string x("Hello");

// output the string using a standard C++ function
puts(x); // automatic conversion to char *
```

As you probably know, a conversion function is automatically executed when object is involved in an expression for which the conversion is defined. In this case, because the prototype for the **puts( )** function tells the compiler that its argument is of type **char** *, the conversion from **string** to **char** * is automatically performed, causing a pointer to the string contained within **x** to be returned. Because of the conversion function, you can use a **string** object in place of a normal C-like string as an argument to any function that takes an argument of type **char** *.

Note: The conversion to **char** * does circumvent encapsulation, because once a function has a pointer to the object's string, it is possible for that function to modify the string directly, bypassing the **string** member functions and without that object's knowledge. For this reason, you must use the conversion to **char** * with care. (If you don't need this conversion, simply delete it from the class specification.) The loss of encapsulation in this case is offset by increased utility and integration with existing library functions. However, this tradeoff is not always warranted.

The Entire string Class

Here is a listing of the entire **string** class along with a short **main( )** function that demonstrates its features:

```
#include "iostream.h"
#include "string.h"
#include "stdlib.h"
#include "conio.h"
#include "stdio.h"

class string {
  char *p;
  int size;
public:
  string(char *str);
  string();
  string(const string &o);  // copy constructor

  ~string() {delete p;}

  friend ostream &operator<<(ostream &stream, string &o);
  friend istream &operator>>(istream &stream, string &o);

  string operator=(string &o);  // assign a string object
  string operator=(char *s);  // assign a quoted string

  string operator+(string &o); // concatenate a string
  string operator+(char *s); // concatenate a quoted string
  friend string operator+(char *s, string &o); /* concatenate
          a quoted string with a string object */

  string operator-(string &o); // subtract a substring
  string operator-(char *s);  // subtract a quoted substring

  // relational operations between string objects
  int operator==(string &o) {return !strcmp(p, o.p);}
  int operator!=(string &o) {return strcmp(p, o.p);}
  int operator<(string &o) {return strcmp(p, o.p) < 0;}
  int operator>(string &o) {return strcmp(p, o.p) > 0;}
  int operator<=(string &o) {return strcmp(p, o.p) <= 0;}
  int operator>=(string &o) {return strcmp(p, o.p) >= 0;}

  // operations between string objects and quoted strings
  int operator==(char *s) {return !strcmp(p, s);}
  int operator!=(char *s) {return strcmp(p, s);}
  int operator<(char *s) {return strcmp(p, s) < 0;}
  int operator>(char *s) {return strcmp(p, s) > 0;}
  int operator<=(char *s) {return strcmp(p, s) <= 0;}
  int operator>=(char *s) {return strcmp(p, s) >= 0;}

  int strsize() {return strlen(p);} // return size of string
  void makestr(char *s) {strcpy(s, p);} // make C-like string
```

```
  operator char *() {return p;}   // conversion to char *
};

// No explicit initialization.
string::string() {
  size = 1;   // make room for null terminator
  p = new char[size];
  if(!p) {
    cout << "Allocation error\n";
    exit(1);
  }
  strcpy(p, "");
}

// Initialize using a quoted string.
string::string(char *str) {
  size = strlen(str) + 1;   // make room for null terminator
  p = new char[size];
  if(!p) {
    cout << "Allocation error\n";
    exit(1);
  }
  strcpy(p, str);
}

// Initialize using a string object.
string::string(const string &o) {
  size = o.size;
  p = new char[size];
  if(!p) {
    cout << "Allocation error\n";
    exit(1);
  }
  strcpy(p, o.p);
}

// Output a string.
ostream &operator<<(ostream &stream, string &o)
{
  stream << o.p;
  return stream;
}

// Input a string.
istream &operator>>(istream &stream, string &o)
{
  char t[255];   // arbitrary size - change if necessary
  int len;

  for(len=0; len<255; len++) {
    stream.get(t[len]);
    if(t[len]=='\n') break;
    if(t[len]=='\b')
      if(len) {
        len--;
        cout << "'\b'";
      }
```

```
  }
  t[len] = '\0';
  len++;

  if(len > o.size) {
    delete o.p;
    o.p = new char[len];
    if(!o.p) {
      cout << "Allocation error\n";
      exit(1);
    }
    o.size = len;
  }
  strcpy(o.p, t);
  return stream;
}

// Assign a string object to a string object.
string string::operator=(string &o)
{
  string temp(o.p);

  if(o.size > size) {
    delete p;  // free old memory
    p = new char[o.size];
    if(!p) {
      cout << "Allocation error\n";
      exit(1);
    }
  }

  strcpy(p, o.p);
  strcpy(temp.p, o.p);

  return temp;
}

// Assign a quoted string to a string object.
string string::operator=(char *s)
{
  int len = strlen(s) + 1;
  if(size < len) {
    delete p;
    p = new char[len];
    size = len;
    if(!p) {
      cout << "Allocation error\n";
      exit(1);
    }
  }
  strcpy(p, s);
  return *this;
}

// Concatenate two string objects.
string string::operator+(string &o)
{
```

```
  int len;
  string temp;

  delete temp.p;
  len = strlen(o.p) + strlen(p) + 1;
  temp.p = new char[len];
  temp.size = len;
  if(!temp.p) {
    cout << "Allocation error\n";
    exit(1);
  }
  strcpy(temp.p, p);

  strcat(temp.p, o.p);

  return temp;
}

// Concatenate a string object and a quoted string.
string string::operator+(char *s)
{
  int len;
  string temp;

  delete temp.p;

  len = strlen(s) + strlen(p) + 1;
  temp.p = new char[len];
  temp.size = len;
  if(!temp.p) {
    cout << "Allocation error\n";
    exit(1);
  }
  strcpy(temp.p, p);

  strcat(temp.p, s);

  return temp;
}

// Concatenate a quoted string and a string object.
string operator+(char *s, string &o)
{
  int len;
  string temp;

  delete temp.p;

  len = strlen(s) + strlen(o.p) + 1;
  temp.p = new char[len];
  temp.size = len;
  if(!temp.p) {
    cout << "Allocation error\n";
    exit(1);
  }
  strcpy(temp.p, s);
```

```
    strcat(temp.p, o.p);

    return temp;
}

// Subtract a substring from a string.
string string::operator-(string &substr)
{
  string temp(p);
  char *s1;
  int i, j;

  s1 = p;
  for(i=0; *s1; i++) {
    if(*s1!=*substr.p) { // if not first letter of substring
      temp.p[i] = *s1;    // then copy into temp
      s1++;
    }
    else {
      for(j=0; substr.p[j]==s1[j] && substr.p[j]; j++) ;
      if(!substr.p[j]) { // is substring, so remove it
        s1 += j;
        i--;
      }
      else { // is not substring, continue copying
        temp.p[i] = *s1;
        s1++;
      }
    }
  }
  temp.p[i] = '\0';
  return temp;
}

// Subtract quoted string from a string object.
string string::operator-(char *substr)
{
  string temp(p);
  char *s1;
  int i, j;

  s1 = p;
  for(i=0; *s1; i++) {
    if(*s1!=*substr) { // if not first letter of substring
      temp.p[i] = *s1; // then copy into temp
      s1++;
    }
    else {
      for(j=0; substr[j]==s1[j] && substr[j]; j++) ;
      if(!substr[j]) { // is substring, so remove it
        s1 += j;
        i--;
      }
      else { // is not substring, continue copying
        temp.p[i] = *s1;
        s1++;
      }
    }
  }
```

```
  }
  temp.p[i] = '\0';
  return temp;
}

main()
{
  string s1("A sample session using string objects.\n");
  string s2(s1);
  string s3;
  char s[80];

  cout << s1 << s2;

  s3 = s1;
  cout << s1;

  s3.makestr(s);
  cout << "Convert to a C-like string: " << s;

  s2 = "This is a new string.";
  cout << s2 << endl;

  string s4(" So is this.");
  s1 = s2+s4;
  cout << s1 << endl;

  if(s2==s3) cout << "Strings are equal.\n";
  if(s2!=s3) cout << "Strings are not equal.\n";
  if(s1<s4) cout << "s1 less than s4\n";
  if(s1>s4) cout << "s1 greater than s4\n";
  if(s1<=s4) cout << "s1 less than or equals s4\n";
  if(s1>=s4) cout << "s1 greater than or equals s4\n";

  if(s2 > "ABC") cout << "s2 greater than ABC\n\n";

  s1 = "one two three one two three\n";
  s2 = "two";
  cout << "Initial string: " << s1;
  cout << "String after subtracting two: ";
  s3 = s1 - s2;
  cout << s3;

  cout << endl;
  s4 = "Hi there!";
  s3 = s4 + " C++ strings are fun\n";
  cout << s3;
  s3 = s3 - "Hi there!";
  s3 = "Aren't" + s3;
  cout << s3;

  s1 = s3 - "are ";
  cout << s1;
  s3 = s1;

  cout << "Enter a string: ";
  cin >> s1;
  cout << s1 << endl;
```

```
cout << "s1 is " << s1.strsize() << " characters long.\n";

puts(s1);  // convert to char *

s1 = s2 = s3;
cout << s1 << s2 << s3;

s1 = s2 = s3 = "Bye ";
cout << s1 << s2 << s3;

return 0;
}
```

The preceding program produces this output:

```
A sample session using string objects.
A sample session using string objects.
A sample session using string objects.
Convert to a C-like string: A sample session using string objects.
This is a new string.
This is a new string. So is this.
Strings are not equal.
s1 greater than s4
s1 greater than or equals s4
s2 greater than ABC

Initial string: one two three one two three
String after subtracting two: one  three one  three

Hi there! C++ strings are fun
Aren't C++ strings are fun
Aren't C++ strings fun
Enter a string: I like C++
s1 is 10 characters long.
I like C++
Aren't C++ strings fun
Aren't C++ strings fun
Aren't C++ strings fun
Bye Bye Bye
```

This output assumes that the string "I like C++" was entered by the user when prompted for input.

To have easy access to the **string** class, remove the **main( )** function and put the rest of the preceding listing into a file called **str.h**. Then, just include this header file with any program in which you want to use **strings**.

Using strings

To conclude this chapter, two short examples are given that illustrate how the **string** class can be used to simplify string handling in C++. The first example creates a simple thesaurus by using **string**s. It first creates a two-dimensional array of **string**s. Within each pair of strings, the first contains the key word, which is looked up. The second string contains a list of alternative or related words. The program prompts for a word, and if the word is in the thesaurus, alternatives are displayed. This program is very simple, but notice how clean and clear the string handling is because of the use of the **string** class and its operators. (Remember, the header file **str.h** contains the **string** class.)

```
#include "str.h"
#include "iostream.h"

string thesaurus[][2] = {
  "book", "volume, tome",
  "store", "merchant, shop, warehouse",
  "pistol", "gun, handgun, firearm",
  "run", "jog, trot, race",
  "think", "muse, contemplate, reflect",
  "compute", "analyze, work out, solve"
  "", ""
};

main()
{
  string x;

  cout << "Enter word: ";
  cin >> x;

  int i;
  for(i=0; thesaurus[i][0]!=""; i++)
    if(thesaurus[i][0]==x) cout << thesaurus[i][1];

  return 0;
}
```

The next example uses a **string** object to check to see if there is an executable version of a program, given its file name. (This program assumes a DOS-type operating system.) To use the program, specify the file name without an extension on the command line. The program then repeatedly tries to find an executable file by that name by adding an extension, trying to open that file, and reporting the results. (If the file does not exist, it cannot be opened.) After each extension is tried, the extension is subtracted from the file name and a new extension is added. Again, the **string** class and its operators make the string manipulations clean and easy to follow:

```
#include "str.h"
#include "iostream.h"
#include "fstream.h"
```

```
// executable file extensions
char ext[3][4] = {
  "EXE",
  "COM",
  "BAT"
};

main(int argc, char *argv[])
{
  string fname;
  int i;

  if(argc!=2) {
    cout << "Usage: fname\n";
    return 1;
  }

  fname = argv[1];

  fname = fname + ".";   // add period
  for(i=0; i<3; i++) {
    fname = fname + ext[i];   // add extension
    cout << "Trying " << fname << " ";
    ifstream f(fname);
    if(f) {
      cout << "- Exists\n";
      f.close();
    }
    else cout << "- Not found\n";
    fname = fname - ext[i]; // subtract extension
  }

  return 0;
}
```

For example, if this program is called ISEXEC, and assuming that
TEST.EXE exists, the command line **ISEXEC TEST** produces this
output:

```
Trying TEST.EXE - Exists
Trying TEST.COM - Not found
Trying TEST.BAT - Not found
```

One thing to notice about the program is that a **string** object is
used in the call to **open( )**. This works because the conversion function
operator char *( ) is automatically invoked. As this situation illustrates,
by the careful application of C++ features, you can achieve significant
integration between C++'s standard types and types that you create.

As mentioned at the start of this chapter, C++'s approach to strings
is usually more efficient than the **string** type that is developed in this

chapter. Therefore, when the greatest efficiency and speed are required, you should use normal C++ strings. However, in cases where such demands are not as great, the **string** class can greatly simplify string handling.

A Pop-up Window Class

Pop-up Windows
Creating Some Video Support Functions
The Window Class
Displaying and Removing a Window
Window I/O
The Entire Window System
Modifications

The pop-up window has become an important feature of most commercially successful programs. The pop-up window also provides a classic example of object-oriented programming using C++. For these reasons, this chapter develops a text-based window class and provides all the necessary functions to support window-based I/O.

As you probably know, many C++ compilers already supply a windowing class. You might ask if there is any value (beyond providing a good example of a C++ application) in developing yet another windowing system. The answer is yes, for two reasons.

First, commercial windowing systems have to be "all things to all people." Because of the wide variety of video modes and hardware, the typical commercial windowing system is "bloated." In many cases, commerical windowing systems give you more than you really want or need for your application. By contrast, the windowing system developed in this chapter, however, is narrow in focus and is limited to 80-column, text-only operations. Because it works only in text mode, no bulky graphics support is required, so the system is quite small. The windowing system developed in this chapter may not suit every application, but it is very efficient for the applications that can use it.

The other reason to create your own windowing system is that you are in complete control of a system you create. Because hardware is continually evolving, you can enhance your windowing system to take advantage of new video modes or devices. You can also accommodate specialized devices and extend or enhance the system to fit your exact needs.

TWENTY-TWO

Note: Windowing systems are extremely device dependent. This chapter assumes a PC environment, and several of the functions interface directly with ROM BIOS (Basic I/O System). However, by changing only a few functions, you can modify the window system to work in any environment.

Before beginning, it is important to define what a windowing system will do.

Pop-up Windows

A pop-up window is a portion of the screen that is used for a specific purpose. When the window comes into existence, what is currently on the screen is saved and the window is displayed. When the application using that window is finished, the window is removed and the original contents of the screen are restored. It is possible to have several windows on the screen at the same time.

One important feature of a windowing system is that it must not allow an application using the window to write past the boundaries of the window. Because the size of the window is not necessarily known to the application, it is the job of the window routines, not the application, to prevent overwriting. Therefore, all of C++'s normal console I/O routines (such as **printf( )** and **gets( )**) and the **cout** and **cin** streams cannot be used, and alternative window-specific I/O functions must be substituted. In fact, the window-specific I/O functions form a major part of any windowing system.

To understand how windows might be effectively used, imagine that you have written a text editor that includes some extra features. One of these extra features is a calculator. Because using the calculator is not actually part of text editing, it makes sense to use a pop-up window whenever it is activated. Thus, when the calculator is used, text editing is simply suspended; it is not completely disrupted. Once the calculations have been performed, the calculator window is removed and text editing continues.

Creating Some Video Support Functions

Before creating the window system, it is necessary to develop some support functions. Because the creation of pop-up windows requires direct and intimate control of the screen, specialized functions are needed that perform screen I/O. As stated, it is not possible to use C++'s normal output functions and operators. The specialized functions will bypass both DOS and BIOS and write directly to the video hardware itself. This is the only way that sufficiently fast screen updates can be accomplished.

To begin, here is a short overview of the PC's video system.

Note: The discussion of the PC's video system presented in this chapter is sufficient to understand how the windowing system works. Consult other texts to learn more about the important topic of video interfacing.

The PC Video System

All PCs contain some type of video adapter that outputs images to the monitor. The four most common types of adapters are the monochrome adapter, the color/graphics adapter (CGA), the enhanced graphics adapter (EGA), and the video graphics array (VGA). The CGA, EGA, and VGA have several modes of operation. The windowing system developed in this chapter requires that the video system be in 80-column text mode. This mode is usually the default mode of operation for general-purpose applications. The monochrome adapter uses mode 7 for 80-column text mode. The CGA/EGA/VGA adapters use either mode 2 or mode 3.

The characters displayed on the screen are held in RAM that is reserved for the display adapters. The location of the video RAM used by the monochrome adapter is B000:0000H, and the CGA/EGA/VGA video RAM starts at B800:0000H. Although the CGA, EGA, and VGA function differently in some modes, they are the same in modes 2 and 3.

Each character displayed on the screen requires 2 bytes of video memory. The first byte holds the actual character, and the second holds its *screen attribute*. For color adapters, the attribute byte is interpreted as shown in Table 22-1. The primary colors can be combined to produce

Bit	Binary Value	Meaning When Set
0	1	Blue foreground
1	2	Green foreground
2	4	Red foreground
3	8	Low intensity
4	16	Blue background
5	32	Green background
6	64	Red background
7	128	Blinking character

Table 22-1.   The Video Attribute Byte

additional colors. If you have a CGA, EGA, or VGA, by default the characters are displayed with an attribute byte value of 7. This turns the three foreground colors on, producing white. To produce reverse video, the foreground bits are turned off and the three background bits are turned on, producing a value of 70H.

The monochrome adapter recognizes the blinking and intensity bits. Fortunately, it is designed to interpret an attribute of 7 as normal, and 70H produces reverse video. Also, the value 1 produces underlined characters.

Each adapter actually has four times as much memory as it needs to display text in 80-column mode. The reasons for this are twofold. First, the extra memory is needed for graphics (except in the monochrome adapter, of course). Second, it allows multiple screens to be held in RAM and then simply switched in when needed. Each region of memory is called a *video page*, and the effect of switching the active video page is quite dramatic. By default, page 0 is used when DOS initializes, and virtually all applications use page 0. For this reason it will be used in the routines in this chapter. However, you can use other pages if you desire.

There are three ways to access the video adapter. The first is through DOS calls, a method that is far too slow for pop-up windows. The second way is through BIOS routines, which is quicker, and on faster machines it may be fast enough if the windows are small. The third way is by reading from and writing to the video RAM directly, which is very fast but requires more programming effort. However, in order for pop-up windows to really "pop up," direct access of the video RAM is necessary. Therefore, this is the approach taken in the windowing system developed here.

To allow the windowing system to access the video RAM, a pointer to it is needed. However, since the video RAM lies in a different segment from that used by a typical program, a **far** pointer must be used. If your C++ compiler does not support **far** pointers, you cannot directly access the video RAM. (This would be very rare). **far** pointers can be supported in one of two ways by a C++ compiler. First, the **far** keyword extension is used by many compilers. It allows a pointer to be declared as **far**. The second way is to use a large memory model compiler in which all pointers are **far** by default. The routines used in this chapter use the **far** type modifier. If you like, you can remove it and simply compile the code by using a large memory model compiler.

Accessing the BIOS

Although the video functions that actually read or write information will bypass DOS and BIOS and access the video RAM directly, the BIOS will still be used for a few operations. Calls are made to BIOS by using a software interrupt. The function that generates a software interrupt is **int86( )**. (Some compilers may give this function a different name.) The **int86( )** function is specific to DOS environments. It has this prototype:

int int86(int *num*, union REGS **inregs*, union REGS **outregs*);

The BIOS has several different interrupts for varying purposes, and it is beyond the scope of this chapter to discuss them. However, the one related to the video adapter is interrupt 16 (10H). Like many BIOS interrupts, interrupt 16 has several options, which are selected based upon the value of the AH register. If the BIOS function returns a value, it is generally returned in AX. However, sometimes other registers are used if several values are returned. The return value of **int86( )** is the value of the **AX** register.

The type **REGS** is supplied in the header **dos.h**. The one shown here is defined by Turbo C++; however, it is similar to the one defined by other compilers.

```
/*
    Copyright (c) Borland International 1987,1988,1990,1991
    All Rights Reserved.
*/

struct WORDREGS {
    unsigned int    ax, bx, cx, dx, si, di, cflag, flags;
};

struct BYTEREGS {
    unsigned char   al, ah, bl, bh, cl, ch, dl, dh;
};

union   REGS    {
    struct  WORDREGS x;
    struct  BYTEREGS h;
};
```

As you can see, **REGS** is a union of two structures. Using the **WORDREGS** structure allows you to access the registers of the CPU as 16-bit quantities. **BYTEREGS** gives you access to the individual 8-bit registers.

Determining the Location of the Video RAM

When reading and writing directly to the video RAM, you first need to overcome the problem caused by the fact that the monochrome adapter has its video RAM at B000:0000H, while the others have theirs at B800:0000H. For the window routines to operate correctly for each adapter, they need to know which adapter is in the system. Fortunately, there is an easy way to do this. The BIOS interrupt 16, function 15, returns the current video mode. As stated earlier, the routines developed in this chapter require that the mode be 2, 3, or 7. Modes 2 and 3 can be used only by the CGA, EGA, or VGA, and these adapters cannot use mode 7—only the monochrome adapter can. Therefore, if the current video mode is 7, there is a monochrome adapter in use; otherwise, it is a CGA, EGA, or VGA. For windowing purposes, the CGA, EGA, and VGA function the same in text mode, so it doesn't matter which is in the system. Therefore, using the current video mode, it is possible to set a global **far** pointer to the address of the video RAM. The following functions perform this job:

```
char far *vid_mem; // pointer to screen memory when in text mode

void set_v_ptr()
{
  int vmode;

  vmode = video_mode();
  if((vmode!=2) && (vmode!=3) && (vmode!=7)) {
    cout << "video must be in 80 column text mode";
    exit(1);
  }
  // set proper address of video RAM
  if(vmode==7) vid_mem = (char far *) 0xB0000000;
  else vid_mem = (char far *) 0xB8000000;
}

// Returns the current video mode.
video_mode(void)
{
  union REGS r;

  r.h.ah = 15; // get video mode
  return int86(0x10, &r, &r) & 255;
}
```

The **video_mode( )** function uses BIOS interrupt 16, function 15, to obtain the current video mode. This value is then used to determine where **vid_mem**, declared as a global **char far ***, will point (that is, either to the memory used by the monochrome adapter or the memory used by the other adapters). This pointer will then be used by the window-based routines that access the video RAM.

Writing to the Video RAM

Once the video mode has been determined and a pointer to the video RAM has been obtained, two direct video RAM output functions can be created. These functions are not, per se, part of the windowing system. However, they are needed because they provide extremely fast output. The functions write a character or a string to the specific x,y location. The attribute byte is also written. They are shown here:

```
// Write character with specified attribute.
void write_char(int x, int y, char ch, int attrib)
{
  char far *v;
```

```
    v = vid_mem;
    v += (y*160) + x*2;
    *v++ = ch; // write the character
    *v = attrib; // write the attribute
}

// Display a string with specifed attribute.
void write_string(int x, int y, char *p, int attrib)
{
  register int i;
  char far *v;

  v = vid_mem;
  v += (y*160) + x*2; // compute the address
  for(i=y; *p; i++) {
    *v++ = *p++; // write the character
    *v++ = attrib; // write the attribute
  }
}
```

Because, in 80-column text mode, each line of the screen holds 80 characters, 160 bytes (80 characters plus 80 attribute bytes) are used per line. The address of the correct location in the video RAM is then 160 times the Y coordinate plus 2 times the X coordinate.

Positioning the Cursor

When I/O is performed using direct video RAM I/O, the cursor's location is not automatically updated. This means that the window routines will need to move the cursor manually. The following function performs this operation. (The function is also not actually part of the windowing class, but it is used by it. The function uses BIOS interrupt 16, function 2.)

```
// Send the cursor to the specified X,Y position.
void goto_xy(int x, int y)
{
  union REGS r;

  r.h.ah = 2; // cursor addressing function
  r.h.dl = x; // column coordinate
  r.h.dh = y; // row coordinate
  r.h.bh = 0; // video page
  int86(0x10, &r, &r);
}
```

Many compilers supply a "goto xy" function. If yours does, feel free to substitute it.

The Window Class

Now that the stage has been set, the windowing system can be developed. The windowing system is managed by the **wintype** class. Its declaration is shown here:

```
class wintype {
  // define where window goes on the screen
  int leftx;  // upper left coordinates
  int upy;
  int rightx;  // lower right coordinates
  int downy;

  int border;  // if non-zero, border displayed
  int active;  // non-zero if window is currently on screen
  char *title;  // title message

  int curx, cury;  // current cursor location in window

  char *buf;  // points to window's buffer
  char color;  // text color

  // private functions
  void save_screen();  // save screen so it can be restored
  void restore_screen();  // restore the original screen
  void draw_border();  // draw a window's border
  void display_title();  // display title
public:
  wintype(int lx, int uy,  // upper left
          int rx, int ly,  // lower right
          int b = 1,  // non-zero for border
          char *mess = ""  // title message
  );

  ~wintype() {winremove(); delete buf;};

  void winput();  // display a window
  void winremove();  // remove a window
  int winputs(char *s);  // write a string to the window
  int winxy(int x, int y);  // go to X,Y relative to window
  void wingets(char *s);  // input string from a window
  int wingetche();  // input a character from a window
  void wincls();  // clears the window
  void wincleol();  // clears to end-of-line

  void setcolor(char c) {color = c;}
  char getcolor() {return color;}
  void setbkcolor(char c) {color = color | (c<<4);}
  char getbkcolor() {return (color>>4) & 127;}

  friend wintype &operator<<(wintype &o, char *s);
  friend wintype &operator>>(wintype &o, char *s);
};
```

The position of the window on the screen and its size are determined by the variables **leftx**, **upy**, **rightx**, and **downy**. These hold the coordinates of the upper-left and lower-right corners of the window.

If the window will have a border, then **border** must be set to nonzero. Whenever the window is on the screen, **active** is set to nonzero. When the window is not displayed, **active** is zero. The title to the window (if any) is pointed to by **title**.

The current cursor location within the window is stored in **curx** and **cury**. All output sent to a window is positioned relative to the window. That is, **curx** and **cury** are relative to the window, not to the screen. This means that if **curx** is 5 and **cury** is 3, then no matter where the window is on the screen, the cursor is located at 5,3 *within the window*. Further, the upper-left corner of the window is 0,0.

When a window is displayed, whatever is currently on the screen is saved in the memory pointed to by **buf**. (This memory is dynamically allocated when the window is created.) The color of the text is determined by the value of **color**. It must be one of these enumerated values:

```
/* Text colors, first 7 can also be used to specify
   background color.
*/
const enum clr {black, blue, green, cyan, red, magenta,
                brown, lightgray, darkgray, lightblue,
                lightgreen, lightcyan, lightred,
                lightmagenta, yellow, white, blink=128};
```

The **wintype** constructor function is shown here:

```
// Construct a window.
wintype::wintype(int lx, int uy, // upper left
        int rx, int ly, // lower right
        int b, // non-zero for border
        char *mess // title message
  )
{
  if(lx<0) lx = 0;
  if(rx>79) rx = 79;
  if(uy<0) uy = 0;
  if(ly>24) ly = 24;

  leftx = lx; upy = uy;
  rightx = rx, downy = ly;
  border = b;
  title = mess;
  active = 0;
  curx = cury = 0;
```

```
buf = new char[2*(rightx-leftx+1)*(downy-upy+1)];
if(!buf) {
  cout << "Allocation error\n";
  exit(1);
}
color = white;
}
```

The constructor first makes sure that the four coordinate values are within range. It then initializes the **private** data. It also allocates the memory that will be used to save the current contents of the screen when the window is activated. When the window is deactivated, the original contents will then be restored.

Notice that by default, the text color is white, the cursor is located at 0,0, and the window is inactive.

Note: The **wintype( )** constructor only constructs a window. It does not display that window. Displaying the window is a separate operation from constructing it.

The ~**wintype( )** destructor removes the window (if needed) and then frees the memory pointed to by **buf**.

Displaying and Removing a Window

Once a window has been constructed, it may be displayed by calling **winput( )**. This function is shown here.

```
// Display a window.
void wintype::winput()
{
  // get active window
  if(!active) { // not currently in use
    save_screen(); // save the current screen
    active = 1; // set active flag
  }
  else return;   // already on screen

  if(border) draw_border();
  display_title();

  // position cursor in upper left corner
  goto_xy(leftx + curx + 1, upy + cury + 1);
}
```

This function first checks to see if the window is already on the screen. If the window is active, the call to **winput( )** is ignored. Otherwise, the current contents of the portion of the screen where the window will be displayed are saved by calling **save_screen( )**, and **active** is set to 1. If **border** is nonzero, a border for the window is drawn. Next, the title is displayed. Finally, the cursor is positioned at the current cursor location. Since the values of **curx** and **cury** are relative to the window, they must be added to **leftx** and **upy**, respectively, so that the cursor can be displayed in the correct screen-relative location.

The **save_screen( )** function is shown next. (It is a private function of **wintype( )**.) It simply copies, byte for byte, the contents of the video RAM where the window will be displayed into the memory pointed to by **buf**. It also clears that portion of the screen.

```
// Save screen so it can be restored after window is removed.
void wintype::save_screen()
{
  register int i,j;
  char *buf_ptr;
  char far *v, far *t;

  buf_ptr = buf;
  v = vid_mem;
  for(i=upy; i<downy+1; i++)
    for(j=leftx; j<rightx+1; j++) {
      t = (v + (i*160) + j*2);
      *buf_ptr++ = *t++;
      *buf_ptr++ = *t;
      *(t-1) = ' ';   // clear the window
    }
}
```

The **draw_border( )** and **display_title( )** functions are shown next. These are also private functions of **wintype**.

```
// Draw a border around the window.
void wintype::draw_border()
{
  register int i;
  char far *v, far *t;

  v = vid_mem;
  t = v;
  for(i=leftx+1; i<rightx; i++) {
    v += (upy*160) + i*2;
    *v++ = 196;
    *v = color;
```

```
        v = t;
        v += (downy*160) + i*2;
        *v++ = 196;
        *v = color;
        v = t;
    }
    for(i=upy+1; i<downy; i++) {
        v += (i*160) + leftx*2;
        *v++ = 179;
        *v = color;
        v = t;
        v += (i*160) + rightx*2;
        *v++ = 179;
        *v = color;
        v = t;
    }
    // draw the corners
    write_char(leftx, upy, 218, color);
    write_char(leftx, downy, 192, color);
    write_char(rightx, upy, 191, color);
    write_char(rightx, downy, 217, color);
}

// Display the window's title.
void wintype::display_title()
{
    register int  x, len;

    x = leftx;

    /* Calculate the correct starting position to center
       the title message - if negative, message won't
       fit.
    */
    len = strlen(title);
    len = (rightx - x - len) / 2;
    if(len<0) return; // don't display it
    x = x + len + 1;

    write_string(x, upy,
                  title, color);
}
```

The values 196 and 179 correspond to horizontal and vertical lines in the PC's extended character set. The values used at the end of **draw_border( )** are corner pieces in the extended character set. The title is only displayed if it can fit.

To remove a window from the screen, use the **winremove( )** function, shown here. It copies what is stored in the memory pointed to by **buf** back into the video RAM.

```
// Remove the window and restore prior screen contents.
void wintype::winremove()
{
  if(!active) return; // can't remove a non-active window

  restore_screen(); // restore the original screen
  active = 0; // restore_video
}
```

Aside from setting **active** to zero, the main purpose of the function is to restore the original contents of the screen by calling the **private** **restore_screen( )** function, as shown here:

```
// Restore a portion of the screen.
void wintype::restore_screen()
{
  register int i,j;
  char far *v, far *t;
  char *buf_ptr;

  buf_ptr = buf;   // compute pointer to video RAM
  v = vid_mem;
  t = v;
  for(i=upy; i<downy+1; i++)
    for(j=leftx; j<rightx+1; j++) {
    v = t;
    v += (i*160) + j*2;
    *v++ = *buf_ptr++;   // write the character
    *v = *buf_ptr++;     // write the attribute
    }
}
```

Window I/O

Input from and output to a window may be performed either by calling member functions or by using the overloaded << and >> operators. All window I/O must be performed through window-based functions that prevent the boundaries of the window from being overwritten.

The lowest-level input function is called **wingetche( )**. This function reads a character from the keyboard and echos it to the window, as shown here:

```
/* Input a keystroke inside a window.
   Returns full 16 bit keyboard code.
*/
wintype::wingetche()
{
  union inkey {
    char ch[2];
    int i;
  } c;
  union REGS r;

  if(!active) return 0; // window not active

  winxy(curx, cury);

  r.h.ah = 0; // read a key
  c.i = int86(0x16, &r, &r);

  if(c.ch[0]) {
    switch(c.ch[0]) {
      case '\r': // the ENTER key is pressed
        break;
      case '\b': // back space
        break;
      default:
        if(curx+leftx < rightx-1) {
          write_char(leftx+ curx+1,
          upy+cury+1, c.ch[0], color);
          curx++;
        }
    }
    if(cury < 0) cury = 0;
    if(cury+upy > downy-2)
      cury--;
    winxy(curx, cury);
  }
  return c.i;
}
```

This function calls BIOS interrupt 16, function 0, which waits for a keypress and returns the full 16-bit keyboard code. The keyboard code is divided into two parts: the character and the position code. If the key pressed is a character key, the character is returned in the low-order 8 bits. However, if a special key is pressed for which no character code exists, such as an arrow key, then the low-order byte is zero and the high-order byte contains that key's position code. For example, the position codes for the up and down arrows are 72 and 80. Although none of the window functions make use of the position code, it is provided here because your window applications will very likely need access to both the character and the position codes.

As you can see by examining the function, no keystrokes will be echoed past the boundary of the window. Also, keystrokes are echoed in the color currently defined for the window. Finally, the window must be active.

To read a string from the keyboard, use **wingets( )**, shown here:

```
// Read a string from a window.
void wintype::wingets(char *s)
{
  char ch, *temp;

  temp = s;
  for(;;) {
    ch = wingetche();
    switch(ch) {
      case '\r':  // the ENTER key is pressed
        *s = '\0';
        return;
      case '\b': // backspace
        if(s>temp) {
          s--;
          curx--;
          if(curx<0) curx = 0;
          winxy(curx, cury);
          write_char(leftx+ curx+1,upy+cury+1, ' ', color);
        }
        break;
      default: *s = ch;
        s++;
    }
  }
}
```

This function calls **wingetche( )** to input each character. Because **wingetche( )** prevents keystrokes from overrunning a window boundary, no input from **wingets( )** may overrun a window boundary either.

To output a string to a window use **winputs( )**, shown here:

```
/* Write a string at the current cursor position
   in the specified window.
   Returns 0 if window not active;
   1 otherwise.
*/
int wintype::winputs(char *s)
{
  register int x, y;
  char far *v;

  // make sure window is active
  if(!active) return 0;
```

```
x = curx + leftx + 1;
y = cury + upy + 1;

v = vid_mem;
v += (y*160) + x*2; // compute starting address

for( ; *s;  s++) {
  if(y >= downy) {
    return 1;
  }
  if(x >= rightx) {
    return 1;
  }

  if(*s=='\n') {
    y++;
    x = leftx+1;
    v = vid_mem;
    v += (y*160) + x*2; // compute the address
    cury++;  // increment Y
    curx = 0; // reset X
  }
  else {
    curx++;
    x++;
    *v++ = *s;  // write the character
    *v++ = color; // color
  }
  winxy(curx, cury);
 }
 return 1;
}
```

This function outputs the specified string beginning at the current cursor location (as defined by **curx** and **cury**) in the current color. No output will be allowed beyond the bounds of the window.

As mentioned, in addition to the I/O member functions, you may also output a string by using << and input a string by using >>. These overloaded operators are shown here. Their operation is straightforward.

```
// Output to a window.
wintype &operator<<(wintype &o, char *s)
{
  o.winputs(s);
  return o;
}

// Input from a window.
wintype &operator>>(wintype &o, char *s)
{
  o.wingets(s);
  return o;
}
```

If you want to input other types of data, simply overload << and >> again.

Three additional window output functions are **wincls( )**, which clears the window, **wincleol( )**, which clears from the current cursor position to the end of the line, and **winxy( )**, which positions the cursor at the window-relative XY position. These functions are shown here:

```
// Clear a window.
void wintype::wincls()
{
  register int i,j;
  char far *v, far *t;

  v = vid_mem;
  t = v;
  for(i=upy+1; i<downy; i++)
    for(j=leftx+1; j<rightx; j++) {
      v = t;
      v += (i*160) + j*2;
      *v++ = ' ';  // write a space
      *v = color;  // in background color
    }
  curx = 0;
  cury = 0;
}

// Clear to end of line.
void wintype::wincleol()
{
  register int i, x, y;

  x = curx;
  y = cury;
  winxy(curx, cury);

  for(i=curx; i<rightx-1; i++)
    winputs(" ");
  winxy(x, y);
}

/* Position cursor in a window at specified location.
   Returns 0 if out of range; non-zero otherwise.
*/
int wintype::winxy(int x, int y)
{
  if(x<0 || x+leftx >= rightx-1)
    return 0;
  if(y<0 || y+upy >= downy-1)
    return 0;
  curx = x;
  cury = y;
  goto_xy(leftx+x+1, upy+y+1);
  return 1;
}
```

You can set the foreground color by using **setcolor( )** and the background color by using **setbkcolor( )**. These functions are defined inside the declaration of **wintype**. For **setcolor( )**, you can use any color specified in the **clr** enumeration. For **setbkcolor( )**, you can use the first seven colors. The functions **getcolor( )** and **getbkcolor( )** return the foreground and background colors, respectively. These functions are defined inline within the **wintype** class.

The Entire Window System

Here is the entire windowing system plus support functions and a **main( )** function that demonstrates the window functions:

```
// A window class.

#include "iostream.h"
#include "conio.h"
#include "stdlib.h"
#include "string.h"
#include "dos.h"
#include "bios.h"

// Global functions
int video_mode(void);
void goto_xy(int x, int y);
void set_v_ptr();
void write_char(int x, int y, char ch, int attrib);
void write_string(int x, int y, char *p, int attrib);

/* Text colors, first 7 can also be used to specify
   background color. */
const enum clr {black, blue, green, cyan, red, magenta,
                brown, lightgray, darkgray, lightblue,
                lightgreen, lightcyan, lightred,
                lightmagenta, yellow, white, blink=128};

char far *vid_mem; // pointer to screen memory when in text mode

class wintype {
  // define where window goes on the screen
  int leftx;  // upper left coordinates
  int upy;
  int rightx; // lower right coordinates
  int downy;
```

```
     int border;  // if non-zero, border displayed
     int active;  // non-zero if window is currently on screen
     char *title; // title message

     int curx, cury; // current cursor location in window

     char *buf; // points to window's buffer

     char color; // text color

     // private functions
     void save_screen(); // save screen so it can be restored
     void restore_screen(); // restore the original screen
     void draw_border(); // draw a window's border
     void display_title(); // display title
   public:
     wintype(int lx, int uy, // upper left
             int rx, int ly, // lower right
             int b = 1, // non-zero for border
             char *mess = "" // title message
     );

     ~wintype() {winremove(); delete buf;};

     void winput(); // display a window
     void winremove(); // remove a window
     int winputs(char *s); // write a string to the window
     int winxy(int x, int y); // go to X,Y relative to window
     void wingets(char *s); // input string from a window
     int wingetche();   // input a character from a window
     void wincls(); // clears the window
     void wincleol(); // clears to end-of-line

     void setcolor(char c) {color = c;}
     char getcolor() {return color;}
     void setbkcolor(char c) {color = color | (c<<4);}
     char getbkcolor() {return (color>>4) & 127;}

     friend wintype &operator<<(wintype &o, char *s);
     friend wintype &operator>>(wintype &o, char *s);
};

// Construct a window.
wintype::wintype(int lx, int uy, // upper left
          int rx, int ly, // lower right
          int b, // non-zero for border
          char *mess // title message
  )
{
   if(lx<0) lx = 0;
   if(rx>79) rx = 79;
   if(uy<0) uy = 0;
   if(ly>24) ly = 24;
```

```
  leftx = lx; upy = uy;
  rightx = rx, downy = ly;
  border = b;
  title = mess;
  active = 0;
  curx = cury = 0;

  buf = new char[2*(rightx-leftx+1)*(downy-upy+1)];
  if(!buf) {
    cout << "Allocation error\n";
    exit(1);
  }
  color = white;
}

// Display a window.
void wintype::winput()
{
  // get active window
  if(!active) { // not currently in use
    save_screen(); // save the current screen
    active = 1; // set active flag
  }
  else return;   // already on screen

  if(border) draw_border();
  display_title();

  // position cursor in upper left corner
  goto_xy(leftx + curx + 1, upy + cury + 1);
}

// Remove the window and restore prior screen contents.
void wintype::winremove()
{
  if(!active) return; // can't remove a non-active window

  restore_screen(); // restore the original screen
  active = 0; // restore_video
}

// Draw a border around the window.
void wintype::draw_border()
{
  register int i;
  char far *v, far *t;

  v = vid_mem;
  t = v;
  for(i=leftx+1; i<rightx; i++) {
    v += (upy*160) + i*2;
    *v++ = 196;
    *v = color;
```

```
      v = t;
      v += (downy*160) + i*2;
      *v++ = 196;
      *v = color;
      v = t;
   }
   for(i=upy+1; i<downy; i++) {
      v += (i*160) + leftx*2;
      *v++ = 179;
      *v = color;
      v = t;
      v += (i*160) + rightx*2;
      *v++ = 179;
      *v = color;
      v = t;
   }
   // draw the corners
   write_char(leftx, upy, 218, color);
   write_char(leftx, downy, 192, color);
   write_char(rightx, upy, 191, color);
   write_char(rightx, downy, 217, color);
}

// Display the window's title.
void wintype::display_title()
{
   register int  x, len;

   x = leftx;

   /* Calculate the correct starting position to center
      the title message - if negative, message won't
      fit.
   */
   len = strlen(title);
   len = (rightx - x - len) / 2;
   if(len<0) return; // don't display it
   x = x + len + 1;

   write_string(x, upy, title, color);
}

// Save screen so it can be restored after window is removed.
void wintype::save_screen()
{
   register int i,j;
   char *buf_ptr;
   char far *v, far *t;

   buf_ptr = buf;
   v = vid_mem;
   for(i=upy; i<downy+1; i++)
      for(j=leftx; j<rightx+1; j++) {
```

```
      t = (v + (i*160) + j*2);
      *buf_ptr++ = *t++;
      *buf_ptr++ = *t;
      *(t-1) = ' ';   // clear the window
    }
}

// Restore a portion of the screen.
void wintype::restore_screen()
{
  register int i,j;
  char far *v, far *t;
  char *buf_ptr;

  buf_ptr = buf;  // compute pointer to video RAM
  v = vid_mem;
  t = v;
  for(i=upy; i<downy+1; i++)
    for(j=leftx; j<rightx+1; j++) {
      v = t;
      v += (i*160) + j*2;
      *v++ = *buf_ptr++;  // write the character
      *v = *buf_ptr++;     // write the attribute
    }
}

/* Write a string at the current cursor position
   in the specified window.
   Returns 0 if window not active;
   1 otherwise.
*/
int wintype::winputs(char *s)
{
  register int x, y;
  char far *v;

  // make sure window is active
  if(!active) return 0;

  x = curx + leftx + 1;
  y = cury + upy + 1;

  v = vid_mem;
  v += (y*160) + x*2; // compute starting address

  for( ; *s;  s++) {
    if(y >= downy) {
      return 1;
    }
    if(x >= rightx) {
      return 1;
    }
```

```
      if(*s=='\n') {
        y++;
        x = leftx+1;
        v = vid_mem;
        v += (y*160) + x*2; // compute the address
        cury++;  // increment Y
        curx = 0; // reset X
      }
      else {
        curx++;
        x++;
        *v++ = *s;  // write the character
        *v++ = color; // color
      }
      winxy(curx, cury);
    }
    return 1;
}

/* Position cursor in a window at specified location.
   Returns 0 if out of range; non-zero otherwise.
*/
int wintype::winxy(int x, int y)
{
  if(x<0 || x+leftx >= rightx-1)
    return 0;
  if(y<0 || y+upy >= downy-1)
    return 0;
  curx = x;
  cury = y;
  goto_xy(leftx+x+1, upy+y+1);
  return 1;
}

// Read a string from a window.
void wintype::wingets(char *s)
{
  char ch, *temp;

  temp = s;
  for(;;) {
    ch = wingetche();
    switch(ch) {
      case '\r': // the ENTER key is pressed
        *s = '\0';
        return;
      case '\b': // backspace
        if(s>temp) {
          s--;
          curx--;
          if(curx<0) curx = 0;
          winxy(curx, cury);
          write_char(leftx+ curx+1, upy+cury+1, ' ', color);
```

```
        }
        break;
      default: *s = ch;
        s++;
    }
  }
}

/* Input keystrokes inside a window.
   Returns full 16 bit keyboard code.
*/
wintype::wingetche()
{
  union inkey {
    char ch[2];
    int i;
  } c;
  union REGS r;

  if(!active) return 0; // window not active

  winxy(curx, cury);

  r.h.ah = 0; // read a key
  c.i = int86(0x16, &r, &r);

  if(c.ch[0]) {
    switch(c.ch[0]) {
      case '\r': // the ENTER key is pressed
        break;
      case '\b': // back space
        break;
      default:
        if(curx+leftx < rightx-1) {
          write_char(leftx+ curx+1,
          upy+cury+1, c.ch[0], color);
          curx++;
        }
    }
    if(cury < 0) cury = 0;
    if(cury+upy > downy-2)
      cury--;
    winxy(curx, cury);
  }
  return c.i;
}

// Clear a window.
void wintype::wincls()
{
  register int i,j;
  char far *v, far *t;

  v = vid_mem;
  t = v;
```

```
   for(i=upy+1; i<downy; i++)
     for(j=leftx+1; j<rightx; j++) {
       v = t;
       v += (i*160) + j*2;
       *v++ = ' ';  // write a space
       *v = color;  // in background color
     }
   curx = 0;
   cury = 0;
}

// Clear to end of line.
void wintype::wincleol()
{
  register int i, x, y;

  x = curx;
  y = cury;
  winxy(curx, cury);

  for(i=curx; i<rightx-1; i++)
    winputs(" ");
  winxy(x, y);
}

// Output to a window.
wintype &operator<<(wintype &o, char *s)
{
  o.winputs(s);
  return o;
}

// Input from a window.
wintype &operator>>(wintype &o, char *s)
{
  o.wingets(s);
  return o;
}

main()
{
  char s[80];

  set_v_ptr(); // set the video memory pointer

  wintype w1(1, 10, 20, 20, 1, "My Window #1");
  wintype w2(40, 1, 60, 20, 1, "My Window #2");
  wintype w3(40, 5, 60, 20, 1, "My Window #3");

  w1.winput();
  w2.winput();
  w1.setcolor(blue);
  w2.setcolor(green);
```

```
  w1 >> s;
  w1.winxy(0, 0);
  w1.winputs("Hi there\n");
  w1.winputs("Windows are fun");
  w1 << "\n";
  w1 >> s;
  w1 << "This \nis " << "a test" << "\n";
  w2 << "this is a test";
  w2.winxy(3, 4);
  w2 << "at location 3, 4";
  w1 << "This is another test for you to see\n";
  w1 >> s;

  w3.winput();  // overlap another window
  w3 >> s;
  w3.winremove();

  w1.winxy(0, 0);
  w1.setcolor(red);
  w1.setbkcolor(cyan);
  w1.winputs("PROMPT: ");
  w1.setcolor(white);
  w1.setbkcolor(black);
  w1 >> s;
  w2.winxy(0, 4);
  w2.setcolor(yellow);
  w2.setbkcolor(green);
  w2.winputs(s);
  w2 >> s;
  w2.wincls();
  w1.winxy(5, 0);
  w1.wincleol();
  w2 >> s;
  w1.winremove();
  w2.winremove();
  w1.winput();
  w1 >> s;
}

void set_v_ptr()
{
  int vmode;

  vmode = video_mode();
  if((vmode!=2) && (vmode!=3) && (vmode!=7)) {
    cout << "video must be in 80 column text mode";
    exit(1);
  }
  // set proper address of video RAM
  if(vmode==7) vid_mem = (char far *) 0xB0000000;
  else vid_mem = (char far *) 0xB8000000;
}
```

```
// Returns the current video mode.
video_mode(void)
{
  union REGS r;

  r.h.ah = 15;  // get video mode
  return int86(0x10, &r, &r) & 255;
}

// Write character with specified attribute.
void write_char(int x, int y, char ch, int attrib)
{
  char far *v;

  v = vid_mem;
  v += (y*160) + x*2;
  *v++ = ch; // write the character
  *v = attrib; // write the attribute
}

// Send the cursor to the specified X,Y position.
void goto_xy(int x, int y)
{
  union REGS r;

  r.h.ah = 2; // cursor addressing function
  r.h.dl = x; // column coordinate
  r.h.dh = y; // row coordinate
  r.h.bh = 0; // video page
  int86(0x10, &r, &r);
}

// Display a string with specified attribute.
void write_string(int x, int y, char *p, int attrib)
{
  register int i;
  char far *v;

  v = vid_mem;
  v += (y*160) + x*2; // compute the address
  for(i=y; *p; i++) {
    *v++ = *p++; // write the character
    *v++ = attrib; // write the attribute
  }
}
```

This program produces the output shown in Figure 22-1.

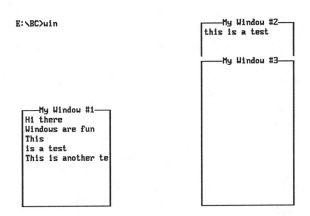

Figure 22-1.   Output from the sample window program

Modifications

Although the windowing system is fully functional, there are some modifications you might want to try. As it stands, when a window is removed, the contents of that window are lost. It is possible, however, to save the contents of the window so they can be restored when the window is redisplayed. This modification may prove valuable for some situations. You might want to overload the << and >> operators so that they can handle more types of data than just strings. Finally, you might want to overload the = operator relative to objects of type **wintype**.

A Linked List Class

A Doubly Linked List Class
Creating a Generic Doubly Linked List Base Class
Other Implementations

The final chapter in this book examines the issues that arise when implementing a doubly linked list using a class. Although a doubly linked list is just one of several methods used to store information, the problems and solutions associated with managing a doubly linked list using a class can be generalized to any storage method.

This chapter explores two different ways of implementing a doubly linked list class. The first implementation creates a doubly linked list for a specific type of data—that is, the data held by the list is hard-coded into the class that manages the list. The second implementation explores one way to create a generic linked list base class that can help construct classes that manage specific types of data.

A Doubly Linked List Class

As you almost certainly know, each item stored in a doubly linked list contains three parts: a pointer to the next element in the list, a pointer to the previous element in the list, and the information that is stored in the list. Figure 23-1 depicts a doubly linked list. A doubly linked list can store any data type, including structures, classes, and unions. The doubly linked list class developed here simply stores strings (for ease of illustration), but any other type of data can be stored.

All linked lists share these two fundamental operations: putting an item on the list and removing an item from the list. In addition to these operations, the doubly linked list class developed in this chapter supports several other operations. The list can be searched, an item can be modified, and the information associated with an item can be retrieved. The list also overloads the << and >> operators and provides two

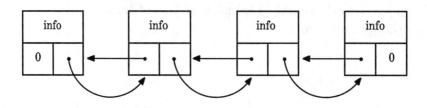

Figure 23-1.   A doubly linked list

functions that display the contents of the list in either a forward or backward direction.

The **dblink** doubly linked list class declaration is shown here:

```
const int STRSIZE = 80;

class dblink {
  char info[STRSIZE]; // information
  dblink *next;  // pointer to next object
  dblink *prior; // pointer to previous object
public:
  dblink() {
    next = NULL;
    prior = NULL;
  };
  dblink(char *s) {
    if(strlen(s)<STRSIZE) strcpy(info, s);
    else *info = NULL;
    next = NULL;
    prior = NULL;
  }

  void store(dblink **start, dblink **end);
  void remove(dblink **start, dblink **end); // delete entry
  void frwdlist(); // display the list from beginning
  void bkwdlist(); // display the list from the end

  dblink *getnext() {return next;}
  dblink *getprior() {return prior;}

  int change(char *s);  // change an element

  void getinfo(char *s) {strcpy(s, info);}

  dblink *find(char *s); // return pointer to matching element
```

```
// Overload << for object of type dblink.
friend ostream &operator<<(ostream &stream, dblink o)
{
  stream << o.info << "\n";
  return stream;
}
// Overload << for pointer to object of type dblink.
friend ostream &operator<<(ostream &stream, dblink *o)
{
  stream << o->info << "\n";
  return stream;
}

// Overload >> for dblink references.
friend istream &operator>>(istream &stream, dblink &o)
{
  cout << "Enter information: ";
  stream >> o.info;
  return stream;
}
};
```

The data member **info** holds the string stored by the list. As stated, this class is designed specifically to maintain a linked list of strings. However, the same general mechanism can be used to maintain a list of any data type. The **next** pointer will point to the next element in the list, and **prior** will point to the previous element in the list.

When each object is constructed, the **prior** and **next** fields are initialized to **NULL**. These pointers are null until the object is put into a list. If an initializer is included, it is copied into **info**.

The **getnext( )** function returns a pointer to the next element in the list. This will be **NULL** if the end of the list has been reached. The **getprior( )** function returns the previous element in the list, if it exists; it returns **NULL** otherwise.

Notice that the ≪ operator is overloaded for both objects of type **dblink** and pointers to objects of **dblink**. This is because it is extremely common, when using a linked list, to access members of the list using a pointer. Therefore it is necessary to overload ≪ so that it operates when given a pointer to the object. However, since there is no reason to preclude an object being output, the second form, which operates directly on an object, is also included.

The store( ) Function

The **store( )** function adds a **dblink** object to the list. It is implemented as shown here:

```
// Add the next entry.
void dblink::store(dblink **start, dblink **end)
{

  if(*start==NULL) { // first element in list
    next = NULL;
    prior = NULL;
    *end = *start = this;
  }
  else { // put on end
    next = NULL;
    prior = *end;
    (*end)->next = this;
    *end = this;
  }
}
```

This function causes the object pointed to by **o** to be added to the end of the list. It is passed the addresses of the pointers that point to the beginning and end of the list. These pointers are created elsewhere in your program. They are updated automatically by **store( )**. The **start** and **end** pointers must be **NULL** when your program begins. When the first item is added to the list, both **start** and **end** will point to it. Each subsequent addition causes **end** to be updated. In this way, **start** and **end** will always point to the beginning and end of the list.

The following fragment shows how to declare the **start** and **end** pointers and add objects to a list:

```
dblink a("One"), b("Two"), c("Three");
dblink *start, *end;

end = start = NULL; // initialize start and end pointers
a.store(&start, &end);
b.store(&start, &end);
c.store(&start, &end);
```

Because objects are always added to the end of the list, the list is not sorted. However, you can modify **store( )** so that it maintains a sorted list if you like.

The pointers to the beginning and end of the list are not members of the **dblink** class. They are simply pointers to objects of type **dblink** defined elsewhere in your program. Therefore, you may maintain two or more linked lists in the same program by keeping separate beginning and ending pointers for each list.

As the **store( )** function makes clear, the linked list managed by the **dblink** class maintains a list of *objects of type* **dblink**. The type of data stored within an object of type **dblink** is irrelevant to the **store( )** function. That is, the fact that, as currently defined, **dblink** contains a data field that holds an 80-character array is not relevant to the **store( )** function. (This fact will be used later to help construct a doubly linked list base class.)

The remove( ) Function

The **remove( )** function removes an object from the list. It is shown here:

```
/* Remove an element from the list and update start and
   end pointers.
*/
void dblink::remove(dblink **start, dblink **end)
{
  if(prior) { // not deleting first element
    prior->next = next;
    if(next) // not deleting last element
      next->prior = prior;
    else // otherwise, are deleting last element
      *end = prior;  // update end pointer
  }
  else { // deleting first element
    if(next) { // list not empty
      next->prior = NULL;
      *start = next;
    }
    else // list now empty
      *start = *end = NULL;
  }
}
```

The **remove( )** function deletes the object for which it is called. There are three places where an item to be deleted can be located. (See Figure 23-2.) It can be the first item, the last item, or somewhere in between. The **remove( )** function handles all three cases. It must be called with the addresses of the pointers that point to the start and end of the list. For example, if **ob** is in the list, then this line removes it:

```
ob.remove(&start, &end);
```

Keep in mind that **remove( )** removes an object from the list, but that object is not destroyed. It is simply "delinked."

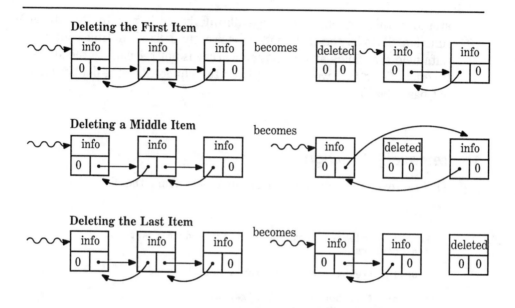

Figure 23-2.   Removing an object from a doubly linked list

Like **store( )**, the operation of **remove( )** does not depend upon the type of data actually stored in the list.

Displaying the List

The functions **frwdlist( )** and **bkwdlist( )** display the contents of the list in a forward and backward direction, respectively. These functions are included to illustrate how the **dblink** class works. They also make convenient debugging aids. However, they may not be applicable to all situations.

```
// Walk through list in forward direction.
void dblink::frwdlist()
{
  dblink *temp;

  temp = this;
  do {
    cout << temp->info << " ";
```

```
      temp = temp->next;
   } while(temp);
   cout << "\n";
}

// Walk through list in backward direction.
void dblink::bkwdlist()
{
   dblink *temp;

   temp = this;
   do {
     cout << temp->info << " ";
     temp = temp->prior;
   } while(temp);
   cout << "\n";
}
```

Changing and Finding an Object in the List

To change the string stored in a object, use the **change( )** function, shown here:

```
// Change contents of info.
int dblink::change(char *s) {
   if(strlen(s)<STRSIZE) {
     strcpy(info, s);
     return 1; // successful
   }
   else
     return 0;  // failed
}
```

This function changes the contents of the string stored in the **info** array of the object that generates the call.

The **find( )** function returns a pointer to the object in the list containing a string that matches that pointed to by **s**:

```
// Find an object given info.
dblink *dblink::find(char *s)
{
   dblink *temp;

   temp = this;

   while(temp) {
     if(!strcmp(temp->info, s)) return temp; // found
     temp = temp->getnext();
```

```
   }
   return NULL; // not in list
}
```

The Entire dblink Class and Sample Program

Here is the entire **dblink** class along with a **main( )** function that
illustrates it:

```
// A doubly linked list class

#include "iostream.h"
#include "string.h"

const int STRSIZE = 80;

class dblink {
  char info[STRSIZE]; // information
  dblink *next;  // pointer to next object
  dblink *prior; // pointer to previous object
public:
  dblink() {
    next = NULL;
    prior = NULL;
  };
  dblink(char *s) {
    if(strlen(s)<STRSIZE) strcpy(info, s);
    else *info = NULL;
    next = NULL;
    prior = NULL;
  }

  void store(dblink **start, dblink **end);
  void remove(dblink **start, dblink **end); // delete entry
  void frwdlist(); // display the list from beginning
  void bkwdlist(); // display the list from the end

  dblink *getnext() {return next;}
  dblink *getprior() {return prior;}

  int change(char *s);  // change an element

  void getinfo(char *s) {strcpy(s, info);}

  dblink *find(char *s); // return pointer to matching element

  // Overload << for object of type dblink.
  friend ostream &operator<<(ostream &stream, dblink o)
  {
    stream << o.info << "\n";
    return stream;
  }
  // Overload << for pointer to object of type dblink.
```

```
  friend ostream &operator<<(ostream &stream, dblink *o)
  {
    stream << o->info << "\n";
    return stream;
  }

  // Overload >> for dblink references.
  friend istream &operator>>(istream &stream, dblink &o)
  {
    cout << "Enter information: ";
    stream >> o.info;
    return stream;
  }
};

// Add the next entry.
void dblink::store(dblink **start, dblink **end)
{

  if(*start==NULL) { // first element in list
    next = NULL;
    prior = NULL;
    *end = *start = this;
  }
  else { // put on end
    next = NULL;
    prior = *end;
    (*end)->next = this;
    *end = this;
  }
}

/* Remove an element from the list and update start and
   end pointers.
*/
void dblink::remove(dblink **start, dblink **end)
{
  if(prior) { // not deleting first element
    prior->next = next;
    if(next) // not deleting last element
      next->prior = prior;
    else // otherwise, are deleting last element
      *end = prior;  // update end pointer
  }
  else { // deleting first element
    if(next) { // list not empty
      next->prior = NULL;
      *start = next;
    }
    else // list now empty
      *start = *end = NULL;
  }
}

// Walk through list in forward direction.
void dblink::frwdlist()
{
  dblink *temp;
```

```
    temp = this;
    do {
      cout << temp->info << " ";
      temp = temp->next;
    } while(temp);
    cout << "\n";
}

// Walk through list in backward direction.
void dblink::bkwdlist()
{
    dblink *temp;

    temp = this;
    do {
      cout << temp->info << " ";
      temp = temp->prior;
    } while(temp);
    cout << "\n";
}

// Find an object given info.
dblink *dblink::find(char *s)
{
    dblink *temp;

    temp = this;

    while(temp) {
      if(!strcmp(temp->info, s)) return temp; // found
      temp = temp->getnext();
    }
    return NULL; // not in list
}

//  Change contents of info.
int dblink::change(char *s) {
    if(strlen(s)<STRSIZE) {
      strcpy(info, s);
      return 1; // successful
    }
    else
      return 0;  // failed
}

main()
{
    dblink a("One"), b("Two"), c("Three");
    dblink *start, *end, *p;
    char s[STRSIZE];

    end = start = NULL; // initialize start and end pointers
    a.store(&start, &end);
    b.store(&start, &end);
    c.store(&start, &end);
```

```
// use member functions to display the list
start->frwdlist();
end->bkwdlist();

// "manually" walk through the list
p = start;
while(p) {
  p->getinfo(s);
  cout << s << endl;
  p = p->getnext(); // get next one
}

// look for an item
p = start->find("Two");
if(p) {
  p->getinfo(s);
  cout << "Found: " << s << endl;
}

// remove an item
b.remove(&start, &end);
start->frwdlist();
end->bkwdlist();

// add a dynamically allocated entry
p = new dblink("Four");
p->store(&start, &end);
start->frwdlist();
end->bkwdlist();

// change information
p->change("This is a new string");
start->frwdlist();

// demonstrate << and >>
cin >> b;
cout << b;
b.store(&start, &end);  // put on end of list

// remove head of list
a.remove(&start, &end);
start->frwdlist();
end->bkwdlist();

// remove end of list
end->remove(&start, &end);
start->frwdlist();

cout << start;

return 0;
}
```

Here is the output produced by this example. (When the program prompted for input, **TEST** was entered.)

```
One Two Three
Three Two One
One
Two
Three
Found: Two
One Three
Three One
One Three Four
Four Three One
One Three This is a new string
Enter information: TEST
TEST
Three This is a new string TEST
TEST This is a new string Three
Three This is a new string
Three
```

Creating a Generic Doubly Linked List Base Class

Although the linked list class created in the preceding section is perfectly valid, it can be used only to manage a list of strings because this is the type of data defined by **dblink**. If you wanted to store another type of data, you would need to change several of the functions to accommodate the new data type. However, there are four operations that are not in any way dependent on the type of data that the list holds. These functions are **store( )**, **remove( )**, **getnext( )**, and **getprior( )**. This section will make use of this fact to create a generic doubly linked list base class that can be used as the foundation from which a derived class defines a specific type of list.

One advantage of creating a generic doubly linked list base class is that it decouples the mechanism (that is, the linked list maintenance) from the data. Thus, the mechanism can be enhanced or modified, and any derived classes will automatically be able to make use of the change (after recompiling, of course). Another advantage of using a generic base class is that it prevents another programmer from tampering with the fundamentals of its operation. You can keep these private. Finally, by creating a doubly linked list base class, you prevent the unwarranted duplication of code and its attendant inefficiencies from being present in your programs.

Note: There are many ways to define a doubly linked list base class. This is one way, but you should experiment on your own with other solutions.

The Doubly Linked Base Class

The doubly linked list base class is shown here:

```
// Generic doubly linked list base class.
class dblink {
  dblink *next;   // pointer to next object
  dblink *prior;  // pointer to previous object
public:
  dblink() {
    next = NULL;
    prior = NULL;
  };

  void store(dblink **start, dblink **end);
  void remove(dblink **start, dblink **end);

  dblink *getnext() {return next;}
  dblink *getprior() {return prior;}
};
```

The implementations of **store( )** and **remove( )** are the same as those used earlier.

Notice that there is no provision for storing data inside this version of **dblink**. The type of data held by the list must be defined by a class derived from **dblink**.

Defining a Specific Doubly Linked List Class

It is very easy to derive a specific type of doubly linked list class from **dblink**. For example, using the generic **dblink** as a base, you can create a derived class that implements a linked list for floating-point values. This class is called **myclass**, and its declaration is shown here:

```
/* This class inherits dblink and creates a
   doubly linked list that stores floating point values.
*/
class mylink : public dblink {
  double info;   // store a double
public:
  mylink () {info = 0.0;}
  mylink(double f) {info = f;}

  mylink *find(double d); // find an item

  void change(double f) {info = f;} // change an item
```

```
double getinfo() {return info;} // return value

// Overload << for mylink objects.
friend ostream &operator<<(ostream &stream, mylink o)
{
  stream << o.info;
  return stream;
}

// Overload << for mylink pointers.
friend ostream &operator<<(ostream &stream, mylink *o)
{
  stream << o->info << " ";
  return stream;
}

// Overload >> for mylink references.
friend istream &operator>>(istream &stream, mylink &o)
{
  stream >> o.info;
  return stream;
}

  void frwdlist(); // display list in forward direction
  void bkwdlist(); // display list in backward direction
};
```

This class contains those functions that are dependent upon the type of data stored in the list. It relies entirely upon the **dblink** base class for the functions that actually maintain the list.

The entire **mylink** implementation is shown in the following program. (The implementation of each function should be obvious.)

```
#include "iostream.h"
#include "string.h"
#include "stdio.h"

// Generic doubly linked list base class.
class dblink {
  dblink *next;  // pointer to next object
  dblink *prior; // pointer to previous object
public:
  dblink() {
    next = NULL;
    prior = NULL;
  };

  void store(dblink **start, dblink **end);
  void remove(dblink **start, dblink **end);

  dblink *getnext() {return next;}
  dblink *getprior() {return prior;}
};
```

```
/* This class inherits dblink and creates a
   doubly linked list that stores floating point values.
*/
class mylink : public dblink {
  double info;
public:
  mylink () {info = 0.0;}
  mylink(double f) {info = f;}

  mylink *find(double d); // find an item

  void change(double f) {info = f;} // change an item

  double getinfo() {return info;} // return value

  // Overload << for mylink objects.
  friend ostream &operator<<(ostream &stream, mylink o)
  {
    stream << o.info;
    return stream;
  }

  // Overload << for mylink pointers.
  friend ostream &operator<<(ostream &stream, mylink *o)
  {
    stream << o->info << " ";
    return stream;
  }

  // Overload >> for mylink references.
  friend istream &operator>>(istream &stream, mylink &o)
  {
    stream >> o.info;
    return stream;
  }

  void frwdlist(); // display list in forward direction
  void bkwdlist(); // display list in backward direction
};

// Add the next entry.
void dblink::store(dblink **start, dblink **end)
{

  if(*start==NULL) { // first element in list
    next = NULL;
    prior = NULL;
    *end = *start = this;
  }
  else { // put on end
    next = NULL;
    prior = *end;
    (*end)->next = this;
    *end = this;
  }
}
```

```
// Delete an object; update start and end pointers.
void dblink::remove(dblink **start, dblink **end)
{
  if(prior) {
    prior->next = next;
    if(next)
      next->prior = prior;
    else
      *end = prior;
  }
  else {
    if(next) {
      next->prior = NULL;
      *start = next;
    }
    else // list now empty
      *start = *end = NULL;
  }
}

// Display list in forward direction.
void mylink::frwdlist()
{
  mylink *temp;

  temp = this;
  do {
    cout << temp->info << " ";
    temp = (mylink *) temp->getnext();
  } while(temp);
  cout << "\n";
}

// Display the list in backward direction.
void mylink::bkwdlist()
{
  mylink *temp;

  temp = this;
  do {
    cout << temp->info << " ";
    temp = (mylink *) temp->getprior();
  } while(temp);
  cout << "\n";
}

// Look for matching info and return pointer to it.
mylink *mylink::find(double d)
{
  mylink *p;

  p = this;

  while(p) {
    if(d == p->info) return p;
    p = (mylink *) p->getnext();
```

```
  }
  return NULL;
}

main()
{
  mylink a(123.2), b(99.043), c(0.303);
  dblink *start, *end;
  mylink *p;

  end = start = NULL;
  a.store(&start, &end);
  b.store(&start, &end);
  c.store(&start, &end);

  // display forwards and backwards
  ((mylink *) start)->frwdlist();
  ((mylink *) end)->bkwdlist();

  // look for an item
  p = a.find(123.2);
  if(p) cout << "Found " << p << "\n";

  // "manually" walk through list
  p = (mylink *) start;
  while(p) {
    cout << p << "\n";
    p = (mylink *) p->getnext();
  }

  // delete b
  b.remove(&start, &end);
  p = (mylink *) start;
  p->frwdlist();

  // add a dynamically allocated item
  p = new mylink(1000.12);
  p->store(&start, &end);
  p->frwdlist();

  // delete first item on list
  a.remove(&start, &end);
  p->frwdlist();

  // demonstrate << and >> operators
  cin >> c;
  cout << c << endl;

  // change c
  c.change(1000.034);
  cout << c << endl;

  // get value of c
  double f;
  f = c.getinfo();
  cout << f;
```

```
  return 0;
}
```

Other Implementations

As stated earlier in this chapter, there are many ways to implement a linked list class. You may want to experiment on your own, trying different approaches. Here are some ideas you can start with.

First, if you won't be needing more than one linked list of any specific type per program, you can store the **start** and **end** pointers inside **dblink** as **statics**. This means that you would no longer have to pass them explicitly to the **store( )** and **remove( )** functions. Remember, static data defined within a class *is shared by all objects* of that class. Therefore, each object will automatically have access to the beginning and end pointers.

The lists in this chapter simply add objects to the end of the list. For many applications, this is acceptable (indeed, desirable). However, you might want to modify **store( )** so that it creates a sorted list. Along these lines, you can create another version of **store( )** that adds elements to the beginning of the list.

Here are some other functions that you might want to add to the **dblink** class:

Function	Purpose
getfirst( )	Returns pointer to first element
getlast( )	Returns pointer to last element
getlength( )	Returns number of objects in list

One final thought: Although the linked lists developed in this chapter store strings and floating-point numbers, remember that any type of data can be stored. You might find it fun to create a simple mailing list database program that uses the doubly linked list shown in this chapter as its storage mechanism.

Some Common Classes

The Complex Class
A BCD Class

Most C++ compilers provide some predefined class libraries that, although they are not technically part of the C++ language, can make your programming tasks easier. The most common class libraries are the I/O classes described in Chapters 17, 18, and 19. In addition, many compilers provide classes for maintaining lists of objects, such as queues, stacks, and linked-list classes. Because these classes vary from implementation to implementation, they are not discussed here. Also, some C++ compilers provide multitasking management classes. However, these classes require a multitasking environment (which not all operating systems provide), and they also vary among host environments. For this reason, the multitasking classes are not discussed here either. (Refer to your compiler's user manual for information on these classes.) There are, however, two class libraries that are typically included with a C++ compiler: a complex class and a BCD class. This appendix briefly examines these two classes.

The Complex Class

As you may know, a *complex number* has two parts: a real half and an imaginary half. The real half is an ordinary number; the imaginary half is a multiple of the square root of −1. To use the **complex** class, you must include **complex.h** in your program.

To construct a complex number, use the **complex** constructor function. It has this prototype:

```
complex(double real_part, double imaginary_part);
```

The << and >> operators are overloaded relative to complex numbers. For example, this program constructs an imaginary number and displays it on the screen:

```
#include <iostream.h>
#include <complex.h>

main(void)
{
  complex num(10, 1);

  cout << num;

  return 0;
}
```

The program outputs the following:

```
(10, 1)
```

This output also illustrates the general format used for displaying complex numbers.

You may mix complex numbers with any other type of number, including integers, **float**s, and **double**s. The arithmetic operators +, −, *, and / are overloaded relative to complex numbers, as are the relational operators == and !=. This program illustrates how complex and regular numbers can be mixed in an expression:

```
#include <iostream.h>
#include <complex.h>

main(void)
{
  complex num(10, 1);

  num = 123.23 + num / 3;

  cout << num;

  return 0;
}
```

The **complex** class overloads many mathematical functions, such as sin( ) (which returns the sine of its argument) relative to complex numbers. It also defines several functions that apply specifically to complex numbers. The complex functions are shown in Table A-1.

Name	Purpose
complex abs(complex n)	Returns the absolute value of n
double acos(complex n)	Returns the arc cosine of n
double arg(complex n)	Returns the angle of n in the complex coordinate plane
complex asin(complex n)	Returns the arc sine of n
complex atan(complex n)	Returns the arc tangent of n
double conj(complex n)	Returns the conjugate of n
complex cos(complex n)	Returns the cosine of n
complex cosh(complex n)	Returns the hyperbolic cosine of n
complex exp(complex n)	Returns e to the nth
double imag(complex n)	Returns the imaginary part of n
complex log(complex n)	Returns the natural log of n
complex log10(complex n)	Returns the log base 10 of n
double norm(complex n)	Returns the square of n
complex polar(double magnitude, double angle)	Returns the complex number given its polar coordinates
complex pow(complex x, complex y) complex pow(complex x, double y) complex pow(double x, complex y)	Returns x to the y power
double real(complex n)	Returns the real part of n
complex sin(complex n)	Returns the sine of n
complex sinh(complex n)	Returns the hyperbolic sine of n
complex sqrt(complex n)	Returns the square root of n
complex tan(complex n)	Returns the tangent of n
complex tanh(complex n)	Returns the hyperbolic tangent of n

Table A-1.   The Complex Functions

A BCD Class

Real numbers can be represented inside the computer in a variety of different ways. The most common is as binary floating-point values. However, another way to represent a real number is to use *binary coded decimals*, or BCD for short. In BCD, base 10, rather than base 2, is used to represent a number. The major advantage to the BCD representation is that no round-off errors occur. For example, using binary floating-point, the number 100.23 cannot be accurately represented and is rounded to 100.230003. However, using BCD, no rounding occurs. For this reason, BCD numbers are often used in accounting programs. The major disadvantage of BCD numbers is that BCD calculations are slower than binary floating-point calculations. To use BCD numbers you must include **bcd.h** in your programs.

The **bcd** class has these constructor functions:

bcd(int *n*)
bcd(double *n*)
bcd(double *n*, int *digits*)

The first two are self explanatory. The last one creates a BCD number that uses *digits* number of digits after the decimal point.

To convert a number from BCD format to normal binary floating-point format, use **real( )**. Its prototype is

long double real(bcd *n*)

The **bcd** class overloads the arithmetic and relational operators as well as the functions shown in Table A-2.

Here is a sample program that illustrates the advantage of BCD numbers when the prevention of round-off errors is important:

```
#include <iostream.h>
#include <bcd.h>

main(void)
{
```

```
    float f = 100.23, f1 = 101.337;
    bcd b(100.23), b1(101.337);

    cout << f+f1 << " " << b+b1;

    return 0;
}
```

This program displays

201.567001 201.567

on the screen.

Name	Purpose
bcd abs(bcd n)	Returns the absolute value of n
bcd acos(bcd n)	Returns the arc cosine of n
bcd asin(bcd n)	Returns the arc sine of n
bcd atan(bcd n)	Returns the arc tangent of n
bcd cos(bcd n)	Returns the cosine of n
bcd cosh(bcd n)	Returns the hyperbolic cosine of n
bcd exp(bcd n)	Returns e to the nth
bcd log(bcd n)	Returns the natural log of n
bcd log10(bcd n)	Returns the log base 10 of n
bcd pow(bcd x, bcd y)	Returns x to the y power
bcd sin(bcd n)	Returns the sine of n
bcd sinh(bcd n)	Returns the hyperbolic sine of n
bcd sqrt(bcd n)	Returns the square root of n
bcd tan(bcd n)	Returns the tangent of n
bcd tanh(bcd n)	Returns the hyperbolic tangent of n

Table A-2.   The BCD Functions

The manuscript for this book was prepared and submitted
to Osborne/McGraw-Hill in electronic form.
The acquisitions editor for this project was Jeffrey Pepper,
the technical reviewer was Werner Feibel,
and the project editor was Janis Paris.

Text design is by Marcela Hancik and Michelle Salinaro,
using Century Expanded for text body
and Eras demibold for display.

Cover art by Bay Graphics Design, Inc. Book printed and
bound by R.R. Donnelley & Sons Company,
Crawfordsville, Indiana.

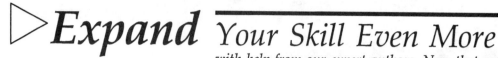

Object-Oriented Programming: An Introduction
by Greg Voss

This significant programming advancement and its methodologies are clearly presented in *Object-Oriented Programming: An Introduction*. Greg Voss compares and contrasts OOP with traditional programming techniques and teaches you how and when to use object-oriented programming techniques instead of traditional structured programming. Object-oriented design is stressed. You'll learn how OOP is used in the real world through examples and exercises that are written in C++ as well as object-oriented Turbo Pascal® and QuickPASCAL®.

$29.95p ISBN: 0-07-881682-3, 600 pp., 7 3/8 X 9 1/4

Born to Code in C
by Herbert Schildt

This book is for all C programmers—especially those who want to know all the secrets of C from the pros. Each chapter contains a profile of a world-class C programmer who reveals the strategies and methodologies that have put him at the top. Topics include icon-based interfaces, super-charging terminate-and-stay-resident programs, and advanced mouse interfacing. Each chapter includes extensive code examples.

$28.95p ISBN: 0-07-881468-5, 526 pp., 7 3/8 X 9 1/4

C: Power User's Guide
by Herbert Schildt

Make your C programs sizzle! All the bells, whistles, and slick tricks used to get professional results in commercial software are unveiled to serious programmers. Build a Borland type interface, develop a core for a database, create memory resident programs, and more. C programming expert Schildt combines theory, background, and code in an even mix as he excites experienced C programmers with new features and approaches.

$22.95p ISBN: 0-07-881307-7, 384 pp., 7 3/8 X 9 1/4
Available in Spanish, ISBN:84-76153813

C: The Pocket Reference
by Herbert Schildt

Here's the best remedy for computer user's memory loss. This handy little guide to C is organized alphabetically so that you can easily find the information you need.

$5.95p ISBN: 0-07-881321-2, 128 pp., 4 1/4 X 7
Available in Spanish ISBN: 84-76152175 **Available Now**

▶ _____Osborne **McGraw-Hill** ■ Available at local book and computer stores.

OS/2 Presentation Manager Programming Primer
by Asael Dror and Robert Lafore

Programmers working with OS/2 as well as those with no previous OS/2 programming experience can get up to speed fast on Presentation Manager, OS/2's graphical user interface. This easy-to-understand approach offers short, clear, programming examples. The book's expert authors offer detailed explanations of features ranging from windows to dynamic data exchange.
$28.95p ISBN: 0-07-881467-7, 626 pp., 7 3/8 X 91/4
Covers Version 1.1

QuickBASIC: The Complete Reference
by Steven Nameroff

This comprehensive guide is written for users at all levels of programming ability. A quick introduction to BASIC programming is followed by a complete command reference section and a discussion of QuickBASIC functions, procedures, files, and graphics. Advanced techniques are grouped together for the professional programmer.
$26.95p ISBN: 0-07-881362-X, 593 pp., 7 3/8 X 9 1/4
Covers Version 4.5
Available in Spanish ISBN: 84-76154488

Teach Yourself C
by Herbert Schildt

Herb Schildt, the widely recognized C expert, is back with another clear, concise volume on the programming language of the 1990s. *Teach Yourself C* uses numerous exercises and skill checks to make sure your programming abilities grow lesson by lesson. By the final chapter, you will possess a solid command of C programming principles, preparing you to work with OS/2, UNIX, and other programs written in C.
$19.95p ISBN: 0-07-881596-7, 681 pp., 7 3/8 X 9 1/4

Using ANSI C In UNIX
by Werner Feibel

If you're already using UNIX, here's the perfect opportunity to learn how to program with the ANSI C standard in the UNIX environment. Feibel, an instructor at Boston University, teaches ANSI C from scratch in this clear, well-written guide. Basic C concepts are presented in detail, the focus then shifts to intermediate and more advanced programming techniques. Feibel emphasizes the creation of small, specialized functions and programs and on making them work together. The book ends with a brief summary of C++.
$24.95p ISBN: 0-07-881631-9, 626 pp., 7 3/8 X 9 1/4

Using QuickPASCAL
by Steven Nameroff

Both students and professionals will benefit from this complete, practical guide to Microsoft's new Pascal programming environment, with a comprehensive discussion of object-oriented programming principles and a thorough Pascal Tutorial. Equally comprehensive are descriptions of Quick PASCAL's program structure, data types, procedures, functions, and more.
$24.95p ISBN: 0-07-881520-7, 475 pp., 7 3/8 X 9 1/4
Covers Version 1.0

QuickC: The Complete Reference
by Werner Feibel

QuickC: The Complete Reference focuses on release 2.5 of the QuickC language, including such productivity enhancements as a built-in editor and assembler, a large library of ready routines, and a hypertext on-line reference system. *QuickC: The Complete Reference* starts with a brief overview of QuickC features, then works through every QuickC function to build a thorough understanding of the integrated QuickC environment.
$24.95p ISBN: 0-07-881661-0, 800 pp., 7 3/8 X 9 1/4

DOS 5 Made Easy
by Herbert Schildt

DOS 5 delivers the upgrade that DOS users have been waiting for, and you'll find out all about it in the ideal one-volume tutorial on the operating system's features and functions. Written by best-selling author Herb Schildt, this book starts with DOS 5's new graphical user interface and file system basics, works through I/O and configuration options, the editor, and concludes with a discussion of hard disk management.
$19.95p ISBN: 0-07-881690-4, 412 pp., 7 3/8 X 9 1/4

C: The Complete Reference
by Herbert Schildt

This renowned reference guide, revised to comply with the new ANSI C standard, is the best and most complete source on ANSI C. C programmers at every level can take adavantage of Schildt's expanded sections on the C language and the ANSI libraries. Comprehensive reference sections are conveniently organized by topic for quick fact-finding.
$28.95p ISBN: 0-07-881538-X, 823 pp., 7 3/8 X 9 1/4

▶ _____Osborne **McGraw-Hill** ■ **Available at local book and computer stores.**

DOS Made Easy
by Herbert Schildt

Previous computer experience is not necessary to understand this concise, well-organized introduction that's filled with short applications and exercises. Begin with an overview of a computer system's components and a step-by-step account of how to run DOS for the first time. Edit text files, use the DOS directory structure, and create batch files.
$19.95p ISBN: 0-07-881295-X, 385 pp., 7 3/8 x 9 1/4 Covers MS-DOS/PC-DOS Version 3.3

Turbo C®/C++: The Complete Reference
by Herbert Schildt

Herb Schildt, author of the runaway best seller *Turbo C®: The Complete Reference*, has written a new book devoted to Borland's Turbo C® 2.0 and Turbo C++® with object-oriented programming. Programmers at every skill level can benefit from this desktop encyclopedia which covers every Turbo C and Turbo C++ command, function, and programming technique. Schildt also discusses the ANSI standard, the integrated Turbo Debugger®, and the Turbo Assembler® in this comprehensive reference.
$29.95p ISBN: 0-07-881535-5, 1000 pp., 7 3/8 X 9 1/4

Turbo Pascal® 6: The Complete Reference
by Stephen K. O'Brien

The most complete single resource ever published for all Turbo Pascal programmers is now available in a special edition that covers all the new features of Borland's recently released version 6. The revolutionary Turbo Vision application framework is also covered so you can use this new tool to write professional-quality applications. Whether you're a beginner or an expert programmer, you'll find the information you need on every Turbo Pascal 6 feature, command, and programming technique.
$29.95p, ISBN: 0-07-881703-X, 1008 pp., 7 3/8 X 9 1/4

Using C++
by Bruce Eckel

This fast-paced, hands-on guide will help you get up to speed on C++, the leading-edge, object-oriented language. Learn the key capabilities that set C++ apart from C including operator and function overloading, references, and encapsulating and hiding data for program clarity. The book discusses many fascinating advanced topics.
$24.95p ISBN:0-07-881522-3, 617 pp., 7 3/8 X 9 1/4, Covers Version 2.0

▶ _____Osborne **McGraw-Hill** ■ **Available at local book and computer stores.**

Windows Programming: An Introduction
by William H. Murray, III and Chris H. Pappas

This guide is a down-to-earth introduction to Windows 3, a program that gives users of IBM PCs and compatibles a graphical interface capability. The authors take you from simple windowing concepts to the creation of sophisticated Windows programs. Best of all, you'll learn how to migrate programming concepts from Windows to OS/2 Presentation Manager.
$28.95 ISBN: 0-07-881536-3, 651 pp., 7 3/8 X 9 1/4

Using Turbo C++®
by Herbert Schildt

Borland's Turbo C++® with object-oriented programming is thoroughly covered in Schildt's introductory guide for all C programmers. Since Turbo C++ can be used with or without its C++ object-oriented extensions, Schildt has carefully structured the book to cover both environments so you have the option to learn either one. Schildt, Osborne's premier C author with a track record of 15 books on C, has perfected the best way to build programming fundamentals into more sophisticated skills.
$24.95p ISBN: 0-07-881610-6, 500 pp., 7 3/8 X 9 1/4

i860™ Microprocessor Architecture
by Neal Margulis
Foreword by Les Kohn

This is the most complete book on Intel®'s i860™ RISC (Reduced Instruction Set Computing) microprocessor—the first one-million transistor chip! Written by Neal Margulis, Intel's chief applications engineer for the i860 processor project, this book begins with the evolution of the architecture and philosophy, followed by a comprehensive look at the i860 microprocessor and its operations. Plenty of example programs and clear explanations are included, along with tips for getting the best performance from the i860 microprocessor.
$29.95p ISBN: 0-07-881645-9, 631 pp., 7 3/8 X 9 1/4

Using QuickBASIC® 4.5, Second Edition
by Don Inman and Bob Albrecht

Here's an excellent programming guide to Microsoft's version 4.5 of QuickBASIC®, written by two programming professionals. They approach QuickBASIC's programming environment in three stages so beginning and experienced BASIC programmers can find the appropriate level of instruction. Learn about subprograms, libraries, metacommands, dynamic debugging, and more.
$22.95p ISBN: 0-07-881514-2, 432 pp., 7 3/8 X 9 1/4